Survival of a Nation

Printed in the United States of America

by **THE ROHR JEWISH LEARNING INSTITUTE**
822 Eastern Parkway, Brooklyn, NY 11213

(888) YOUR-JLI/718-221-6900
WWW.MYJLI.COM

ב"ה

Survival of a Nation:

Exploring Israel through the Lens of the Six-Day War

STUDENT TEXTBOOK

The Rohr Jewish Learning Institute acknowledges the generous support of the following individuals and foundations:

PRINCIPAL BENEFACTOR

GEORGE ROHR
New York, NY

ADVISORY BOARD OF GOVERNORS

YAAKOV AND KAREN COHEN
Potomac, MD

YITZCHOK AND JULIE GNIWISCH
Montreal, QC

BARBARA HINES
Aspen, CO

DANIEL B. MARKSON
S. Antonio, TX

DANIEL AND ROSIE MATTIO
Seattle, WA

DAVID MINTZ
Tenafly, NJ

DR. STEPHEN F. SERBIN
Columbia, SC

LEONARD A. WIEN, JR.
Miami Beach, FL

PILLARS OF JEWISH LITERACY

KEVIN BERMEISTER
Sydney, Australia

PABLO AND SARA BRIMAN
Mexico City, Mexico

YOSEF GOROWITZ
Redondo Beach, CA

DR. VERA KOCH GROSZMANN
S. Paulo, Brazil

HERSCHEL LAZAROFF
Baltimore, MD

JENNY LJUNGBERG
New York, NY

DAVID MAGERMAN
Gladwyne, PA

DR. MICHAEL MALING
Deerfield, IL

YITZCHAK MIRILASHVILI
Herzliya, Israel

LARRY SIFEN
Virginia Beach, VA

YAIR SHAMIR
Savyon, Israel

PARTNERING FOUNDATIONS

WILLIAM DAVIDSON FOUNDATION

MEROMIM FOUNDATION

KOHELET FOUNDATION

CRAIN-MALING FOUNDATION

WORLD ZIONIST ORGANIZATION

AVI CHAI FOUNDATION

OLAMI WORLDWIDE—WOLFSON FOUNDATION

RUDERMAN FAMILY FOUNDATION

THE ESTATE OF ELLIOT JAMES BELKIN

SPONSORS

MARK AND REBECCA BOLINSKY
Long Beach, NY

DANIEL AND ETA COTLAR
Houston, TX

SHMUEL AND SHARONE GOODMAN
Chicago, IL

FRANK (A"H) AND FRUMETH POLASKY
Saginaw, MI

DR. ZE'EV RAV-NOY
Los Angeles, CA

ALAN ZEKELMAN
Bloomfield Hills, MI

THE ROHR JEWISH LEARNING INSTITUTE

gratefully acknowledges
the pioneering support of

George and Pamela Rohr

Since its inception,
the Rohr JLI has been
a beneficiary of the vision, generosity,
care, and concern
of the Rohr family.

In the merit of
the tens of thousands of hours of Torah study
by JLI students worldwide,
may they be blessed with health,
Yiddishe nachas from all their loved ones,
and extraordinary success
in all their endeavors.

DEDICATED TO

Dr. Ze'ev and Mrs. Varda Rav-Noy

הרה"ח ר' **שאלתיאל זאב** שיחי'

וזוגתו מרת **ורדה פייגא בלומא** תחי'

רב-נוי

With deep appreciation for their leadership
and partnership with JLI in bringing Torah study
to all corners of the world

May they go from strength to strength and enjoy
good health, happiness, *nachas* from their loved ones,
and success in all their endeavors
לאורך ימים ושנים טובות.

Endorsements

I would like to extend my heartfelt congratulations for the initiative to develop your new course, *Survival of a Nation*, which outlines Israel's ongoing efforts to confront the numerous and significant challenges it faces through the lens of the fiftieth anniversary of the Six-Day War.

For several reasons, this war was a defining moment in the history of the State of Israel. Israel's position changed within an extremely short time period from existential concern for its fate to a sense of elation, success, and salvation. Many viewed these events—especially the swift victory and the restoration of the ancient holy sites to Jewish sovereignty—as part of the redemption of the Jewish people. The result was a spiritual awakening among Jews throughout the world and across the religious spectrum who were overjoyed by the opportunity to once again visit the Wailing Wall and the Old City of Jerusalem.

At the same time, over the past fifty years, the outcome of the war, which brought extensive areas in Judea and Samaria under Israeli control, has become a significant issue in the conflict between Israel and its neighbors—and among Israelis themselves—over the proper way to treat this land and its Arab population.

I examined the course content and saw that it not only provides students a comprehensive and important overview of these critical events and their ramifications but also clarifies a number of concepts that can help them strengthen their identification with the State of Israel. As such, this course does the Jewish people an important service. Next year in the rebuilt city of Jerusalem!

MK YULI-YOEL EDELSTEIN
Speaker of the Knesset

To understand the complex challenges of Israel's security and survival requires a thorough and nuanced education of the issues that affect it. *Survival of a Nation* is a six-week course reflecting on the social, political and religious issues that were shaped by the historic Six-Day War. This course is a special opportunity for Jews around the world to gain insight and identify with the struggles and triumphs of their brothers and sisters in Eretz Yisrael.

MK ELI BEN-DAHAN
Deputy Minister of Defense

Learning about the Six-Day War is essential for anyone who is trying to understanding Israeli society, politics, or culture. After only six days of fighting, the 1967 victory resulted in a massive change to Israel's landscape which led to further implications and challenges. The Rohr Jewish Learning Institute's course, *Survival of a Nation: Exploring Israel through the Lens of the Six-Day War*, puts modern Israel in the context of history and allows for a deeper understanding of some of the major dilemmas experienced during that period—some of which Israel is still dealing with today. Taking this class provides a unique opportunity to understand how our past is connected to our present, thereby allowing us to recognize our role in the next chapter of the story of the Jewish people.

DANI DAYAN
Consul General of Israel, New York

The Six-Day War constitutes a defining moment, in many ways, in the modern history of the people of Israel and of the State of Israel. This short war caused changes of the highest import whose implications continue to endure and unfold even today, fifty years after this event that lasted a mere six days.

This course presented by the Rohr Jewish Learning Institute addresses the issues in a broad and elemental way. It broadens our knowledge and understanding of the events. I give my blessing to the Rohr Institute for taking the initiative in the study of this important subject—so central to the history of the people of Israel who have returned to their land—and in its consequences for Diaspora Jewry.

AVRAHAM DUVDEVANI
Chairman, World Zionist Organization

It is an honor to congratulate you on the launch of your latest educational course, *Survival of a Nation*, explaining and navigating the many challenges Israel faces today, fifty years since its victory in the Six-Day War.

That week in June 1967 was a historic moment not only for the State of Israel, but for all Jewish people. Those days brought with them the return to our ancestral Land and the strategic depth Israel previously lacked. They ended with Jerusalem, the heart of the nation, once again under Jewish control—after almost 2,000 years of exile.

When Israel defeated larger and better equipped armies it proved to the world the Jewish state was strong, causing Jews in Argentina, Canada, and France to hold their heads high. The sound of the shofar blown at the Western Wall was so great it penetrated the Iron Curtain and reached millions of Jews who were fighting for the right to remain Jewish.

History, however, did not stop with that miraculous victory. Until today the outcome impacts our lives. Our right to live in, and cultivate, Judea and Samaria is no longer an axiom, and international bodies have the audacity to spread lies and question our 3,800-year-old connection to Jerusalem.

The lessons I have seen from this latest course present students with much of the information needed to fully understand the complex issues facing Israel. By explaining basic terminology and drawing on a range of sources, your material is capable of enriching Jews of different backgrounds and connecting them to our common heritage and homeland.

And, as we study about Israel, let us always remember the generation-old prayer uniting Jews around the world: Next year in Jerusalem.

MK NAFTALI BENNETT
Minister of Education
Minister of Diaspora Affairs

Today, as the BDS movement spreads throughout the world and in Europe in particular, it is very important to learn about Israel and its history as well as about its role as the sole democratic country in the Middle East.

In order to gain the knowledge to defend Israel, it is very important to understand the obstacles overcome at its founding, the struggle of its society, and the state of its security, its social makeup, economy, and more.

MK MERAV BEN-ARI
Member of the Knesset

Israel's long history of being attacked by its neighbors has shaped our resistance and perseverance and created the strong state we have today.

It is easier for the world to show Israel as a problem on the international scene. These controversies deflect from Israel's impressive contributions to humanity in the areas of human rights, technological and scientific advancements, and ethical and moral standards.

Despite its youth, Israel has thrived. And despite the controversies, it will continue to innovate and demonstrate its strong contributions to the world.

This course shows the relationship between Israel's past and the Israeli history being written today. It is the Jewish faith that symbolizes our relationship to our history, our identity, and our religious heritage. It will demonstrate to everyone the connection of the Jewish Diaspora to their homeland, Israel.

Our country needs the Jewish people from around the world to explain how Israel is strong and how Israel won't ever forsake the Jews in the Diaspora. This is the fact: Israel is everywhere and a part of each of us, even if the international organizations are trying to show Israel as a problem. They will never sever the relationship between the Jewish people and their Land!

MK SHARREN HASKEL
Member of the Knesset

"Lift up your eyes and look about you: All assemble and come to you; your sons come from afar, and your daughters are carried on the hip" (Isaiah 60:4).

Even though the common use of this phrase is in regards to making *aliyah*, I chose to write it here to remind us that Israel is not merely a geographical area; it is first and foremost a vision, an idea. It started with the idea of a shared nationality for all Jews. A peoplehood. With the belief that we are stronger and better together.

This is the feeling that ties me to you as I am writing this. We are one people, no matter where we are. And this connection between Jews in Israel and around the world makes us all better. Your involvement in Israel's reality makes a great impact—whether it is being done here or in the countries you live in. The connection with your communities enriches our perspective about how Israel is today, and how it should be. I believe and hope it also affects you and your families, knowing that you too have a homeland, being proud of your homeland, and having the ability to impact it.

I am happy about the opportunity provided by JLI's new course, *Survival of a Nation*. Jews throughout the world will be able to learn about Israel and deepen their connection to the Land and the people.

MK ORLY LEVY-ABEKASIS
Member of the Knesset

To understand today's Israel, it is critical to understand the events and trends that created today's challenges and successes, and to appreciate the degree to which many of the choices Israel faces today are similar to those it has faced in the past. The Rohr Jewish Learning Institute's course *Survival of a Nation* illustrates the manifold and critical ways in which the Six-Day War, one of the turning points in Israel's history, both shaped the modern Middle East and was, at the same time, the product of realities that Israel has faced since even before its creation.

DANIEL GORDIS
Author of *Israel: A Concise History of a Nation Reborn*
Winner of Jewish Book Council 2016 Award for Book of the Year

The Rohr JLI has proven again its noted ability to choose topics that are present in the soul of the people of Israel and, with perfect timing, to engage them. When nations of the world cast doubt on the legitimacy of the Jewish state, and the UN and UNESCO negate the connection of the Jewish people to the Eternal City, Jerusalem, this course comes and, in six lessons, succeeds in focusing on the main issues that connect all Jews to their historical homeland. The course staff finds a way to simplify and clarify a complex topic and to present it in a professional and experiential mode. I have no doubt that this course will fulfill its objectives. Wishing you success.

DR. SIMCHA ASAF LEIBOVITZ

Director, World Center for Leadership, Mt. Herzl

Perhaps even more than the 1948–49 War of Independence, the 1967 Six-Day War represents a turning point in Jewish history. Jews worldwide were chilled by the possibility that the nascent Jewish state, so tentatively perched on the edge of the Mediterranean, would be utterly destroyed by the surrounding Arab nations. In a victory that invites biblical comparisons, however, Israel's sudden and overwhelming victory shocked the international community. The eternal city of Jerusalem was unified under Jewish control for the first time in nearly two millennia, and Israel secured its borders virtually from Damascus to Cairo.

Coming so soon after the devastation of the Holocaust, the ever-renewing Jewish people found new strength in this triumph, sparking a return to their physical homeland in Israel and spiritual homeland in the Torah. The events of June 1967 did not go uncontested, however, and the borders remain a central aspect of the lingering Israeli-Palestinian conflict. This new JLI course is a welcome addition to the curriculum, promoting wider awareness of this complex and important event in Jewish history.

DR. HENRY ABRAMSON

Dean, Lander College of Arts and Sciences
Touro College

The Six-Day War was a watershed not only for the State of Israel, but for Jewish and world history, as well. For Jews the world over it was seen as nothing less than a miraculous deliverance. In its aftermath, questions and conflicts arose which still stand at the center of both the world's and the Jewish agendas. The Rohr JLI course is a superb opportunity both to study and appreciate a remarkable historical event, and to gain a deeper understanding of the world in which we live.

PROFESSOR JEFFREY WOOLF

Bar-Ilan University

The fiftieth anniversary of the Six-Day War is certain to be accompanied by a massively organized effort to delegitimize Israel's presence in Jerusalem and other areas it liberated from Jordanian occupation. The JLI's course is crucial for those who wish to understand the events in their true historical perspective, without the great revisionism of recent years. And the course makes clear that understanding what happened then, and why, is essential to understanding the situation of Israel and the Jewish people today.

PROFESSOR EUGENE KONTOROVICH

Northwestern University School of Law

As an Israeli tour guide and educator, I am thrilled to see this latest in a series of outstanding and relevant JLI courses. This promises to be an exciting course that will play an indispensable role in connecting Jews to the reality and miracles of the Land and people of Israel.

DR. LISA AIKEN

Clinical psychologist
Israeli tour guide
Author of *To Be a Jewish Woman* and other books

ראש הממשלה
PRIME MINISTER

March 12, 2017

Dear Friends,

I send warm greetings from Jerusalem to the Rohr Jewish Learning Institute.

For nearly twenty years, JLI has worked to bring Jews from around the world closer to our shared heritage and tradition. Through your interactive and advanced courses, Jews of all backgrounds and affiliations can deepen their knowledge and understanding of our history and explore the diverse issues that affect Jewish life today.

Your new course about the Six Day War coincides with the 50th anniversary of the reunification of Jerusalem. With the liberation of the Western Wall and the Old City in 1967, the prayers of generations of Jews were finally answered.

The liberation of Jerusalem was a watershed in Jewish and Zionist history. Breaking the stranglehold on the then-divided city left it stronger and more prosperous. The IDF's sweeping victory also united and energized Jews in Israel and abroad, and was followed by a significant increase in immigration to Israel.

I wish you much success with this project. I have no doubt it will help people better understand the importance of this fateful event.

Sincerely,

Benjamin Netanyahu

Jerusalem, Israel

Contents

MAP OF ISRAEL

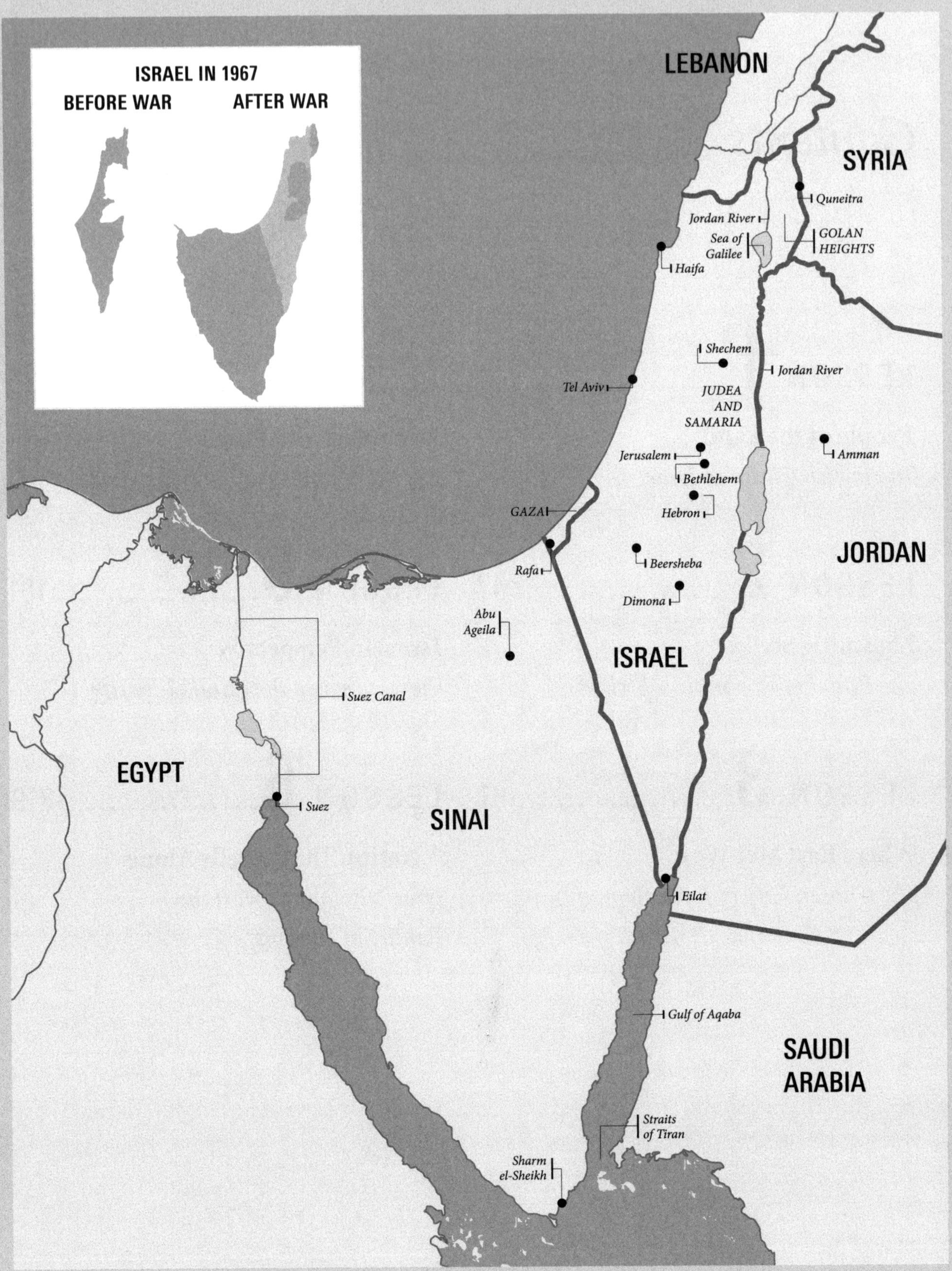

ISRAEL AND ITS NEIGHBORING ARAB AND MUSLIM COUNTRIES

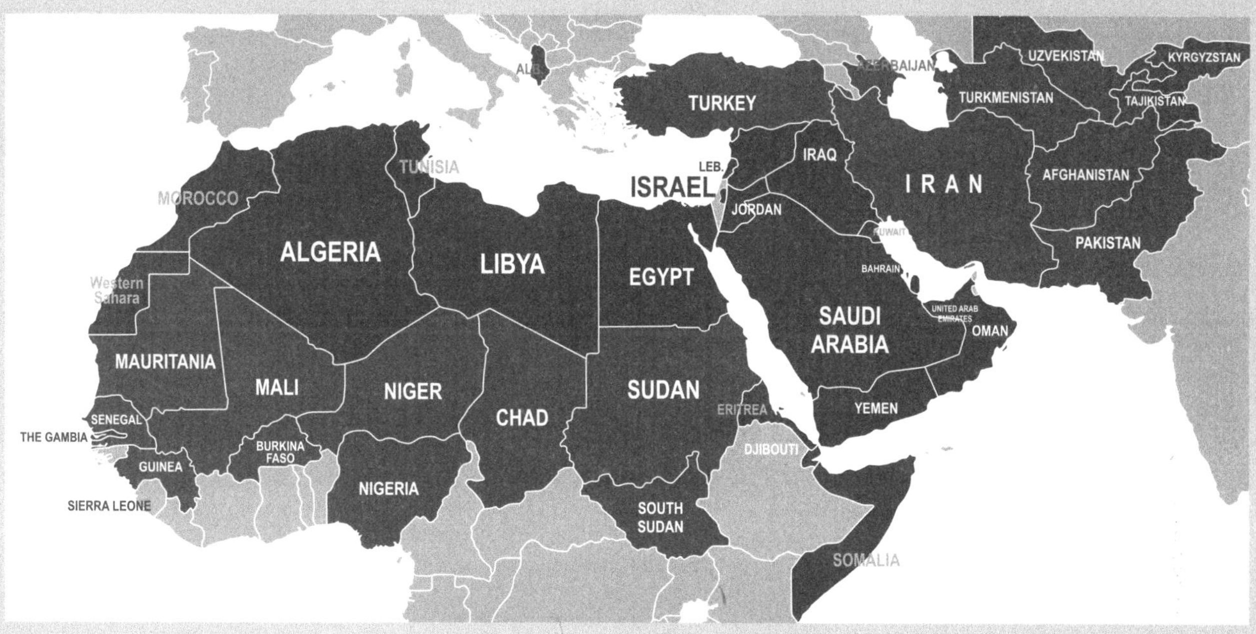

Land Mass Comparison (in square miles)

Algeria	919,600	South Sudan	239,285	Eritrea	45,406
Saudi Arabia	830,000	Yemen	203,891	Jordan	34,495
Sudan	728,200	Turkmenistan	189,657	Azerbaijan	33,436
Libya	679,400	Uzbekistan	173,351	U.A.E.	32,278
Iran	636,400	Morocco	172,414	Sierra Leone	27,699
Chad	495,800	Iraq	168,754	Albania	11,100
Niger	489,200	Oman	119,499	Djibouti	8,958
Mali	478,800	Burkina Faso	105,869	**Israel**	**8,019**
Mauritania	397,700	Western Sahara	102,703	Kuwait	6,880
Egypt	390,120	Guinea	94,926	Qatar	4,468
Nigeria	356,669	Kyrgyzstan	77,182	Gambia	4,127
Pakistan	307,374	Senegal	75,951	Lebanon	4,036
Turkey	302,535	Syria	71,500	Comoros	785
Afghanistan	252,072	Tunisia	63,170	Bahrain	295
Somalia	246,201	Tajikistan	55,251		

1949–1956

Hundreds of Israelis killed by Arab fedayeen that infiltrate from Egyptian-controlled Gaza and Sinai, and Jordanian territory.

July 26, 1956

Egypt nationalizes the Suez Canal; bars passage to Israeli ships.

July 14, 1966

Syria shells Israel. Israeli Air Force downs Syrian MiG-21.

November 4

Egypt and Syria sign mutual defense pact.

November 13

Samu raid: Israeli troops retaliate for the November 10 killing of 3 Israeli soldiers by a landmine. The attack kills 15 Jordanian soldiers and 3 civilians; destroys many Arab houses in Jordanian-held Samu.

January–April, 1967

63 Arab attacks (Syrian tank fire, mines, more than 200 mortar shells, Palestinian terror attacks) heighten anxiety in Israel.

April 7, 1967

Israel responds to Syrian shelling. The IAF shoots down 6 Syrian MiGs.

May 13, 1967

USSR plants disinformation about impending Israeli attack on Syria.

May 17, 1967

Two Egyptian MiGs fly over Israeli nuclear plant in Dimona.

May 23, 1967

Egypt closes the Straits of Tiran to Israeli shipping. U.S. President Johnson calls blockade illegal and disastrous for peace.

May 26, 1967

President Johnson warns Israel not to attack first.

May 24–June 4, 1967

Four Arab countries (Egypt, Syria, Jordan, and Iraq) deploy more than 230,000 troops close to Israel's borders.

May 30, 1967

Jordan and Egypt sign mutual defense pact.

LEADING UP TO THE WAR

October 29–November 7, 1956

Sinai Campaign. Israel invades and conquers the Sinai, while the British and French wrest control of the Suez Canal. Eventually, Israel retreats from the Sinai, a UN Peacekeeping Force is installed in the Sinai, with the U.S. guaranteeing Israel's freedom of passage through the Straits of Tiran. Relative quiet ensues on the Egypt-Israel border.

November 18, 1959

Israel begins work on the National Water Carrier Project, to divert waters of the Jordan River to the Negev, taking its share of water in accordance with the Johnston Plan. The project is successfully completed in June 1964.

January 14–17, 1964

Reacting to the National Water Carrier Project, Arab leaders unite to plan the destruction of Israel.

Per the agreement at the Arab summit, Syria begins to divert the Jordan River headwaters.

May 14, 1967

After fourteen Syrian attacks, Israeli PM Eshkol warns Syria of retaliation.

Egypt mobilizes thousands of its troops in and around the Suez Canal.

May 16, 1967

Egypt moves into the Sinai, and demands that the UN peacekeepers withdraw.

THE WAR

Day 1, Monday, June 5, 1967

Egyptian Front

In a surprise preemptive strike, Israel destroys most of Egypt's air force and airfields.

IDF Forces enter Gaza and Sinai.

Jordanian Front

Israel sends a message to Jordan's King Hussein: Despite the outbreak of war, it would not attack Jordanian territory if it remained quiet on that front.

Jordan bombards Jerusalem and Central Israel. Jordanian artillery shells Tel Aviv. Iraqi and Jordanian aircraft try to bomb Tel Aviv and other targets.

Israel bombs airfields in Mafraq and Amman.

Battle for East Jerusalem begins.

Israeli forces enter the West Bank.

Syrian Front

Syrian aircraft attack targets in northern Israel. IAF aircraft attack Syrian airbases, destroying most of the Syrian air force.

Syrian artillery bombards Rosh Pina.

SIX-DAY WAR TIMELINE

Day 2, Tuesday, June 6, 1967

Egyptian Front

Israeli conquest of Gaza complete, IDF moves into the Sinai.

General retreat ordered for the Egyptian army.

Jordanian Front

Battle for Jerusalem continues.

Israel makes great advances in the West Bank.

General retreat from West Bank ordered for the Jordan Legion.

Syrian Front

Syrian artillery continues barrage on Israeli border communities.

Day 3, Wednesday, June 7, 1967

Egyptian Front

Battle and Israeli conquests continue in the Sinai.

Nasser turns down UN Security Council ceasefire initiative.

Blockade of the Straits of Tiran broken as Israel Navy arrives at Sharm el Sheikh.

Jordanian Front

Israeli conquest of the Old City of Jerusalem, the Temple Mount, and the Western Wall completed.

Shechem (Nablus), Gush Etzion, Bethlehem, and Jericho conquered.

Syrian Front

Syrian artillery bombardments continue all along the northern border.

Day 4, Thursday, June 8, 1967

Egyptian Front

IDF arrives at the Suez Canal.

Egypt agrees to a ceasefire.

Jordanian Front

Hebron conquered.

IDF destroys Jordan River bridges.

Syrian Front

Syrian artillery bombardments continue all along the northern border with Golan.

IAF attacks Syrian defenses.

General

IAF and the Israeli Navy attack the USS Liberty, a U.S. Navy surveillance ship sailing off the coast of Gaza, resulting in the deaths of 34 crew members and injuring 171. Israeli and U.S. government inquiries concluded that the attack was the result of Israel mistakenly identifying the Liberty as an Egyptian vessel. Others believe that the attack was deliberate.

Day 5, Friday, June 9 ,1967

Egyptian Front

Nasser delivers a speech blaming the U.S. for the Egyptian defeat, insisting that the U.S. helped Israel, and announces his resignation. The speech is followed by huge demonstrations of support, causing Nasser to retract the resignation.

Syrian Front

Israeli attack on the Syrian-held Golan Heights begins.

Day 6, Shabbat (Saturday), June 10,1967

Syrian Front

Golan conquered.

Israel agrees to a ceasefire with Syria.

AFTER THE WAR

June 14,1967

In honor of the holiday of Shavuot, the Western Wall opens to Israeli civilians. Hundreds of thousands flock to the Old City and the Wall.

June 28–29,1967

Israel annexes East Jerusalem. Arab residents of East Jerusalem are given permanent resident status in Israel.

June 19,1967

Israeli cabinet decides on a secret offer, to be delivered to the Syrians and Egyptians through the Americans, calling for the return of conquered land in return for peace.

September 1,1967

Arab leaders at the Khartoum Conference say no to peace. They announce "The Three Nos": No peace with Israel, no negotiations with Israel, and no recognition of Israel.

Lesson 1

PEOPLE OF THE LAND

THE JEWISH CLAIM TO ISRAEL

Israeli Army Chief of Staff Yitzhak Rabin on a flight over the Suez Canal region during the Sinai campaign of the Six-Day War, 1967. (Photo credit: Magnum Photos; Micha Bar Ami, photographer)

The 1967 conflict resulted from the argument, espoused by Egypt's Gamal Abdel Nasser and most leaders in the Arab world, that Israel's existence was illegitimate, having been founded on stolen Arab territory. What is Israel's response to this argument? What is her right to exist as a Jewish state in the heart of the Middle East? And what is the justification for associating Judaism—an ethereal religion of beliefs and ideas—with a specific territory?

TEXT 1

DANIEL 6:11

> כְּדִי יְדַע דִּי רְשִׁים כְּתָבָא, עַל לְבַיְתֵהּ וְכַוִּין פְּתִיחָן לֵהּ בְּעִלִּיתֵהּ נֶגֶד יְרוּשְׁלֶם, וְזִמְנִין תְּלָתָה בְיוֹמָא הוּא בָּרֵךְ עַל בִּרְכוֹהִי וּמְצַלֵּא וּמוֹדֵא קֳדָם אֱלָהֵהּ, כָּל קֳבֵל דִּי הֲוָא עָבֵד מִן קַדְמַת דְּנָה.

Upon learning that the decree had been written, Daniel went to his home, where in the upstairs room there were windows open facing Jerusalem. Three times a day he kneeled and prayed and gave thanks to his God, just as he had done beforehand.

TEXT 2

SIDDUR TEHILAT HASHEM, *AMIDAH* PRAYER

> תְּקַע בְּשׁוֹפָר גָּדוֹל לְחֵרוּתֵנוּ, וְשָׂא נֵס לְקַבֵּץ גָּלֻיּוֹתֵינוּ, וְקַבְּצֵנוּ יַחַד מֵאַרְבַּע כַּנְפוֹת הָאָרֶץ לְאַרְצֵנוּ. בָּרוּךְ אַתָּה ה' מְקַבֵּץ נִדְחֵי עַמּוֹ יִשְׂרָאֵל.

Sound the great *shofar* for our freedom, raise a banner to gather our exiles, and gather us from the four corners of the earth into our Land. Blessed are You . . . Who gathers the dispersed of His people Israel.

SIDDUR TEHILAT HASHEM

One of the prayer books that follow the tradition of the Arizal, as established by Rabbi Shne'ur Zalman of Liadi. It was first published in New York in 1945.

TEXT 3a

PSALMS 137:1–6

עַל נַהֲרוֹת בָּבֶל שָׁם יָשַׁבְנוּ גַם בָּכִינוּ בְּזָכְרֵנוּ אֶת צִיּוֹן.

עַל עֲרָבִים בְּתוֹכָהּ תָּלִינוּ כִּנֹּרוֹתֵינוּ.

כִּי שָׁם שְׁאֵלוּנוּ שׁוֹבֵינוּ דִּבְרֵי שִׁיר וְתוֹלָלֵינוּ שִׂמְחָה: "שִׁירוּ לָנוּ מִשִּׁיר צִיּוֹן!"

אֵיךְ נָשִׁיר אֶת שִׁיר ה' עַל אַדְמַת נֵכָר?

אִם אֶשְׁכָּחֵךְ יְרוּשָׁלָם תִּשְׁכַּח יְמִינִי.

תִּדְבַּק לְשׁוֹנִי לְחִכִּי אִם לֹא אֶזְכְּרֵכִי, אִם לֹא אַעֲלֶה אֶת יְרוּשָׁלַם עַל רֹאשׁ שִׂמְחָתִי.

By the rivers of Babylon we sat and wept as we remembered Zion.

We hung our harps on willows in its midst.

For there our captors asked of us to sing songs, our tormentors [insisted on] joyful tunes. "Sing for us of the songs of Zion!" [they demanded].

How can we sing the song of God on foreign soil?

If I forget you, O Jerusalem, may my right hand forget [its skill].

May my tongue cleave to my palate if I do not remember you, if I do not recall Jerusalem at the height of my joy.

TEXT 3b

PSALMS 126:1–2

> שִׁיר הַמַּעֲלוֹת, בְּשׁוּב ה' אֶת שִׁיבַת צִיּוֹן הָיִינוּ כְּחֹלְמִים.
>
> אָז יִמָּלֵא שְׂחוֹק פִּינוּ וּלְשׁוֹנֵנוּ רִנָּה. אָז יֹאמְרוּ בַגּוֹיִם, "הִגְדִּיל ה' לַעֲשׂוֹת עִם אֵלֶּה"!

A song of ascents: When God returns the returnees of Zion, we will have been like dreamers.

Our mouths will then be filled with laughter, and our tongues with song. They will then say among the nations, "God has done amazing things for this nation."

TEXT 3c

SIDDUR TEHILAT HASHEM, GRACE AFTER MEALS.

רַחֵם ה' אֱלֹקֵינוּ עַל יִשְׂרָאֵל עַמֶּךָ, וְעַל יְרוּשָׁלַיִם עִירֶךָ, וְעַל צִיּוֹן מִשְׁכַּן כְּבוֹדֶךָ, וְעַל מַלְכוּת בֵּית דָּוִד מְשִׁיחֶךָ, וְעַל הַבַּיִת הַגָּדוֹל וְהַקָּדוֹשׁ שֶׁנִּקְרָא שִׁמְךָ עָלָיו ... וּבְנֵה יְרוּשָׁלַיִם עִיר הַקֹּדֶשׁ בִּמְהֵרָה בְיָמֵינוּ.

Our God, have compassion on Your people Israel, on Your city Jerusalem, on Zion the dwelling place of Your glory, on the kingship of the House of David Your anointed one, and on the great and holy house upon which Your name is called. . . . Rebuild Jerusalem, the holy city, speedily in our days.

NOTABLE *ALIYAHS* THROUGH THE CENTURIES

1738 BCE

God commands Abraham: "Go from your land, and from your birthplace, and from your father's house, to the land that I will show you." Abraham journeys from Haran and settles in the Land of Canaan.

1273 BCE

Forty years after their Exodus from Egypt, the Children of Israel enter the Promised Land under the leadership of Joshua.

371 BCE

Under a mandate from Cyrus of Persia, the Judean prince Zerubbabel returns to the Land with 42,000 Jews from the Babylonian exile, and initiates construction of the Second Temple.

348 BCE

Ezra leads a second group of 1,500 returnees from Babylon.

335 BCE

Nehemiah arrives from Babylon and oversees the rebuilding of the walls of Jerusalem.

32 BCE

Hillel, a descendant of the royal House of David, arrives in the Holy Land from Babylon and is appointed nasi (president) of the Sanhedrin—an office his descendants would hold for the next 460 years.

2nd century CE

Rabbi Chiya "the Great" makes *aliyah* from his native Babylon and assists Rabbi Yehudah Hanasi in his compilation of the Mishnah.

614 CE

During the brief Persian conquest of the Holy Land, Jews are allowed to settle in Jerusalem for the first time in nearly 500 years.

1141

Rabbi Yehudah Halevi arrives in the Land of Israel.

1165

Fleeing religious persecution in North Africa, Maimonides arrives in the Land of Israel, but after a few months, settles in Egypt. Upon his passing, his body is brought to Israel and buried in Tiberias.

1173

Benjamin of Tudela visits the Holy Land and authors a report of the state of its Jewish population.

1211

"*Aliyah* of the Tosafists": Following Saladin's expulsion of the Crusaders, he issues an invitation to Jews to settle in the Holy Land. A large group of English and French/German Jews arrives in the Land, including 300 Talmudic scholars.

1267

Nachmanides makes *aliyah* from his native Spain to the Holy Land and resurrects the Jewish community in Jerusalem, which had been ravaged during the Mongol raids 23 years earlier.

c. 1290

Groups of German Jews come to Jerusalem.

1570

Rabbi Yitschak Luria ("Ari") arrives in Safed, securing its role as a center of Kabbalah.

1700

Rabbi Yehudah HaChasid ("The Pious") makes *aliyah* with 700 followers.

1740–1747

Beginning of the Chasidic *aliyah*: A number of Rabbi Yisrael Ba'al Shem Tov's disciples, traveling as individuals, move to the Holy Land, including his brother-in-law Rabbi Gershon of Kitov. The Ba'al Shem Tov himself makes several attempts to reach the Holy Land but encounters many obstacles and is forced to return to Mezhibuzh, in the Ukraine.

1742

Aliyah of Rabbi Chaim ibn Attar of Morocco (the "Or Hachayim").

1764

First organized group *aliyah* of Chasidim, led by Rabbi Menachem Mendel of Premishlan.

1777

Large group of Chasidic families make *aliyah* under the leadership of Rabbi Menachem Mendel of Vitebsk, Rabbi Avraham of Kalisk, and Rabbi Yisrael of Polotsk, settling in Safed, Tiberias, and Hebron.

1777

A group of 130 Tunisian Jews make *aliyah* and settle in the Galilee.

1798

Rabbi Nachman of Breslov visits the Holy Land.

1808

Several hundred disciples of Rabbi Eliyahu, the Ga'on of Vilna, make *aliyah* and eventually settle in Jerusalem.

1869

Founding of Nachalat Shiva, a self-sustaining community outside the walls of the Old City of Jerusalem.

1878

Petah Tikva is founded as an agricultural settlement by religious pioneers from Europe, with the financial help of Baron Edmond de Rothschild.

1881

Yemenite *aliyah*: Jews had traveled to Israel from Yemen, whose ancient Jewish community dates back to the First Temple era, for many centuries. In 1881, conditions in the Ottoman Empire make travel to Israel less prohibitive, and the trickle becomes a flood, with some walking many miles through the desert to realize their lifelong dream of living in the Holy Land. Thousands make *aliyah* in the ensuing decades.

1882

With the advent of the modern Zionist movement, and the rise of antisemitism and the persecution of Jews in Europe, the migration of Diaspora Jews to Israel increases exponentially. Between 1882 and 1939, close to half a million Jews emigrate from Eastern Europe to the Land of Israel.

1884

Hovevei Zion movement organizes support for Jewish return to the Land and its settlement.

1901–1902

Agricultural settlements founded in Sejera, Mescha, Menachemia, and Yavne'el.

1909

Founding of the first kibbutz, Degania, and the first modern Israeli city, Tel Aviv.

1933–1948

The British strictly limit the number of Jews allowed to immigrate to the Land of Israel, sealing the fate of many Jews seeking to escape the Nazi threat in Europe. More than 100,000 Jews attempt to enter the Land clandestinely during this period; most are intercepted by the British and sent back to Europe or interned in British detention camps.

1948–1971

Aliyah from Arab countries: Between 1948 and 1971, about 900,000 Jews leave, flee, or are expelled from Arab and Muslim countries and make *aliyah*, including 255,000 Jews from Morocco; 128,000 from Iraq; 57,000 from Iran; 83,000 from Libya and Tunisia; and 4,000 from Afghanistan.

1949–1950

Nearly 50,000 Yemenite Jews are airlifted to Israel in "Operation Magic Carpet," orchestrated by the newly established State of Israel.

1973

Exodus of Soviet Jewry: Israel's victory in the Six-Day War sparks a renaissance of Jewish identity among the Jews of the Soviet Union, accompanied by a movement to immigrate to Israel. Most of those who apply for exit visas are refused, fired from their jobs, and persecuted by the Soviet regime; leading "refuseniks" are jailed and exiled to the gulag. In the early 1970s, the Soviets relent, and tens of thousands are allowed to leave for Israel.

1984–1991

Ethiopian *aliyah*: In the late 1970s, a clandestine operation by the Mossad is implemented to rescue the Beta Israel community of Ethiopia, threatened by famine and persecution. About 17,000 members of the community are airlifted to Israel in the 1980s, and 45,000 more in the next decade, including 14,325 flown in on 34 aircraft in a single day on May 24, 1991 in "Operation Solomon."

1991

Following the collapse of the Soviet Union in 1991, close to 1,000,000 immigrate to Israel.

TEXT 4

MAIMONIDES, *MISHNEH TORAH*, LAWS OF KINGS 5:10–11

גְּדוֹלֵי הַחֲכָמִים הָיוּ מְנַשְּׁקִין עַל תְּחוּמֵי אֶרֶץ יִשְׂרָאֵל וּמְנַשְּׁקִין אֲבָנֶיהָ וּמִתְגַּלְגְּלִין עַל עֲפָרָהּ. וְכֵן הוּא אוֹמֵר, "כִּי רָצוּ עֲבָדֶיךָ אֶת אֲבָנֶיהָ וְאֶת עֲפָרָהּ יְחוֹנֵנוּ" (תְּהִלִּים קב, טו) . . .

וְאֵינוֹ דוֹמֶה קוֹלַטְתּוֹ מֵחַיִּים לְקוֹלַטְתּוֹ אַחַר מוֹתוֹ. וְאַף עַל פִּי כֵן, גְּדוֹלֵי הַחֲכָמִים הָיוּ מוֹלִיכִים מֵתֵיהֶם לְשָׁם. צֵא וּלְמַד מִיַּעֲקֹב אָבִינוּ וְיוֹסֵף הַצַּדִּיק.

The great sages would kiss the boundaries of the Land of Israel [upon arrival], kiss its stones, and roll in its dust. Indeed it is written (PSALMS 102:15), "Your servants cherish her stones and favor her dust." . . .

Although one cannot compare being received by the Holy Land during one's lifetime to being received by it after one's death, nevertheless, the greatest sages would bring their dead to be buried in the Holy Land, as can be learned from the example of our father Jacob and the righteous Joseph.

RABBI MOSHE BEN MAIMON (MAIMONIDES, RAMBAM) 1135–1204

Halachist, philosopher, author, and physician. Maimonides was born in Cordoba, Spain. After the conquest of Cordoba by the Almohads, he fled Spain and eventually settled in Cairo, Egypt. There, he became the leader of the Jewish community and served as court physician to the vizier of Egypt. He is most noted for authoring the *Mishneh Torah*, an encyclopedic arrangement of Jewish law, and for his philosophical work, *Guide for the Perplexed*. His rulings on Jewish law are integral to the formation of halachic consensus.

Jerusalem from the Mount of Olives, Edward Lear, c. 1859 (The Israel Museum, Jerusalem)

TEXT 5

RABBI YEHUDAH HALEVI, *SHIREI RABBI YEHUDAH HALEVI* (NEW YORK: OGEN PUBLISHING HOUSE OF THE HISTADRUT IVRITH, 1944), ED. SIMON BERNSTEIN, SONG 211

לִבִּי בְמִזְרָח, וְאָנֹכִי בְּסוֹף מַעֲרָב.
אֵיךְ אֶטְעֲמָה אֵת אֲשֶׁר אֹכַל וְאֵיךְ יֶעֱרָב?

אֵיכָה אֲשַׁלֵּם נְדָרַי וֶאֱסָרַי,
בְּעוֹד צִיּוֹן בְּחֶבֶל אֱדוֹם וַאֲנִי בְּכֶבֶל עֲרָב?

יֵקַל בְּעֵינַי עֲזֹב כָּל טוּב סְפָרַד,
כְּמוֹ יֵקַר בְּעֵינַי רְאוֹת עַפְרוֹת דְּבִיר נֶחֱרָב.

My heart is in the East,
and I am at the ends of the West.
How can I taste what I eat,
and how could it be savored?

How shall I render my vows and my bonds,
while Zion is yet in the fetters of Rome,
and I am in the shackles of Arabia?

It shall be as easy for me
to forsake all the bounty of Spain,
as it is precious for me to behold
the dust of the desolate Abode.

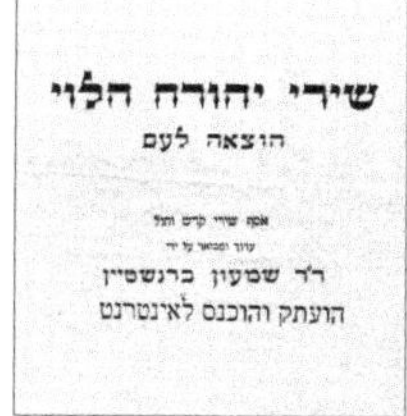

שירי יהודה הלוי
הוצאה לעם
ד"ר שמעון ברנשטיין
הועתק והוכנס לאינטרנט

RABBI YEHUDAH HALEVI
CA. 1075–1141

Noted author, physician, and poet. Rabbi Yehudah Halevi is best known as the author of the *Kuzari*, a philosophical work, written in the form of a discussion between a Jew, a Christian, and a Muslim before the King of the Khazars. In addition to the *Kuzari*, he wrote thousands of poems, of which only a few hundred survive today.

QUESTION FOR DISCUSSION

How does Israel's situation today compare with its situation in the months before the Six-Day War? Is it better? Worse? Essentially the same?

TEXT 6

MACCABEES I, 15:33–34

claim 22 Hundred years ago

Simon answered [Antiochus' messenger] and said to him:

"It is not a foreign land that we have conquered, neither is it the possession of others over which we rule. It is the heritage of our ancestors, which was for some time unjustly conquered, which we, upon obtaining the power to do so, have restored to ourselves."

MACCABEES

Apocryphal and pseudepigraphical work. I Maccabees and II Maccabees contain the history of Simon the Hasmonean and Judah Maccabee. Claiming to be the condensation of a history of the Maccabees by Jason of Cyrene, II Maccabees is a devout treatment of Judas Maccabeus' career and of the Jews' persecution at the hands of Antiochus. It was probably composed in Greek late in the first century BCE by a Jewish author.

Figure 1.2

Timeline of Jewish Presence in Israel

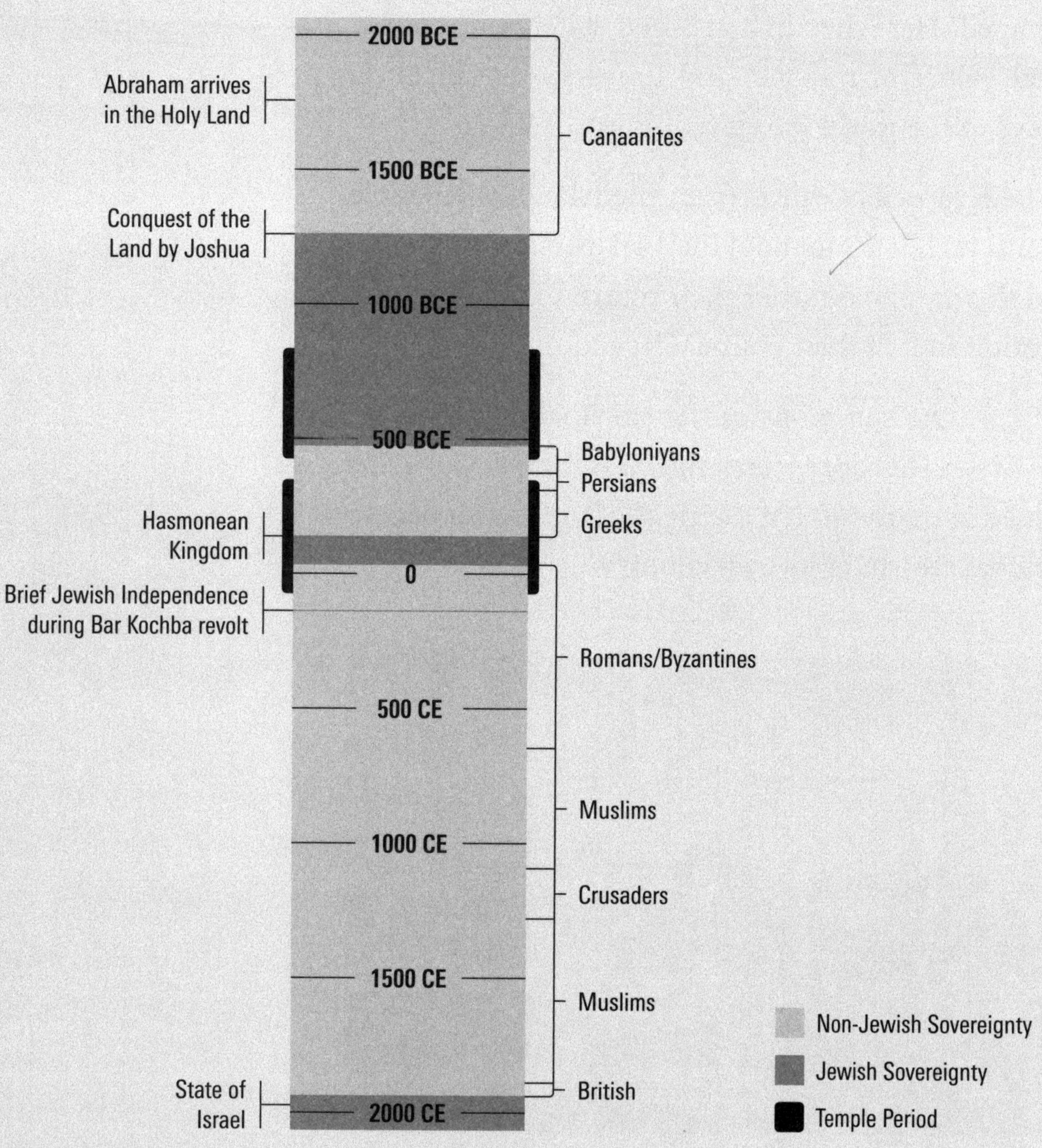

TEXT 7a

ISRAEL'S DECLARATION OF INDEPENDENCE, MAY 14, 1948

The Land of Israel was the birthplace of the Jewish people. Here their spiritual, religious, and political identity was shaped. Here they first attained statehood, created cultural values of national and universal significance, and gave to the world the eternal Book of Books.

After being forcibly exiled from their land, the people kept faith with it throughout their Dispersion and never ceased to pray and hope for their return to it and for the restoration in it of their political freedom. . . .

In 1897, at the summons of the spiritual father of the Jewish State, Theodore Herzl, the First Zionist Congress convened and proclaimed the right of the Jewish people to national rebirth in its own country.

Declaration of State of Israel, 1948. (Photo credit: Israel Ministry of Foreign Affairs; Rudi Weissenstein, photographer)

TEXT 7b

IBID.

This right was recognized in the Balfour Declaration of the 2nd November, 1917, and re-affirmed in the Mandate of the League of Nations which, in particular, gave international sanction to the historic connection between the Jewish people and the Land of Israel and to the right of the Jewish people to rebuild its National Home. . . .

On the 29th November, 1947, the United Nations General Assembly passed a resolution calling for the establishment of a Jewish State in the Land of Israel; the General Assembly required the inhabitants of the Land of Israel to take such steps as were necessary on their part for the implementation of that resolution. This recognition by the United Nations of the right of the Jewish people to establish their State is irrevocable.

TEXT 7C

IBID.

The catastrophe which recently befell the Jewish people—the massacre of millions of Jews in Europe—was another clear demonstration of the urgency of solving the problem of its homelessness by re-establishing in the Land of Israel the Jewish State, which would open the gates of the homeland wide to every Jew and confer upon the Jewish people the status of a fully privileged member of the comity of nations.

TEXT 8

RASHI, GENESIS 1:1

אָמַר רַבִּי יִצְחָק: לֹא הָיָה צָרִיךְ לְהַתְחִיל [אֶת] הַתּוֹרָה אֶלָּא מֵ"הַחוֹדֶשׁ הַזֶּה לָכֶם" (שְׁמוֹת יב, ב), שֶׁהִיא מִצְוָה רִאשׁוֹנָה שֶׁנִּצְטַווּ [בָּהּ] יִשְׂרָאֵל. וּמַה טַעַם פָּתַח בִּבְרֵאשִׁית?

מִשּׁוּם "כֹּחַ מַעֲשָׂיו הִגִּיד לְעַמּוֹ, לָתֵת לָהֶם נַחֲלַת גּוֹיִם" (תְּהִלִּים קיא, ו). שֶׁאִם יֹאמְרוּ אוּמּוֹת הָעוֹלָם לְיִשְׂרָאֵל, "לִסְטִים אַתֶּם! שֶׁכְּבַשְׁתֶּם אַרְצוֹת שִׁבְעָה גוֹיִם", הֵם אוֹמְרִים לָהֶם, "כָּל הָאָרֶץ שֶׁל הַקָּדוֹשׁ בָּרוּךְ הוּא הִיא. הוּא בְּרָאָהּ וּנְתָנָהּ לַאֲשֶׁר יָשַׁר בְּעֵינָיו. בִּרְצוֹנוֹ נְתָנָהּ לָהֶם, וּבִרְצוֹנוֹ נְטָלָהּ מֵהֶם וּנְתָנָהּ לָנוּ".

Rabbi Yitschak said: The Torah ought to have begun [with the verse] "This month shall be to you, etc." (EXODUS 12:2), the first mitzvah commanded to the people of Israel. Why, then, does it begin with "In the beginning, [God created the heavens and the earth]"? . . .

"The strength of His works He related to His people, to give them the inheritance of the nations" (PSALMS 111:6). If the nations of the world will say to Israel, "You are thieves for having conquered the lands of the seven nations," Israel will reply, "The entire world is God's; He created it and granted it to whomever He desired. It was His will to give it to the [seven nations], and it was His will to take it from them and give it to us."

RABBI SHLOMO YITZCHAKI (RASHI) 1040–1105

Most noted biblical and Talmudic commentator. Born in Troyes, France, Rashi studied in the famed *yeshivot* of Mainz and Worms. His commentaries on the Pentateuch and the Talmud, which focus on the straightforward meaning of the text, appear in virtually every edition of the Talmud and Bible.

TEXT 9

NACHMANIDES, LEVITICUS 18:25

הוּא מַאֲמָרָם (כְּתוּבּוֹת קי, ב) "כָּל הַדָּר בְּחוּצָה לָאָרֶץ דוֹמֶה כְּמִי שֶׁאֵין לוֹ אֱלוֹקַהּ, שֶׁנֶּאֱמַר, 'לָתֵת לָכֶם אֶת אֶרֶץ כְּנַעַן לִהְיוֹת לָכֶם לֵאלֹקִים' (וַיִּקְרָא כה, לח)". . . כִּי עִיקָּר כָּל הַמִּצְוֹת לְיוֹשְׁבִים בְּאֶרֶץ ה'.

The sages of the Talmud (KETUBOT 110B) declared: "Anyone who lives outside of the Land is comparable to one who has no God, as it is written, '. . . to give to you the Land of Canaan, to be a God for you' (LEVITICUS 25:38)." . . . For all the *mitzvot* of the Torah were given primarily to be fulfilled by those who dwell in the Land of God.

RABBI MOSHE BEN NACHMAN (NACHMANIDES, RAMBAN) 1194–1270

Scholar, philosopher, author, and physician. Nachmanides was born in Spain and served as leader of Iberian Jewry. In 1263, he was summoned by King James of Aragon to a public disputation with Pablo Cristiani, a Jewish apostate. Though Nachmanides was the clear victor of the debate, he had to flee Spain because of the resulting persecution. He moved to Israel and helped reestablish communal life in Jerusalem. He authored a classic commentary on the Pentateuch and a commentary on the Talmud.

Offering of the first fruits, brought to the Temple of Jerusalem, illustration from Dictionnaire Historique et Critique de la Bible *(Author: A. A. Calmet), publ. in Amsterdam, c. 1725. (Artist unknown)*

TEXT 10

RABBI JONATHAN SACKS, *COVENANT & CONVERSATION*, "THE G-D OF CREATION AND THE LAND OF ISRAEL," WWW.RABBISACKS.ORG

Why should a religion be tied to a land? It sounds absurd, especially in the context of monotheism. Surely the G-d of everywhere can be served anywhere. . . .

Judaism is not primarily about personal salvation, the relationship between the individual and G-d in the inner recesses of the soul. It is about collective redemption. . . . We are social animals. Therefore we find G-d in society. That is what we discover when we reflect on the basic structure of the Torah's many commands. They include laws about the administration of justice, the conduct of war, ownership of land, employer-employee relationships, the welfare of the poor, [and] the periodic cancellation of debts. . . .

Laws shape a society, and a society needs space. A sacred society needs sacred space, a holy land. Hence Jews and Judaism need their own land.

In four thousand years, for much of which Jews lived in exile, the people of the covenant were scattered over the face of the earth. There is no land in which Jews have never lived. Yet in all those centuries, there was only one land where they were able to do what almost every other nation takes for granted: create their own society in accordance with their own beliefs.

RABBI JONATHAN SACKS, PHD
1948–

Former chief rabbi of the United Kingdom. Rabbi Sacks attended Cambridge University and received his doctorate from King's College, London. A prolific and influential author, his books include *Will We Have Jewish Grandchildren?* and *The Dignity of Difference.* He received the Jerusalem Prize in 1995 for his contributions to enhancing Jewish life in the Diaspora, was knighted and made a life peer in 2005, and became Baron Sacks of Aldridge in 2009.

The premise of the Torah is that G-d must be found somewhere in particular if He is to be found everywhere in general.

TEXT 11

RABBI ARYEH KAPLAN, *JERUSALEM: EYE OF THE UNIVERSE* (NEW YORK: NATIONAL CONFERENCE OF SYNAGOGUE YOUTH, 1976), PP.77–78

If you look at a map, you will see that the geographical location of the Land of Israel virtually guaranteed that it would play a key role in the tides of civilization. The Old World consisted of two great land masses, Eurasia (Europe and Asia) and Africa. It was impossible to travel from Eurasia to Africa without passing through the Holy Land. Therefore, every conqueror, every civilization that passed from one continent to the other, had to pass through the Holy Land and come in contact with the Jew. . . .

Besides being a gateway between north and south, the Holy Land is part of the keystone link between east and west. . . . In the past, most caravan routes linking the Atlantic and Pacific passed directly through the Holy Land.

The Land of Israel was therefore literally the crossroads of civilization.

RABBI ARYEH KAPLAN
1934–1983

American rabbi, author, and physicist. Rabbi Kaplan authored more than 50 volumes on Torah, Talmud, Jewish mysticism, and philosophy, many of which have become modern-day classics. He is best known for his popular translation and elucidation of the Bible, *The Living Torah*, and his translation of the Ladino biblical commentary, *Me'am Lo'ez*.

TEXT 12

RUTH GAVISON, "THE JEWS' RIGHT TO STATEHOOD: A DEFENSE," *AZURE*, SUMMER 2003

Is it possible to justify the existence of a Jewish state? This question, raised with increased frequency in recent years, is not just a theoretical one. Israel will endure as a Jewish state only if it can be defended, in both the physical and the moral sense. . . .

Over the many years in which I have participated in debates about Israel's constitutional foundations and the rights of its citizens, I did not generally feel this question to be particularly urgent. Indeed, I believed that there was no more need to demonstrate the legitimacy of a Jewish state than there was for any other nation state, and I did not take claims to the contrary very seriously. Those who denied the legitimacy of Israel as a Jewish state were, in my eyes, little different from the radical ideologues who dismiss all national movements as inherently immoral, or who insist that Judaism is solely a religion with no right to national self-expression; their claims seemed marginal and unworthy of systematic refutation.

Today I realize that my view was wrong. The repudiation of Israel's right to exist as a Jewish state is now a commonly held position, and one that is increasingly seen as legitimate. Among Israeli Arabs, for example, it is nearly impossible to find anyone willing to endorse, at least

RUTH GAVISON
1945–

Israeli legal scholar. Ruth Gavison was born and raised in Israel, studied law at Hebrew University, and received her doctorate in philosophy of law from Oxford University. Gavison currently serves as a law professor at Hebrew University. Gavison served as President of the Israeli Association for Civil Rights and now heads the Metzila Center, an institute she established to promote the legitimacy of Israel as a Jewish and democratic state.

publicly, the right of Jews to national self-determination in the land of Israel. Rejection of the Jewish state has in fact become the norm among most representatives of the Arab public—including those who have sworn allegiance as members of Knesset. . . .

More worrisome, perhaps, is the fact that many Jews in Israel agree with this view, or at least show a measure of sympathy for it.

Painting made by students and teachers, found in a Gaza school room during the Six-Day War, 1967. (Photo credit: Magnum Photos; Leonard Freed, photographer)

TEXT 13

RABBI JONATHAN SACKS, *COVENANT & CONVERSATION*, "THE G-D OF CREATION AND THE LAND OF ISRAEL," OP. CIT.

Today the overwhelming majority of those who challenge Israel's right to exist believe in Israel's G-d, that is to say, the G-d of Abraham. They belong to the large family of faith known as the Abrahamic monotheisms.

To them, we must humbly say: when it comes to political conflict, let us search for a political solution. Let us work together in pursuit of peace. But when it comes to religion, let us not forget that without Judaism, there would be no Christianity and no Islam. Unlike Christianity and Islam, Judaism never sought to convert the world and never created an empire. All it sought was one tiny land, promised to the children of Israel by the creator of the universe, in whom Jews, Christians and Muslims all believe.

Sadly, Rabbi Isaac was right, and Rashi was right to quote him at the beginning of his Torah commentary. The Jewish people would be challenged on its right to the land, by people who claimed to worship the same G-d. That same G-d summons us today to the dignity of the human person, the sanctity of human life, and the imperative of peace. And that same G-d tells us that in a world of 82 Christian nations and 56 Muslim ones, there is room for one small Jewish state.

KEY POINTS

1 Although God is everywhere, Israel is the physical location that serves as the epicenter of the Jewish people's relationship with God.

2 Israel has been the homeland of the Jewish people for more than 3000 years. In every generation, even while the Land was under foreign rule, there were Jews living there.

3 Despite suffering millennia of exile and dispersion, the Land of Israel has always remained foremost in our nation's consciousness and the object of our love and yearning. We recall the Holy Land at every Jewish event and every life milestone.

4 Throughout the centuries, we have longed for the day we would return to the Holy Land. Every time we pray, we face Jerusalem and beseech God to return us to our ancestral homeland. Over the centuries, many Jews have made *aliyah*; many more, who could not, have chosen to be buried in Israel's soil.

5 The establishment of the State of Israel in 1948 provided the opportunity for many Jews to realize the dream of living in the Holy Land. Though the State of Israel stands on a firm legal foundation under international law, Israel's Arab neighbors refused to recognize the legitimacy of the Jewish state.

6 In May 1967, Egypt expelled the UN peacekeepers stationed in the Sinai Peninsula and announced a blockade of Israel's access to the Red Sea via the Straits of Tiran. Arab armies massed, and the Arab world openly pronounced their intention to "push the Jews into the sea." Israel was on the precipice of unspeakable tragedy.

7 Despite the Jews' seemingly well-founded claim to the Land of Israel—a claim that is certainly at least as valid as any other nation's right to their land—Israel's legitimacy is still being questioned by wide segments of the world community.

8 Our ultimate and truest claim to the Land lies in the Scriptures, whose entire narrative reads as the Jewish people's "title deed" to the Holy Land. God made a covenant with Abraham, Isaac, and Jacob and entrusted them and their descendants with a special mission. The covenant and mission are inexorably bound up with the promise of the Land.

9 Our purpose in life is to sanctify the physical world. To that end, God assigned a specific land to us, and tasked us to create there a very mundane—but divinely perfect—society. Our example radiates, and ultimately transforms, the entire world.

10 In order to be able to tell the world why the Land of Israel is ours, we first need to know ourselves why we need a land, and what our truest claim to the Land is.

Appendix

PRE-SIX-DAY WAR ARAB INCITEMENT AGAINST ISRAEL

"Every one of the hundred million Arabs has been living for the past nineteen years on one hope—to live to see the day Israel is liquidated. . . . There is no life, no peace nor hope for the gangs of Zionism to remain in the occupied land. As of today, there no longer exists [the UN] international emergency force to protect Israel. . . . The sole method we shall apply against Israel is a total war which will result in the extermination of Zionist existence"

—*Sawt al-Arab* ("Voice of Arabs"), Cairo Radio, May 18, 1967

"Our forces are now entirely ready not only to repulse any aggression, but to initiate the act ourselves, and to explode the Zionist presence in the Arab homeland of Palestine. The Syrian army, with its finger on the trigger, is united. I believe that the time has come to begin a battle of annihilation."

—Syrian Defense Minister Hafez Assad (later to be Syria's president), May 20, 1967

"We are ready to enter a general war with Israel. The battle will be a general one and our basic objective will be to destroy Israel."

—Egyptian President Gamel Abdel Nasser, in a speech to the General Council of the International Confederation of Arab Trade Unions, May 26, 1967

"We will not accept any . . . coexistence with Israel. . . . Today the issue is not the establishment of peace between the Arab states and Israel. . . . The war with Israel is in effect since 1948."

—Gamel Abdel Nasser, at a press conference before several hundred of the world's press, May 28, 1967

"The existence of Israel is an error which must be rectified. This is our opportunity to wipe out the ignominy, which has been with us since 1948. Our goal is clear—to wipe Israel off the map."

—Iraqi President Abdul Rahman Arif, May 31, 1967

"Those who survive will remain in Palestine. I estimate that none of them will survive."

—Ahmed Shukairy, chairman of the PLO in Jordanian Jerusalem, in a June 1, 1967, news interview, in response to the question, "What will happen to the Israelis if there is a war?"

"The men into the sea, the women for us."

—Popular chant at Arab rallies in the weeks leading up to the war, popularized by Ahmed Said, director and chief announcer of *Sawt al-Arab*

TEXT 14

TRAVELOGUE OF BENJAMIN OF TUDELA (CIRCA 1170)

From Tyre it is one day's travel to Acre, the Acco of Scripture, on the boundary of the tribe of Asher. It is the frontier of the Land of Israel. Because of its situation on the shore of the Mediterranean and its large port, it is the principal place of disembarkation of all pilgrims who come to Jerusalem by sea. . . . There are about two hundred Jewish inhabitants here, whose leaders are R. Zadok, R. Jepheth, and R. Jonah.

Three parasangs farther is Haifa. . . . One side of this city is situated on the coast, on the other it is overlooked by Mount Carmel. Under the mountain are many Jewish gravesites, and near the summit is the cavern of Elijah the Prophet. The Christians have built a place of worship near this site, which they call St. Elias. On the summit of the hill you may still trace the site of the altar which was rebuilt by Elijah in the time of King Ahab, and the circumference of which is about four yards. The Kishon River runs down the mountain and along its base.

It is four parasangs hence to Kfar Nachum, identical with Meon, the place of abode of Nabal the Carmelite. Six parasangs brings us to Cesarea . . . inhabited by about ten Jews and two hundred Samaritans. . . . To Kakun, the Keilah of Scripture, is half a day's journey; in this place are no Jews. To St. George, the ancient Luz,

BENJAMIN OF TUDELA
12TH CENTURY

Medieval traveler. Benjamin was born in Tudela, Spain, and little is known of his personal life. In 1165, he embarked on a journey that took him across Europe to Israel and the Middle East, continuing on through the Arabian Peninsula and North Africa and arriving back in Spain in 1173. In his journey, Benjamin visited virtually every medieval Jewish community, and his record of his travels, *Masa'ot Binyamin*, is an important source of medieval history and geography.

half a day's journey; one Jew only, a dyer, lives here. To Sebaste, one day's journey. This is the ancient Samaria, where you may still trace the site of the palace of the Israelite King Ahab. It was formerly a very strong city, and is situated on a mount, in a fine country, richly watered, and surrounded with gardens, orchards, vineyards, and olive-groves. No Jews live here.

It is two parasangs farther to Shechem (Nablus), situated in the valley between Mount Gerizim and Mount Ebal. It is the abode of about one thousand Cutheans, who observe the Mosaic law only, and are called Samaritans. . . . On Passover and holidays they offer burnt-offerings on the altar which they have erected on Mount Gerizim . . . which they claim is the Holy Temple. . . .

Jerusalem is a small city strongly fortified with three walls. It contains a numerous population, composed of Arabs, Jacobites, Arameans, Greeks, Georgians, Franks, and indeed of people of all tongues. The dyeing-house is rented by the year, and the exclusive privilege of dyeing is purchased from the king by the Jews of Jerusalem, two hundred of whom dwell in one corner of the city, under the tower of David. . . . The city contains no edifice stronger than the tower of David. There are two buildings there. One is a hospital that affords shelter to the sick; these are provided with everything they may want, both during life and in death. The second they call "Temple," being the palace originally built by King Solomon, which harbors and furnishes four hundred knights, who are ever ready to wage war. . . . In Jerusalem is the large place of worship, called Sepulcher, containing the sepulcher of "that man," visited by all pilgrims.

Jerusalem has four gates, called the gates of Abraham, David, Zion, and Jehoshaphat. The latter stands opposite the site of the Holy Temple. . . . Omar Ben Al-Khataab erected a large and handsome cupola over it; the gentiles do not put any idols or images in this place, but only come there to pray. In front of it you see the western wall, one of the walls of the Holy Temple . . . it is called the Gate of Mercy, and all Jews come there to pray. . . .

If you leave the city by the gate of Jehoshaphat, you may see the pillar erected on Absalom's place, and the grave of King Uzziah, and the great spring of Shiloah, which runs into the brook Kedron. Over this spring is a large building erected in the times of our forefathers. Very little water is found at Jerusalem; the inhabitants generally drink rain-water, which they collect in their houses.

From the Valley of Jehoshaphat the traveler immediately ascends the Mount of Olives. . . . From hence the Dead Sea is distinctly visible. Two parasangs from the sea stands the salt pillar into which Lot's wife was metamorphosed; and although the goats continually lick it, the pillar grows again, and retains its original state. You also have a prospect over the whole valley of the Dead Sea, and of the brook of Shittim, even as far as Mount Nebo. . . .

Two parasangs from Jerusalem is Bethlehem of Judea; and within half a mile of it, at a crossroads, stands the monument of the grave of Rachel. This monument is constructed of eleven stones, equal to the number of the children of Jacob. It is covered by a cupola, which rests upon four pillars; and every Jew who passes there inscribes his name on the stones of the monument. Twelve Jews, dyers by profession, live at Bethlehem. The country abounds with rivulets, wells, and springs of water.

Six parasangs farther is Hebron. The ancient city of that name was situated on the hill, and lies in ruins at present; in the valley is the Machpelah field and cave, and there the city is situated today. Here is the large place of worship called St. Abram de Bron, which during the time of the Mohammedans was a synagogue. The Gentiles have erected six sepulchers in this place, which they pretend to be those of Abraham and Sarah, of Isaac and Rebecca, and of Jacob and Leah; the pilgrims are told that they are the sepulchers of the patriarchs, and money is extorted from them. But if any Jew comes, who gives an additional fee to the keeper of the cave, an iron door is opened, which dates from the times of our forefathers who rest in peace, and with a burning candle in his hands the visitor descends into a first cave, which is empty, traverses a second in the same state, and at last reaches a third, which contains six graves, those of Abraham, Isaac, and Jacob, and of Sarah, Rebecca, and Leah, one opposite the other. . . . A lamp burns in the cave and upon the graves continually, both night and day; and you there see tubs filled with the bones of Israelites, for it was their custom to bring there the bones of their forefathers, and to leave them there. . . .

In Ramleh you still find walls erected by our forefathers, as is evident from the inscriptions upon the stones. The city contains about three hundred Jews. It was formerly very considerable, for a Jewish cemetery in its vicinity is two miles in extent.

Five parasangs hence to Jaffa, the Japho of Scripture, on the coast; one Jew only, a dyer by profession, lives here. Three parasangs to Ibelin, the ancient Jabneh, where the site of the school may still be traced; it contains no Jews. . . .

Ascalon, which is in fact the New Ascalon, built on the coast by Ezra the Priest . . . is very large and handsome; and merchants from all parts resort to it, on account of its convenient situation on the border of Egypt. There are here about two hundred Jews, of whom the principals are R. Tzemach, R. Aaron, and R. Solomon, besides about forty Karaites, and about three hundred Cutheans or Samaritans. In the city is a fountain called Bir Ibrabim-al-Khahil, and it is said that this is the well dug by Abraham in the time of the Philistines.

In Sepphoris, the Tzippori of antiquity, are the gravesites of Rabbi Judah HaNasi, Rabban Gamliel, of R. Chiya, who came back from Babylon, and of Jonah the son of Amittai the prophet. . . . From Sepphoris it is five parasangs to Tiberius, a city situated between two mountains on the shore of the Sea of Kinereth, which is a river large and wide as a lake; the Jordan flows into it, and then emerges from it and flows through planes to a place called Ashdoth-Pisga, and then empties itself into the Dead Sea. Tiberius contains about fifty Jews, the leaders of whom are R. Abraham the astronomer, R. Muchthar, and R. Isaac. The hot waters, which spout forth from underground, are called the hot springs of Tiberias.

TEXT 15

THE REBBE, RABBI MENACHEM M. SCHNEERSON, ROSH HASHANAH MESSAGE, DAYS OF *SELICHOTH* 5717 (1957)

בִּסְקִירָה פְּשׁוּטָה אֶפְשָׁר בְּנָקֵל לִמְצוֹא אֶת הַצַּד הַשָּׁוֶה, הַקַּו הַמְיֻחָד, שֶׁהָיָה תָּמִיד אֵצֶל בְּנֵי יִשְׂרָאֵל בְּכָל הַתְּקוּפוֹת וְהַמְּאוֹרָעוֹת הַשּׁוֹנִים, שֶׁבּוֹ קְשׁוּרָה עֶצֶם הַמַּהוּת וְהַקִּיּוּם שֶׁל עַם יִשְׂרָאֵל.

סְקִירָה אוֹבְּיֶיקְטִיבִית, לְלֹא דֵּעָה קְדוּמָה, לְאוֹרֶךְ הַהִיסְטוֹרְיָה שֶׁל עַם יִשְׂרָאֵל, מוּכְרַחַת לְהָבִיא לִידֵי מַסְקָנָא, שֶׁקִּיּוּמוֹ שֶׁל עַמֵּנוּ בְּוַדַּאי אֵינוֹ קָשׁוּר בְּשֶׁפַע חוּמְרִי אוֹ עוֹצְמָה פִיזִית. אֲפִילוּ בַּזְּמַנִּים הַטּוֹבִים בְּיוֹתֵר, תַּחַת הַמַּמְלָכָה הַמְאוּחֶדֶת שֶׁל שְׁלֹמֹה הַמֶּלֶךְ, הָיָה עַם יִשְׂרָאֵל וּמַלְכוּת יִשְׂרָאֵל - מִבְּחִינָה פּוֹלִיטִית וְכַלְכָּלִית - קְטַנִּים בְּהַשְׁוָאָה לִמְלוּכוֹת הָעוֹלָם בִּזְמַן הַהוּא, מִצְרַיִם, אַשּׁוּר וּבָבֶל. כְּמוֹ כֵּן בָּרוּר, שֶׁלֹּא שִׁלְטוֹן הַמְּלוּכָה וְלֹא הַשֶּׁטַח הַגִּיאוֹגְרָפִי [הַגֵּאוֹגְרָפִי] הִבְטִיחוּ אֶת קִיּוּמֵנוּ, כִּי הַהִיסְטוֹרְיָה שֶׁלָּנוּ בְּתוֹר עַם בַּעַל מְדִינָה בְּאַרְצוֹ, הִיא קְצָרָה בְּיוֹתֵר בְּהַשְׁוָאָה עִם הַהִסְטוֹרְיָה הַגָּלוּתִית שֶׁלָּנוּ, לְלֹא מְלוּכָה וּלְלֹא אֶרֶץ. כְּמוֹ כֵן לֹא יְכוֹלָה הַשָּׂפָה לְהֵחָשֵׁב יְסוֹד חִיּוּנִי בְּקִיּוּמֵנוּ, כִּי עוֹד בִּימֵי קֶדֶם שִׁמְּשָׁה אֲרָמִית כִּשְׂפַת דִּיבּוּר שֶׁל הָעָם: חֲלָקִים שֶׁל הַתַּנַ"ךְ, כִּמְעַט כָּל תַּלְמוּד בַּבְלִי, הַזֹּהַר וְעוֹד, נִכְתְּבוּ בַּלָּשׁוֹן הָאֲרָמִית. בִּימֵי ר' סַעֲדְיָה גָּאוֹן וְהָרַמְבַּ"ם הָיְתָה הַשָּׂפָה הָעַרְבִית שְׂפָתָם שֶׁל רוֹב הֲמוֹנֵי הָעָם, וּלְאַחַר מִכֵּן אִידִישׁ וְשָׂפוֹת אֲחֵרוֹת. כְּמוֹ כֵּן אִי אֶפְשָׁר לוֹמַר שֶׁמִּין תַּרְבּוּת אוֹ מַדָּע כְּלָלִיִּים הִבְטִיחוּ אֶת קִיּוּם אוּמָּתֵנוּ, כִּי דְּבָרִים אֵלֶּה נִשְׁתַּנּוּ בְּתַכְלִית מִתְּקוּפָה לִתְקוּפָה.

נִשְׁאַר רַק דָּבָר אֶחָד, שֶׁהוּא הַצַּד הַשָּׁוֶה לְכָל הַזְּמַנִּים, כָּל הָאֲרָצוֹת וְכָל הַתְּנָאִים שֶׁבְּדִבְרֵי יָמֵינוּ - הַתּוֹרָה וְהַמִּצְווֹת שֶׁשָּׁמְרוּ בְּנֵי יִשְׂרָאֵל בְּחַיֵּיהֶם הַיּוֹם-יוֹמִיִּים בִּמְסִירוּת נֶפֶשׁ גְּדוֹלָה בְּיוֹתֵר . . .

כִּי קִיּוּם עַמֵּנוּ תָּלוּי אַךְ וְרַק בְּקִיּוּם הַתּוֹרָה וְהַמִּצְווֹת בְּחַיֵּי יוֹם יוֹם, שֶׁל הַיָּחִיד וְשֶׁל הַצִּיבּוּר.

סוֹד קִיּוּמֵנוּ כְּעַם הוּא "הֵן עַם לְבָדָד יִשְׁכּוֹן", שֶׁכָּל יָחִיד, אִישׁ, אִשָּׁה וְיֶלֶד, עוֹבְדִים רַק אֶת ה' אֶחָד, עַל פִּי תּוֹרָתֵנוּ תּוֹרָה אַחַת, שֶׁהִיא נִצְחִית וְאֵינָהּ יְכוֹלָה לְהִשְׁתַּנּוֹת חַס וְשָׁלוֹם. הַ"שּׁוֹנִי שֶׁלָּנוּ" אֵינוֹ חוּלְשָׁה שֶׁלָּנוּ, אֶלָּא הַתּוֹקֶף שֶׁלָּנוּ. רַק בְּדֶרֶךְ הַתּוֹרָה וְהַמִּצְווֹת יְכוֹלִים אָנוּ לְמַלֵּא אֶת תַּפְקִידֵנוּ הָעִיקָּרִי וְהַמַּהוּתִי שֶׁהוּא לְפִי צִיוּוּיוֹ שֶׁל בּוֹרֵא הָעוֹלָם כּוּלּוֹ - לִהְיוֹת "מַמְלֶכֶת כֹּהֲנִים וְגוֹי קָדוֹשׁ" וְעַל יְדֵי זֶה גַּם סְגוּלָה לָאֱנוֹשׁוּת כּוּלָּהּ.

RABBI MENACHEM MENDEL SCHNEERSON 1902–1994

The towering Jewish leader of the 20th century, known as "the Lubavitcher Rebbe," or simply as "the Rebbe." Born in southern Ukraine, the Rebbe escaped Nazi-occupied Europe, arriving in the U.S. in June 1941. The Rebbe inspired and guided the revival of traditional Judaism after the European devastation, impacting virtually every Jewish community the world over. The Rebbe often emphasized that the performance of just one additional good deed could usher in the era of Mashiach. The Rebbe's scholarly talks and writings have been printed in more than 200 volumes.

By a process of simple elimination, we can easily ascertain what factors have been essential to [the Jewish people's] existence and survival, and thus [also] determine the essential character and function of our people.

An objective, unprejudiced survey of the long history of our people will at once bring to light the fact that it was not material wealth, nor physical strength, that helped us to survive. Even during the most prosperous times under the united monarchy of King Solomon, the Jewish people and state were materially insignificant by comparison with such contemporary world empires as Egypt, Assyria and Babylonia. That it was not statehood or homeland—is clear from the fact that most of the time, by far, our people possessed no independent state and has lived in the diaspora. That it was not the language, is likewise clear from the fact that even in Biblical times Aramaic began to supplant the Holy Tongue as the spoken language; parts of the Scripture and almost all of our Babylonian Talmud, the Zohar, etc., are written in that language. In the days of Saadia and Maimonides, Arabic was the spoken language of most Jews, while, later, Yiddish and other languages. Nor was it any common secular culture that preserved our people, since that changed radically from one era to another.

The one and only common factor which has been present with Jews throughout the ages, in all lands, and under all circumstances, is the Torah [and] Mitzvoth, which Jews have observed tenaciously in their daily life. . . .

The essential factor of our existence and survival is our adherence to the Torah and the practice of its precepts in our everyday life.

The secret of our existence is in our being "a people that dwell alone" (NUM. 23:9), every one of us, man or woman, believing in the One G-d, leading a life according to the one Torah, which is eternal and unchangeable. Our "otherness" and independence of thought and conduct are not our weakness but our strength. Only in this way can we fulfill our function imposed on us by the Creator, to be unto G-d a "kingdom of priests and a holy nation," thereby being also a "segulah" for all humanity.

TEXT 16

RABBI YEHUDAH HALEVI, *KUZARI* 2:9–12

אָמַר הַכּוּזַרִי: אָמְרְךָ "לְעַמּוֹ" כְּבָר נִתְבָּאֵר לִי, אֲבָל אָמְרְךָ "בְּאַרְצוֹ" קָשֶׁה עָלַי לְקַבְּלוֹ.

אָמַר הֶחָבֵר: אֵין זֶה קָשֶׁה לְקַבֵּל יִחוּד אֶרֶץ מִכְּלַל הָאֲרָצוֹת, וַהֲרֵי אַתָּה רוֹאֶה מְקוֹמוֹת נִבְחָרִים לְצֶמַח מְסוּיָּים בִּלְעָדֵי צֶמַח אַחֵר, וּמַתָּכוֹת בִּלְעָדֵי מַתָּכוֹת, וּבַעֲלֵי חַיִּים בִּלְעָדֵי בַּעֲלֵי חַיִּים, וְיִתְיַחֲדוּ אֲנָשָׁיו בְּצוּרוֹת וּמִדּוֹת בִּלְעָדֵי זוּלָתָם, בְּאֶמְצָעוּת הַמֶּזֶג, כִּי לְפִי הַמֶּזֶג תִּהְיֶה שְׁלֵמוּת הַנֶּפֶשׁ וּמִגְרַעְתָּהּ.

אָמַר הַכּוּזַרִי: אֲבָל לֹא שָׁמַעְתִּי עַל תּוֹשָׁבֵי אֶרֶץ יִשְׂרָאֵל מַעֲלָה עַל שְׁאָר בְּנֵי אָדָם.

אָמַר הֶחָבֵר: כָּךְ הַרְכֶּם זֶה, אַתֶּם אוֹמְרִים שֶׁהוּא מַצְלִיחַ בּוֹ הַכֶּרֶם, וְאִלּוּ לֹא נִיטְעוּ בּוֹ הַדְּלָיוֹת וְנֶעֶבְדָה בּוֹ הָאֲדָמָה כָּרָאוּי לָהּ, לֹא הָיָה מֵנִיב עֲנָבִים. וְהִנֵּה הַיִּחוּד הָרִאשׁוֹן לָעַם אֲשֶׁר הֵם סְגוּלָּה וְהַבְּחִירִים, כְּפִי שֶׁאָמַרְתָּ. וְאַחַר כָּךְ לָאֶרֶץ יֵשׁ בְּכָךְ עֵזֶר עִם הַמַּעֲשִׂים וְהַמִּצְוֹות הַצְּמוּדִים לָהֶם, אֲשֶׁר הֵם כַּעֲבוֹדָה לְכֶּרֶם. אֲבָל לֹא יִתָּכֵן לָאֵלֶּה הַסְּגוּלָּה לְהִדָּבֵק בַּדָּבָר הָאֱלֹקִי בְּזוּלַת הַמָּקוֹם הַזֶּה, כְּפִי שֶׁנִּתְבָּרֵר הַהַצְלָחָה לְכֶרֶם בְּזוּלַת הָהָר הַזֶּה.

The Kuzari: You speak of "a Godly people in a Godly land." Regarding a "Godly people," the meaning is clear to me. But the idea of a "Godly land" is difficult to accept.

The Rabbi: It should not be difficult to see how one land may be unique amongst others in a certain respect. There are places where particular plants, metals, or animals are found, or whose inhabitants are distinguished in their physiology and character.

The Kuzari: But I have not heard that there is anything special about the people living in the Land of Israel in comparison with other peoples.

הכוזרי

RABBI YEHUDAH HALEVI
CA. 1075–1141

Noted author, physician, and poet. Rabbi Yehudah Halevi is best known as the author of the *Kuzari*, a philosophical work, written in the form of a discussion between a Jew, a Christian, and a Muslim before the King of the Khazars. In addition to the *Kuzari*, he wrote thousands of poems, of which only a few hundred survive today.

The Rabbi: How about that hill on which you say that vines thrive so well? It will not produce choice wine unless one plants grapevines in it and does all the necessary vinicultural work. The first thing that is required is a people with the unique qualities; then the land, and the actions taken in it (in this case, the *mitzvot* tied to the Holy Land, which can be compared to the cultivation of the vineyard) will also play a part in their greatness. Yet unlike the grapevine, which could conceivably produce grapes in other locales as well, the chosen people can cleave to the divine ideal only in this land.

Additional Readings

THE HEBRON PURCHASE

RABBI YANKI TAUBER, BASED ON THE TEACHINGS OF THE REBBE

In chapter 23 of Genesis, we read of the first tract in the Land of Israel to enter into Jewish possession.

Sixty years earlier, G-d had told Abraham: "The entire land that you see, I will give to you and your descendants forever . . . Arise and traverse the land, in its length and in its breadth, for to you I shall give it" (Genesis 13:15, 17). But this was a promise concerning the future; the land was not yet his, and Abraham took care not to even allow his sheep to graze on Canaanite property. (Indeed, this was the cause of the split between Abraham and his nephew Lot—see Rashi on Genesis 13:7.) The first part of the Land of Israel to belong to the Jewish people in the actual and legal sense was the "Machpelah field and its cave" in the heart of Hebron, which Abraham purchased from Ephron the Hittite.

As our sages point out, there are three parts of Israel over which the Jewish right of ownership is most powerfully established. Even one who denies the divine promise quoted above—and reiterated by G-d tens of times throughout the Bible—cannot contest the Jewish right over the Temple Mount in Jerusalem, purchased by King David from Aravnah the Jebusite (as related in the closing verses of II Samuel); the section of Shechem (Nablus) purchased by Jacob from the family of the Canaanite ruler Hamor (Genesis 33:19); and the Machpelah field of Hebron, of which we read:

> *And Abraham weighed to Ephron the silver, which he had named in the hearing of the sons of Heth, four hundred shekels of silver in negotiable currency. . . .*
>
> *Then Abraham buried Sarah his wife in the cave of the field of Machpelah before Mamre, that is Hebron, in the land of Canaan.*

The Torah recounts the Ephron-Abraham sale in great detail, including the sum of the purchase price—four hundred silver shekels. Based on this figure, the thirteenth-century sage Rabbi Yitzchak bar Yehudah (author of *Paaneach Raza*) makes an interesting calculation. According to Leviticus 27:16, the value of land in biblical times was 50 silver shekels for a *beit kor*, or 75,000 square *amot* (cubits). Thus, the area purchased by Abraham was eight *beit kor*, or 600,000 square cubits. A square cubit is the approximate area occupied by an upright human being.

The generation of Jews which left Egypt and received the Torah at Mount Sinai numbered some 600,000 heads of households. Our sages tell us that the Jewish nation consists of 600,000 souls, and that the soul of every Jew who ever lived is an offshoot of one of these 600,000 "general" souls. Thus the Torah contains 600,000 letters (counting the spaces between letters), for each Jew possesses something of the Torah.

The same is true of the Land of Israel. Israel is the eternal inheritance of the Jewish people, equally the property of every individual Jew. And so it has been from the very first moment of Jewish ownership of the Holy Land: the first plot of land obtained by the first Jew included a share for every Jewish soul.

Chabad.org

RABBI YANKI TAUBER, 1965–

Chasidic scholar and author. A native of Brooklyn, NY, Rabbi Tauber is an internationally renowned author who specializes in adapting the teachings of the Lubavitcher Rebbe. He is a member of the JLI curriculum development team, and has written numerous articles and books, including *Once Upon a Chassid* and *Beyond the Letter of the Law*.

LAND OWNERSHIP IN PALESTINE, 1880–1948

MOSHE AUMANN

A great deal has been spoken and written over the years on the subject of land ownership in Israel—or, before 1948, Palestine. Arab propaganda, in particular, has been at pains to convince the world, with the aid of copious statistics, that the Arabs "own" Palestine, morally and legally, and that whatever Jewish land ownership there may be is negligible. From this conclusions have been drawn (or implied) with regard to the sovereign rights of the State of Israel and the problem of the Arab refugees.

The Arab case against Israel, in the matter of Jewish land purchases, rests mainly on two claims: (1) that the Palestinian Arab farmer was peacefully and contentedly working his land in the latter part of the 19th century and the early part of the 20th when along came the European Jewish immigrant, drove him off his land, disrupted the normal development of the country and created a vast class of landless, dispossessed Arabs; (2) that a small Jewish minority, owning an even smaller proportion of Palestinian lands (5 per cent as against the Arabs' 95 per cent), illegally made itself master of Palestine in 1948.

Our purpose in this pamphlet is to set the record straight by marshalling the facts and figures pertaining to this very complex subject, on the basis of the most reliable and authoritative information available, and to trace the history of modern Jewish resettlement purely from the point of view of the sale and purchase of land.

MOSHE AUMANN, 1926–

Diplomat and author. Born in Frankfurt, Germany, Moshe Aumann's family fled Nazi Germany to the United States, where he attained his degrees in journalism and social sciences from the City College of New York. In 1950 he made *aliyah* to Israel and worked as a journalist. Aumann served for 35 years in Israel's Foreign Ministry, and focused on Israeli-Christian relations. He has written about Christian attitudes about Israel, and land ownership in the pre-State of Israel era.

Pre-1948 Conditions in Palestine

A study of Palestine under Turkish rule reveals that already at the beginning of the 18th century, long before Jewish land purchases and large-scale Jewish immigration started, the position of the Palestinian fellah (peasant) had begun to deteriorate. The heavy burden of taxation, coming on top of chronic indebtedness to money-lenders, drove a growing number of farmers to place themselves under the protection of men of wealth or of the Moslem religious endowment fund *(Waqf)*, with the result that they were eventually compelled to give up their title to the land, if not their actual residence upon and cultivation of it.

Until the passage of the Turkish Land Registry Law in 1858, there were no official deeds to attest to a man's legal title to a parcel of land; tradition alone had to suffice to establish such title—and usually it did. And yet, the position of Palestine's farmers was a precarious one, for there were constant blood-feuds between families, clans and entire villages, as well as periodic incursions by rapacious Bedouin tribes, such as the notorious Ben Sakk'r, of whom H. B. Tristram *(The Land of Israel: A Journal of Travels in Palestine,* Society for Promoting Christian Knowledge, London, 1865) wrote that they "can muster 1,000 cavalry and always join their brethren when a raid or war is on the move. They have obtained their present possessions gradually and, in great measure, by driving out the fellahin (peasants), destroying their villages and reducing their rich corn-fields to pasturage." (p. 488.)

Tristram goes on to present a remarkable and highly revealing description of conditions in Palestine on both sides of the Jordan River in the middle of the 19th century—a description that belies the Arab claim of a tranquil, normally developing Palestinian rural economy allegedly disrupted by Jewish immigration and settlement.

> *A few years ago, the whole Ghor was in the hands of the fellahin, and much of it cultivated for corn.*

Now the whole of it is in the hands of the Bedouin, who eschew all agriculture, except in a few spots cultivated here and there by their slaves; and with the Bedouin come lawlessness and the uprooting of all Turkish authority. No government is now acknowledged on the east side; and unless the Porte acts with greater firmness and caution than is his wont . . . Palestine will be desolated and given up to the nomads.

The same thing is now going on over the plain of Sharon, where, both in the north and south, land is going out of cultivation, and whole villages [are] rapidly disappearing from the face of the earth. Since the year 1838, no [fewer] than 20 villages have been thus erased from the map and the stationary population extirpated. Very rapidly the Bedouin are encroaching wherever horse can be ridden; and the Government is utterly powerless to resist them or to defend its subjects. (p. 490)

For descriptions of other parts of the country, we are indebted to the 1937 Report of the Palestine Royal Commission—though, for lack of space, we can quote but the briefest passages. In Chapter 9, para. 43 the Report quotes an eye-witness account of the condition of the Maritime Plain in 1913:

The road leading from Gaza to the north was only a summer track suitable for transport by camels and carts . . . no orange groves, orchards or vineyards were to be seen until one reached Yabna village. . . . Not in a single village in all this area was water used for irrigation. . . .Houses were all of mud. No windows were anywhere to be seen. . . .The ploughs used were of wood. . . . The yields were very poor. . . .The sanitary conditions in the village were horrible. Schools did not exist. . . . The rate of infant mortality was very high. . . .

The area north of Jaffa . . . consisted of two distinctive parts. . . . The eastern part, in the direction of the hills, resembled in culture that of the Gaza-Jaffa area. . . . The western part, towards the sea, was almost a desert. . . . The villages in this area were few and thinly populated. Many ruins of villages were scattered over the area, as owing to the prevalence of malaria, many villages were deserted by their inhabitants.

The Huleh basin, below the Syrian border, is described as "including a number of Arab villages and a large papyrus swamp draining south into Lake Huleh . . . a triangular strip of land some 44 sq. miles in area. . . . This tract is irrigated in a very haphazard manner by a network of small, primitive canals. It is, owing to over-irrigation, now the most malarious tract in all Palestine. It might become one of the most fertile."

With regard to yet another region in Palestine—the Beisan (Beit Shean) area—we quote from the report of Mr. Lewis French, Director of Development appointed by the British Government in 1931:

We found it inhabited by fellahin who lived in mud hovels and suffered severely from the prevalent malaria. . . . Large areas of their lands were uncultivated and covered with weeds. There were no trees, no vegetables. The fellahin, if not themselves cattle thieves, were always ready to harbor these and other criminals. The individual plots of cultivation changed hands annually. There was little public security, and the fellahin's lot was an alternation of pillage and blackmail by their neighbours, the Bedouin.

This, then, was the picture of Palestine in the closing decades of the 19th century and up to the First World War: a land that was overwhelmingly desert, with nomads continually encroaching on the settled areas and its farmers; a lack of elementary facilities and equipment; peasants wallowing in poverty, ignorance and disease, saddled with debts (interest rates at times were as high as 60 per cent) and threatened by warlike nomads or neighbouring clans. The result was a growing neglect of the soil and a flight from the villages, with a mounting concentration of lands in the hands of a small number of large landowners, frequently residing in such distant Arab capitals as Beirut and Damascus, Cairo and Kuwait. Here, in other words, was a social and economic order that had all the earmarks of a medieval feudal society.

Who Dispossessed the Palestinian Peasant?

The Palestinian peasant was indeed being dispossessed, but by his fellow-Arabs: the local sheikh and village elders, the Government tax-collector, the merchants and money-lenders; and, when he was a tenant-farmer (as was usually the case), by the absentee-owner. By the time the season's crop had been distributed among all these, little if anything remained for him and his family, and new debts generally had to be incurred to pay off the old. Then the Bedouin came along and took their "cut", or drove the hapless fellah off the land altogether.

This was the "normal" course of events in 19th-century Palestine. It was disrupted by the advent of the Jewish pioneering enterprise, which sounded the death-knell of this medieval feudal system. In this way the Jews played an objective revolutionary role. Small wonder that it aroused the ire and active opposition of the Arab sheikhs, absentee landowners, money-lenders and Bedouin bandits.

Jewish Land Purchases

It is important to note that the first enduring Jewish agricultural settlement in modern Palestine was founded not by European refugees, but by a group of old-time families, leaving the overcrowded Jewish Quarter of the Old City of Jerusalem. (According to the Turkish census of 1875, by that time Jews already constituted a majority of the population of Jerusalem and by 1905 comprised two-thirds of its citizens. The *Encyclopaedia Britannica* of 1910 gives the population figure as 60,000, of whom 40,000 were Jews.)

In 1878 they founded the village of Petah Tikva in the Sharon Plain—a village that was to become known as the "Mother of Jewish Settlements" in Palestine. Four years later a group of pioneering immigrants from Russia settled in Rishon le-Zion. Other farming villages followed in rapid succession.

When considering Jewish land purchases and settlements, four factors should be borne in mind:

1. Most of the land purchases involved large tracts belonging to absentee owners. (Virtually all of the Jezreel Valley, for example, belonged in 1897 to only two persons: the eastern portion to the Turkish Sultan, and the western part to the richest banker in Syria, Sursuk "the Greek.")
2. Most of the land purchased had not been cultivated previously because it was swampy, rocky, sandy or, for some other reason, regarded as uncultivable. This is supported by the findings of the Peel Commission Report (p. 242): "The Arab charge that the Jews have obtained too large a proportion of good land cannot be maintained. Much of the land now carrying orange groves was sand dunes or swamp and uncultivated when it was purchased . . . there was at the time at least of the earlier sales little evidence that the owners possessed either the resources or training needed to develop the land." (1937)
3. While, for this reason, the early transactions did not involve unduly large sums of money, the price of land began to rise as Arab landowners took advantage of the growing demand for rural tracts. The resulting infusion of capital into the Palestinian economy had noticeable beneficial effects on the standard of living of all the inhabitants.
4. The Jewish pioneers introduced new farming methods which improved the soil and crop cultivation and were soon emulated by Arab farmers.

The following figures show land purchases by the three leading Jewish land-buying organizations and by individual Jews between 1880 and 1935.

Jewish Land Purchases, 1880–1935 (in Dunams[1])

Organization	Total Land Acquired	Government Concessions	From Private Owners	Large Tracts[2] Dunams	Large Tract Percent (approx.)
PICA (Palestine Jewish Colonization Association)	469,407	39,520	429,887	293,545	70
Palestine Land Development Co.	579,492	66,513[3]	512,979	455,169	90
Jewish National Fund[4]	836,396				
Until 1930			270,084	239,170	90
1931–1947			566,312		50
Individual Jews	432,100		432,100		50

From the above table it will be seen that the proportion of the land purchased from large (usually absentee) owners ranged from about 50 to 90 per cent.

"The total area of land in Jewish possession at the end of June 1947," writes A. Granott in *The Land System in Palestine* (Eyre and Spottiswoode, London, 1952, p. 278), "amounted to 1,850,000 dunams, of this 181,100 dunams had been obtained through concessions from the Palestinian Government, and about 120,000 dunams had been acquired from Churches, from foreign companies, from the Government otherwise than by concessions, and so forth. It was estimated that 1,000,000 dunams and more, or 57 per cent, had been acquired from large Arab landowners, and if to this we add the lands acquired from the Government, Churches, and foreign companies, the percentage will amount to seventy-three. From the fellaheen there had been purchased about 500,000 dunams, or 27 per cent, of the total acquired. The result of Jewish land acquisitions, at least to a considerable part, was that properties which had been in the hands of large and medium owners were converted into holding of small peasants."

The League of Nations Mandate

When the League of Nations conferred the Mandate for Palestine upon Great Britain in 1922, it expressly stipulated that "The Administration of Palestine . . . shall encourage, in cooperation with the Jewish Agency . . . close settlement by Jews on the land, including State lands and waste lands not acquired for public purposes" (Article 6), and that it "shall introduce a land system appropriate to the needs of the country, having regard, among other things, to the desirability of promoting the close settlement and intensive cultivation of the land." (Article 11)

British policy, however, followed a different course, deferring to the extremist Arab opposition to the above-mentioned provision of the Mandate. Of some 750,000 dunams of cultivable State lands, 350,000, or nearly half, had been allotted by 1949 to Arabs and only 17,000 dunams to Jews. This was in clear violation of the terms of the Mandate. Nor, ironically enough, did it help the Arab peasants for whose benefit these transactions were ostensibly carried out. The glaring examples of this policy are the case of the Besian lands and that of the Huleh Concession.

Besian Lands

Under the Ghor-Mudawwarra Agreement of 1921, some 225,000 dunams of potentially fertile wasteland in the Besian (Beit Shean) area were handed over to Arab farmers on terms severely condemned not only by Jews but also by such British experts as Lewis French and Sir John Hope-Simpson. More than half of the land was irrigable, and, according to the British experts, eight dunams of irrigated land per capita (or 50–60 dunams per family) were sufficient to enable a family to maintain itself on the land. Yet many farmers received far more than that: six families, of whom two lived in Syria, received a combined area of about 7,000 dunams; four families (some living in Egypt) received a combined area of 3,496 dunams ; another received 3,450 and yet another, 1,350.

Thus the Ghor-Mudawwarra Agreement was instrumental in creating a new group of large landowners. Possessing huge tracts, most of which they were unable to till, these owners began to sell the surplus lands at speculative prices. In his 1930 Report, Sir Hope-Simpson wrote of the Agreement that it had deprived the Government of "the control of a large area of fertile land eminently suited for development and for which there is ample water for irrigation," and that "the grant of the land has led to speculation on a considerable scale."

Huleh Area

For twenty years (from 1914 to 1934) the Huleh Concession—some 57,000 dunams of partly swamp-infested but potentially highly fertile land in northeastern Palestine—was in Arab hands. The Arab concessionaires were to drain and develop the land so as to make additional tracts available for cultivation, under very attractive terms offered by the Government (first Turkish, then British). However, this was never done, and in 1934 the concession was sold to a Jewish concern, the Palestine Land Development Company, at a huge profit. The Government added several onerous conditions concerning the amount of land (from the drained and newly developed tracts) that had to be handed over—without reimbursement for drainage and irrigation costs—to Arab tenant-farmers in the area.

All told, hundreds of millions of dollars were paid by Jewish buyers to Arab landowners. Official records show that in 1933 £854,796 was paid by Jewish individuals and organizations for Arab land, mostly large estates; in 1934 the figure was £1,647,836 and in 1935, £1,699,488. Thus, in the course of only three years £4,202,180 (more than 20 million dollars at the prevailing rate of exchange) was paid out to Arab landowners (Palestine Royal Commission Report, 1937).

To understand the magnitude of the prices paid for these lands, we need only look at some comparative figures. In 1944, Jews paid between $1,000 and $1,100 per acre in Palestine, mostly for arid or semi-arid land; in the same year rich black soil in the state of Iowa was selling for about $110 per acre (U.S. Department of Agriculture).

Effects on Arab Population

In those instances where as a result of such transactions Arab tenant-farmers were displaced (on one year's notice), compensation in cash or other land was paid, as required by the 1922 Protection of Cultivators Ordinance; the Jewish land-buying associations often paid more than the law required (Pollack and Boehm, *The Keren Kayemeth Le-Israel).* Of 688 such tenants between 1920 and 1930, 526 remained in agricultural occupations, some 400 of them finding other land (Palestine Royal Commission Report, 1937, Chapter 9, para. 61).

Investigations initiated in 1931 by Mr. Lewis French disposed of the charge that a large class of landless or dispossessed Arab farmers was created as a result of Jewish land purchases. According to the British Government report (Memoranda prepared by the Government of Palestine, London 1937, Colonia No. 133, p. 37), the total number of applications for registration as landless Arabs was 3,271. Of these, 2,607 were rejected on the ground that they did not come within the category of landless Arabs. Valid claims were recognized in the case of 664 heads of families, of whom 347 accepted the offer of resettlement by the Government. The remainder refused either because they had found satisfactory employment elsewhere or because they were not accustomed to irrigated cultivation or the climate of the new areas (*Peel Report*, Chapter 9, para. 60).

Purchases of land by Jews in the hill country had always been very small and, according to the investigations by Mr. French, of 71 applications by Arabs claiming to be landless, 68 were turned down.

Arab Population Changes Due to Jewish Settlement

Another Arab claim disproved by the facts is that Zionist "colonialism" led to the disruption and ruin of the Arab Palestinian society and economy.

Statistics published in the Palestine Royal Commission Report (p. 279) indicate a remarkable phenomenon: Palestine, traditionally a country of Arab emigration, became after World War I a country of

Arab immigration. In addition to recorded figures for 1920-36, the Report devotes a special section to illegal Arab immigration. While there are no precise totals on the extent of Arab immigration between the two World Wars, estimates vary between 60,000 and 100,000. The principal cause of the change of direction was Jewish development, which created new and attractive work opportunities and, in general, a standard of living previously unknown in the Middle East.

Another major factor in the rapid growth of the Arab population was, of course, the rate of natural increase, among the highest in the world. This was accentuated by the steady reduction of the previously high infant mortality rate as a result of the improved health and sanitary conditions introduced by the Jews.

Altogether, the non-Jewish element in Palestine's population (not including Bedouin) expanded between 1922 and 1929 alone by more than 75 per cent. The *Royal Commission Report* makes these interesting observations:

> *The shortage of land is, we consider, due less to the amount of land acquired by Jews than to the increase in the Arab population, (p. 242) We are also of the opinion that up till now the Arab cultivator has benefited, on the whole, both from the work of the British administration and from the presence of Jews in the country. Wages have gone up; the standard of living has improved; work on roads and buildings has been plentiful. In the Maritime Plains some Arabs have adopted improved methods of cultivation. (p. 241)*

Jewish development served as an incentive not only to Arab entry into Palestine from Lebanon, Egypt, Syria and other neighbouring countries, but also to Arab population movements within the country—to cities and areas where there was a large Jewish concentration. Some idea of this phenomenon may be gained from the following official figures:

Changes in towns: The Arab population in predominantly Arab towns rose only slightly (if at all) between the two World Wars: in Hebron—from 16,650 in 1922 to 22,800 in 1943; Nablus—from 15,931 to 23,300; Jenin—from 2,737 to 3,900; Bethlehem—from 6,658 to 8,800. Gaza's population actually decreased from 17,426 in 1922 to 17,045 in 1931.

On the other hand, in the three major Jewish cities the Arab population shot up during this period, far beyond the rate of natural increase: Jerusalem—from 28,571 in 1922 to 56,400 (97 percent); Jaffa—from 27,437 to 62,600 (134 per cent); Haifa—from 18,404 to 58,200 (216 per cent).

Changes in rural areas: The population of the predominantly Arab Beersheba district dropped between 1922 and 1939 from 71,000 to 49,000 (the rate of natural increase should have resulted in a rise to 89,000). In the Bethlehem district the figure increased from 24,613 to about 26,000 (after falling to 23,725 in 1929). In the Hebron area it went up from 51,345 to 59,000 (the natural increase rate dictated a rise to 72,000).

In contrast to these declines or comparatively slight increases in exclusively Arab-inhabited areas, in the Nazareth, Beit Shean, Tiberias and Acre districts—where large-scale Jewish settlement and rural development was underway—the figure rose from 89,600 in 1922 to some 151,000 in 1938 (by about 4.5 per cent per annum, compared with a natural increase rate of 2.5–3 per cent).

In the largely Jewish Haifa area the number of Arab peasants increased by 8 per cent a year during the same period. In the Jaffa and Ramla districts (heavily Jewish populated), the Arab rural population grew from 42,300 to some 126,000—an annual increase of 12 per cent, or more than four times as much as can be attributed to natural increase (L. Shimony, *The Arabs of Palestine,* Tel-Aviv, 1947, pp. 422–23).

One reason for the Arab gravitation toward Jewish-inhabited areas, and from neighbouring countries to Palestine, was the incomparably higher wage scales paid there, as may be seen from the following table.

Daily Wage Scales, 1943 (in mils)[5]

	Unskilled Labour	Skilled Labour
Palestine	220–250	350–600
Egypt	30–50	70–200
Syria	80–100	150–200
Iraq	50	70–200

The capital received by Arab landowners for their surplus holdings was used for improved and intensive cultivation or invested in other enterprises. Turning again to the Report of the Palestine Royal Commission (p. 93), we find the following conclusions: "The large import of Jewish capital into Palestine has had a general fructifying effect on the economic life of the whole country. . . . The expansion of Arab industry and citriculture has been largely financed by the capital thus obtained. . . . Jewish example has done much to improve Arab cultivation. . . . The increase in Arab population is most marked in areas affected by Jewish development."

During World War II, the Arab population influx mounted apace, as is attested by the *UNRWA Review*, Information Paper No. 6 (September 1962):

A considerable movement of people is known to have occurred, particularly during the Second World War, years when new opportunities of employment opened up in the towns and on military works in Palestine. These wartime prospects and, generally, the higher rate of industrialization in Palestine attracted many new immigrants from the neighbouring countries, and many of them entered Palestine without their presence being officially recorded.

Land Ownership in 1948

The claim is often made that in 1948 a Jewish minority owning only 5 per cent of the land of Palestine made itself master of the Arab majority, which owned 95 per cent of the land.

In May 1948 the State of Israel was established in only part of the area allotted by the original League of Nations Mandate. 8.6 percent of the land was owned by Jews and 3.3 per cent by Israeli Arabs, while 16.9 per cent had been abandoned by Arab owners who imprudently heeded the call from neighbouring countries to "get out of the way" while the invading Arab armies made short shrift of Israel. The rest of the land—over 70 per cent—had been vested in the Mandatory Power, and accordingly reverted to the State of Israel as its legal heir. (Government of Palestine, *Survey of Palestine, 1946*, British Government Printer, p. 257.)

The greater part of this 70 per cent consisted of the Negev, some 3,144,250 acres all told, or close to 50 per cent of the 6,580,000 acres in all of Mandatory Palestine. Known as Crown or State Lands, this was mostly uninhabited arid or semi-arid territory, inherited originally by the Mandatory Government from Turkey. In 1948 it passed to the Government of Israel.

These lands had not been owned by Arab farmers—neither under the British Mandate nor under the preceding regime. Thus it is obvious that the contention that 95 per cent of the land—whether of Mandatory Palestine or of the State of Israel—had belonged to Arabs has absolutely no foundation in fact.

There is perhaps no better way of concluding and summing up this study than to quote from an article entitled *Is Israel a Thorn or a Flower in the Near East?* by Abdul Razak Kader, the Algerian political writer, now living in exile in Paris *(Jerusalem Post*, Aug. 1, 1969):

"The Nationalists of the states neighbouring on Israel, whether they are in the government or in business, whether Palestinian, Syrian or Lebanese, or town dwellers of tribal origin, all know that at the beginning of the century and during the British Mandate the marshy plains and stone hills were sold to the Zionists by their fathers or uncles for gold, the very gold which is often the origin of their own political or commercial careers. The nomadic or seminomadic peasants who inhabited the frontier regions know full well what the green plains, the afforested hills and the flowering fields of today's Israel were like before.

"The Palestinians who are today refugees in the neighbouring countries and who were adults at the time of their flight know all this, and no anti-Zionist propaganda—pan-Arab or pan-Moslem—can make them forget that their present nationalist exploiters are the worthy sons of their feudal exploiters of yesterday and that the thorns of their life are of Arab, not Jewish, origin."

Aumann, Moshe. "Appendix 2: Land Ownership in Palestine, 1880–1948", from Leibler, Isi. *The Case for Israel.* Melbourne, Victoria: Executive Council of Australian Jewry, 1972.

Reprinted with permission from the publisher.

Endnotes

1 dunams = 1 acre.

2 The large tracts often belonged to absentee landlords.

3 Land situated in the sandy Beersheba and marshy Huleh districts.

4 ". . . created on December 25, 1901, to ensure that land would be purchased for the Jewish workers who were to be personally responsible for its cultivation.

"Since the J.N.F. was as concerned with conforming to socialist ideals as with intensive economic exploitation of land, its Charter was opposed to the use of lands purchased by it as private property. The J.N.F. retained the freehold of the lands, while the people working it are only life tenants. . . .

"The capital of the Jewish National Fund was essentially raised from small regular donations from millions of Jewish craftsmen, labourers, shop-owners and intellectuals in Central and Eastern Europe where the shadow of genocide was already apparent, who felt concerned about the return of Jews to Zion. . . .

"Contrary to colonialist enterprises, which were seeking an exorbitant profit from land extorted from the colonized peoples, Zionist settlement discouraged private capital as its enterprise was of a socialist nature based on the refusal to exploit the worker." (Kurt Niedermaler, *Colonisation without Colonialism,* Youth and Hechalutz Dept., Jewish Agency, Jerusalem, 1969).

5 Source: A. Khoushy, *Brit Poali Eretz-Israel,* 1943, p. 25.

Lesson 2

Remnants of a destroyed Russian-made helicopter on the Egyptian air force base of Bir Gafgafa in the Sinai Israeli-occupied zone, 1967. (Photo credit: Magnum Photos; Rene Burri, photographer)

LIGHTNING STRIKE

THE ETHICS OF PREEMPTIVE STRIKES

As Arab armies mobilized along its borders, Israel faced immense international pressure not to launch a preemptive strike. She ignored these warnings and struck first. What are the ethics of preemptive strikes? What weight should be given to political considerations—as opposed to purely security/military concerns—in rendering such decisions? And how do these deliberations apply to the host of mortal threats that Israel faces today?

TEXT 1a

MAIMONIDES, *MISHNEH TORAH*, LAWS OF CHANUKAH 4:14

> גָדוֹל הַשָּׁלוֹם שֶׁכָּל הַתּוֹרָה נִיתְּנָה לַעֲשׂוֹת שָׁלוֹם בָּעוֹלָם, שֶׁנֶּאֱמַר, "דְּרָכֶיהָ דַּרְכֵי נֹעַם וְכָל נְתִיבוֹתֶיהָ שָׁלוֹם" (מִשְׁלֵי ג, יז).

Great is peace, for the entire Torah was given to engender peace in the world, as it is stated [regarding the Torah]: "Her ways are pleasant ways, and all her paths are peace" (PROVERBS 3:17).

RABBI MOSHE BEN MAIMON (MAIMONIDES, RAMBAM) 1135–1204

Halachist, philosopher, author, and physician. Maimonides was born in Cordoba, Spain. After the conquest of Cordoba by the Almohads, he fled Spain and eventually settled in Cairo, Egypt. There, he became the leader of the Jewish community and served as court physician to the vizier of Egypt. He is most noted for authoring the *Mishneh Torah*, an encyclopedic arrangement of Jewish law, and for his philosophical work, *Guide for the Perplexed*. His rulings on Jewish law are integral to the formation of halachic consensus.

TEXT 1b

ETHICS OF THE FATHERS 1:12

> הִלֵּל אוֹמֵר: הֱוֵי מִתַּלְמִידָיו שֶׁל אַהֲרֹן, אוֹהֵב שָׁלוֹם וְרוֹדֵף שָׁלוֹם, אוֹהֵב אֶת הַבְּרִיּוֹת וּמְקָרְבָן לַתּוֹרָה.

Hillel would say: Be of the disciples of Aaron—a lover of peace, a pursuer of peace, one who loves people and draws them close to Torah.

***PIRKEI AVOT* (ETHICS OF OUR FATHERS)**

A 6-chapter work on Jewish ethics that is studied widely by Jewish communities, especially during the summer. The first 5 chapters are from the Mishnah, tractate Avot. Avot differs from the rest of the Mishnah in that it does not focus on legal subjects; it is a collection of the sages' wisdom on topics related to character development, ethics, healthy living, piety, and the study of Torah.

TEXT 2

MAIMONIDES, *MISHNEH TORAH*, LAWS OF KINGS AND BATTLES 6:1

אֵין עוֹשִׂין מִלְחָמָה עִם אָדָם בָּעוֹלָם עַד שֶׁקּוֹרְאִין לוֹ שָׁלוֹם . . . שֶׁנֶּאֱמַר, "כִּי תִקְרַב אֶל עִיר לְהִלָּחֵם עָלֶיהָ, וְקָרָאתָ אֵלֶיהָ לְשָׁלוֹם" (דְבָרִים כ, י).

War may not be waged against any human being in the world before extending an overture of peace . . . as it is stated: "When you approach a city to fight against it, you shall offer it terms of peace" (DEUTERONOMY 20:10).

TEXT 3a

GENESIS 32:7–8

וַיָּשֻׁבוּ הַמַּלְאָכִים אֶל יַעֲקֹב לֵאמֹר, "בָּאנוּ אֶל אָחִיךָ אֶל עֵשָׂו, וְגַם הֹלֵךְ לִקְרָאתְךָ וְאַרְבַּע מֵאוֹת אִישׁ עִמּוֹ".

וַיִּירָא יַעֲקֹב מְאֹד וַיֵּצֶר לוֹ.

The angels returned to Jacob, saying, "We came to your brother Esau, and he is coming toward you, and four hundred men are with him."

Jacob was very frightened, and he was distressed.

TEXT 3b

RASHI, AD LOC.

"וַיִּירָא" - שֶׁמָּא יֵהָרֵג.
"וַיֵּצֶר לוֹ" - אִם יַהֲרוֹג הוּא אֶת אֲחֵרִים.

He was *frightened* lest he be killed.

He was *distressed* that he might be compelled to kill others.

RABBI SHLOMO YITZCHAKI (RASHI)
1040–1105

Most noted biblical and Talmudic commentator. Born in Troyes, France, Rashi studied in the famed *yeshivot* of Mainz and Worms. His commentaries on the Pentateuch and the Talmud, which focus on the straightforward meaning of the text, appear in virtually every edition of the Talmud and Bible.

TEXT 4a

DEUTERONOMY 23:10

כִּי תֵצֵא מַחֲנֶה עַל אֹיְבֶיךָ וְנִשְׁמַרְתָּ מִכֹּל דָּבָר רָע.

When your camp goes forth against your enemies, be on guard against all forms of impropriety.

TEXT 4b

RABBI MOSHE BEN NACHMAN, AD LOC.

> וְהַנָּכוֹן בְּעֵינַי בְּעִנְיַן הַמִּצְוָה הַזֹּאת, כִּי הַכָּתוּב יַזְהִיר בְּעֵת אֲשֶׁר הַחֵטְא מָצוּי בּוֹ. וְהַיָּדוּעַ בְּמִנְהֲגֵי הַמַּחֲנוֹת הַיּוֹצְאוֹת לְמִלְחָמָה כִּי . . . יִגְזְלוּ וְיַחְמְסוּ וְלֹא יִתְבּוֹשְׁשׁוּ אֲפִילוּ בְּנִיאוּף וְכָל נְבָלָה, הַיָּשָׁר בִּבְנֵי אָדָם בְּטִבְעוֹ יִתְלַבֵּשׁ אַכְזָרִיּוּת וְחֵמָה כְּצֵאת מַחֲנֶה עַל אוֹיֵב. וְעַל כֵּן הִזְהִיר בּוֹ הַכָּתוּב, "וְנִשְׁמַרְתָּ מִכֹּל דָּבָר רָע".

In my estimation, the meaning of this commandment is as follows. The Torah admonishes us to be careful at a time when sin is prevalent. The practice of army battalions is well known: when they go to battle, they routinely . . . rob and plunder, and engage in illicit and licentious behavior and all that is despicable without a modicum of shame. The traits of cruelty and fury are aroused in soldiers—even those who are otherwise decent human beings—when they descend upon the enemy. Therefore, the verse admonishes: "Be on guard against all forms of impropriety."

RABBI MOSHE BEN NACHMAN (NACHMANIDES, RAMBAN)
1194–1270

Scholar, philosopher, author, and physician. Nachmanides was born in Spain and served as leader of Iberian Jewry. In 1263, he was summoned by King James of Aragon to a public disputation with Pablo Cristiani, a Jewish apostate. Though Nachmanides was the clear victor of the debate, he had to flee Spain because of the resulting persecution. He moved to Israel and helped reestablish communal life in Jerusalem. He authored a classic commentary on the Pentateuch and a commentary on the Talmud.

TEXT 5

THE TRIAL OF THE MAJOR WAR CRIMINALS BEFORE THE INTERNATIONAL MILITARY TRIBUNAL SITTING AT NUREMBERG, GERMANY, 14 NOVEMBER 1945–1 OCTOBER 1946
OFFICIAL TEXT, ENGLISH LANGUAGE (THE BLUE SERIES, GETZVILLE, NY: WILLIAM S. HEIN AND CO., INC.) VOLUME 1 (1947), JUDGMENT, P. 186, OCTOBER 1, 1946

The charges in the Indictment that the defendants planned and waged aggressive wars are charges of the utmost gravity. War is essentially an evil thing. Its consequences are not confined to the belligerent states alone, but affect the whole world.

To initiate a war of aggression, therefore, is not only an international crime; it is the supreme international crime differing only from other war crimes in that it contains within itself the accumulated evil of the whole.

Defendants in the dock at the International Military Tribunal trial of war criminals in Nuremberg, Germany, Nov. 1945. (Photo credit: USHMM Photo Archives; Raymond D'Addario, photographer)

QUESTION FOR DISCUSSION

Are there circumstances under which initiating a "war of aggression" would be justified? If yes, what would those circumstances be?

TEXT 6

PRESIDENT JOHN F. KENNEDY, TELEVISED ADDRESS TO THE NATION, OCTOBER 22, 1962

Neither the United States of America nor the world community of nations can tolerate deliberate deception and offensive threats on the part of any nation, large or small. We no longer live in a world where only the actual firing of weapons represents a sufficient challenge to a nation's security to constitute maximum peril. . . .

The 1930s taught us a clear lesson. Aggressive conduct, if allowed to go unchecked and unchallenged, ultimately leads to war.

PRESIDENT JOHN F. KENNEDY
1917–1963

American politician. Born in Massachusetts, Kennedy studied international affairs at Harvard University. A scion of the prominent Kennedy family, he was elected to the U.S. Congress and later to the Senate. Kennedy was elected President of the U.S. in 1960, a position he held until his assassination in 1963. Kennedy is best known for his handling of the Cuban missile crisis and his "New Frontier" economic and social programs.

TEXT 7

ALAN M. DERSHOWITZ, *PREEMPTION: A KNIFE THAT CUTS BOTH WAYS* (NEW YORK: W.W. NORTON, 2007), P. 60

There is little in the way of an accepted jurisprudence or morality of anticipatory self-defense in the military context. What we see instead are a series of ad hoc decisions made over time and place, some of which have been validated by the verdict of history, others condemned. Not surprisingly, history's judgment seems to depend in large part on whether the action that was taken turned out, in retrospect, to be right rather than on whether it was justified on the basis of what was reasonably believed at the time it was taken. Since we can never know for certain how a preventive or preemptive military action will turn out—indeed, we do not even have a shared definition of "success"—these ad hoc verdicts of history provide little in the way of prospective guidance to what sorts of anticipatory military actions are legally or morally justified.

At one extreme is the total annihilation of a perceived enemy who has taken no outward steps toward mounting an attack or even preparing for one. Throughout history, nations and tribes have set out to destroy their enemies before they became strong enough to pose a realistic military threat. . . . At the other extreme is waiting to be absolutely certain that the enemy is about to attack and simply beating him to the punch. (That was

ALAN M. DERSHOWITZ
1938–

American lawyer, jurist, and political commentator. Mr. Dershowitz was a professor of law at Harvard University for half a century; he achieved that position at the age of 28, the youngest full professor of law in the history of the school. Dershowitz is an advocate of Israel and an activist civil liberties lawyer who takes half of his cases *pro bono*. He has written 20 books, including *The Case for Israel*.

Israel's claim when it preemptively attacked the Egyptian and Syrian air forces at the beginning of the Six-Day War of 1967.)

TEXT 8

KENNETH ADELMAN, CITED IN "SIX DEGREES OF PREEMPTION," *THE WASHINGTON POST*, SEPTEMBER 29, 2002

The most wonderful example of preemption in the modern era was Israel's attack in June of 1981 on the Osirak nuclear plant that would have had nuclear weapons in Iraq's hands by probably 1985, 1986. For my sins, I was at the United Nations when the new Reagan administration went along with a resolution in the Security Council, condemning Israel for that. I'm mortified to think back at it. It was a big mistake. . . .

I thought it was absolutely right at the time to condemn Israel. But thank God Israel did that, looking back at it. The idea of Saddam Hussein being the main Arab leader with nuclear weapons since 1985 is frightful.

KENNETH ADELMAN
1946–

Diplomat and policy analyst. Adelman received his degrees in foreign service studies and political theory from Georgetown University. Adelman served in multiple U.S. Republican administrations, including positions in the Department of Defense and as deputy ambassador to the U.N. Adelman is considered a prominent neoconservative.

TEXT 9

MICHAEL R. GORDON, "PAPERS FROM IRAQI ARCHIVE REVEAL CONSPIRATORIAL MIND-SET OF HUSSEIN," *THE NEW YORK TIMES*, OCTOBER 25, 2011

Mr. Hussein said he was not surprised that Israel felt threatened by Iraq, which he asserted would defeat Iran and emerge with a military that was stronger than ever. "Once Iraq walks out victorious [in its war against Iran], there will not be any Israel," he said in a 1982 conversation. "Technically, they are right in all of their attempts to harm Iraq."

Illustration of Israeli fighter jets bombing the Osirak nuclear reactor in Iraq, 1981. (Artist: Rick Herter)

TEXT 10

REPORT TO THE PRESIDENT OF THE UNITED STATES BY THE COMMISSION ON THE INTELLIGENCE CAPABILITIES OF THE UNITED STATES REGARDING WEAPONS OF MASS DESTRUCTION, MARCH 31, 2005, P. 3

On the brink of war, and in front of the whole world, the United States government asserted that Saddam Hussein had reconstituted his nuclear weapons program, had biological weapons and mobile biological weapon production facilities, and had stockpiled and was producing chemical weapons. All of this was based on the assessments of the U.S. Intelligence Community. And not one bit of it could be confirmed when the war was over. . . .

This failure was in large part the result of analytical shortcomings; intelligence analysts were too wedded to their assumptions about Saddam's intentions. But it was also a failure on the part of those who collect intelligence. . . . In the end, those agencies collected precious little intelligence for the analysts to analyze, and much of what they did collect was either worthless or misleading. Finally, it was a failure to communicate effectively with policymakers; the Intelligence Community didn't adequately explain just how little good intelligence it had—or how much its assessments were driven by assumptions and inferences rather than concrete evidence.

TEXT 11

HENRY KISSINGER, *DIPLOMACY*, (NEW YORK, NY: SIMON AND SCHUSTER [TOUCHSTONE SERIES REPRINT OF 1994 FIRST EDITION], 1995), P. 294

No one has stated the result of the Western Allies' hesitancy to confront Hitler better than Joseph Goebbels, Hitler's diabolical propaganda chief. In April 1940, on the eve of the Nazi invasion of Norway, he told a secret briefing:

> Up to now we have succeeded in leaving the enemy in the dark concerning Germany's real goals, just as before 1932 our domestic foes never saw where we were going or that our oath of legality was just a trick. . . . They could have suppressed us. They could have arrested a couple of us in 1925 and that would have been that, the end. No, they let us through the danger zone. That's exactly how it was in foreign policy too. . . . In 1933 a French premier ought to have said (and if I had been the French premier I would have said it): "The new Reich Chancellor is the man who wrote *Mein Kampf*, which says this and that. This man cannot be tolerated in our vicinity. Either he disappears or we march!" But they didn't do it. They left us alone and let us slip through the risky zone, and we were able to sail around all dangerous reefs. *And when we were done, and well armed, better than they, then they started the war!* [Italics in original]

HENRY KISSINGER
1923–

Diplomat and political scientist. Born in Furth, Germany, to a Jewish family, Kissinger fled Nazi persecution with his family, arriving in New York. Kissinger received his degree in political science from Harvard University. He was appointed Secretary of State by President Nixon, a position he continued to hold in the Ford administration. As Secretary of State, Kissinger pioneered the policy of détente with the U.S.S.R. and orchestrated the opening of relations with China. Kissinger has written a number of books about foreign policy, and his advice continues to be sought by U.S. leaders.

TEXT 12

AMNON BARZILAI, "GOLDA MEIR'S NIGHTMARE," *HAARETZ*, MARCH 10, 2003

Before daybreak on Yom Kippur, October 6, 1973, Golda Meir had a bad night's sleep. She had a premonition that something dreadful was about to happen. . . . At 4 A.M. on that 1973 Yom Kippur, the phone rang in the prime minister's home. Golda Meir's nightmare became a reality. Her military secretary, Brigadier General Yisrael Lior, was on the line. He told her, concisely: "Information has come saying that the Egyptians and Syrians will launch a combined attack on Israel in the afternoon."

Before she left her house that Saturday morning, Meir asked her military secretary to convene a meeting with Israel Defense Forces Chief of Staff David ("Dado") Elazar, and ministers Moshe Dayan, Yigal Allon, and Yisrael Galili. Participants were to gather in her office before 7 A.M., but the meeting was delayed. At about 8 A.M., two matters were brought to Meir's attention by Elazar and Dayan, the defense minister.

Israeli Prime Minister Golda Meir gestures at a news conference as she arrived for talks with U.S. President Nixon in Washington, D.C. Feb. 26, 1973. (Source: AP)

The men disagreed about the two subjects—the scope of the reservist call-up, and whether or not a preemptive strike should be ordered. . . . The issue of whether or not to deliver a preemptive blow was more complicated. Elazar claimed that launching such a strike would save many lives. Dayan counseled that the chance of such a blow succeeding, at a time when the army had yet to be called up for deployment, was slight. The prime minister refused to go ahead with the preemptive strike. As Meir recalled: "'Dado,' I said, 'I know all the arguments in favor of a preemptive strike, but I am against it. We don't know, any of us, what the future will hold, but there is always the possibility that we will need help, and if we strike first, we will get nothing from anyone.'"

Three years later, two young Jewish researchers, Steven Rosen and Martin Indyk (the future U.S. ambassador to Israel), wrote a study entitled "The Temptation of Preemption in the Fifth Arab-Israel War." Their research probed the price paid by Israel as a result of the decision not to go ahead with the preemptive strike. Had Meir authorized such a strike against Syria's missiles and air force, the pair wrote, it could have destroyed 90 percent of Syria's missile bases within three to six hours, at a price of less than 10 lost Israeli planes.

"Clearly, this result would have had a decisive impact on air force losses later on, and also (and this is still more significant) on the efficiency of tens of thousands of air force sorties conducted during the war. Israeli fatalities on the ground would have been reduced, the wearing down of Arab artillery, and of tanks and fortified vehicles from Arab armies, would have accelerated, and strikes against Egyptian bridges on the [Suez] canal would have been more efficient," the study argued.

Kenneth Keating, the U.S. ambassador to Israel, arrived at the prime minister's office while the meeting was still in session. Meir adjourned it, and briefed Keating about the joint Egyptian-Syrian attack. Later, the ambassador delivered a message from Henry Kissinger, warning Israel's government against taking the first steps to start a war.

In her autobiography, Meir wrote that she was at peace with her decision, which, she claimed, clinched America's airlift to Israel. Indyk and Rosen, however, disputed this interpretation. In their view, had Israel launched a preemptive strike, its action would not have influenced the White House's policy. . . .

Military historian Meir Pail was appointed after the Yom Kippur War to serve on a research team formed by the IDF's history department (the team was commissioned to investigate the strategic handling of the war). As Pail sees it, Meir was right not to launch a preemptive strike. In an interview with Haaretz, he said: "Could the air force have acted against Egypt, as it had during the War of Attrition? At a time when there was a cease-fire? When we had no pretext to act? And against Syria? That morning, we didn't know for certain that a war would erupt. Nor did the world know about Syria and Egypt's mobilization for war. In order to engage [in] a preventive strike, you need a pretext, a cause, that the outside world can understand. That especially holds true with respect to the U.S. The world would have accused us of being paranoid. What reason would we have given to explain why we were attacking Syria?"

TEXT 13

MAIMONIDES, *MISHNEH TORAH*, LAWS OF KINGS AND BATTLES 4:2

וְאֵי זוֹ הִיא מִלְחֶמֶת מִצְוָה? זוֹ מִלְחֶמֶת . . . וְעֶזְרַת יִשְׂרָאֵל מִיַּד צָר שֶׁבָּא עֲלֵיהֶם.

What is considered an obligatory war? A war . . . to defend a Jewish community against an enemy that comes to attack them.

TEXT 14a

TALMUD, ERUVIN 45A

נָכְרִים שֶׁצָּרוּ עַל עֲיָירוֹת יִשְׂרָאֵל, אֵין יוֹצְאִין עֲלֵיהֶם בִּכְלֵי זַיְינָן וְאֵין מְחַלְּלִין עֲלֵיהֶן אֶת הַשַּׁבָּת . . . בַּמֶּה דְבָרִים אֲמוּרִים? כְּשֶׁבָּאוּ עַל עִסְקֵי מָמוֹן. אֲבָל בָּאוּ עַל עִסְקֵי נְפָשׁוֹת, יוֹצְאִין עֲלֵיהֶן בִּכְלֵי זַיְינָן וּמְחַלְּלִין עֲלֵיהֶן אֶת הַשַּׁבָּת.

וּבְעִיר הַסְמוּכָה לַסְּפָר, אֲפִילוּ לֹא בָּאוּ עַל עִסְקֵי נְפָשׁוֹת אֶלָּא עַל עִסְקֵי תֶּבֶן וְקַשׁ, יוֹצְאִין עֲלֵיהֶן בִּכְלֵי זַיְינָן וּמְחַלְּלִין עֲלֵיהֶן אֶת הַשַּׁבָּת.

If Gentiles besiege Jewish cities, we do not initiate a military offensive against them, nor do we desecrate the Shabbat [to prepare a defense]. . . . This rule applies if the enemy's goal is solely monetary; if, however, they threaten lives, we initiate a military offensive against them, and we desecrate the Shabbat if necessary.

If the city abuts the border, even if the enemy does not seek to take any lives, rather, they only want to plunder straw and hay, we initiate a military offensive even if this entails desecrating the Shabbat.

BABYLONIAN TALMUD

A literary work of monumental proportions that draws upon the legal, spiritual, intellectual, ethical, and historical traditions of Judaism. The 37 tractates of the Babylonian Talmud contain the teachings of the Jewish sages from the period after the destruction of the 2nd Temple through the 5th century CE. It has served as the primary vehicle for the transmission of the Oral Law and the education of Jews over the centuries; it is the entry point for all subsequent legal, ethical, and theological Jewish scholarship.

TEXT 14b

RABBI YITSCHAK BEN MOSHE, *OR ZARU'A*, VOL. 2, LAWS OF SHABBAT, CH. 84

וְטַעֲמָא דְמִילְתָא, שֶׁמָא יִלְכְּדוּהָ וּמִשָּׁם תְּהֵא נוֹחָה לִיכְבֹּשׁ כָּל הָאָרֶץ לִפְנֵיהֶם . . .

וְאֵין לְחַלֵק בֵּין הֵיכָא שֶׁצָרוּ כְּבַר לְאוֹמְרִים שֶׁרוֹצִים לָבוֹא לִשְׁלוֹל, אֶלָא כְּשֶׁהַקוֹל יוֹצֵא שֶׁרוֹצִים לָבוֹא לִשְׁלוֹל אַף עַל פִּי שֶׁלֹא בָּאוּ עֲדַיִין, מוּתָּר לִלְבּוֹשׁ כְּלֵי זַיִין לִשְׁמוֹר וְלַעֲשׂוֹת קוֹל בָּעִיר כְּדֵי שֶׁלֹא יָבוֹאוּ דְאֵין מְדַקְדְקִין בְּפִקוּחַ נֶפֶשׁ.

Halachah views a city alongside the border differently for fear that if the enemy conquers it, it will be a launching pad that will allow them to conquer the entire land with greater ease. . . .

There is no difference if the enemy has already besieged the city or if they have only declared their intention to come and plunder the city. As soon as reports arrive that the enemy intends to come and plunder, even though they have not yet arrived, it is permitted to don arms [even on Shabbat], be on guard, and mobilize the city residents to prevent the enemy from coming. For when lives are potentially at risk, we do not require absolute proof in order to prompt action.

RABBI YITSCHAK BEN MOSHE OF VIENNA
CA. 1180–1250

Student of the German tosafists. His fame stems primarily from his influential halachic work and commentary to the Talmud, *Or Zaru'a*, which was subsequently quoted by many halachic authorities. His son Rabbi Chaim wrote a compendium of his father's work, which for many generations was the only widely used version of the *Or Zaru'a*. In the 19th century, the original work was found and published. Among his students was the Maharam of Rothenburg.

TEXT 14C

RABBI J. DAVID BLEICH, "PREEMPTIVE WAR IN JEWISH LAW," *TRADITION* 21:1, SPRING 1983, PP. 3–41

The Gemara [Talmud], Eruvin 45a, sanctions defensive action, on the Sabbath as well as on weekdays, against heathens who besiege a border settlement even though the marauding forces seek only "straw and hay," i.e., they are intent only upon looting or exacting economic concessions. It is clear that in such situations there exists no imminent danger; it is not at all certain that any life will be endangered. There is, however, reason to fear that even if the aggressors' immediate pecuniary or economic goals are achieved without resistance, having penetrated border defenses, the enemy may engage in warfare at some future time and thereby endanger Jewish lives. The loss of fortified border settlements would leave the entire country exposed and defenseless. Hence defensive measures are warranted.

RABBI DR. J. DAVID BLEICH
1936–

Expert on Jewish law, ethics, and bioethics. Rabbi Bleich serves as professor of Talmud at the Rabbi Isaac Elchanan Theological Seminary, an affiliate of Yeshiva University, as well as head of its postgraduate institute for the study of Talmudic jurisprudence and family law. A noted author, he is most famous for his 7-volume *Contemporary Halakhic Problems.*

Exercise

There were four events that precipitated the Six-Day War: (a) The closing of the Straits of Tiran to Israeli shipping, (b) the removal of the UN peacekeeping force from the Sinai Desert, (c) the massing of Arab armies in the Sinai and on Israel's borders, and (d) the poisonous rhetoric and threats voiced by the Arab leadership at the time.

Based on the halachic texts we just studied, was Israel justified in taking preemptive military action? Do the following events justify a preemptive strike from the standpoint of Jewish law?

	YES	NO	UNSURE
The closing of the Straits of Tiran			
The removal of the UN peacekeeping force			
The massing of troops			
The rhetoric and threats			

TEXT 15

RABBI SHLOMO YOSEF ZEVIN, *LE'OR HAHALACHAH* (JERUSALEM: KOL MEVASER, 2004), P. 88

נִמְצֵינוּ לְמֵדִים מִלְחֶמֶת אִיסּוּר בִּמְדִינַת יִשְׂרָאֵל אֵינָהּ אֶלָּא בַּתֵּיאוּרִים בִּבְחִינַת הֵיכִי תִּמְצָא, לוּ יְצוּיַּיר כַּךְ וְכַךְ . . . אֲבָל לְמַעֲשֶׂה, כָּל שָׁלֹשׁ הַמִּלְחָמוֹת שֶׁל מְדִינַת יִשְׂרָאֵל - הָעַצְמָאוּת, וְסִינַי, וְשֵׁשֶׁת הַיָּמִים וְהַהֶמְשֵׁךְ שֶׁל שֵׁשֶׁת הַיָּמִים - כּוּלָּן הֵן מַמָּשׁ עֶזְרַת יִשְׂרָאֵל מִיַּד צָר הַבָּא עֲלֵיהֶם . . . כָּךְ הָיָה הַמַּצָּב בְּכָל שָׁלֹשׁ הַמִּלְחָמוֹת וְכָךְ הוּא גַּם עַכְשָׁיו וְאֵין לְךָ מִלְחֶמֶת חוֹבָה וּמִצְוָה גְּדוֹלָה מִזּוֹ.

RABBI SHLOMO YOSEF ZEVIN
1890–1978

Editor in chief of the *Talmudic Encyclopedia*. Rabbi Zevin was born in Kazimirov, Belarus, and was ordained by numerous prominent rabbis, including Rabbi Yosef Rosen of Rogatchov and Rabbi Michel Epstein. In 1934, he immigrated to Israel.

Hypothetically, there are circumstances under which Israel would be forbidden to go to war. . . . In actuality, however, the three wars that Israel has waged—the War of Independence, the Sinai Campaign, and the Six-Day War (and the War of Attrition that followed)—were fought "to defend a Jewish community against an enemy that comes to attack them." . . . This was the situation in all three of the wars, and the same is true today. There is no greater obligatory "mitzvah" war than these.

TEXT 16

TALMUD, SANHEDRIN 72A

וְהַתּוֹרָה אָמְרָה: אִם בָּא לְהוֹרְגְךָ, הַשְׁכֵּם לְהוֹרְגוֹ.

The Torah instructs us: If one is coming to kill you, rise up to kill him [first].

TEXT 17

RABBI SHNE'UR ZALMAN OF LIADI, *LIKUTEI TORAH, KI TETSE* 35C

אִיתָא בְּזוֹהַר, "שְׁעַת צְלוֹתָא שְׁעַת קְרָבָא"... שֶׁבְּכָל דוֹר וָדוֹר וּבְכָל יוֹם
וָיוֹם צָרִיךְ לִהְיוֹת מִלְחָמָה זוּ בְּנֶפֶשׁ הָאָדָם, כִּי זֶה לְעוּמַּת זֶה עָשָׂה אֱלֹקִים:
נֶפֶשׁ דִקְדוּשָּׁה, מַעֲשֶׂה דִבּוּר וּמַחְשָׁבָה מִדּוֹת וְשֵׂכֶל דִקְדוּשָּׁה; וּכְנֶגְדָּהּ
נֶפֶשׁ הַחִיּוּנִית הַבַּהֲמִיּוּת כוּ'. וּלְאוֹם מִלְאוֹם יֶאֱמָץ, וְצָרִיךְ הָאָדָם לְהַגְבִּיר
נֶפֶשׁ דִקְדוּשָּׁה. וְשְׁעַת מִלְחָמָה הִיא שְׁעַת הַתְּפִלָּה.

The Zohar states, "The time of prayer is the time of battle." . . . In every generation and every day, we must wage an internal spiritual battle. For "this opposite this did God create" (ECCLESIASTES 7:14): within every one of us there is a holy soul—from which emanates holy deeds, words, thoughts, emotions, and perceptions—and an unholy soul. Both these souls strive for dominance, and it is up to the individual to empower the holy soul to defeat its opponent. This battle is waged during the daily prayers.

RABBI SHNE'UR ZALMAN OF LIADI (ALTER REBBE) 1745–1812

Chasidic rebbe, halachic authority, and founder of the Chabad movement. The Alter Rebbe was born in Liozna, Belarus, and was among the principal students of the Magid of Mezeritch. His numerous works include the *Tanya*, an early classic containing the fundamentals of Chabad Chasidism, and *Shulchan Aruch HaRav*, an expanded and reworked code of Jewish law.

TEXT 18

RABBI ABRAHAM BEN DAVID, *BA'ALEI HANEFESH, SHA'AR HAKEDUSHAH*

אֵין דֶּרֶךְ לַיֵּצֶר הָרַע עָלָיו אֶלָּא מִדֶּרֶךְ הַהֶיתֵּר, וּפֶתַח דַּרְכּוֹ מִן הַמּוּתָּר אֶצְלוֹ, וְאִם יִשְׁמוֹר אֶת הַפֶּתַח אֵינוֹ צָרִיךְ שִׁימּוּר אַחֵר . . . כִּי דֶּרֶךְ הַיּוֹעֵץ הַבְּלִיַּעַל הַהוּא, מְיַעֲצוֹ לְמַלְאוֹת תַּאֲוָתוֹ מִן הַמּוּתָּר לוֹ, וְאַחֲרֵי הִרְגִּילוּ אוֹתוֹ לְמַלֵּא תַּאֲוָתוֹ בְּהֶיתֵּר וְהִשִּׁיא אֶת נַפְשׁוֹ לִהְיוֹת שׁוֹקֵקָה כָּל עֵת וְלִהְיוֹתָהּ עוֹרֶגֶת אֶל רַעֲבוֹנָהּ, אָז יְסִיתֶנָּה אֶל הָאָסוּר הַקַּל, וּמִן הַקַּל אֶל הֶחָמוּר כַּאֲשֶׁר אָמַרְתִּי לְךָ.

וְעַל זֶה הִזָּהֵר בְּהֶיתֵּר, וְאִם תִּגְדּוֹר בּוֹ אֶת עַצְמְךָ וּתְמַעֵט תַּאֲוָתְךָ מִן הַמּוּתָּר לְךָ, מוּבְטָח אַתָּה שֶׁלֹּא יְסִיתְךָ עוֹד יִצְרְךָ אֶל הָאָסוּר.

The *yetser* (evil inclination) finds its opening by enticing a person to engage in permitted pleasures. One who guards that opening need not fear being enticed to do the forbidden. . . . For this is the *modus operandi* of the wicked counsel-giver: First he advises a person to engage in non-forbidden pleasures. After he has habituated a person to filling his heart's desires in permitted areas, and has caused him to crave pleasures and be attentive to his hunger for gratification, he induces him to commit a minor transgression. The temptation for major indiscretions soon follows.

Be careful, therefore, not to overly indulge in permitted pleasures. If you rein in your temptations and minimize your permitted indulgences, you are assured that the *yetser* will not be able to entice you to do the forbidden.

RABBI ABRAHAM BEN DAVID
CA. 1120–1198

Talmudic commentator and kabbalist. Rabbi Abraham ben David, known by the acronym of his name "Ra'avad," was a 12th-century rabbi, talmudist and kabbalist in Provençe, France. Ra'avad is best known for his critical comments on Maimonides' *Mishneh Torah* as well as his criticisms of the earlier authority Rabbi Yitschak Alfasi (Rif). Ra'avad also wrote responsa and commentaries to many tractates of the Talmud, and is considered one of the important transmitters of the kabbalistic tradition.

KEY POINTS

1 The USSR provided Egypt with false information about an impending Israeli invasion of Syria. In response, Egypt mobilized for war, expelled the UN peacekeepers from the Sinai, and blocked Israel's access to the Straits of Tiran. Arab armies massed at Israel's borders, and the Arab world pronounced its intention to annihilate Israel.

2 Israel made extensive diplomatic efforts to avert war and, when they failed, Israel launched a preemptive strike against Egypt, destroying its air force and commencing the Six-Day War.

3 "To initiate a war of aggression . . . is not only an international crime; it is the supreme international crime." Nevertheless, it is almost universally accepted that a preemptive strike is justified in an instance when not attacking, and instead absorbing the first blow, poses a mortal danger.

4 The Torah commands us to seek peace before resorting to unpeaceful options. Nevertheless, according to Torah law, we must preempt the enemy and strike first if we have information of the enemy's intention to attack.

5 The Six-Day War is often contrasted to the 1973 Yom Kippur War, that cost more than 2,500 Israeli lives, when Israel chose not to strike first. During the Six-Day War, however, Israel did not have a buffer zone to absorb the enemy attack.

6 With regard to today's threats to Israel, from the Torah's perspective, once all reasonable avenues for peace are exhausted, Israel should preemptively eliminate any threat, provided that the military assesses that the attack will be successful and effective.

7 Nonmilitary experts often lack sufficient information or knowledge to determine Israel's correct course of action.

Appendices

TEXT 19

ABBA EBAN, *PERSONAL WITNESS: ISRAEL THROUGH MY EYES* (NEW YORK: G.P. PUTNAM'S SONS, 1992), PP. 353–354

Since Israeli responses to Syrian violence weakened the Damascus regime, which the Kremlin wished to protect, Moscow had another bright idea. It would attempt to get Egypt to accept the burden of protecting Syria against the consequences of its own aggression.

On May 12 and 13, in Moscow, an Egyptian parliamentary delegation had been told to expect "an Israeli invasion of Syria immediately after Independence Day, with the aim of overthrowing the Damascus regime." . . .

Later in the month of May, when we were visibly on the verge of war, Nasser frankly explained his military actions in terms of Soviet advice. His announcement on May 22 of the decision to blockade the Straits of Tiran included these sentences, which are full of significance for the historian:

> On May 13, we received accurate information that Israel was concentrating on the Syrian border huge armed forces of about 11 to 13 brigades. . . . The decision made by Israel at the time was to carry out an attack on Syria, starting on May 17. On May 14, we took action, discussed the matter, and

ABBA EBAN
1915–2002

Israeli diplomat and politician. Born in South Africa, Eban was raised and educated in the U.K. and served as an intelligence officer for the British Army in Mandatory Palestine. After the establishment of the State of Israel, Eban served as Israel's ambassador to the U.N. and the U.S. In 1959 he returned to Israel and served in the Knesset for almost 30 years, including 8 years as foreign minister. Eban was considered Israel's foremost advocate in the international arena and was renowned for his passion, eloquence, and wit.

contacted our Syrian brothers. The Syrians also had this information.

TEXT 20

ANTHONY CLARK AREND, "INTERNATIONAL LAW AND THE PREEMPTIVE USE OF MILITARY FORCE," *THE WASHINGTON QUARTERLY* (26:2), SPRING 2003, PP. 91–93

As the Second World War was coming to an end, the delegates from 51 states assembled in San Francisco in the spring of 1945 to draft the charter of the new global organization. Pledging to "save succeeding generations from the scourge of war," the framers of the UN Charter sought to establish a normative order that would severely restrict the resort to force. Under Article 2(4) of the charter, states were to "refrain in their international relations from the threat or use of force against the territorial integrity or political independence of any State or in any other manner inconsistent with the Purposes of the United Nations." In the charter, there were only two explicit exceptions to this prohibition: force authorized by the Security Council and force in self-defense. Under Article 39, the council is empowered to determine if there is a "threat to the peace, breach of the peace, or act of aggression." If the Security Council so determines, it

ANTHONY CLARK AREND
1958–

Scholar on international law. Arend received his degree in foreign affairs from the University of Virginia, and currently serves as Professor of Government and Foreign Service at Georgetown University. He specializes in international law and relations and has published a number of books on these topics.

can authorize the use of force against the offending state under Article 42.

The critical provision relating to the other exception, self-defense, is Article 51, which provides in part:

> Nothing in the present Charter shall impair the inherent right of individual or collective self-defence if an armed attack occurs against a Member of the United Nations, until the Security Council has taken measures necessary to maintain international peace and security. Measures taken by Members in the exercise of this right of self-defence shall be immediately reported to the Security Council and shall not in any way affect the authority and responsibility of the Security Council under the present Charter to take at any time such action as it deems necessary in order to maintain or restore international peace and security.

Although the basic contours of Article 51 seem straightforward, its effect on the customary right of anticipatory self-defense is unclear. If one reviews the scholarly literature on this provision, writers seem to be divided into two camps. On one hand, some commentators—"restrictionists" we might call them—claim that the intent of Article 51 was explicitly to limit the use of force in self-defense to those circumstances in which an armed attack has actually occurred. Under this logic, it would be unlawful to engage in any kind of preemptive actions. A would-be victim would first have to become an actual victim before it would be able to use military force in self-defense. Even though Article 51 refers to an "inherent right" of self-defense, restrictionists would argue that, under the charter, that inherent right could now be exercised only following a clear, armed attack.

Other scholars, however, would reject this interpretation. These "counter-restrictionists" would claim that the intent of the charter was not to restrict the preexisting customary right of anticipatory self-defense. Although the arguments of specific counter-restrictionists vary, a typical counter-restrictionist claim would be that the reference in Article 51 to an "inherent right" indicates that the charter's framers intended for a continuation of the broad pre-UN Charter customary right of anticipatory self-defense. The occurrence of an "armed attack" was just one circumstance that would empower the aggrieved state to act in self-defense. As the U.S. judge on the International Court of Justice (ICJ), Stephen Schwebel, noted in his dissent in *Nicaragua v. U.S.*, Article 51 does not say "if, and only if, an armed attack occurs." It does not explicitly limit the exercise of self-defense to only the circumstance in which an armed attack has occurred.

Unfortunately, despite Schwebel's willingness to express his views on anticipatory self-defense, neither the ICJ nor the UN Security Council has authoritatively determined the precise meaning of Article 51. Indeed, in the *Nicaragua* case, the ICJ made a point of noting that, because "the issue of the lawfulness of a response to the imminent threat of armed attack has not been raised . . . the Court expresses no view on the issue." As a consequence, the language of the charter clearly admits of two interpretations about the permissibility of preemptive force.

TEXT 21

JONATHAN STEELE, "THE BUSH DOCTRINE MAKES NONSENSE OF THE UN CHARTER," *THE GUARDIAN*, JUNE 6, 2002

The world was outraged by Israel's raid on June 7 1981. "Armed attack in such circumstances cannot be justified. It represents a grave breach of international law," Margaret Thatcher thundered. Jeane Kirkpatrick, the US ambassador to the UN and as stern a lecturer as Britain's then prime minister, described it as "shocking" and compared it to the Soviet invasion of Afghanistan. American newspapers were as fulsome. "Israel's sneak attack . . . was an act of inexcusable and short-sighted aggression," said *The New York Times*. The *Los Angeles Times* called it "state-sponsored terrorism".

The greatest anger erupted at the UN. Israel claimed Saddam Hussein was trying to develop nuclear weapons and it was acting in self-defence, which is legal under Article 51 of the UN charter. Other countries did not agree. They saw no evidence that Iraq's nuclear energy programme, then in its infancy and certified by the International Atomic Energy Agency as peaceful, could be described as military, aggressive or directed against a particular country. In any case, pre-emptive action by one country against another country which offers no imminent threat is illegal.

The UN security council unanimously passed a resolution condemning the Israeli raid. The US usually vetoes UN attempts to censure Israel but this time Washington joined in. The Reagan administration even blocked deliveries of new F-16s to its close ally. . . . Policymakers and ordinary people around the world clearly sensed that Israel's pre-emptive strike took us all to the top of a slippery slope. If pre-emption was accepted as legal, the fragile structure of international peace would be undermined. Any state could attack any other under the pretext that it detected a threat, however distant.

JONATHAN STEELE
1941–

Journalist and author. Born and raised in the U.K., Steele studied at the University of Cambridge and Yale. Steele has served as a foreign correspondent and editor at *The Guardian* since 1975. He has published a number of books about Soviet Russia and also writes extensively about the Middle East.

TEXT 22a

TALMUD, PESACHIM 25B

> כִּי הַהוּא דְאָתָא לְקַמֵיה דְרָבָא. אָמַר לֵיה: "מָרֵי דוּרַאי אָמַר לִי, 'זִיל קַטְלֵיה לִפְלַנְיָא וְאִי לֹא קַטְלִינָא לָךְ'".
>
> אָמַר לֵיה: "לִיקְטְלוּךְ וְלֹא תִיקְטוֹל. מַאי חָזֵית דְדָמָא דִידָךְ סוּמָק טְפֵי, דִילְמָא דָמָא דְהַהוּא גַבְרָא סוּמָק טְפֵי?"

A man once came before Rava and said: "The ruler of my city has told me, 'Go kill so-and-so, and if you do not, I will kill you.'"

Rava said to him: "Let him kill you rather than you kill the other. What makes you think that your blood is more red than his? Maybe his blood is redder?"

TEXT 22b

MAIMONIDES, *MISHNEH TORAH*, LAWS OF MURDERERS AND PRESERVATION OF LIFE 1:6

> הָרוֹדֵף אַחַר חֲבֵרוֹ לְהוֹרְגוֹ, אֲפִילוּ הָיָה הָרוֹדֵף קָטָן, הֲרֵי כָּל יִשְׂרָאֵל מְצוּוִין לְהַצִּיל הַנִרְדָף מִיַד הָרוֹדֵף, וַאֲפִילוּ בְּנַפְשׁוֹ שֶׁל רוֹדֵף.

If one is pursuing another with the intention of killing him or her—even if the pursuer is a minor—every Jew is commanded to come to the rescue of the pursued, even if it is necessary to kill the pursuer in order to save the threatened individual.

Additional Readings

THE SOVIET UNION AND THE SIX-DAY WAR: REVELATIONS FROM THE POLISH ARCHIVES

URI BAR-NOI

Introduction

Thirty-six years have passed since the June 1967 war between the State of Israel and its Arab neighbors. Despite the passage of time, the role played by the Kremlin, in the events which led to this armed conflict and during the war, remains to this day an enigma. Scholars have debated the question of the extent to which the Union of Soviet Socialist Republics (USSR) was responsible for the outbreak of hostilities in the Middle East on 5 June 1967. Some researchers have argued that Moscow instigated the war in order to increase Arab dependence on Soviet aid, as well as to unify progressive forces in the Middle East and to further consolidate its position in the region.[1] According to one historian, Soviet leaders sought a limited Arab-Israeli war and had no desire to bring about the destruction of Israel. They saw no major risk in a limited armed conflict between Israel and Arab countries, and thought that " . . . it would be useful to shake up their Arab clients a bit. . . ." Their conception was that the Arab armed forces were well-equipped and sufficiently prepared for any armed conflict with the Israeli Defense Forces (IDF).[2]

Other scholars contend that the Soviet leadership was divided on Middle East policy as a result of a power struggle between members of the collective leadership which had overthrown Nikita Khrushchev in October 1964. According to this interpretation, Soviet Premier Alexei Kosygin, President of the Supreme Soviet Nikolae Podgorny, and Minister for Foreign Affairs Andrei Gromyko were skeptical as to whether their Arab clients were prepared to go to war against Israel. They all supposedly advocated a cautious policy towards the Middle East designed to avert the danger of an armed conflict between the USSR and the United States following a war between Israel and Arab countries. The Secretary of the Soviet Communist Party (CPSU), Leonid Brezhnev and his new political ally, Defense Minister Marshall Andrei Grechko, however, pursued an adventurous policy course which led to escalation of the Arab-Israeli conflict. Hence, according to this view, the Six-Day War was a conspiracy designed to precipitate an armed conflict in the Middle East and to improve the domestic position of both Brezhnev and Grechko.[3]

Nikita Khrushchev's memoirs, as well as the reminiscences of Soviet military and intelligence personnel, also indicate that Moscow indeed sought escalation of Middle Eastern tensions leading to the outbreak of another war between Israel and its Arab neighbors. The Soviet high command seemed to have encouraged high-ranking Egyptian and Syrian officers to go to war against Israel, and persuaded the political leadership to support its designs. Moreover, the Soviet military took practical steps to assist Syria in stopping the advance of Israeli troops into Syrian territory toward the end of the war. These steps included a naval landing, airborne reinforcements and air support for ground operations. Military operations were, however, eventually aborted for fear of American retaliation and due to dissension within the Kremlin.[4]

A third interpretation argues that Moscow had no desire to encourage its Arab clients to wage war against Israel. By contrast, it wished to avert the danger of a potential Israeli military attack on Syria. But

URI BAR-NOI

Historian. Bar-Noi received his degree in international history from the London School of Economics and Political Science, and currently serves as a history professor at Bar-Ilan University in Jerusalem. He specializes in the history of the Cold War and has written extensively on this topic.

Egyptian President Gamal Abd el-Nasser misinterpreted Moscow's intentions and blocked the Gulf of Aqaba without the Kremlin's knowledge, or at least without its full consent. This action served as a casus belli for the Israeli Government and led to the outbreak of hostilities in the region.[5]

New archival evidence from Poland sheds light on the role played by the USSR in the events leading up to the outbreak of the Six-Day War and during the conflict. This evidence is based on Leonid Brezhnev's secret report at a plenary session of the Central Committee of the Soviet Communist Party (CC CPSU) held on June 20, 1967 entitled "On Soviet Policy Following the Israeli Aggression in the Middle East." A copy of Brezhnev's brief was translated into Polish and subsequently circulated among the leadership of the Polish Communist Party. This Polish record was acquired as part of a recent research project on the Cold War in the Middle East undertaken by the Chaim Herzog Center for Middle East Studies and Diplomacy at Ben-Gurion University of the Negev in Israel in cooperation with CWIHP.[6]

Brezhnev's report shows that Moscow had no intention of inciting an armed conflict in the Middle East and that the June 1967 war was the result of grave miscalculations and of Soviet inability to control the Arabs, rather than a conspiracy. The brief documents that throughout April–May, 1967, the Kremlin suspected that Israel was planning an act of aggression against Syria. Determined to forestall the Israeli offensive and to rescue the new radical-left regime in Damascus, the Soviet government informed Egypt that Israel had mobilized its armed forces on the border with Syria. By doing so, Moscow hoped to manipulate Nasser into assisting Syria by concentrating his armed forces on Egypt's border with Israel. The Kremlin estimated—mistakenly, as it turned out—that Israel was militarily weak and could not cope with a war on two fronts. Subsequently, Moscow consented to the ejection of United Nations (UN) peacekeeping forces from outposts on the Israeli-Egyptian border, and to the concentration of Egyptian troops on the Sinai Peninsula and the Gaza Strip.

Brezhnev's account suggests that after the situation in the Middle East deteriorated in May 1967, Moscow was no longer able to control the crisis. The Soviets were taken aback when Nasser blocked the Gulf of Aqaba without having consulted them. Israel's surprise attack and rapid victory within six days alarmed the Soviet leadership. Moscow, however, was not inclined to take any military action against Israel. Nor was it willing to airlift weapons to its Arab clients while hostilities continued. The Soviet leaders doubted that their Arab clients were capable of fighting any further. They concentrated instead on the diplomatic front and sought a cease-fire agreement mediated by the UN. Such an accord would stop the Israeli offensive, restore the status quo ante in the Middle East, and force Israel to withdraw to the prewar border. It was only when the occupation of the Syrian capital by the IDF seemed imminent that the Kremlin sharply increased pressure upon Israel and even resorted to military threats. At that point President Lyndon B. Johnson intervened in the conflict and persuaded the Israeli Government to stop the fighting.

Soviet Perceptions of Israel and the Six-Day War

The first part of Brezhnev's report indicates that the Soviet leader's perception of the Six-Day War was rigidly defined by his doctrinaire outlook on international affairs. As the document clearly demonstrates, Brezhnev perceived the Israeli attack on Egypt and Syria as an act of aggression supported by the US and West European powers. He dismissed Western attempts to portray the Six-Day War as a local conflict resulting from the protracted quarrel between Arabs and Jews. He vigorously claimed that the Israeli attack was part of a worldwide campaign designed to suppress the anti-colonial struggle and hamper the turn to socialism in the progressive societies of Asia, Greece, Africa and Latin America.

Brezhnev described Israel as a tool in the hands of Western imperialism, and claimed that the Israeli assault had been planned carefully by the West. According to him, Israel's military campaign aimed at overthrowing the progressive regimes in the Middle East, diminishing the influence of the USSR on its Arab clients, and restoring the predominant position which Western powers had held in this region until the mid-1950s. To support this thesis, the Soviet leader claimed that prior to the June 1967 war, Israel had received massive military supplies from the West and its armed forces had been equipped with the most modern assault weapons.[7]

In the brief, Brezhnev dismissed allegations that the Soviet government had encouraged both the Egyptians and the Syrians to threaten Israel. He claimed that Moscow's military aid to its Arab clients was mainly designed to assist them in their protracted struggle against colonialism, to consolidate their independence, and to improve their capability to defend themselves against both external and internal dangers. Moreover, the Soviet leader indicated that his government feared that a potential suppression of regimes in Cairo and Damascus might lead to the collapse of the anti-colonialist movement in the Middle East. Subsequently, the regional and global balance of power would tilt in favor of the West.[8]

Soviet Miscalculations and Failure to Control the Mid-May 1967 Crisis

In his overview of events which led to the outbreak of hostilities on 5 June 1967, Brezhnev pointed out that in mid-May 1967, Moscow had received information that Israel was contemplating a military campaign against Syria and other Arab countries. In light of this information, the Politburo of the CPSU decided to inform the Egyptian and Syrian governments of Israel's plans for aggression. Unfortunately, Brezhnev refrained from revealing critical information about the controversial Soviet warnings regarding the build-up of an Israeli assault against Syria. He limited himself to saying that " . . . there were many signs that led us to conclude that a serious international crisis was in the making and that Israel had prepared an act of aggression supported by Western powers . . . ."[9]

Before the CPSU Plenum Brezhnev stressed the fact that the Kremlin had no desire to incite war between Israel and its Arab neighbors. Moscow only intended to contain the State of Israel and to forestall its aggressive plans. The brief reveals that the Soviet government gave its consent to Egyptian actions which led to the withdrawal of UN forces and to the concentration of troops along the 1949 armistice line between Egypt and Israel. It shared the Egyptian government's view that these steps would deter Israel from waging war against Syria. However, Moscow's reaction to the closure of Straits of Tiran was lukewarm. Brezhnev considered the action misconceived, and he deplored the fact that Nasser had failed to consult the Kremlin before taking such a step. While the Soviet leader agreed that the ill-advised closure of the Gulf of Aqaba had indeed brought some prestige to the Egyptian president, he claimed that it provoked Israel to conduct a wider military campaign against its Arab neighbors.

Brezhnev's report indicates that following the closure of the Straits of Tiran, Moscow was determined to avert further deterioration in the Middle East and to foil Israeli and Western plans for aggression. Fear that the blockade of the Gulf of Aqaba might provoke Israel into war led Moscow to exert diplomatic pressure upon the Israeli government. Simultaneously, Moscow did its utmost to tone down the belligerent rhetoric of Egyptian and Syrian leaders and to assure that no further provocation be taken against Israel. Brezhnev revealed that during a meeting of the CC CPSU held on 30 May 1967, Syrian President Nur al-Din Atassi, then on an official visit to Moscow, had been asked to avoid taking any steps which could be used by Israel as a pretext to wage war against Syria. A similar request was conveyed in a note to Nasser on 26 May 1967. The Egyptian president was asked to do his utmost to prevent armed conflict with Israel. Both Nasser and his Minister of War, Shams al-Din Badran, who visited the Soviet capital on 28 May 1967, assured Soviet officials on several occasions that Egypt did not plan to resort to armed conflict or to provoke Israel to wage war.[10]

Restraint and Concentration on the Diplomatic Front

Brezhnev's report reveals that Israel's surprise attack on three fronts and the rapid victory over Egypt, Syria and Jordan was a bombshell for Moscow. Prior to the outbreak of hostilities, Soviet leadership operated under the illusion that Arab armed forces could easily repel any Israeli offensive and defeat the IDF on the battlefield. In retrospect, Brezhnev assured his audience that the armed forces of Egypt, Syria, Algeria and Iraq were superior to the IDF in number of troops and amount of tanks, planes, ships and armaments. They had been equipped with the most modern weapons, and had received high-level training from Soviet and other East European instructors. However, their fighting capacity and morale were very low. They were backwards, undisciplined and poorly organized. In spite of their alleged superiority over Israel in arms and military personnel, the Arabs lost most of their air power during the initial phase of the Israeli offensive. Left without an air umbrella and anti-aircraft defense, their ground forces suffered heavy losses.[11]

Brezhnev's account of the events clearly shows that following the disintegration of the Egyptian army and the rapid advance of Israeli troops into Sinai, Moscow decided to pursue a policy course designed to stop the offensive and to guarantee the survival of Nasser's regime. The Kremlin, however, had no desire to intervene actively in the fighting on the side of its Arab clients. Nor did it plan to supply them with arms to replace weapon systems destroyed in the fighting. Instead, Moscow concentrated on the diplomatic front. According to Brezhnev, the Kremlin sought an early cease-fire to stop the Israeli offensive. Then it planned to force an Israeli withdrawal to the prewar borders.

Brezhnev's brief reveals that on midnight of 7 June 1967, Egyptian Vice-President Marshal Amr informed the Soviet ambassador in Cairo that the situation on the Egyptian-Israeli front was critical and asked that a cease-fire agreement between his country and Israel be achieved within five hours. One hour later, members of the CPSU Politburo held an emergency session to discuss ways to help Egypt out of this difficult situation. According to Brezhnev's report, members of the Politburo were fully aware that the Egyptian army was in a state of chaos and confusion, and that it could not repel the Israeli attack. They ruled out the possibility of airlifting military supplies to Egypt while hostilities continued, something that would be impossible to arrange within a short period of time. Moreover, they were skeptical whether Soviet aircraft carrying supplies could safely land on Egyptian airfields which had been destroyed by the Israeli Air Force.[12]

The report clearly shows that the Politburo feared that Nasser's regime would not survive the Israeli offensive. Therefore, the Soviet leadership was determined to achieve an early cease-fire agreement, mediated by the UN. On June 7, 1967, the UN Security Council adopted a draft resolution which called for an immediate cease-fire in the Middle East. The IDF continued the offensive, despite this appeal and a second UN resolution calling for an early cease-fire. Subsequently, Moscow issued a stern warning to the Israeli government threatening to reassess its relations with Israel and to consider other means if the offensive continued.

But Brezhnev's report reveals that Nasser, too, was not ready to accept a cease-fire as yet. As the brief indicates, the Soviet leader deplored Nasser's vacillation that in itself served as an obstacle to Moscow's attempts to ensure Israeli compliance with UN resolutions. Only on 9 June 1967, did the Egyptian government announce its willingness to agree to a cease-fire but it was too late. By this time, the IDF had completed its occupation of the entire Sinai desert and had launched an offensive against Syria.

To Moscow policy makers, the offensive against Syria was another stage in the imperialist campaign against radical-left regimes in the Middle East. Determined to save Syria from a humiliating defeat and occupation, the Soviet government attempted to force Israel to comply with the two Security Council resolutions. On 8 June 1967, it instructed its ambassador to the UN to draft another resolution calling for an immediate cessation of hostilities and the withdrawal of Israeli troops to the 5 June 1967 border. The next day, heads of government and the leaders of communist parties in Eastern Europe gathered to discuss the Middle East crisis. At the end of this urgently convened conference, held in Moscow, a communiqué was issued by the Communist delegations condemning Israel as an aggressor, and calling upon the Israeli government to stop the offensive and pull its troops out of Syrian territory without delay.[13]

Brezhnev relates that this communiqué made little impression upon Israel, which continued its campaign against Syria. On 10 June 1967, the IDF captured the town of El-Quneitra, one of the Syrian army's main strongholds on the road to Damascus. Syria's panicked foreign minister informed the Soviet

Government that Israeli tanks, supported by aircraft, were advancing on the Golan Heights in the direction of the Syrian capital. He asked that all possible measures be taken by Moscow to forestall the attack, otherwise it would be too late for his country.

The Soviet Government perceived the occupation of El-Quneitra as another critical turning point in the June 1967 war. Subsequently, it rushed to stop the Israeli offensive entirely. A Soviet missile cruiser and a number of submarines based in the Mediterranean Sea were ordered to set sail immediately for the Syrian coast. On the afternoon of 10 June 1967, the Soviet government broke off diplomatic relations with Israel. In a note to the Israeli government, Moscow accused Israel of being responsible for the brutal violation of successive UN resolutions calling for a cease-fire in the Middle East. The Soviet government also threatened to impose sanctions upon Israel if it did not stop immediately the military campaign.

Other Eastern European countries followed suit and broke off diplomatic relations with Israel. In retrospect, Brezhnev claimed that this was a spontaneous action, and that it had not been planned or discussed by the Soviet and Eastern European leaders during their urgent consultations in Moscow. The USSR and other Eastern European countries felt a sense of urgency following the defeat of their Arab allies. Therefore, they were willing to take concerted action to stop the penetration of Israeli troops into Arab territories.[14]

Brezhnev's report indicates that Moscow simultaneously conveyed an ultimatum to President Johnson. The first part of the Soviet ultimatum was a strongly-worded complaint about Israel's non-compliance with the UN resolutions which called for an immediate cease-fire in the Middle East. The Soviet government then urged the US president to persuade the Israeli government to halt the offensive without delay. It threatened to take any necessary action, including military action, if Israel failed to stop the fighting within the next few hours.

According to Brezhnev's report, this ultimatum bore fruit. Faced with Soviet pressure, Washington forced the Israeli government to comply with the Security Council resolutions and stop the advance of its armed forces into the heart of Syria. Johnson informed Brezhnev that Secretary of State Dean Rusk had sent to the Israeli government an urgent message demanding that Israel immediately implement all Security Council resolutions. In response, the Israeli government expressed its willingness to comply with UN resolutions and, subsequently, ended its offensive against Syria on the evening of 10 June 1967.[15]

Conclusion

Brezhnev's confidential report to the CC CPSU does not shed light on the controversial information regarding the concentration of Israeli troops on the Syrian border, conveyed to the Egyptians by the Soviet government in mid-May 1967. Nor does it link this action with the outbreak of hostilities in the Middle East a few weeks later. The report seems apologetic in tone, with the Soviet leader attempting to avoid being held accountable for the provocation which led Arab leaders to resort to bellicose actions. In turn, these actions spurred the Israeli preemptive attack and resulted in the humiliating defeat of both Egypt and Syria, the disintegration of their armed forces and the occupation of the entire Sinai desert, West bank and Golan Heights by Israel. As the brief indicates, the Soviet leader held Nasser solely responsible for this catastrophe. He claimed that the reckless closing of the Tiran Straits to the passage of Israeli ships provoked Israel to conduct a wider military campaign against its Arab neighbors.

The report suggests that the Kremlin had no desire to incite an armed conflict between its Arab clients and the State of Israel, and that the June 1967 war was a result of Moscow's clumsy diplomacy, grave miscalculations and inability to control the crisis which it had provoked. It grew out of a determination to foil Israel's aggressive plans against Syria and to frustrate what it suspected was a joint Israeli-imperialist scheme to suppress progressive forces in the Middle East. The Kremlin assumed that these plans were part of a Western campaign aimed to overthrow radical-left regimes in the Middle East and to undermine the predominant position which the USSR had maintained in the region since the mid-1950s. The brief demonstrates that Moscow operated under the illusion that Israel was militarily weak and could not risk war on two fronts. It estimated that preventive action would deter Israel from waging war against Syria.

This Polish record indicates that after the outbreak of hostilities, Moscow had no plan to actively intervene in the fighting on the side of its Arab clients, nor did it take any steps to invade Israel, as suggested by some scholars. Brezhnev's account of the Six-Day War reveals that during this armed conflict, the Kremlin's occupants preferred the diplomatic front to military action. They were not even willing to deliver vital supplies of armaments, tanks and airplanes to their Arab clients while hostilities continued. Politburo members were fully aware that Egypt's armed forces had disintegrated and could not continue fighting. Brezhnev's brief suggests that Moscow's sole plan was to exert diplomatic pressure upon Israel to agree to an early cease-fire and pull its armed forces out of occupied territories. By pursuing this plan, Moscow hoped to stall the Israeli offensive and guarantee the survival of the radical-left regimes in the Middle East. With the Israeli government defiant and reluctant to comply with a series of UN resolutions calling for an immediate cease-fire, the USSR and the majority of its Eastern European satellites responded in what Brezhnev described as a spontaneous act of breaking off diplomatic relations with Israel. Simultaneously, the Soviet government concentrated a small naval contingent near the Syrian coast. It also put pressure upon the US president to use his influence with the Israeli government to persuade it to stop its military operation against Syria without delay.

I am grateful to Dr. Dror Ze'evi, former Chairman of the Chaim Herzog Center for the Study of Middle East and Diplomacy (CHC) at Ben-Gurion University of the Negev for his encouragement and support, as well as for granting me access to Soviet and East European documents held in this center. The document was obtained from the Polish Archives by CHC researchers. Document translated by Gennady Pasechnik for the CHC.

"The Soviet Union and the Six-Day War: Revelations from the Polish Archives," The Wilson Center: Cold War International History Project. July 7, 2011. https://www.wilsoncenter.org/publication/the-soviet-union-and-the-six-day-war-revelations-the-polish-archives#0.

Endnotes

1 Michael Oren, *Six Days of War: June 1967 and the Making of the Modern Middle East* (Oxford, 2002), pp.54–55; Jon D. Glassman, *Arms for the Arabs: The Soviet Union and War in the Middle East* (Baltimore, 1975), pp. 35–36; Peter Mangold, *Superpower Intervention in the Middle East* (London, 1978), pp. 116–117; Galia Golan, *Soviet Policies in the Middle East: From World War II to Gorbachev* (Cambridge, 1990), p. 58; Richard Parker (ed.), *The Six-Day War: A Retrospective* (Gainesville, 1996), p. 36.

2 Alexei Vassiliev, *Russian Policy in the Middle East: from Messianism to Pragmatism* (Reading, 1993), pp. 65–66.

3 Avraham Ben-Zur, *Gormim Sovietim ve Milkhemet Sheshet Hayamim* [trans. from Hebrew: *Soviet Elements and the Six-Day War*] (Tel-Aviv, 1975), pp. 174–215; Pedro Ramet, *The Soviet-Syrian Relationship since 1955: A Troubled Alliance* (Boulder, 1990), pp. 43–44; Richard Parker (ed.), *The Six-Day War*, pp. 46–48.

4 Isabella Ginor, "The Russians Were Coming: The Soviet Military Threat in the 1967 Six-Day War", Middle Eastern Review of International Affairs [Israel] 4(4) December 2000: 44–59; Christopher Andrew and Vasili Mitrokhin, *The Mitrokhin Archive: The KGB in Europe and the West* (London, 1999), pp.473–475; Nikita S. Khrushchev, *Vremya, ludi, vlast* (Moskva, 1999g.), tom 3, l. 435; tom 4, l. 460.

5 Yaacov Ro'i, *From Encroachment to Involvement: A Documentary Study of Soviet Foreign Policy in the Middle East, 1945–1973* (Jerusalem, 1974), xxxiii-xxxiv; Karen Dawisha, *Soviet Foreign Policy Towards Egypt* (London, 1977), pp. 37–43; Patrick Seale, "Syria", in *The Cold War and the Middle East* (eds.) Yezid Sayigh and Avi Shlaim (Oxford, 1997), pp. 59–62; Richard B. Parker, "The June 1967 War: Some Mysteries Explored", *Middle East Journal* 46(2) 1992: 177–197; Walter Laqueur, *The Road to War 1967: The Origins of the Arab-Israeli Conflict* (London, 1968), pp. 230, 235; Fawaz Gerges, *The Superpower and the Middle East: Regional and International Politics, 1955-1967* (Boulder, Colo., 1994), p. 216; Chaim Herzog, *The Arab-Israeli Wars: War and Peace in the Middle East from the War of Independence to Lebanon* (London, 1982), pp. 148–149.

6 This research project found on certain documents from Russian and Eastern European archives.

7 AAN KC PZPR 2632, pp. 359–360.

8 Ibid., pp. 360–362.

9 Ibid., pp. 366–367.

10 Ibid., pp. 368-369.

11 Ibid., pp. 370-372.

12 Ibid., pp. 372-373.

13 Ibid., pp. 376–379.

14 Ibid., pp. 379–383.

15 Ibid., pp. 383–385.

TO PREEMPT OR NOT TO PREEMPT
A COMPARISON BETWEEN THE SIX-DAY AND YOM KIPPUR WARS

ALAN DERSHOWITZ

In both 1967 and 1973 Israel faced the decision whether to preempt an expected imminent attack or to absorb the first blow and then respond. Each decision has, with the benefit of hindsight, been criticized as wrong,[1] but at the time the decisions had to be made both may well have been correct. A comparison between them affords unusual insight into the appropriate criteria for preemption in the military context.

The Six-Day War

Israel had to decide whether to attack preemptively in 1967, when Egypt, in coordination with Syria, again closed the Strait of Tiran, expelled UN peacekeepers, massed its regular army on the border and threatened a genocidal war. According to Nasser, the war was to be not over the Strait of Tiran but over Israel's "existence," and "The objective will be Israel's destruction."

Hafiz al-Assad ordered his Syrian soldiers to "strike the enemy's [civilian] settlements, tum them into dust, pave the Arab roads with the skulls of Jews. Strike them without mercy." He characterized the forthcoming attack on Israel as a "battle of annihilation." Damascus Radio incited its listeners: "Arab masses, this is your day. Rush to the battlefield. . . . Let them know that we shall hang the last imperialist soldier with the entrails of the last Zionist."[2]

Israel attacked preemptively, destroying the Egyptian and Syrian air forces on the ground, and went on to win a decisive victory in six days. Although it also feared an attack from Jordan, it did not act preemptively against that enemy to the east. Indeed, on the morning of June 5, 1967, it passed to Jordan through a UN envoy a message that it would not attack Jordanian forces if Jordan did not attack first. Instead it absorbed the first blows from Jordanian artillery against civilian targets in West Jerusalem and military targets near Tel Aviv and Ramat David.[3] Jordanian ground forces also took control of Government House in Jerusalem, threatening Mount Scopus. Israeli authorities believed that "if [the Jordanian Army] could take Mount Scopus and encircle Jewish Jerusalem,"[4] it would hold a strong military position. Israel then responded with ground and air attacks. It defeated Jordan as well, though with considerable casualties.[5]

Much of the world accepted the necessity of, and justification for, Israel's preemptive attack of 1967, because Israel was seen as an underdog surrounded by hostile Arab nations threatening its destruction. Moreover, Egypt had been the first to commit a casus belli, an act of war, by denying Israeli shipping access to an international waterway and then threatening a large-scale attack by expelling UN peacekeepers, and by massing its troops on the border. The Egyptian Air Force also flew over Israel's nuclear facility in Dimona, raising the specter of an aerial attack on Israel's nuclear capacity.[6] Nasser had earlier threatened that "the Arabs would take preemptive action" in order to stop Israel from developing nuclear weapons.[7] It was Israel, however, that fired the first shot, because as Israeli Prime Minister Levi Eshkol told his cabinet, a war in which "the first five minutes will be decisive" was inevitable, and "[t]he question is who will attack the other's airfields first."[8] The Israeli Air Force attacked the Egyptian airfields first, and Israel's air superiority was assured. Its swift and decisive ground victory resulted in fewer civilian casualties than in any comparable modem war.[9] The number of Israeli civilians and soldiers who might have been killed in

ALAN M. DERSHOWITZ, 1938–

American lawyer, jurist, and political commentator. Mr. Dershowitz was a professor of law at Harvard University for half a century; he achieved that position at the age of 28, the youngest full professor of law in the history of the school. Dershowitz is an advocate of Israel and an activist civil liberties lawyer who takes half of his cases pro bono. He has written 20 books, including *The Case for Israel.*

an initial attack from the combined Arab armies was estimated to be quite high.[10] It is not absolutely certain, however, that the Egyptians would necessarily have attacked despite their provocative actions.

In his influential book *Just and Unjust Wars*, Michael Walzer has noted that Nasser intended to make Israel believe that a catastrophic attack was imminent, so as to require it to call up its reserves and destroy its economy as well as its self-confidence. He cited Egyptian documents captured by Israel during the war that suggested a plan by Nasser to maintain "his army on Israel's border without [actual] war." This would have achieved "a great victory" because it would have kept the Strait of Tiran permanently closed to Israeli shipping and because "of the strain it would have placed on the Israeli defense system." Walzer pointed to the "basic asymmetry in the structure of forces: [T]he Egyptians could deploy. . . .their large army of long-term regulars on the Israeli border and keep it there indefinitely; the Israelis could only counter their deployment by mobilizing reserve formations, and reservists could not be kept in uniform for very long. . . ."[11] He also pointed to the failure of international diplomacy that made clear "the unwillingness of the Western powers to pressure or coerce the Egyptians. . . . Day by day, diplomatic efforts seemed only to intensify Israel's isolation." Finally, he cited the psychological factors: "Egypt was in the grip of a war fever, familiar enough from European history, a celebration in advance of expected victories. The Israeli mood was very different, suggesting what it means to live under the threat: rumors of coming disasters were endlessly repeated; frightened men and women raided food shops, buying up their entire stock, despite government announcements that there were ample reserves; thousands of graves were dug in the military cemeteries; Israel's political and military leaders lived on the edge of nervous exhaustion."[12]

Despite the after-the-fact uncertainty whether Egypt would actually have attacked, Walzer believed that Israeli leaders experienced "just fear" and that Egyptian leaders intended "to put it in danger."[13] Accordingly, Walzer concluded: "The Israeli first strike is, I think, a clear case of legitimate anticipation."[14]

The Six-Day War ended with the capture and subsequent occupation of the West Bank, Gaza, and the Golan Heights, a situation that changed international opinion and made future preemptive actions more problematic.

Walzer is plainly correct as a matter of law. In the context of both domestic individual self-defense and international military preemption, the action must be judged by what was known and reasonably believed at the time the action was taken, not by what was later learned or even what was "objectively" true.[15] By that criterion Israel's preemptive attack was a lawful instance of anticipatory self-defense in response to a deliberate provocation and threatened attack by Egypt and Syria.

The Yom Kippur War

In 1973 Israel again faced a coordinated attack from Egypt and Syria. The intelligence concerning its enemies' intentions was not as good as in 1967, and the threat was not perceived as so grave because of the buffer provided by the territories conquered in 1967 and because the threat was not as overt. Perhaps the knowledge, obtained in the aftermath of the Six-Day War, that Nasser may not have intended to attack in June 1967, led some to believe that Sadat did not intend to strike. Moreover, in this case Sadat intended to make Israel believe that it was not planning to attack. Nonetheless, there was a brief opportunity for a preemptive attack against the Egyptian and Syrian air forces, despite the reality that they were better protected than they had been in 1967. At 4:00 a.m. on October 6, 1973, Israeli intelligence received a report from a high-level Egyptian official who was spying for Israel that an Egyptian-Syrian attack was imminent. Several military leaders proposed preemptive action. Indeed, Israel's Chief of Staff David Elazar "ordered the commander of the air force . . . to prepare a preemptive strike and issued a standby order to attack at 11:00 in the morning."[16] But Defense Minister Moshe Dayan "adamantly opposed a preemptive strike," observing that "we're in a political situation in which we can't do what we did in 1967."[17]

In the hours leading up to the Egyptian-Syrian attack, the proposal for preemption was debated in front of Israel's prime minister, Golda Meir. The case for preemption was presented by General Elazar, who argued that it would save many lives: "Elazar entered Mrs. Meir's office on that Saturday morning with some persuasive arguments in favor of a pre-emptive air-strike, namely, that a first strike could disrupt and retard the enemy offensive, allow Israel's army more time to mobilize, destroy at least part of the enemy air-defense systems, and limit Israeli casualties.[18]

The negative case was argued by Dayan, who said that a preemptive attack by Israel would make it more difficult to secure American support if needed. He believed that the "political damage Israel would incur by striking first would be far greater, and accordingly he opposed pre-emption."[19] When the presentations were completed, "the prime minister hemmed uncertainly for a few moments but then came to a clear decision. There would be no preemptive strike. Israel might be needing American assistance soon and it was imperative that it not be blamed for starting the war. 'If we strike first we won't get help from anybody,' she said."[20]

At the close of the war, U.S. Secretary of State Henry Kissinger told Dayan that Israel "had been wise not to stage a preemptive strike on Yom Kippur. If it had . . . it would not have received so much as a nail from the United States."[21] Because Israel was willing to absorb the first blow, and because it suffered enormous losses—in both life and in equipment[22]—the United States agreed to supply it with considerable replacement armaments. Most of the American weapons arrived too late for actual use in the war, but the knowledge that they were on the way allowed the Israeli Army to use all available weapons and ammunition without fear of running out.[23]

The immediate military cost to Israel of having not preempted is impossible to calculate, but some experts have estimated that the number of casualties suffered by Israel—2,656 dead and 7,250 wounded—would have been considerably lower.[24] During the 1967 war, fewer than 800 Israeli soldiers were killed and approximately 2,500 wounded.[25] More significant, the ratios of dead and wounded between Israel and its enemies was very different in the two wars. The ratio in the Yom Kippur War was between four to one and seven to one in Israel's favor, depending on whose figures are credited,[26] whereas the ratio during the Six-Day War was "approximately 25 to 1 in Israel's favor."[27]

Military historians and analysts have studied the Israeli decision not to preempt and have concluded that the cost of not preempting was high. U.S. Air Force specialists estimated that "had the air force been permitted to pre-empt, the destruction of 90 percent of the SAM [surface-to-air missile) sites could have been accomplished in a period of three to six hours for the loss of under ten aircraft." This would have reduced "Israeli losses on the ground" considerably: "Preemptive air strikes on front-line missiles and troop concentrations could certainly have been expected to disrupt the enemy offensive and its communications. Some authoritative writers have argued that the IAF [Israeli Air Force] could have delivered three thousand tons of bombs on enemy targets before the Arab attack reached full strength."[28]

One reason why it is impossible to come up with precise estimates of how many lives might have been saved by a preemptive attack is that such an attack could have changed the entire course of the war, perhaps even prevented the attack by Egypt and Syria.[29] This must remain highly speculative, especially with regard to the Yom Kippur War because Egypt's goal was not to win a full-blown military victory in traditional terms but rather to restore its honor by inflicting heavy casualties on the Israeli Army and regaining some of its lost territories before a cease-fire could be imposed. That is why, despite its eventual military defeat, "for Egypt, the war was a towering accomplishment,"[30] and its president, Anwar el-Sadat, the man who started the war, emerged as "the clearest victor."[31] Egypt's "victory" in the Ramadan War (as the Yom Kippur War is called in the Arab world) is still celebrated, despite massive military losses. ·

It is precisely with regard to wars that are not subject to the usual deterrent calculi of military costs and benefits that preemption becomes an attractive option. Deterrence, at least in theory, is always a preferable way of preventing a war since it relies on the sword of Damocles' hanging rather than dropping. However, for enemies who do not fear the sword dropping, preemption may be the only realistic option. It will probably always be a matter of degree since almost no enemy is completely oblivious to the threat of retaliation.

The calculations that went into the decisions regarding the Yom Kippur War went well beyond short-term military advantages and disadvantages. Israel would almost certainly have gained considerable short-term military benefits from a preemptive strike against Egypt and Syria.[32] But the longer-term risks would have been considerable, especially in regard to its relations with its major ally, the United States.[33] One important reason why the risks of preemption would have been so high for Israel was that it had successfully employed that tactic six years earlier and had won an overwhelming victory. Because it now was perceived as so strong, and because it had been criticized in some quarters for starting the shooting in the Six-Day War, Israel was in a difficult position with regard to preempting once again. It feared—understandably, as it turned out—that the international community would not believe that it was in fact acting preemptively once again to ward off an inevitable and imminent attack, but rather that it was using the excuse of preventive self-defense to wage an aggressive war.

This suggests another important potential cost of preemption: that once done—even successfully—it becomes difficult to repeat. This is so for a variety of practical reasons. First, an enemy who is aware of the prior preemptive act can better prepare for a repetition. Sadat went to great efforts to mask his intentions on the eve of the Yom Kippur War so as to deny Israel the opportunity to take effective preemptive measures. (We shall see how Israel's preemptive attack against Iraq's nuclear reactor in 1981 caused Iran to take precautions against a similar attack later.) Second, a successful preemptive attack makes it difficult to justify—on moral, legal, political, and diplomatic grounds—a subsequent attack. We saw this in Dayan's argument against a repeat in 1973 of what Israel had done successfully in 1967. Finally, and related to the second reason, if a nation repeatedly preempts following an initial successful preemption, the propriety of its initial preemption will be retrospectively challenged. This too was part of Dayan's concerns. We shall see that the United States' preventive attack on Iraq in 2003 (and its subsequent occupation) have made it more difficult to justify a preventive attack against Iran's nuclear facilities, even though Iran appears to be much closer to developing nuclear weapons than Iraq was.

Another related factor that may have contributed to Israel's decisions to preempt in 1967 but not in 1973 is that in 1967 Nasser was overtly threatening to attack and took action designed to make Israel, and the world, believe that an attack was imminent (even if it was not). The world would thus be more likely to accept Israel's preemptive justification than it would in 1973, when Sadat intended that Israel, and the world, believe that he was not planning an attack (even though he was). Accordingly, a preemptive attack may be more acceptable in the face of an overt threat, even if intended as a bluff, than in the face of a well-concealed sneak attack.

In sum, therefore, an analysis of the Six-Day and Yom Kippur wars suggests that a major factor in deciding whether to undertake a preemptive attack will generally be the short-term military advantage secured by striking the first blow. As Shimon Peres, the former prime minister and defense minister of Israel, has written, it is the duty of a leader to "meet [war] under the least dangerous conditions," which necessarily must include the option of a preemptive attack.[34] But there will be other considerations as well, including political, diplomatic, legal, moral, humanitarian, and prudential. Moreover, there is always the possibility that firing the first shot—even on the basis of the best intelligence and with the highest of motives—may turn out to provoke a war that would not otherwise have begun.

The burden of justification should always be on the nation that acts preemptively or preventively. In satisfying that burden, the anticipatory actor can point to the certainty of an attack, its imminence, and the extent of the damage it would suffer from absorbing the first blow, both militarily and to its civilian population. Other critical factors include the nature of the preemptive action (a single decisive first strike against a military target as distinguished from a full-scale war with massive casualties and a long-term occupation); the limited damage to noncombatants it would inflict with its preemption (especially as compared with absorbing the first blow and then retaliating); the likelihood of a shorter, less damaging war, if it preempts; and other ineffable factors. In the end the decision will always be dependent on the quality of intelligence and an assessment of probabilities.[35] It will also turn on the comparative values placed on the lives of a nation's own civilians and soldiers and those of its enemies. It will always be a matter of degree and judgment. But no law or rule of morality will ever succeed in prohibiting all preemptive military actions. Nor should it.[36]

Alan M. Dershowitz, *Preemption*: A Knife that Cuts Both Ways (New York: W.W. Norton, 2007).

Reprinted with permission from publisher.

Endnotes

1 See pp. 82–83, 85.
2 Quoted in Dershowitz, *The Case for Israel*, loc. cit., p. 92.
3 Michael B. Oren, *Six Days of War: June 1967 and the Making of the Modern Middle East* (Oxford, U.K.: Oxford University Press, 2002), pp. 186–87
4 Samir A. Mutawi, *Jordan in the 1967 War* (Cambridge, U.K.: Cambridge University Press, 1987), p. 124.
5 See Oren, op. cit., pp. 305–06.
6 Warner D. Farr, "The Third Temple's Holy of Holies: Israel's Nuclear Weapons," *Counterproliferation Papers, Future Warfare Series No. 2*; accessible at http://www. Au.af.mil/au/awc/awcgate/cpc-pubs/farr.htm
7 Michael Karpin, *The Bomb in the Basement* (New York: Simon & Schuster, 2006), p. 276 (of uncorrected proofs).
8 Oren, op. cit., p. 82. Some have argued with the benefit of hindsight, that it is possible that absent Israel's first strike, there would have been no 1967 war. Even if that were true, and it is impossible to be certain that it is, Israel's actions must be judged on the basis of what it knew and reasonably believed *at the time*. As prime minister of Israel Menachem Begin spoke about the uncertainty Israel faced and its motives in launching its preemptive strike: "In June 1967, we again had a choice. The Egyptian Army concentrations in the Sinai approaches do not prove that Nasser was really about to attack us. We must be honest with ourselves. We decided to attack him. This was a war of self-defense in the noblest sense of the term. The Government of National Unity then established and decided unanimously: we will take the initiative and attack the enemy, drive him back, and thus assure the security of Israel and the future of the nation."—"Excerpts from Begin Speech at National Defense College," *New York Times*, August 21, 1982, p. 6.
9 See Oren, op. cit., p. 306: "Casualty rates . . . among civilians was remarkably low [because] much of the fighting took place far from major population centers."
10 Ibid., pp. 162–64
11 Michael Walzer, *Just and Unjust Wars* (New York: Basic Books, 2000), pp. 83–86.
12 Ibid.
13 Ibid., p. 84.
14 See also Eric Hammel, *Six Days in June: How Israel Won the 1967 Arab-Israeli War* (Pacifica, Calif.: Pacifica Press, 2001), p. 29: "[T]he bluff. . . Nasser commenced on May 13, 1967 ensured that the inevitable war would commence sooner rather than later."
15 See, for example, *Washington v. Hazlett*, 113 N.W. (1907), pp. 371, 380–81; and *Washington v. Wanrow*, 88 Wash. 2d 221, 559 P.2d (1977), p. 548.
16 Steven J. Rosen and Martin Indyk, "The Temptation to Pre-empt in a Fifth Arab-Israeli War," *Orbis* (Summer 1976), p. 270.
17 Abraham Rabinovich, The Yom Kippur War: The Epic Encounter That Transformed the Middle East (New York NY: Knopf Doubleday Publishing Group, 1967), p. 87
18 Rosen and Indyk, op. cit., p. 272.
19 Ibid., p. 273. Even in the planning stages for a possible war, preemption was essentially taken of the table:

> In the wake of the 1967 victory new elements were introduced into Israel's calculus. The capture of Sinai, the West Bank, and the Golan Heights for the first time provided her with strategic depth and with what her leaders regarded as defensible borders. Thus it was believe that preemption was no longer a military necessity. Moreover, the political costs of preemption had risen considerably, as America sought stability in the region as a precondition for a negotiated settlement. Accordingly, Defense Minister Dayan ordered the IDF to rely primarily on a non-preemptive strategy. Instead, the Israeli forces depended on early warning of any Arab intention to attack to allow time for mobilization.
> —Ibid., p. 270.

20 Rabinovich, op. cit. p. 89.
21 Ibid., p. 454. Some have questioned this assessment. See p. 304, n.50.
22 There were times during the Yom Kippur War when Moshe Dayan and other feared for the survival of Israel. Abraham Rabinovich wrote: "What [Dayan] sensed now as Israel's mortality and it shook him. He was gripped, he would later write, by an anxiety he had never before known."—Ibid., p. 218.
23 Ibid., p. 491.
24 To put the losses into comparative perspective, Israel "lost almost three times as many men per capita in nineteen days as the United States in Vietnam in close to a decade." Ibid., p. 498.
25 Many of Israeli casualties of the 1967 war occurred on the Jordanian front, and they might have been avoided or reduced had Israel taken preemptive action against Jordan.
26 "Arab casualties as given by a western analyst were 8,528 dead and 19,450 wounded. Israel estimated Arab casualties to be almost twice those figures—15,000 dead . . . and 35,000 wounded . . ." Rabinovich, op. cit., p. 497.
27 Oren, op. cit., p. 305.
28 Rosen and Indyk, op. cit., p. 272.
29 It might also have prevented the subsequent peace treaty between Egypt and Israel—or perhaps facilitated it. No one can know for certain. The contingencies of history, especially military history, always leave much to speculation.
30 Rabinovich, op. cit., p. 55.
31 Ibid., p. 507. At least in short term. He was assassinated several years later by Islamic fundamentalists.
32 The issue is complicated by the fact that Israel did not even call up all its reserve soldiers in the days leading up to the Yom Kippur

attack, as it did in 1967. General Elazar estimated that "if we had mobilized, the war would have lasted three, four, six days."—Ibid., p. 489.

Mobilization, especially by Israel, which relies on reserved, can itself be viewed as a preemptive tactic—or at least as a combination of preemption and deterrence.

33 It turned out, ironically, that "[a]t the initial meeting of the policy makers [in Washington at the beginning of the war], most participants presumed that Israel had started the war"—probably because of its preemptive actions in 1967.—Ibid., p. 322.

This and other factors have led some experts to conclude that Meir was wrong to refuse preemption because of fear of American reaction. "Two influential exponents of this line of reasoning, Edward Luttwak and Water Laqueur, have denigrated the political costs of preemption in arguing: '. . . the moral issue of who fired first did not after all make any difference. Rather the reverse. Most governments blandly accused the Israelis of being aggressors. Clearly only the United States mattered, and it remains an open question whether an Israeli air strike against Arab forces whose offensive have entered the operational phase would have made much of a difference to American opinion.'"—Rosen and Indyk, op. cit., p. 275.

34 Shimon Peres, *From These Men: Seven Founders of the State of Israel* (New York: Wyndham, 1979), p. 55; quoted in William C. Bradford, "The Duty to Defend Them: A Natural Law Justification for the Bush Doctrine of Preventive War," *Notre Dame Law Review*, vol. 79 (2004), p. 1457.

35 For an interesting analysis of how an "abundance of information" may have led Israel "to intelligence hubris," see Efraim Halevy, "In Defense of the Intelligence Services," *Economist*, July 29, 2004.

36 Walzer sought to revise the preexisting paradigm in light of his conclusion justifying Israeli preemption in the Six-Day War:

> To say that [Israel's preemption was justified], however, is to suggest a major revision of the legalist paradigm. For it means that aggression can be made out not only in the absence of any immediate intention to launch such an attack or invasion. The general formula must go something like this: states may use military force in the threats of war, whenever the failure to do would seriously risk their territorial integrity or political independence. Under such circumstances it can fairly be said that they have been forced to fight and that they are victims of aggression. Since there are no police upon whom they can call, the moment at which states are forced to fight probably comes sooner than it would for individuals in a settled domestic society. But if we imagine an unstable society, like the "wild-west" of American fiction, the analogy can be restated: a state under threat is like an individual hunted by an enemy who has announced his intension of killing or injuring him. Surely such a person may surprise his hunter, if he is able to do so. The formula is permissive, but it implies restrictions that can usefully be unpacked only with reference to particular cases. It is obvious, for example, that measures short of war are preferable to war itself whenever they hold out the hope of similar or nearly similar effectiveness. But what those measures might be, or how long they must be tried, cannot be a matter of *priori* stipulation. In the case of the Six-Day war, the "asymmetry in the structure of forces" set a time limit on diplomatic efforts that would have no relevance to conflicts involving other sorts of states and armies. A general rule containing words like "seriously" opens a broad path for human judgement—which it is, no doubt, the purpose of the legalist paradigm to narrow or block altogether. But it is a fact of our moral life that political leaders make such judgements, and that once they are made the rest of us uniformly condemn them. Rather, we weigh and evaluate their actions on the basis of criteria like those I have tried to describe. When we do that we are acknowledging that there are threats with which no nation can be expected to live. And that acknowledgement is an important part of our understanding aggression. —Walzer, op. cit., p. 85.

Lesson 3

WHERE EAST MET WEST

THE CHOSEN CITY OF JERUSALEM

Antique world map as clover leaf showing Jerusalem in the center of the world, c. 1581. (Artist: Heinrich Bunting)

In the course of repulsing Jordanian aggression, Israel captured the Old City of Jerusalem, including its Temple Mount and Western Wall, all of which holds utmost historical, cultural, and spiritual import to the Jewish nation. The return of these sites to Jewish hands triggered a global Jewish spiritual awakening. What is the history and significance of Jerusalem? What allure does it hold for its millions of annual visitors?

PARTITIONED JERUSALEM, 1948–1967

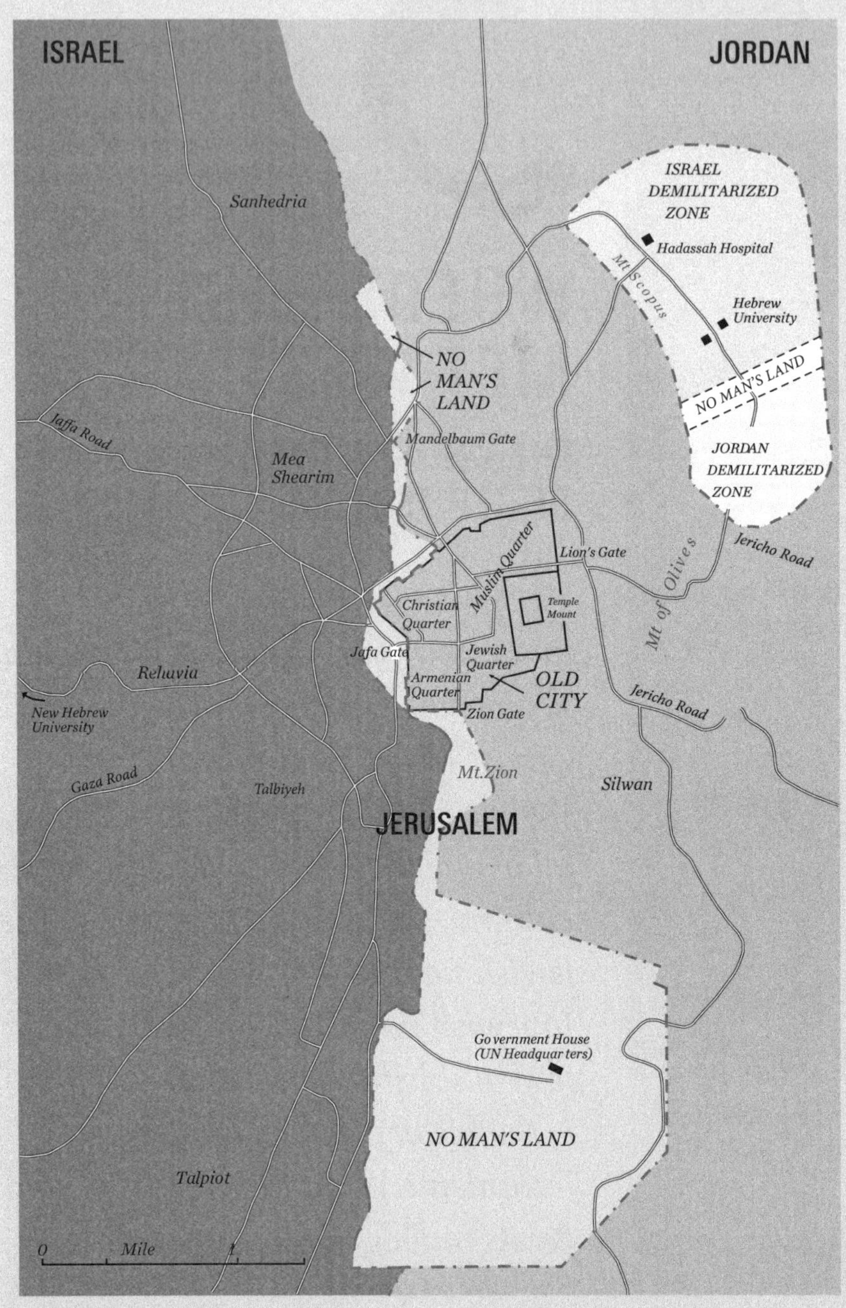

H. M. Sachar, A History of Israel, *Knopf 1979.*

TEXT 1

ISAIAH 62:6–7

> עַל חוֹמֹתַיִךְ יְרוּשָׁלַםִ הִפְקַדְתִּי שֹׁמְרִים כָּל הַיּוֹם וְכָל הַלַּיְלָה, תָּמִיד לֹא יֶחֱשׁוּ, הַמַּזְכִּרִים אֶת ה', אַל דֳּמִי לָכֶם. וְאַל תִּתְּנוּ דֳמִי לוֹ, עַד יְכוֹנֵן וְעַד יָשִׂים אֶת יְרוּשָׁלַםִ תְּהִלָּה בָּאָרֶץ.

O Jerusalem, I have appointed [the exiled Jewish nation as] watchmen over your walls. All day and all night, they shall never cease praying [for your welfare]. Be not silent, [you] who remind God [of Jerusalem's devastation]. Give Him no rest, until He establishes and makes Jerusalem the praise of the earth.

An Israeli soldier walks in front of the Western Wall in Jerusalem's Old City, June 4, 1967. (Photo Credit: Israel Defense Ministry)

TEXT 2

MAIMONIDES, *MISHNEH TORAH*, LAWS OF THE HOLY TEMPLE 2:1–2

וּבַמִּקְדָּשׁ נֶעֱקַד יִצְחָק אָבִינוּ, שֶׁנֶּאֱמַר (בְּרֵאשִׁית כב, ב), "וְלֶךְ לְךָ אֶל אֶרֶץ הַמֹּרִיָּה", וְנֶאֱמַר בְּדִבְרֵי הַיָּמִים (ב ג, א), "וַיָּחֶל שְׁלֹמֹה לִבְנוֹת אֶת בֵּית ה' בִּירוּשָׁלַם בְּהַר הַמּוֹרִיָּה, אֲשֶׁר נִרְאָה לְדָוִיד אָבִיהוּ, אֲשֶׁר הֵכִין בִּמְקוֹם דָּוִיד בְּגֹרֶן אָרְנָן הַיְבוּסִי". וּמַסּוֹרֶת בְּיַד הַכֹּל שֶׁהַמָּקוֹם שֶׁבָּנָה בּוֹ דָוִד וּשְׁלֹמֹה הַמִּזְבֵּחַ בְּגוֹרֶן אֲרַוְנָה הוּא הַמָּקוֹם שֶׁבָּנָה בּוֹ אַבְרָהָם הַמִּזְבֵּחַ וְעָקַד עָלָיו יִצְחָק.

וְהוּא הַמָּקוֹם שֶׁבָּנָה בּוֹ נֹחַ כְּשֶׁיָּצָא מִן הַתֵּיבָה, וְהוּא הַמִּזְבֵּחַ שֶׁהִקְרִיב עָלָיו קַיִן וְהֶבֶל, וּבוֹ הִקְרִיב אָדָם הָרִאשׁוֹן קָרְבָּן כְּשֶׁנִּבְרָא, וּמִשָּׁם נִבְרָא. אָמְרוּ חֲכָמִים: אָדָם מִמָּקוֹם כַּפָּרָתוֹ נִבְרָא.

Isaac was bound [and prepared as a sacrifice] on the Temple's [future] site, as it is said: "Go to the land of Moriah [and offer Isaac there as a sacrifice on a mountain that I will show you]" (GENESIS 22:2), and in (II) Chronicles (3:1), it is said: "Then Solomon began to build the Temple of God in Jerusalem, on Mount Moriah, where God had appeared to his father David, on the site that David had prepared [to build the Temple], on the threshing floor of Araunah the Jebusite." According to unanimous Jewish tradition, the site upon which David and Solomon built the altar, on the threshing floor of Araunah, is the location where Abraham built the altar on which he prepared Isaac for sacrifice.

[Also according to our tradition,] Noah built an altar on this site when he left the ark. Cain and Abel offered their sacrifices on an altar on this site. Adam offered a

RABBI MOSHE BEN MAIMON (MAIMONIDES, RAMBAM) 1135–1204

Halachist, philosopher, author, and physician. Maimonides was born in Cordoba, Spain. After the conquest of Cordoba by the Almohads, he fled Spain and eventually settled in Cairo, Egypt. There, he became the leader of the Jewish community and served as court physician to the vizier of Egypt. He is most noted for authoring the *Mishneh Torah,* an encyclopedic arrangement of Jewish law, and for his philosophical work, *Guide for the Perplexed.* His rulings on Jewish law are integral to the formation of halachic consensus.

sacrifice there after he was created, [in fact,] he was created from soil taken from this location. Our sages said: "Man was created from the place where he [would find] atonement."

TEXT 3

JOSHUA 15:63

וְאֶת הַיְבוּסִי יוֹשְׁבֵי יְרוּשָׁלִַם לֹא יָכְלוּ בְנֵי יְהוּדָה לְהוֹרִישָׁם, וַיֵּשֶׁב הַיְבוּסִי
אֶת בְּנֵי יְהוּדָה בִּירוּשָׁלִַם עַד הַיּוֹם הַזֶּה.

As for the Jebusites that inhabited Jerusalem, the children of Judah could not drive them out. The Jebusites dwelled in Jerusalem alongside the children of Judah to this day.

TEXT 4

MECHILTA, PARASHAT BO, INTRODUCTION

> עַד שֶׁלֹּא נִבְחֲרָה יְרוּשָׁלַיִם, הָיְתָה כָּל אֶרֶץ יִשְׂרָאֵל כְּשֵׁרָה לַמִּזְבְּחוֹת. מִשֶּׁנִּבְחֲרָה יְרוּשָׁלַיִם, יָצְאת אֶרֶץ יִשְׂרָאֵל, שֶׁנֶּאֱמַר, "הִשָּׁמֶר לְךָ פֶּן תַּעֲלֶה עֹלֹתֶיךָ . . . כִּי אִם בַּמָּקוֹם אֲשֶׁר יִבְחַר" (דְּבָרִים יב, יג-יד).

Until Jerusalem was chosen, it was permissible to erect altars anywhere in the Land of Israel. Ever since Jerusalem was chosen, it is unacceptable to erect an altar elsewhere, as the verse says, "Take heed not to offer your burnt offerings [anywhere you please]. Offer them only at the place that God will choose" (DEUTERONOMY 12:13–14).

מכילתא
בווילנא

MECHILTA

A halachic Midrash on the Book of Exodus. Midrash is the designation of a particular genre of rabbinic literature usually forming a running commentary on specific books of the Bible. The name "*Mechilta*" means "rule," and was given to this Midrash because its comments and explanations are based on fixed rules of exegesis. This work is often attributed to Rabbi Yishmael ben Elisha.

Jerusalem from the Mount of Olives, *Charles Théodore Frère, c. 1851. Pilgrims worshipping outside of Jerusalem; oil on canvas. (The Metropolitan Museum of Art, New York)*

Figure 3.1

Mitzvot and Laws Unique to Jerusalem

1	Festival pilgrimage
2	Certain offerings and tithes may be consumed only in its city limits
3	No house rentals
4	A corpse may not remain there overnight
5	No cemeteries or graves
6	Spouses can oblige one another to move there
7	Purim is celebrated a day later

triple Purim if it falls on Sat.

Shushan Purim celebrated in Old City of Jerusalem

TEXT 5

MAIMONIDES, *MISHNEH TORAH*, LAWS OF THE HOLY TEMPLE 6:16

> קְדוּשַּׁת הַמִּקְדָּשׁ וִירוּשָׁלַיִם מִפְּנֵי הַשְּׁכִינָה, וּשְׁכִינָה אֵינָהּ בְּטֵלָה. וַהֲרֵי הוּא אוֹמֵר, "וַהֲשִׁמּוֹתִי אֶת מִקְדְּשֵׁיכֶם" (וַיִּקְרָא כו, לא), וְאָמְרוּ חֲכָמִים: אַף עַל פִּי שֶׁשְּׁמוּמִין, בִּקְדוּשָּׁתָן הֵן עוֹמְדִים.

The Temple and Jerusalem are holy because of the Divine presence [that dwells there], and the Divine presence is everlasting. Thus it says: "I will make your holy places desolate" (LEVITICUS 26:31), and the sages explained this verse to mean: "Even though the places are desolate, they retain their holiness" (TALMUD, MEGILAH 28A).

Former Israeli Prime Minister David Ben-Gurion surveys the newly reclaimed Western Wall, Jerusalem, June 7, 1967. (Photo Credit: Magnum Photos; Micha Bar Am, photographer)

TEXT 6

MAIMONIDES, *GUIDE FOR THE PERPLEXED* 3:45

מַדוּעַ לֹא הִזְכִּירוֹ בְּפֵירוּשׁ בַּתּוֹרָה וְלֹא יִיחֲדוֹ, אֶלָּא נִרְמָז עָלָיו וְנֶאֱמַר אֲשֶׁר יִבְחַר ה׳ וְגוֹ׳? יֵשׁ בְּכָךְ לְדַעְתִּי שָׁלוֹשׁ חָכְמוֹת.

הָאַחַת: כְּדֵי שֶׁלֹּא יַחֲזִיקוּ בּוֹ הָעַמִּים וְיִלְחֲמוּ עָלָיו מִלְחָמָה קָשָׁה, כַּאֲשֶׁר יֵדְעוּ שֶׁהַמָּקוֹם הַזֶּה מַטָּרַת הַתּוֹרָה מִכָּל הָעוֹלָם.

וְהַשֵּׁנִית: שֶׁלֹּא יַשְׁחִיתוּהוּ אוֹתָם שֶׁהוּא בִּידֵיהֶם עַתָּה וִיהַרְסוּהוּ כְּכָל יְכָלְתָּם.

וְהַשְּׁלִישִׁית, וְהִיא הַיּוֹתֵר חֲשׁוּבָה: כְּדֵי שֶׁלֹּא יְבַקֵּשׁ כָּל שֵׁבֶט שֶׁיְּהֵא זֶה בְּנַחֲלָתוֹ וְיִכְבּוֹשׁ אוֹתוֹ, וְיִהְיֶה שָׁם מִן הַמַּחֲלוֹקֶת וְהַקְּטָטָה כְּמוֹ שֶׁאֵירַע בִּדְרִישַׁת הַכְּהוּנָּה. וּלְפִיכָךְ בָּא הַצִּיוּוּי שֶׁלֹּא יִבְנֶה בֵּית הַבְּחִירָה כִּי אִם אַחַר הֲקָמַת מֶלֶךְ, כְּדֵי שֶׁתְּהֵא הַהַחְלָטָה בְּיַד אֶחָד, וְיִסְתַּלְּקוּ הַקְּטָטוֹת.

For three reasons the name of the place is not distinctly stated in the Torah, but alluded to in the phrase "the place that God will choose, etc." (DEUTERONOMY 12:11).

First, if the nations had learned that, in the view of the Torah, this place was the center of the universe, they would have occupied it and ferociously battled to retain it.

Second, those who were then in possession of the city might have, in spite, destroyed and ruined it to the best of their capability [before the Jews took hold of it].

Third, and most importantly, every one of the twelve tribes would have desired to have this place in its borders and under its control. This would have led to rivalry and discord (such as was caused by Korach's desire for the priesthood). Therefore it was commanded that the Temple should not be built before the appointment of a king who would make all the decisions, and thus minimize the discord.

TEXT 7

RABBI CHAIM BEN BETSALEL, *SEFER HACHAYIM, SEFER GE'ULAH VEYESHU'AH*, CH. 1

וּמִפְּנֵי טַעַם זֶה לֹא הוּזְכַּר יְרוּשָׁלַיִם בְּפֵירוּשׁ בְּכָל הַתּוֹרָה, רַק אָמַר סְתָם, "אֶל הַמָּקוֹם אֲשֶׁר יִבְחַר ה'" (דְּבָרִים יב, ה), לְפִי שֶׁכָּל מָקוֹם מוּקְטָר וּמוּגָּשׁ לִשְׁמוֹ וְהַכֹּל בִּכְלָל "הַמָּקוֹם אֲשֶׁר יִבְחַר ה'".

The Torah does not mention the name of the city of Jerusalem; rather the city is referred to ambiguously as "the place that God will choose" (DEUTERONOMY 12:5). Because we serve God and pray to Him in all places, and everywhere we do so, it is "the place that God will choose."

physical and spiritual place of Jerusalem

RABBI CHAIM BEN BETSALEL
C. 1530–1588

Rabbi and author. Rabbi Chaim was the older brother of Rabbi Yehudah Loew, the famed Maharal of Prague. Rabbi Chaim served as rabbi in the communities of Worms and Friedberg, Germany. Rabbi Chaim wrote *Be'er Mayim Chayim*, a supercommentary to Rashi's commentary on the Torah, and *Sefer Hachayim*, a book of ethics.

TEXT 8

MIDRASH TANCHUMA, KEDOSHIM 10

כְּשֵׁם שֶׁהַטַּבּוּר הַזֶּה נָתוּן בְּאֶמְצַע הָאִישׁ, כָּךְ אֶרֶץ יִשְׂרָאֵל נְתוּנָה בְּאֶמְצַע הָעוֹלָם, שֶׁנֶּאֱמַר, "יֹשְׁבֵי עַל טַבּוּר הָאָרֶץ" (יְחֶזְקֵאל לח, יב) . . .

אֶרֶץ יִשְׂרָאֵל יוֹשֶׁבֶת בְּאֶמְצָעִיתוֹ שֶׁל עוֹלָם, וִירוּשָׁלַיִם בְּאֶמְצָעִיתָהּ שֶׁל אֶרֶץ יִשְׂרָאֵל.

Just as the navel is located in the center of the human being, so, too, the Land of Israel is the center of the world, as the verse states, "dwelling on the navel of the earth" (EZEKIEL 38:12). . . .

The Land of Israel sits at the center of the world, and Jerusalem sits at the center of the Land of Israel.

MIDRASH TANCHUMA

A midrashic work bearing the name of Rabbi Tanchuma, a 4th-century Talmudic sage quoted often in this work. Midrash is the designation of a particular genre of rabbinic literature usually forming a running commentary on specific books of the Bible. *Midrash Tanchuma* provides textual exegeses, expounds upon the biblical narrative, and develops and illustrates moral principles. *Tanchuma* is unique in that many of its sections commence with a halachic discussion, which subsequently leads into non-halachic teachings.

meeting point
where physical and spiritual
area meet

Heaven and Earth connect here

Physical and Spiritual should be integrated

TEXT 9

II SAMUEL 24:18–25

וַיָּבֹא גָד אֶל דָּוִד בַּיּוֹם הַהוּא וַיֹּאמֶר לוֹ, "עֲלֵה הָקֵם לַה' מִזְבֵּחַ בְּגֹרֶן אֲרַוְנָה הַיְבֻסִי". וַיַּעַל דָּוִד כִּדְבַר גָּד, כַּאֲשֶׁר צִוָּה ה'.

וַיַּשְׁקֵף אֲרַוְנָה וַיַּרְא אֶת הַמֶּלֶךְ וְאֶת עֲבָדָיו עֹבְרִים עָלָיו, וַיֵּצֵא אֲרַוְנָה וַיִּשְׁתַּחוּ לַמֶּלֶךְ אַפָּיו אָרְצָה. וַיֹּאמֶר אֲרַוְנָה, "מַדּוּעַ בָּא אֲדֹנִי הַמֶּלֶךְ אֶל עַבְדּוֹ?" וַיֹּאמֶר דָּוִד, "לִקְנוֹת מֵעִמְּךָ אֶת הַגֹּרֶן, לִבְנוֹת מִזְבֵּחַ לַה', וְתֵעָצַר הַמַּגֵּפָה מֵעַל הָעָם".

וַיֹּאמֶר אֲרַוְנָה אֶל דָּוִד, "יִקַּח וְיַעַל אֲדֹנִי הַמֶּלֶךְ הַטּוֹב בְּעֵינָיו, רְאֵה הַבָּקָר לָעֹלָה וְהַמֹּרִגִּים וּכְלֵי הַבָּקָר לָעֵצִים", הַכֹּל נָתַן אֲרַוְנָה הַמֶּלֶךְ לַמֶּלֶךְ, וַיֹּאמֶר אֲרַוְנָה אֶל הַמֶּלֶךְ, "ה' אֱלֹקֶיךָ יִרְצֶךָ".

וַיֹּאמֶר הַמֶּלֶךְ אֶל אֲרַוְנָה, "לֹא, כִּי קָנוֹ אֶקְנֶה מֵאוֹתְךָ בִּמְחִיר, וְלֹא אַעֲלֶה לַה' אֱלֹקַי עֹלוֹת חִנָּם".

וַיִּקֶן דָּוִד אֶת הַגֹּרֶן וְאֶת הַבָּקָר בְּכֶסֶף שְׁקָלִים חֲמִשִּׁים, וַיִּבֶן שָׁם דָּוִד מִזְבֵּחַ לַה', וַיַּעַל עֹלוֹת וּשְׁלָמִים, וַיֵּעָתֵר ה' לָאָרֶץ, וַתֵּעָצַר הַמַּגֵּפָה מֵעַל יִשְׂרָאֵל.

The prophet Gad came that day to David and said to him: "Go and build an altar to God on the threshing floor of Araunah the Jebusite." David went as God had commanded through Gad.

Araunah looked out, and he saw the king and his servants approaching. Araunah went out, prostrated himself before the king, and said: "Why has my lord the king come to his servant?" David responded: "[I have come] to purchase the threshing floor from you, to build an altar to God, so that the plague will cease from the people."

Araunah said to David, "Let my lord the king take [the threshing floor and use it as an altar] and offer [to God] that which is pleasing in his eyes. See, [you can take] the oxen for burnt-offerings, and the threshing tools and the [wooden] tools of the oxen for wood." All this Araunah the chieftain [of the Jebusites] wished to give to King David. Araunah said to the king, "May your God accept [your sacrifice]."

"No," David said to Araunah. "I insist on paying for it. I will not offer to my God offerings for which I did not pay."

So David bought the threshing floor and the oxen for fifty silver shekels. He built there an altar and offered various offerings to God. God accepted the offerings, and the plague upon Israel came to an end.

Page from 15th-century illustrated volume of Mishneh Torah, *depicting the sacrifices in the Temple. (The Israel Museum)*

TEXT 10

RABBI YOSEF BABAD, *MINCHAT CHINUCH*, MITZVAH 284

מְבוֹאָר בִּשְׁמוּאֵל ב (כד, יט-כד) וְדִבְרֵי הַיָּמִים א (כא, יט-כה), דְּדָוִד הַמֶּלֶךְ עָלָיו הַשָּׁלוֹם קָנָה אֶת מְקוֹם הַמִּקְדָּשׁ מֵאֲרַוְנָה הַיְבוּסִי . . . צָרִיךְ לוֹמַר דְּהַמָּקוֹם הַזֶּה לֹא נִלְקַח מֵעוֹלָם מֵאֲרַוְנָה. וְהַטַּעַם דְּלֹא נִלְקַח מִיָּדוֹ, דְּאֶפְשָׁר הוּא הִשְׁלִים עִם דָּוִד הַמֶּלֶךְ עָלָיו הַשָּׁלוֹם בְּשָׁעָה שֶׁפָּתַח בְּשָׁלוֹם . . .

וְאֶפְשָׁר לוֹמַר דְּהָיָה עַל יְדֵי סִיבָּה שֶׁלֹּא לְקָחוֹ מֵאִתּוֹ. וְקָרוֹב לוֹמַר, כִּי הָיָה רְצוֹן הַשֵּׁם יִתְבָּרֵךְ שֶׁהַמָּקוֹם הַקָּדוֹשׁ הַזֶּה שֶׁבּוֹ הַשְׁרָאַת שְׁכִינָה לְעוֹלְמֵי עַד לֹא יִהְיֶה בְּחָזְקָה, אֲפִילוּ בְּהֵיתֵּר עַל יְדֵי כִּיבּוּשׁ . . . וַאֲפִילוּ בְּמַתָּנָה לֹא רָצָה דָּוִד הַמֶּלֶךְ עָלָיו הַשָּׁלוֹם לִיקַּח, רַק בְּכֶסֶף מָלֵא. וְרָצָה שֶׁיִּהְיֶה חֵלֶק לְכָל יִשְׂרָאֵל בַּמָּקוֹם הַמְקוּדָּשׁ הַזֶּה.

The Scriptures relate (II SAMUEL 24:19–24, I CHRONICLES 21:19–25) that King David purchased the site of the Temple from Araunah the Jebusite. . . . It is clear that this location was not taken earlier from Araunah, possibly because he had accepted the peace overture of King David. . . .

There is a deeper reason why the site was not previously taken from Araunah. It appears that it was God's will that the holy site where the Divine presence was destined to reside for all eternity should not be taken by force, even permissible force. . . . Moreover, King David did not want to accept the site as a gift; rather, he insisted on paying full market value, and he wanted that all of Israel should thereby have a portion in the holiest of all sites.

ספר
מנחת חנוך
חלק ראשון

RABBI YOSEF BABAD
1801-1874

Rabbi Babad was born in historical Galicia (now western Ukraine-Eastern Poland) and served as Rabbi of a number of communities in the region, eventually appointed Rabbi of the city of Tarnopol, Ukraine. Rabbi Babad is best known for his popular work, *Minchat Chinuch*. Following the order of *Sefer Hachinuch*, *Minchat Chinuch* provides a deep conceptual legal analysis of each of the 613 biblical commandments.

TEXT 11

MIDRASH, *BEREISHIT RABAH* 79:7

שְׁלֹשָׁה מְקוֹמוֹת שֶׁאֵין אוּמוֹת הָעוֹלָם יְכוֹלִין לְהוֹנוֹת אֶת יִשְׂרָאֵל לוֹמַר גְזוּלִים הֵן בְּיֶדְכֶם, וְאֵלוּ הֵן: מְעָרַת הַמַכְפֵּלָה, וּבֵית הַמִקְדָשׁ, וּקְבוּרָתוֹ שֶׁל יוֹסֵף.

מְעָרַת הַמַכְפֵּלָה, דִכְתִיב, "וַיִשְׁמַע אַבְרָהָם אֶל עֶפְרוֹן וַיִשְׁקֹל אַבְרָהָם לְעֶפְרֹן" (בְּרֵאשִׁית כג, טז).

בֵּית הַמִקְדָשׁ, דִכְתִיב, "וַיִתֵּן דָוִיד לְאָרְנָן בַּמָקוֹם וגו'" (דִבְרֵי הַיָמִים א, כא, כה).

וּקְבוּרָתוֹ שֶׁל יוֹסֵף, "וַיִקֶן אֶת חֶלְקַת הַשָׂדֶה" (בְּרֵאשִׁית לג, יט) - יַעֲקֹב קָנָה שְׁכֶם.

There are three locations regarding which the nations of the world cannot harass Israel with the claim that it is stolen: The Cave of Machpelah, the Holy Temple, and the resting place of Joseph [in Shechem].

The Cave of Machpelah, for it is written: "Abraham agreed to Ephron's terms and weighed out for him [the price that Ephron had asked . . . four hundred silver shekels]" (GENESIS 23:16).

The Holy Temple, for it is written, "David paid Araunah for the site" (I CHRONICLES 21:25).

Joseph's burial place, for it is written, "Jacob purchased the plot of land [from the sons of the ruler of Shechem]" (GENESIS 33:19).

BEREISHIT RABAH

An early rabbinic commentary on the Book of Genesis. This Midrash bears the name of Rabbi Oshiya Rabah (Rabbi Oshiya "the Great"), whose teaching opens this work. This Midrash provides textual exegeses and stories, expounds upon the biblical narrative, and develops and illustrates moral principles. Produced by the sages of the Talmud in the Land of Israel, its use of Aramaic closely resembles that of the Jerusalem Talmud. It was first printed in Constantinople in 1512, together with four other Midrashic works on the other four books of the Pentateuch.

TEXT 12

MIDRASH, *SHIR HASHIRIM RABAH* 2:26

"הִנֵּה זֶה עוֹמֵד אַחַר כָּתְלֵנוּ" (שִׁיר הַשִּׁירִים ב, ט), אַחַר כּוֹתֶל מַעֲרָבִי שֶׁל בֵּית הַמִּקְדָּשׁ. לָמָּה? שֶׁנִּשְׁבַּע לוֹ הַקָּדוֹשׁ בָּרוּךְ הוּא שֶׁאֵינוֹ חָרֵב לְעוֹלָם.

"Behold He stands beyond our wall" (SONG OF SONGS 2:9). This refers to the western wall of the Holy Temple, which God swore would never be destroyed.

שיר

SHIR HASHIRIM RABAH

A Midrashic text and exegetical commentary on the book of Song of Songs. This Midrash explicates this biblical book based on the principle that its verses convey an allegory of the relationship between God and the people of Israel. It was compiled and edited in the Land of Israel during the 6th century.

Praying at the Western Wall, Jerusalem, Israel.

TEXT 13

MIDRASH, *PIRKEI RABBI ELIEZER*, CH. 35

הִשְׁכִּים יַעֲקֹב בְּפַחַד גָדוֹל וְאָמַר, "בֵּיתוֹ שֶׁל הַקָדוֹשׁ בָּרוּךְ הוּא בַּמָקוֹם הַזֶה!" שֶׁנֶאֱמַר, "וַיִירָא וַיֹאמַר, 'מַה נוֹרָא הַמָקוֹם הַזֶה'" (בְּרֵאשִׁית כח, יז).

מִכָּאן אַתָּה לָמֵד שֶׁכָּל הַמִתְפַּלֵל בַּמָקוֹם הַזֶה בִּירוּשָׁלַיִם כְּאִילוּ הִתְפַּלֵל לִפְנֵי כִּסֵא הַכָּבוֹד, שֶׁשַׁעַר הַשָׁמַיִם שָׁם הוּא, וּפֶתַח פָּתוּחַ לִשְׁמֹעַ תְּפִלָּה, שֶׁנֶאֱמַר, "וְזֶה שַׁעַר הַשָׁמָיִם" (שָׁם).

Jacob awoke in great fright and said, "God's house is in this place!" As it is written, "Jacob was afraid and said, 'How awesome is this place! [This is none other than the house of God, and this is the gate of heaven]'" (GENESIS 28:17).

From here we learn that all who pray in this place, in Jerusalem, it is as if they pray before God's throne. The entryway to heaven is there, and the door is open for prayers to be heard, as it says, "this is the gate of heaven."

PIRKEI RABBI ELIEZER

A Midrash bearing the name of Rabbi Eliezer ben Hyrcanus, a prominent rabbinic sage living during the 1st and 2nd centuries. *Pirkei Rabbi Eliezer* commences with the story of the early days of Rabbi Eliezer's life, and then chronologically narrates and expounds upon events from the Creation until the middle of the journeys of the Children of Israel in the wilderness.

TEXT 14

RABBI DR. NISSAN MINDEL, *MY PRAYER* (BROOKLYN, NY: KEHOT PUBLICATION SOCIETY, 1972), INTRODUCTION, PP. 6–7

The highest level on the "ladder" of prayer is reached when we are so inspired as to want nothing but the feeling of attachment with G-d. On this level *Tefilah* is related to the verb (used in Mishnaic Hebrew) *tofel*, to "attach," or "join," or "bind together," as two pieces of a broken vessel are pieced together to make it whole again.

Our soul is "truly a part of G-dliness," and it therefore longs to be reunited with, and reabsorbed in, G-dliness; just as a small flame when it is put close to a larger flame is absorbed into the larger flame. We may not be aware of this longing, but it is there nevertheless. Our soul has, in fact, been called the "candle of G-d" (PROVERBS 20:27). The flame of a candle is restless, striving upwards, to break away, as it were, from the wick and body of the candle; for such is the nature of fire, to strive upwards. Our soul, too, strives upwards, like the flame of the candle.

RABBI NISSAN MINDEL, PHD
1912–1999

Secretary to the Lubavitcher Rebbe. Born in Latvia, Rabbi Mindel immigrated to the U.S. where he received a doctorate in Semitic languages from Columbia University. He translated many works into English, including the *Tanya,* the seminal text of Chabad philosophy, and was a prolific writer who authored numerous works including *Philosophy of Chabad* and *My Prayer.*

TEXT 15

MECHILTA, PARASHAT BO, INTRODUCTION

עַד שֶׁלֹּא נִבְחַר בֵּית עוֹלָמִים, הָיְתָה יְרוּשָׁלַיִם רְאוּיָה לַשְּׁכִינָה. מִשֶּׁנִּבְחַר בֵּית עוֹלָמִים, יָצָאת יְרוּשָׁלַיִם, שֶׁנֶּאֱמַר, "כִּי בָחַר ה' בְּצִיּוֹן" (תְּהִלִּים קלב, יג), וְאוֹמֵר, "זֹאת מְנוּחָתִי עֲדֵי עַד" (שָׁם, יד).

Before the Holy Temple was chosen, all of Jerusalem was suitable to host the Divine presence. Once the Holy Temple was chosen, the rest of Jerusalem became ineligible to host the Divine presence, as it is said, "For God has chosen Zion . . . This is My resting place for all eternity" (PSALMS 132:13–14).

Hebrew inscription on a parapet fragment from the Temple Mount, reading "To the place of trumpeting," 1st century BCE. (The Israel Museum)

TEXT 16

RABBI SHNE'UR ZALMAN OF LIADI, *TANYA,* CH.53

וְהִנֵּה, כְּשֶׁהָיָה בַּיִת רִאשׁוֹן קַיָּם, שֶׁבּוֹ הָיָה הָאָרוֹן וְהַלּוּחוֹת בְּבֵית קֹדֶשׁ הַקֳּדָשִׁים, הָיְתָה הַשְּׁכִינָה, שֶׁהִיא מַלְכוּת דַּאֲצִילוּת, שֶׁהִיא בְּחִינַת גִּלּוּי אוֹר אֵין סוֹף בָּרוּךְ הוּא שׁוֹרָה שָׁם וּמְלֻבֶּשֶׁת בַּעֲשֶׂרֶת הַדִּבְּרוֹת, בְּיֶתֶר שְׂאֵת וְיֶתֶר עֹז, בְּגִלּוּי רַב וְעָצוּם, יוֹתֵר מִגִּלּוּיָהּ בְּהֵיכְלוֹת קָדְשֵׁי הַקֳּדָשִׁים שֶׁלְּמַעְלָה בְּעוֹלָמוֹת עֶלְיוֹנִים. כִּי עֲשֶׂרֶת הַדִּבְּרוֹת הֵן כְּלָלוּת הַתּוֹרָה כֻּלָּהּ, דְּנָפְקָא מִגּוֹ חָכְמָה עִלָּאָה, דִּלְעֵלָּא לְעֵלָּא מֵעָלְמָא דְּאִתְגַּלְיָא. וּכְדֵי לְחָקְקָן בְּלֻחוֹת אֲבָנִים גַּשְׁמִיִּים, לֹא יָרְדָה מִמַּדְרֵגָה לְמַדְרֵגָה כְּדֶרֶךְ הִשְׁתַּלְשְׁלוּת הָעוֹלָמוֹת עַד עוֹלָם הַזֶּה הַגַּשְׁמִי. כִּי עוֹלָם הַזֶּה הַגַּשְׁמִי מִתְנַהֵג בְּהִתְלַבְּשׁוּת הַטֶּבַע הַגַּשְׁמִי. וְהַלּוּחוֹת מַעֲשֵׂה אֱלֹקִים הֵמָּה, וְהַמִּכְתָּב מִכְתַּב אֱלֹקִים הוּא, לְמַעְלָה מֵהַטֶּבַע שֶׁל עוֹלָם הַזֶּה הַגַּשְׁמִי.

In the First Temple, the Ark and the Tablets were housed in the "Holy of Holies" chamber. The *Shechinah*, that is the revelation of God's Infinite Light, was manifest there and was expressed in the Ten Commandments [etched in the Tablets]. The level of Godly light that was manifest in the Holy of Holies greatly exceeded that of analogous spiritual "Holy of Holies" chambers in supernal worlds. For the Ten Commandments comprise the principles of the whole Torah, and the Torah derives from God's wisdom that wholly transcends the Divine energy that is invested in Creation. Moreover, the engraving of the Ten Commandments on material stone tablets did not entail any metamorphosis or diminishment of the Divine wisdom. Thus, while this material world functions through the garment of the physical laws of nature, the Tablets are "the handiwork of God, and the writing [upon it] is the writing of God" (EXODUS 32:16). The Tablets defied the nature of this material world.

RABBI SHNE'UR ZALMAN OF LIADI (ALTER REBBE) 1745–1812

Chasidic rebbe, halachic authority, and founder of the Chabad movement. The Alter Rebbe was born in Liozna, Belarus, and was among the principal students of the Magid of Mezeritch. His numerous works include the *Tanya*, an early classic containing the fundamentals of Chabad Chasidism, and *Shulchan Aruch HaRav*, an expanded and reworked code of Jewish law.

TEXT 17

TALMUD, BERACHOT 8A

> מִיּוֹם שֶׁחָרַב בֵּית הַמִּקְדָּשׁ, אֵין לוֹ לְהַקָּדוֹשׁ בָּרוּךְ הוּא בְּעוֹלָמוֹ אֶלָּא אַרְבַּע אַמּוֹת שֶׁל הֲלָכָה בִּלְבָד.

Since the day the Temple was destroyed, God has no place in this world aside from the "four cubits" of [the study of] Halachah.

Engraving of Jerusalem besieged by Titus, 1682. (Artist: Jan Luyken, Rijks Musuem Amsterdam)

BABYLONIAN TALMUD

A literary work of monumental proportions that draws upon the legal, spiritual, intellectual, ethical, and historical traditions of Judaism. The 37 tractates of the Babylonian Talmud contain the teachings of the Jewish sages from the period after the destruction of the 2nd Temple through the 5th century CE. It has served as the primary vehicle for the transmission of the Oral Law and the education of Jews over the centuries; it is the entry point for all subsequent legal, ethical, and theological Jewish scholarship.

TEXT 18

ZACHARIAH 8:3–5

> כֹּה אָמַר ה׳, "שַׁבְתִּי אֶל צִיּוֹן וְשָׁכַנְתִּי בְּתוֹךְ יְרוּשָׁלָם . . . עֹד יֵשְׁבוּ זְקֵנִים וּזְקֵנוֹת בִּרְחֹבוֹת יְרוּשָׁלָם וְאִישׁ מִשְׁעַנְתּוֹ בְּיָדוֹ מֵרֹב יָמִים. וּרְחֹבוֹת הָעִיר יִמָּלְאוּ יְלָדִים וִילָדוֹת מְשַׂחֲקִים בִּרְחֹבֹתֶיהָ".

God has said: "I will return to Zion, and I will dwell in the midst of Jerusalem. . . . Old men and women shall once again sit in the streets of Jerusalem, each with their staff in hand because of old age. The streets of the city shall be filled with boys and girls playing there."

KEY POINTS

1 King David captured Jerusalem and made it the capital of Israel. Ever since, Jerusalem is the spiritual center of the universe and the permanent abode of the Divine presence.

2 Although some of the pivotal events described in the Five Books of Moses occurred in Jerusalem, the name Jerusalem does not appear in these books. Instead, the Torah makes reference to the "place that God will choose." One of the reasons for this omission is that Jerusalem represents a spiritual center that is accessible to anyone, regardless of physical location.

3 Jerusalem is the meeting point between heaven and earth, where our physical existence fuses with our spiritual purpose and mission. It is the "place that God will choose" that is at the center of our being.

4 The Temple Mount is located on the site of a threshing floor that King David purchased from Araunah the Jebusite. David bought, rather than conquered, the land, for the Temple is a symbol of peace. David bought it with funds collected from all of Israel, for the Temple is a symbol of Jewish unity.

5 Due to ritual purity concerns, certain areas of the Temple Mount may not be accessed today.

6 The Western Wall is part of the retaining wall that enclosed the Temple Mount, built by King Herod during the Second Temple Era. According to the Midrash, God vowed that this wall would never be destroyed, and that the Divine presence would be forever present there.

7 Prayers recited at the Western Wall are especially effective because the Temple Mount is the gateway to heaven for all prayers. Prayer represents our relationship with God, which resides at the center of (both the physical and spiritual) Jerusalem.

8 The Holy Temple, at the center of Jerusalem and the Temple Mount, represents our relationship with God that transcends the limitations inherent in human effort (symbolized by prayer). Today, Torah study is the vehicle for experiencing this degree of unity with God.

Additional Readings

SARAH NACHSHON AND THE ANCIENT JEWISH CEMETERY IN HEBRON

NOAM ARNON

A baby boy was born to Baruch and Sarah Nachshon in 1975. Baruch, a famous Hasidic artist and his wife Sarah were among the first Jews to return to Hebron. Following the establishment of Kiryat Arba the Nachshons celebrated the birth of a son and decided to perform the brit milah inside the cave of the Machpelah—burial place of Abraham and Sarah, Isaac and Rebecca, and Jacob and Leah. The baby was named Avraham Yedidya.

Three months later, Sarah found Avraham Yedidya dead in his crib. The young mother was beside herself. Why should her new son, brought into the covenant of Abraham in Hebron in the most ancient city of the Jewish People in the Land of Israel, be taken from her after only three months? Everything in this world has a purpose. What was the purpose of her three-month-old son?

Sarah decides that Avraham Yedidya would be buried in the ancient Jewish cemetery in Hebron. The cemetery had been last used to inter the 67 Jews slaughtered in the 1929 riots in Hebron. It is minutes from the traditional graves of Ruth and Jesse and overlooks the Cave of the Machpelah. Perhaps, Sarah thinks, this was the purpose of the baby, to take part in a sad but vital part of renewing Jewish Hebron. After almost fifty years, the Jewish cemetery of Hebron would again be utilized as a Jew's last resting place.

Late afternoon: the funeral procession leaves Kiryat Arba for the ancient Jewish cemetery in Hebron. Then, suddenly the mourners encounter soldiers and roadblocks! The cars come to a halt. Soldiers begin scouring the site, opening car doors, searching for something. "No, you may not proceed to the cemetery," the soldiers order the mourners, "The cemetery is off-limits". One of the car doors opens. A women gets out with a bundle in her arms.

She addresses the soldiers, "Are you looking for me—are you looking for my baby? My name is Sarah Nachshon. Here is my baby, in my arms. If you won't let us drive to the cemetery we will walk!"

Men with shovels and flashlights, and women, Kiryat Arba residents, walk through ancient Hebron as night falls. They pass the Cave of the Machpelah. They pass the 450-year-old Abraham Avinu synagogue, left in ruins, destroyed by the Jordanian conquerors in 1948. Blockades, set up to stop the crowd, are pushed aside. Senior officers give orders over their walkie-talkies: "Stop them—don't let them proceed"—but the soldiers, overcome by the scene, radio back: "We can't stop them. If you want to stop them come down here and do it yourselves".

The procession continues, past Beit Romano, Beit Schneerson, home of Menucha Rachel Schneerson Slonim, granddaughter of the "Ba'al HaTanya," up the steep hill to the ancient cemetery.

Moonlight illuminates the field. Sarah Nachshon releases the body of her tiny son, Avraham Yedidya, and it is lowered into the freshly dug grave. The grave site is only meters from the mass grave of 1929. Mustering her voice, Sarah utters: "Four thousand years ago our Patriarch Abraham purchased Hebron for the Jewish People by burying his wife Sarah here. Tonight Sarah is repurchasing Hebron for the Jewish People by burying her son Avraham here".

"Sarah Nachshon and the Ancient Jewish Cemetery in Hebron." www.Hebron.com

THE CANDLE OF GOD

RABBI ADIN EVEN-ISRAEL STEINSALTZ

The First Temple was built to house the Holy Ark and the tablets of the Ten Commandments. The structure could thus be considered the dwelling place of the Shechinah, which is the Malchut of Atzilut or the manifestation of Divine light. And indeed, for centuries, the spiritual power emanating from the tablets of the Decalogue in the Holy of Holies on earth was stronger and more effective than the emanations from the shrine centers of holiness in the upper worlds. Difficult as this may be to comprehend, these Ten Commandments inscribed by God radiated a certain depth and fullness of spiritual power that was more influential than that which came from the spiritual worlds themselves. This was possible precisely because they were engraved on stone, the most material of substances, and because the Ten Commandments are the essence of all of the Torah, which is the direct expression of Divine Wisdom. The Temple simply contained the Revelation, which had not yet descended and changed from world to world, but which had been written on stone and given to the people through Moses.

There are two things here that arouse our incredulity. One is the fact that this world to which the Divine revealed His Wisdom is a material world and relatively dense to penetration of spirit. The other is the fact that this material world is a natural world, with laws of its own. In a sense, however, the stone tablets of the Decalogue were not a part of the material world, even though they were certainly of substance; they did not abide by the laws of nature. The letters were indeed engraved on stone, but they were forces of an entirely different order; they belonged to the dimension of Divine light and emanated an influence that was higher than anything else in the World of Action where they were kept.

In accordance with the original order of things, the World of Action is influenced by the light of the Shechinah through its own "Holy of Holies" or brain center, which in turn descends from the higher worlds. When the Ten Commandments were given to the Children of Israel and subsequently were housed in the Holy of Holies of the Temple, another source of Revelation intervened. The stone tablets do not diffuse their revelation and scatter it in all directions like the light from the higher worlds, which descends from gradation to gradation until it penetrates the World of Action and all its material parts in accordance with natural law. The Ten Commandments made a great leap; originating in Divine Wisdom, they burst through all the intervening worlds—or rather bypassed them—in order to reveal themselves to the material world without paying any attention to the laws of nature in this world. They avoided the various processes of contraction and change that characterize the evolvement of this world; and altogether, it was something that did not belong to this world. It was a material concretization of a much higher mode of existence; its light was far beyond anything else that the world had ever experienced. That is to say, the tablets of the Ten Commandments belonged to the dimension of miracle, an act of God.

Nevertheless, they were limited in space and substance, so that the Shechinah was present only when they were still kept ritually safeguarded in the First Temple. After they were removed, in the time of the Second Temple, the Shechinah was no longer manifest in the same way. The tablets of the Ten Commandments were the last physical remnant of the Divine descent to the people of Israel; they represented enlightenment at its highest level, when Divine revelation burst through the clouds of the rigid reality

RABBI ADIN EVEN-ISRAEL STEINSALTZ, 1937–

Talmudist, author, and philosopher. Rabbi Even-Israel Steinsaltz is considered one of the foremost Jewish thinkers of the 20th century. Praised by Time magazine as a "once-in-a-millennium scholar," he has been awarded the Israel Prize for his contributions to Jewish study. He lives in Jerusalem and is the founder of the Israel Institute for Talmudic Publications, a society dedicated to the translation and elucidation of the Talmud.

of worlds upon worlds of existence, and came to the people without altering itself by contraction, deformation, or concealment.

During the period of the Second Temple, therefore, the Shechinah was not dwelling among the people in the same way as when the tablets were present. Nevertheless, the Shechinah did dwell in the Holy of Holies in the way that Divine influence is ordinarily focused—by gradual descent through the intervening worlds and by assuming the forms, or putting on the garments of the Kingdoms of Emanation, Creation, Formation, and finally, of the World of Action. Consequently the light from the Holy of Holies in the time of the Second Temple belonged to the essence of holiness as transmitted through the brain center (Holy of Holies) of the World of Action. It was a light that originated beyond the reality of this world and radiated to all the world, while the Temple itself was the crossroads of the life of this world. No one could enter therein (the Holy of Holies) unless he was the High Priest, and even he was permitted to enter only on the Day of Atonement. Thus, even if the manifestation was not the same as in the time of the First Temple, the Second Temple could still be considered the dwelling place of the highest sanctity.

But when the Second Temple was destroyed, it could no longer function as a focal point of Divine holiness and, as it is written, God transferred this function to the confines of the Halachah. "Hence, each individual who sits by himself and occupies himself with Torah (in thought, word, and action), the Shechinah is with him" (*Brachot* 8a). The phrase "the Shechinah is with him" means in the order of the gradual descent and investment of the Malchut of Atzilut in the Malchut of Briah, of Yetzirah, and of Asiyah. In other words, it is not a revelation experience—even if the Shechinah is present. The light and inspiration that follows the presence of the Shechinah simply depends on the amount of holiness the person is able to bring down.

What is more, this occupation with Torah is, for the most part, a very practical matter. Most of the 613 commandments are active precepts, even if only in the sense that one must pray and study with one's lips and voice, recite certain blessings aloud, keep the Sabbath by doing or refraining from doing definite actions, and so on. Torah is related to this world directly by thoughts, speech, and deeds. One cannot be said to have fulfilled one's obligations by contemplating noble concepts or aspiring to spiritual heights; it is the doing that counts.

"The Lord by Wisdom founded the earth" (Proverbs 3:19) indicates that Divine Wisdom has established this world of ours and that His Shechinah is part of it. For man, this Shechinah is symbolized by speech, which is the word of the mouth; and "saying" Torah expresses His Wisdom. As the Zohar puts it: "The father (Wisdom) begat the daughter (Malchut) which is Oral Law" (Zohar III, 187a), and the Oral Law is the Halachah, or the way of life according to the commandments.

This brings us back to the recognition that the basis of all things is Divine Wisdom that reveals itself in Torah. To say that God's light is now focused in the narrow confines of Halachah means that the Divine manifests His Will in the ordinary realities of the world. Once, in the period of the First Temple, His Will was manifested through the tablets of the Ten Commandments, bringing His Wisdom to the people directly from the highest height; and in the time of the Second Temple this was accomplished by the Divine light descending through all the higher worlds, with all the distortion and contractions this involved. Now, the Holy of Holies is to be found in the only place left to the Divine sanctity in the study of Torah and the deeds of Torah.

This is what is meant by the passage "always let your clothes be white, and let there be no lack of oil on your head" (Ecclesiastes 9:8), which the Zohar explains. For the supernal light that is kindled on one's head, namely the Shechinah, requires oil, and oil is the symbol of being clothed in wisdom, namely the 613 commandments of the Torah. Man is here likened to a candle of God; the fire is the Shechinah, giving light in all directions, and the part that burns is the wick, or the animal-soul. What maintains the burning is the oil—the holy symbol of wisdom—the good deeds or the mitzvot of the Torah. In other words, the physical life and the body of man have to be burning in the fire of right action in order to enable the Shechinah to give light. The burning of the animal-soul is not a total destruction, however, because the soul which gives life to the being cannot be demolished. It is rather a transformation, a transmutation from darkness to light, from bitterness to sweetness, which in turns brings about that which is called "ascent of the feminine waters," the ascent of the lower, passive aspects of the universe toward the higher revealed forces above them. Such is the work of the Tzadik—a conversion of evil to good by transforming the animal-soul. That is, the animal-soul remains; it is not annihilated, but its desires and lusts are converted from one extreme to the other. The animal-soul of the Tzadik no longer knows the desires of the flesh; it wants only the holiness of its own consummation. It seeks the transformation of the garments or shells of the animal being in thought, word, and deed, making them into sparks of Divine light.

In this way, the Tzadik removes himself from the eternal conflict between the animal-soul and the Divine Soul and manages to remain fixed in his own essence on the level of the Divine within him. He achieves it by worshipping God with both his bad impulse and his good impulse. The bad impulse thus ceases to be evil and becomes a part of the totality of the Divine oneness in a man.

The person who is not a Tzadik, he who is a Benoni, has to continue to struggle. His life can, nevertheless, be just as holy, for he also demolishes the garments of the animal-soul in all their manifestations in thought, word, and deed. The steady devotion to God extricates the shells from the realm of the animal and transmutes them into instruments of holiness. Indeed, every Jewish person who is occupied wholly with matters that are connected with such devotion, whose speech and actions are directed from within to God, will undergo such a transformation. The sacrificial fire of Divine worship may not be able to change the essence of the animal-soul in a person, but the expressions of his soul are transmuted into something else.

The difference between the Tzadik and the Benoni would then be in the way the essence of the soul is changed. The Tzadik achieves it inwardly; from his own essential being, he effects a total transformation of his animal-soul. The Benoni is more concentrated on the outward manifestations of his animal-soul, even though, as he progresses, the animal-soul changes and becomes something other than what it was. The soul of the Benoni is extricated from the darkness of the shells; it is not annihilated in the light of Divine Wisdom, only its garments in thought, word, and deed are transformed in the 613 mitzvot of the Torah. Thus, the Benoni keeps changing himself constantly; he has to keep transmuting his inner essence by working on the outer manifestations of his being. His efforts are directed to a vigilant struggle to transform his animal-soul; and this is possible because the animal-soul is of Klipat Nogah, which is basically a spiritual category, even if it is not holy.

The core of the difference would, therefore, appear to be bound up with the animal-soul of man. The point is that this animal-soul is not necessarily of the essence of evil; it is of an undefined essence which, if not treated at all, belongs, like everything else neglected by man, to the realm of formlessness or to the realm of the shells. But when such essences are privileged to be corrected by man, they are raised to a higher level and undergo changes that are of the nature of transformation. This happens whenever the animal-soul, which is of Klipat Nogah, is so refined; there is a transformation from darkness to light, from bitterness to sweetness, whether in the fullness of perfection or only in external expression. In a certain sense, with every mitzvah, be it sanctified thought or action, at least at the moment of performance, man is transformed into a vessel of the Shechinah, an intermediary of the Divine light within him. At the same time, he becomes a means for the ascension of the "feminine waters," and in this ascension, and in response to it, there also occurs an augmentation or an extension of the light of the Shechinah, which is a revelation of Divine light in the brain of the head. It is in such manner that the Divine light is drawn to the soul—at the moment when the lamp seems to be burning out, the flame clutches at the oil rising in the wick and reinforces itself again. It is thus that the soul functions as a candle of God.

Indeed, the soul of man, in its wholeness, is an expression of the truth that "the Lord your God is a consuming fire." For "the Lord your God" is that which works on the reality of the world like a consuming fire; it utterly destroys all that it meets, and there is a constant process of such confrontation and burning. Earthly reality is fuel to the flame of Divine reality; everything is consumed by God. But earthly reality is not only matter and animality; it is also man. We too belong to the world. The difference is that the soul of man is capable of using this fire in order to transform and not to annihilate. Man raises things up to a higher level and thus preserves them. We are letting the previous essence burn up and, as in every burning, which is actually an essential chemical change, we are changing the composition of the reality of the world.

For the Lord your God is a consuming fire to be manifested by you. This demands contact with the world. Revelation is not an abstract Heavenly experience; it is a process of correct self-nullification in the greater dimension of an all-embracing reality. The Benoni is he who makes himself a candle of Divine light. He is not simply the average or middle between the good and the evil. He is intermediate between the one who has succeeded in transforming the entire essence of his soul and the one who is still changing. In terms of his daily existence the advanced Benoni behaves like a Tzadik, in spite of the fact that he is in inner conflict. The justification of his life is that, at every moment, he burns in the consuming fire of the Lord, for his soul is the candle of God.

Steinsaltz, Adin. *The Long Shorter Way: Discourses on Chasidic Thought*, ch. 53, pp. 351–357. New Milford, CT: Maggid Books, 2014

THE SHOFAR AND THE WALL

RABBI MOSHE SEGAL

Editor's Note: The Holy Temple in Jerusalem was twice destroyed—by the Romans in the year 69 CE, and by the Babylonians on the same date in 423 BCE. One wall remains standing as a living symbol of the Jewish people's ownership over the Land of Israel and the city of Jerusalem—the Kotel HaMaaravi or "Western Wall."

What follows is an excerpt (translated from the Hebrew) from the memoir of Rabbi Moshe Segal (1904-1985), a Lubavitcher Chassid who was active in the struggle to free the Holy Land from British rule.

In those years, the area in front of the Kotel did not look as it does today. Only a narrow alley separated the Kotel and the Arab houses on its other side. The British Government forbade us to place an Ark, tables or benches in the alley; even a small stool could not be brought to the Kotel. The British also instituted the following ordinances, designed to humble the Jews at the holiest place of their faith: it is forbidden to pray out loud, lest one upset the Arab residents; it is forbidden to read from the Torah (those praying at the Kotel had to go to one of the synagogues in the Jewish quarter to conduct the Torah reading); it is forbidden to sound the *shofar* on Rosh Hashanah and Yom Kippur. The British Government placed policemen at the Kotel to enforce these rules.

On Yom Kippur of that year [1930] I was praying at the Kotel. During the brief intermission between the *musaf* and *minchah* prayers, I overheard people whispering to each other: "Where will we go to hear the shofar? It'll be impossible to blow here. There are as many policemen as people praying. . . . " The Police Commander himself was there, to make sure that the Jews will not, G-d forbid, sound the single blast that closes the fast.

RABBI MOSHE TSVI SEGAL, 1904–1984

Religious Zionist activist. Born in Ukraine, Rabbi Segal studied in local yeshivas and was active in Zionist youth movements. He made *aliyah* to Israel in 1924, was active in the Jewish underground opposing the British Mandate, and was famously arrested for blowing the shofar at the Western Wall after Yom Kippur, in defiance of a British ordinance. After the Six-Day War, Rabbi Segal was the first Jew to settle in the Jewish Quarter of Jerusalem's Old City.

I listened to these whisperings, and thought to myself: Can we possibly forgo the sounding of the shofar that accompanies our proclamation of the sovereignty of G-d? Can we possibly forgo the sounding of the shofar, which symbolizes the redemption of Israel? True, the sounding of the shofar at the close of Yom Kippur is only a custom, but "A Jewish custom is Torah!" I approached Rabbi Yitzchak Horenstein, who served as the Rabbi of our "congregation," and said to him: "Give me a shofar."

"What for?"

"I'll blow."

"What are you talking about? Don't you see the police?"

"I'll blow."

The rabbi abruptly turned away from me, but not before he cast a glance at the prayer stand at the left end of the alley. I understood: the *shofar* was in the stand. When the hour of the blowing approached, I walked over to the stand and leaned against it.

I opened the drawer and slipped the shofar into my shirt. I had the shofar, but what if they saw me before I had a chance to blow it? I was still unmarried at the time, and following the Ashkenazic custom, did not wear a *tallit*. I turned to a person praying at my side, and asked him for his *tallit*. My request must have seemed strange to him, but the Jews are a kind people, especially at the holiest moments of the holiest day, and he handed me his *tallit* without a word.

I wrapped myself in the *tallit*. At that moment, I felt that I had created my own private domain. All around me, a foreign government prevails, ruling over the people of Israel even on their holiest day and at their holiest place, and we are not free to serve our G-d; but under this *tallit* is another domain. Here I am under no dominion save that of my Father in Heaven; here I shall do as He commands me, and no force on earth will stop me.

When the closing verses of the *Neillah* prayer—"Hear O Israel," "Blessed be the name" and "The L-rd is G-d"—were proclaimed, I took the shofar and blew a long, resounding blast. Everything happened very quickly. Many hands grabbed me. I removed the *tallit* from over my head, and before me stood the Police Commander, who ordered my arrest.

I was taken to the kishla, the prison in the Old City, and an Arab policeman was appointed to watch over me. Many hours passed; I was given no food or water to break my fast. At midnight, the policeman received an order to release me, and he let me out without a word.

I then learned that when the chief rabbi of the Holy Land, Rabbi Avraham Yitzchak Kook, heard of my arrest, he immediately contacted the secretary of High Commissioner of Palestine, and asked that I be released. When his request was refused, he stated that he would not break his fast until I was freed. The High Commissioner resisted for many hours, but finally, out of respect for the rabbi, he had no choice but to set me free.

For the next eighteen years, until the Arab conquest of the Old City in 1948, the shofar was sounded at the Kotel every Yom Kippur. The British well understood the significance of this blast; they knew that it will ultimately demolish their reign over our land as the walls of Jericho crumbled before the shofar of Joshua, and they did everything in their power to prevent it. But every Yom Kippur, the shofar was sounded by men who know they would be arrested for their part in staking our claim on the holiest of our possessions.

"The Shofar and the Wall," Chabad.org
Reprinted with permission from the publisher.

Lesson **4**

OCCUPIED WITH PEACE

ON THE VIABILITY OF LAND FOR PEACE

Israeli soldiers pose with captured Jordanian flags in front of the mosque of the Dome of the Rock, near the site of the Temple Mount, now in the hands of Israel, June 7, 1967. (Photo credit: Magnum Photos; Micha Bar Am, photographer)

Israel's pre-1967 borders subsequently became known as the "Green Line," to distinguish them from territories captured during the Six-Day War. Israel immediately offered to return her newly acquired territories in exchange for lasting peace, but the Arab world rejected the offer. Subsequent attempts at exchanging land for peace have failed to resolve the issues surrounding these territories. Should Israel hold on to them no matter the cost? Is there an authentic way to trade land for a lasting and sustainable peace?

TIMELINE OF "LAND FOR PEACE" EFFORTS

July 7, 1937

The Peel Commission, a British Commission of Inquiry appointed in 1936 to investigate the causes of unrest in Mandatory Palestine, recommends partition. The Arabs unanimously oppose the idea of a Jewish state and condemn the partition plan.

November 29, 1947

The UN General Assembly adopts "The United Nations Partition Plan for Palestine," recommending the creation of independent Arab and Jewish states and a special international regime for Jerusalem. The plan is accepted by the Zionist leadership but rejected by Arab governments.

June 10, 1967

Six-Day War concludes.

June 19, 1967

The Israeli cabinet determines the conditions for giving back territories. The final document reads: "Israel is offering to make peace with Egypt (and Syria) based on international borders and the security requirements of Israel." The wording is deliberately vague, and no specific territories are named. It is meant to leave room for negotiations.

June 28, 1967

Israel annexes East Jerusalem. Its Arab residents are given permanent Israeli resident status.

September 1, 1967

Arab leaders at the Khartoum Conference articulate the "three noes": "No peace, no recognition, and no negotiations with Israel."

September 27, 1967

Jewish settlers return to Gush Etzion, a block of settlements destroyed by the Jordanians in 1948.

April 11, 1968

A group of Jews celebrate the Passover seder in Hebron and refuse to leave. In August 1971, after a lengthy legal battle, they establish a nearby settlement called Kiryat Arba.

July 17, 1968

The PLO charter is amended. It continues to invalidate Israel's right to exist and includes the principle of armed struggle for the liberation of Palestine. (Thirty years later, the PLO changes its charter, recognizing Israel.)

November 22, 1968

UN Security Council Resolution 242 demands the "withdrawal of Israeli armed forces from territories occupied in the recent conflict," and effectively creates the land-for-peace paradigm. Israel accepts the resolution.

May, 1973

The settlement of Katif (later Netzer Hazani) is established. It is the first of 21 Gush Katif settlements in Gaza.

September, 1973

The Israeli government approves building plans for the city of Yamit in northern Sinai Peninsula.

October 6, 1973

The Yom Kippur War is launched. Israel retains all the territories it conquered in 1967.

February 9, 1974

The Gush Emunim (Block of the Faithful) movement is formed to promote Jewish settlement on the West Bank.

November 19, 1977

Egyptian President Anwar Sadat visits Jerusalem and begins the process that leads to the Camp David Accords.

September 17, 1978

Israel and Egypt sign the Camp David Accords, frameworks that aspire to broker a comprehensive peace in the Middle East, and include both Palestinian and Egyptian demands. (The Palestinian framework stalls due to the lack of a cooperative Palestinian representative.)

March 26, 1979

A peace treaty is signed by Israeli Prime Minister Menachem Begin, Egyptian President Anwar Sadat, and U.S. President Jimmy Carter. Egypt agrees to peace with Israel in exchange for Israel's withdrawal from Sinai. Israel also pledges to expand Palestinian self-government in the West Bank and Gaza. The treaty is ratified by the Knesset.

July 30, 1980

Israel passes the Jerusalem Law, making united Jerusalem the official capital of Israel.

December 14, 1981

Israel passes the Golan Heights Law, which applies Israeli "laws, jurisdiction, and administration" to the Golan Heights, yet stops short of full-fledged annexation.

April 21–25, 1982

The Israeli settlement of Yamit in the Sinai Peninsula is evacuated in accordance with the Egyptian–Israeli peace treaty. With this, Israel completes its withdrawal from the Sinai.

1987–1991

The first Palestinian Intifada takes place in the Gaza Strip and the West Bank.

October 30, 1991

The U.S.-Soviet sponsored Madrid Conference brings together Israeli, Lebanese, Syrian, Jordanian, and Palestinian representatives for peace talks.

June 23, 1992

The Labor party returns to power under Yitzhak Rabin, pledges to halt Jewish settlement expansion, and opens secret talks with the PLO.

September 13, 1993

The first Oslo Accords are signed in the presence of Yitzhak Rabin, Yasser Arafat, and U.S. President Bill Clinton. Violence and terrorism continue by Palestinian groups that reject the accords.

October 26, 1994

Following decades of secret negotiations, a peace agreement between Israel and Jordan is signed by King Hussein and Yitzhak Rabin. Israel returns 300 square kilometers of territory. Jordan establishes full diplomatic relations with Israel.

May–July, 1994

Israel withdraws from the West Bank city of Jericho and most of Gaza, and allows Yasser Arafat to move PLO administration from Tunis and set up the Palestinian National Authority.

October 14, 1994

The 1994 Nobel Peace Prize is jointly awarded to Shimon Peres, Yitzhak Rabin, and Yasser Arafat "for their efforts to create peace in the Middle East."

September 28, 1995

Yitzhak Rabin and Yasser Arafat sign an interim agreement for transfer of further power and territory to the PA. This agreement forms the basis for the 1997 Hebron Protocol, the 1998 Wye River Memorandum, and the internationally sponsored "Road Map for Peace" of 2003.

November 4, 1995

Yigal Amir, a Jewish extremist, assassinates Yitzhak Rabin. Shimon Peres takes over as prime minister.

2000–2005

The second Palestinian Intifada breaks out. As a result of the increase of suicide bombing attacks, Israel begins the construction of the West Bank fence, significantly reducing the incidence of suicide bombings. The barrier's construction is a major issue of contention.

June 24, 2002

George W. Bush becomes the first U.S. president to publicly endorse the notion of a Palestinian state.

April 30, 2003

The Quartet (the U.S., E.U., Russia, and the UN) proposes a road map to resolve the Israeli-Palestinian conflict. The plan includes an independent Palestinian state. Israel and the PA accept the plan.

July 9, 2005

The global BDS ("Boycott, Divestment, and Sanctions") campaign is launched. BDS attempts to place economic and political pressure on Israel to meet the demands of the Palestinians and UN resolutions.

August–September, 2005

Israel unilaterally "disengages" from Gaza and forcibly evacuates 25 Jewish settlements.

February 25, 2006

Hamas wins the Palestinian parliamentary elections and takes control of Gaza. Rocket attacks on Israel from Gaza escalate. Over the following years, these attacks are met with frequent Israeli raids and incursions.

November 27–28, 2007

The Annapolis Conference establishes the "two-state solution" as the basis for future talks between Israel and the PA.

December 27, 2008–January 18, 2009

Operation Cast Lead: IDF forces conduct a large-scale military operation in Gaza in response to ongoing rocket fire.

November 14–21, 2012

Operation Pillar of Defense: IDF forces conduct a large-scale military operation in Gaza in response to ongoing rocket fire.

July 8 August 26, 2014

Operation Protective Edge: IDF forces conduct a large-scale military operation in Gaza in response to major rocket attacks targeting large Israeli cities including Tel Aviv and Jerusalem.

1992–present

New settlements have been "frozen" by the government. Media reports about Israeli construction beyond the green line refer to new housing in Jerusalem or new neighborhoods in existing settlements. New settlements, referred to as *ma'achazim*, are illegal and usually evacuated quickly.

December 23, 2016

UN Security Council Resolution 2334 condemns Israel for expanding settlements in the West Bank. The U.S. abstains.

TEXT 1

UNITED NATIONS SECURITY COUNCIL RESOLUTION 2334, ADOPTED DECEMBER 23, 2016

Condemning all measures aimed at altering the demographic composition, character and status of the Palestinian Territory occupied since 1967, including East Jerusalem. . . .

Reiterating its vision of a region where two democratic States, Israel and Palestine, live side by side in peace within secure and recognized borders,

Stressing that the status quo is not sustainable and that significant steps, consistent with the transition contemplated by prior agreements, are urgently needed in order to (i) stabilize the situation and to reverse negative trends on the ground, which are steadily eroding the two-State solution and entrenching a one-State reality, and (ii) to create the conditions for successful final status negotiations and for advancing the two-State solution through those negotiations and on the ground,

1. *Reaffirms* that the establishment by Israel of settlements in the Palestinian territory occupied since 1967, including East Jerusalem, has no legal validity and constitutes a flagrant violation under international law and a major obstacle to the achievement of the two-State solution and a just, lasting and comprehensive peace. . . .

3. *Underlines* that it will not recognize any changes to the 4 June 1967 lines, including with regard to Jerusalem, other than those agreed by the parties through negotiations.

No Man's Land between Israel and Jordan during the Six-Day War, 1967. (Photo credit: Magnum Photos; Leonard Freed, photographer)

Exercise 1

Provide three reasons why Israel should allow for the creation of a Palestinian state and three reasons why Israel should not:

Israel should allow for the creation of a Palestinian state because:

1.

2.

3.

Israel should not allow for the creation of a Palestinian state because:

1.

2.

3.

QUESTION FOR DISCUSSION

In the course of negotiating peace, should Israel treat Jerusalem—East Jerusalem and/or the Old City and the Western Wall—differently from the other captured territories?

TEXT 2a

NUMBERS 33:53

וְהוֹרַשְׁתֶּם אֶת הָאָרֶץ וִישַׁבְתֶּם בָּהּ, כִּי לָכֶם נָתַתִּי אֶת הָאָרֶץ לָרֶשֶׁת אֹתָהּ.

You shall vacate the Land [of its inhabitants] and settle in it, for I have given the Land to you to inherit.

Yitzhak Rabin and David Ben-Gurion lead a group of soldiers past the Dome of the Rock June 7, 1967. (Photo credit: Magnum Photos; Micha Bar Am, Photographer)

TEXT 2b

RABBI MOSHE BEN NACHMAN, *HASAGOT AL SEFER HAMITZVOT*

שֶׁנִּצְטַוִּינוּ לָרֶשֶׁת הָאָרֶץ אֲשֶׁר נָתַן הָאֵ-ל יִתְעַלֶּה לַאֲבוֹתֵינוּ, לְאַבְרָהָם לְיִצְחָק וּלְיַעֲקֹב, וְלֹא נַעַזְבָהּ בְּיַד זוּלָתֵנוּ מִן הָאוּמוֹת אוֹ לִשְׁמָמָה. וְהוּא אָמְרוֹ לָהֶם, "וְהוֹרַשְׁתֶּם אֶת הָאָרֶץ וִישַׁבְתֶּם בָּהּ, כִּי לָכֶם נָתַתִּי אֶת הָאָרֶץ לָרֶשֶׁת אוֹתָהּ" . . .

וְאוֹמֵר אֲנִי כִּי הַמִּצְוָה שֶׁחֲכָמִים מַפְלִיגִים בָּהּ, וְהוּא דִּירַת אֶרֶץ יִשְׂרָאֵל, עַד שֶׁאָמְרוּ "כָּל הַיּוֹצֵא מִמֶּנָּה וְדָר בְּחוּצָה לָאָרֶץ יְהֵא בְּעֵינֶיךָ כְּעוֹבֵד עֲבוֹדָה זָרָה" (כְּתוּבּוֹת ק, ב) . . . וְזוּלַת זֶה הַפְלָגוֹת גְּדוֹלוֹת שֶׁאָמְרוּ בָּהּ, הַכֹּל הוּא מִמִּצְוַת עֲשֵׂה הוּא שֶׁנִּצְטַוִּינוּ לָרֶשֶׁת הָאָרֶץ לָשֶׁבֶת בָּהּ.

אִם כֵּן הִיא מִצְוַת עֲשֵׂה לְדוֹרוֹת, מִתְחַיֵּיב כָּל אֶחָד מִמֶּנּוּ וַאֲפִילוּ בִּזְמַן גָּלוּת.

We have been commanded to take possession of the Land that God gave to our forefathers, to Abraham, Isaac, and Jacob, and not to leave the Land in the hands of any other nation or allow it to remain unpopulated. Thus, God instructed the Children of Israel: "You shall vacate the Land [of its inhabitants] and settle in it, for I have given the Land to you to inherit." . . .

The sages greatly extolled the importance of the mitzvah of dwelling in the Land. On top of their many lavish praises, they went so far as to say: "Whoever leaves the Land and dwells in the Diaspora is analogous to an idol worshiper" (TALMUD, KETUBOT 100B). . . . It is my contention that all this praise is due to the biblical commandment to take possession of the Land and dwell in it.

This commandment applied to all generations; and every one of us is obligated to fulfill it, even in times of exile.

RABBI MOSHE BEN NACHMAN (NACHMANIDES, RAMBAN) 1194–1270

Scholar, philosopher, author, and physician. Nachmanides was born in Spain and served as leader of Iberian Jewry. In 1263, he was summoned by King James of Aragon to a public disputation with Pablo Cristiani, a Jewish apostate. Though Nachmanides was the clear victor of the debate, he had to flee Spain because of the resulting persecution. He moved to Israel and helped reestablish communal life in Jerusalem. He authored a classic commentary on the Pentateuch and a commentary on the Talmud.

TEXT 3

RABBI SHLOMO DURAN, *RESPONSA* 2

אֵין סָפֵק שֶׁהַדִּירָה בְּאֶרֶץ יִשְׂרָאֵל הִיא מִצְוָה גְדוֹלָה בְּכָל זְמַן, בֵּין בִּפְנֵי הַבַּיִת בֵּין שֶׁלֹא בִּפְנֵי הַבַּיִת, וַאֲדוֹנִי זְקֵנִי הָרַמְבַּ"ן זַ"ל מָנָה אוֹתָהּ מִכְּלַל מִצְוֹת עֲשֵׂה, כְּמוֹ שֶׁנֶּאֱמַר, "וִירִשְׁתֶּם אוֹתָהּ וִישַׁבְתֶּם בָּהּ"...

אָמְנָם, מִצְוָה זוּ אֵינָהּ מִצְוָה כּוֹלֶלֶת לְכָל יִשְׂרָאֵל בְּגָלוּת הַחֵל הַזֶּה, אֲבָל הִיא נִמְנַעַת כְּלָל... אָמְנָם מִצְוָה הִיא עַל כָּל יָחִיד לַעֲלוֹת לָדוּר שָׁם.

Undoubtedly, to dwell in the Land of Israel is a great mitzvah. This is true in all generations, whether or not the Holy Temple is standing in Jerusalem. My grandfather, Nachmanides, lists this mitzvah among the 613 biblical commandments, citing the verse, "You shall vacate the Land [of its inhabitants] and settle in it." . . .

However, this obligation does not lie collectively upon the exiled nation of Israel; in fact, while in exile, the collective is enjoined from fulfilling this mitzvah. . . . Currently, the mitzvah is incumbent upon the individual: every individual is urged to go and dwell in the Land.

RABBI SHLOMO DURAN (RASHBASH)
CA. 1400–1470

Halachic authority. Born in Algiers, Rashbash was the son and successor of Rabbi Shimon ben Tsemach Duran, and like his father, he authored many responsa. In 1437, he composed a defense of the Talmud, which was published under the title *Milchemet Chovah*. Additionally, Duran also defended Judaism against Christian theological polemics in his treatise, *Setirat Emunat Hanotsrim*.

Israeli settlers of Atzmona picking the last crop of tomatoes shortly before the evacuation of the settlement, 1982. (Photo credit: Magnum Photos; Micha Bar Am, photographer)

TEXT 4a

DEUTERONOMY 7:1–2

כִּי יְבִיאֲךָ ה' אֱלֹקֶיךָ אֶל הָאָרֶץ אֲשֶׁר אַתָּה בָא שָׁמָּה לְרִשְׁתָּהּ, וְנָשַׁל גּוֹיִם
רַבִּים מִפָּנֶיךָ, הַחִתִּי וְהַגִּרְגָּשִׁי וְהָאֱמֹרִי וְהַכְּנַעֲנִי וְהַפְּרִזִּי וְהַחִוִּי וְהַיְבוּסִי,
שִׁבְעָה גוֹיִם רַבִּים וַעֲצוּמִים מִמֶּךָ. . . לֹא תִכְרֹת לָהֶם בְּרִית וְלֹא תְחָנֵּם.

When your God brings you into the Land you are entering to possess, He will cast away from before you many nations—the Hittites, Girgashites, Amorites, Canaanites, Perizzites, Hivvites, and Jebusites—seven nations that are more numerous and powerful than you. . . . Do not make a covenant with them, nor be gracious to them.

TEXT 4b

RABBI YOSEF CARO, *SHULCHAN ARUCH, YOREH DE'AH* 151:8

אֵין מוֹכְרִים לָהֶם בָּתִּים וְשָׂדוֹת בְּאֶרֶץ יִשְׂרָאֵל; אֲבָל מַשְׂכִּירִין לָהֶם בָּתִּים,
וְלֹא שָׂדוֹת.

It is forbidden to sell to idolaters houses and fields in the Land of Israel; however, it is permitted to rent out to them houses, but not fields.

RABBI YOSEF CARO (MARAN, *BEIT YOSEF*) 1488–1575

Halachic authority and author. Rabbi Caro was born in Spain, but was forced to flee during the expulsion in 1492 and eventually settled in Safed, Israel. He authored many works including the *Beit Yosef, Kesef Mishneh*, and a mystical work, *Magid Meisharim*. Rabbi Caro's magnum opus, the Shulchan Aruch (Code of Jewish Law), has been universally accepted as the basis for modern Jewish law.

TEXT 5

RABBI TSADOK HAKOHEN RABINOWITZ, *POKED AKARIM* 4

וְהַהוֹדָאָה עַל יְשׁוּעָה, דָבָר זֶה חִידְשָׁה לֵאָה בְּהוּלֶּדֶת יְהוּדָה, דְעַל כֵּן קְרָאָתוֹ כֵּן. וְעַל שְׁמוֹ נִקְרְאוּ כֵּן כָּל יִשְׂרָאֵל. דְזֶה כָּל כֹּחַ יִשְׂרָאֵל הַנִבְדָלִים מֵהָעַמִים שֶׁהֵם מַכִּירִים בְּכָל דָבָר שֶׁהוּא מֵהַשֵּׁם יִתְבָּרֵךְ הַמוֹשִׁיעָם, וּמוֹדִים לוֹ עַל זֶה.

Upon giving birth to her fourth son, Leah became the first to express gratitude to God for His deliverance, and she therefore named her son Judah. All of Israel is called by his name because the uniqueness of the Jewish people is that they recognize that everything comes from God, their Deliverer, and they express their gratitude to Him for this.

ספר

פרי צדיק

חלק ראשון

קדושת שבת

שביתת שבת

צדוק הכהן

RABBI TSADOK HAKOHEN RABINOWITZ OF LUBLIN
1823–1900

Chasidic master and thinker. Rabbi Tsadok was born into a Lithuanian rabbinic family and later joined the Chasidic movement. He was a follower of the Chasidic leaders, Rabbi Mordechai Yosef Leiner of Izbica and Rabbi Leibel Eiger. He succeeded Rabbi Eiger after his passing and became a rebbe in Lublin, Poland. He authored many works on Jewish law, Chasidism, Kabbalah, and ethics, as well as scholarly essays on astronomy, geometry, and algebra.

Engraving of the Tomb of the Patriarchs, Hebron. David Roberts, 1838. The mosque above the tomb was built by the Turks.

TEXT 6

MAIMONIDES, *MISHNEH TORAH*, LAWS OF KINGS 10:12

> צִוּוּ חֲכָמִים לְבַקֵּר חוֹלֵיהֶם וְלִקְבֹּר מֵתֵיהֶם עִם מֵתֵי יִשְׂרָאֵל, וּלְפַרְנֵס עֲנִיֵּיהֶם בִּכְלַל עֲנִיֵּי יִשְׂרָאֵל, מִפְּנֵי דַּרְכֵי שָׁלוֹם. הֲרֵי נֶאֱמַר, "טוֹב ה' לַכֹּל וְרַחֲמָיו עַל כָּל מַעֲשָׂיו" (תְּהִילִים קמה, ט), וְנֶאֱמַר "דְּרָכֶיהָ דַרְכֵי נֹעַם וְכָל נְתִיבוֹתֶיהָ שָׁלוֹם" (מִשְׁלֵי ג, יז).

In the interest of maintaining peaceful relations, our sages instructed us to visit the non-Jewish sick, bury their dead, and give charity to their poor, just as we do for our fellow Jews. [The imperative to be kind to non-Jews is based on the Scriptures.] For it is written, "God is good to all, and His compassion extends to all His creations" (PSALMS 145:9), and it is written, "The ways [of the Torah] are sweet, and all her paths are peaceful" (PROVERBS 3:17).

RABBI MOSHE BEN MAIMON (MAIMONIDES, RAMBAM) 1135–1204

Halachist, philosopher, author, and physician. Maimonides was born in Cordoba, Spain. After the conquest of Cordoba by the Almohads, he fled Spain and eventually settled in Cairo, Egypt. There, he became the leader of the Jewish community and served as court physician to the vizier of Egypt. He is most noted for authoring the *Mishneh Torah*, an encyclopedic arrangement of Jewish law, and for his philosophical work, *Guide for the Perplexed*. His rulings on Jewish law are integral to the formation of halachic consensus.

TEXT 7

MAIMONIDES, *MISHNEH TORAH,* LAWS OF SHABBAT 2:3

> הָא לָמַדְתָּ, שֶׁאֵין מִשְׁפְּטֵי הַתּוֹרָה נְקָמָה בָּעוֹלָם, אֶלָּא רַחֲמִים וְחֶסֶד וְשָׁלוֹם בָּעוֹלָם. וְאֵלּוּ הָאֶפִּיקוֹרְסִים שֶׁאוֹמְרִים שֶׁאָסוּר לְחַלֵּל שַׁבָּת אֲפִילּוּ לְצוֹרֶךְ פִּיקּוּחַ נֶפֶשׁ, עֲלֵיהֶם הַכָּתוּב אוֹמֵר: "וְגַם אֲנִי נָתַתִּי לָהֶם חוּקִּים לֹא טוֹבִים וּמִשְׁפָּטִים לֹא יִחְיוּ בָּהֶם" (יְחֶזְקֵאל כ, כה).

This teaches that the laws of the Torah are not vengeful; rather they bring compassion, kindness, and peace to the world. As for those heretics who say that [administering life-saving treatment] constitutes a forbidden violation of the Shabbat, one may apply to them the verse: "I gave them harmful statutes and laws by which they cannot live" (EZEKIEL 20:25).

TEXT 8

RABBI OVADIAH YOSEF, "CEDING TERRITORIES FROM THE LAND OF ISRAEL TO SAVE LIVES," *TECHUMIN,* VOL. X, P. 47

אִם יִתְבָּרֵר לְמַעֲלָה מִכָּל סָפֵק שֶׁיִּהְיֶה שָׁלוֹם אֱמֶת בֵּינֵינוּ לְבֵין שְׁכֵנֵינוּ הָעֲרָבִים אִם יוּחְזְרוּ לָהֶם הַשְּׁטָחִים, וּלְעוּמַת זֹאת קַיֶּמֶת סַכָּנַת מִלְחָמָה מִיָּדִית אִם לֹא יוּחְזְרוּ לָהֶם הַשְּׁטָחִים, יֵשׁ לְהַחְזִיר לָהֶם הַשְּׁטָחִים, מִשּׁוּם שֶׁאֵין לְךָ דָּבָר הָעוֹמֵד בִּפְנֵי פִּיקּוּחַ נֶפֶשׁ.

If it were determined beyond any doubt that returning the territories to our Arab neighbors would result in true peace, and that the immediate threat of war looms if the territories are not returned, we must then return the territories. For nothing is of greater importance than saving lives.

RABBI OVADIAH YOSEF
1920–2013

Talmudic scholar and former Sephardic chief rabbi of Israel. Born in Basra, Iraq, Rabbi Yosef was recognized as a great authority in Halachah. His responsa are highly regarded within rabbinic circles and are considered binding in many Sephardic communities. Rabbi Yosef was also a major political figure in Israel, serving as the spiritual leader of the Shas party. Among his most popular works are *Yabi'a Omer* and *Yechaveh Da'at*.

QUESTION FOR DISCUSSION

In your estimation, does exchanging land for peace and/or allowing for the creation of a Palestinian state endanger lives, or save lives?

TEXT 9a

AMNON RESHEF, FROM AN ADDRESS DELIVERED AT THE COMMANDERS FOR ISRAEL'S SECURITY CONFERENCE, OCTOBER 22, 2015

Israel's security and her Jewish-democratic nature can only be secured through parting ways with the Palestinians. This is a national security interest of the highest order. . . . The agreement with the Palestinians will be based on the "two states for two nations" principle and founded on the 1967 borders.

AMNON RESHEF
1938–

Israeli army general and peace advocate. Born and raised in Israel, Reshef rose through the IDF ranks in the armored corps, reaching the rank of major general. Following his military service, Reshef has been active in advocating for peace by means of the two-state solution, establishing and leading Commanders for Israel's Security, an organization of ex-security officials supporting this position.

TEXT 9b

YAAKOV AMIDROR, *GEVULOT BENEI HAGANAH: TNAI HECHRECHI LEBITACHON HA'ARETS* (JERUSALEM: HOTSA'AT HAMERKAZ HAYERUSHALMI LE'INYANEI TSIBUR UMEDINAH, 2005), P. 28

Regarding the question of Israel's borders, from a professional military viewpoint, an Israeli withdrawal to the pre-1967 lines will endanger Israel, for the following reasons:

- Israel will not be able to defend itself against a future conventional military threat. Considering the current situation in the Middle East, no one can guarantee that such a threat will not materialize.
- Israel's ability to prevent the destruction of its national infrastructure in the event of missile attacks will be greatly reduced, and its retaliatory capacity will also be significantly restricted.
- As a result of these two weaknesses, the likelihood will increase that Israel's enemies will utilize their newfound advantage to attack Israel in one or both of these ways.
- A security buffer zone beyond the border barrier is a vital component of border security, increasing the barrier's effectiveness in preventing terrorist infiltration.

YA'AKOV AMIDROR
1948–

Israeli general and security expert. Born and raised in Israel, Amidror served in the IDF during the Six-Day and Yom Kippur Wars, rising to the rank of Major General. From 2011–2013, Amidror served as the head of Israel's National Security Council. He currently serves as a researcher at the Jerusalem Center for Public Affairs.

TEXT 10

SHAUL ARIELI, "THE DANGERS OF ANNEXING THE WEST BANK," *HA'ARETZ*, JANUARY 25, 2017

The commanders, I among them, can see the reality taking form right in front of us. We seek only to warn the Zionist public against the unilateral annexation that the government is initiating. In the name of messianic nationalism, these steps threaten the Zionist vision of a democratic state for the Jewish people with equal rights for all. . . .

In 1967, the government annexed 70 square kilometers [of East Jerusalem] on which 69,000 Palestinians lived at the time, constituting just 26 percent of the combined city's population. By 2015 these numbers had reached 320,000 and almost 40 percent.

Because of Jewish migration from the city, because of its many tensions, within two decades Israel's capital will clearly become a city with a Jewish minority. If the Palestinians change their policy and decide to take part in local elections, the mayor and most of the city council will be Palestinian. . . .

Much the same would happen with "united Israel" if we succumb to the annexation longings of Habayit Hayehudi's Naftali Bennett and Bezalel Smotrich. At the time of annexation, the proportion of Jews would be about 60 percent, but within 15 years the country would

SHAUL ARIELI
1959–

Israeli activist. Born and raised in Israel, Arieli served in the IDF, achieving the rank of colonel. He served in the administrations of successive Israeli Prime Ministers in positions related to Israeli-Palestinian negotiations. He was one of the architects of the "Geneva Initiative" and has written a number of books advocating a two-state solution to the Israeli-Palestinian conflict.

have an Arab majority. We would wake up into the reality that David Ben-Gurion warned about in 1947 even before Israel existed: "There can be no stable and strong Jewish state so long as it has a Jewish majority of only 60 percent."

TEXT 11

RABBI SHNE'UR ZALMAN OF LIADI, *SHULCHAN ARUCH HARAV, ORACH CHAYIM* 618:2

וַאֲפִילּוּ אִם הַחוֹלֶה אוֹמֵר, "אֵינִי צָרִיךְ לֶאֱכוֹל", וְיֵשׁ שָׁם רוֹפֵא - אֲפִילּוּ הוּא נָכְרִי - וְאוֹמֵר שֶׁהוּא צָרִיךְ לֶאֱכוֹל, מַאֲכִילִין אוֹתוֹ עַל פִּיו, וְהוּא שֶׁיְּהֵא בָּקִי.

If a patient maintains that he or she does not need to eat, but a doctor—even a non-Jewish doctor—insists that the patient must eat, we feed the patient, as per the doctor's instructions. This is provided that the doctor is an expert medical practitioner.

RABBI SHNE'UR ZALMAN OF LIADI (ALTER REBBE) 1745–1812

Chasidic rebbe, halachic authority, and founder of the Chabad movement. The Alter Rebbe was born in Liozna, Belarus, and was among the principal students of the Magid of Mezeritch. His numerous works include the *Tanya*, an early classic containing the fundamentals of Chabad Chasidism, and *Shulchan Aruch HaRav*, an expanded and reworked code of Jewish law.

Exercise 2

THE NEW YORK TIMES, WEDNESDAY, JULY 27, 2016 A5

In a Turbulent World Israel's Security Chiefs Agree:

SEPARATION INTO TWO STATES
Is Essential for Israel's Security

CHIEFS OF STAFF FROM THE ISRAEL DEFENSE FORCES:

SHAUL MOFAZ
"Time is not in favor of the state of Israel… The generation of the leaders today should decide. This year, next year — we have to decide."
Washington Post, 7/19/12

DAN HALUTZ
"The question is whether there is a leadership who is willing to go the extra step to maintain a Jewish state, because the alternative is a bi-national state."
Arutz Sheva, 4/8/11

AMNON LIPKIN-SHAHAK, Z"L
"I am afraid that it might come to a point in which it will be impossible to go back to a two-state solution, and then it's going to be a chaotic situation."
J Street, 12/21/12

GABI ASHKENAZI
Israel will one day be "forced to separate from the Palestinians, in one way or another…time is not on our side."
Jerusalem Post, 9/12/12

BENNY GANTZ
"This issue is important to us, it is important for ourselves, it is important for our connections with the international community."
Times of Israel, 2/6/15

EHUD BARAK
"A two-state solution is the only viable long-term solution. It is a compelling imperative for us, in order to secure our identity and our future as a Jewish and democratic state; it's not a favor for the Palestinians."
Haaretz, 3/4/13

SHIN BET (ISRAEL'S DOMESTIC SECURITY AGENCY) DIRECTORS:

AVI DICHTER
"Any intelligent person realizes that a one-state solution with the six million Jews and seven million non-Jews — mostly Muslims — is irresponsible"
Arutz Sheva, 12/29/14

YUVAL DISKIN
"[T]he unsolved Israeli-Palestinian conflict represent[s] an existential threat…we need to reach an agreement now, before we reach the 'point of no return.'"
Geneva Initiative 10 Year Conference, 12/4/13

AMI AYALON
"[T]he only way to sustain Zionism — by which I mean the perpetuation of a Jewish, democratic Israel in the spirit of the Declaration of Independence — is by making the two-state solution a reality."
Jerusalem Post, 4/8/14

AVRAHAM SHALOM, Z"L
"If we do not turn away from adhering to the entire land of Israel [including the West Bank and Gaza] and begin to understand the other side, we will not get anywhere…If we don't change this there will be nothing there."
The Guardian, 11/29/03

JACOB PERRY
"We're dealing with fateful issues in Israel, the peace process is deadlocked and we're heading rapidly towards a bi-national state. This is the end of Zionism, we need new leadership."
Ynet News, 6/9/12

HEADS OF THE MOSSAD (ISRAEL'S INTELLIGENCE AGENCY):

MEIR DAGAN, Z"L
Netanyahu and Bennett "are leading us to a binational state which is a disaster and dangerous to Zionism."
Arutz Sheva, 6/3/15

TAMIR PARDO
"The biggest threat [to Israel] is the Palestinian issue."
Haaretz, 6/5/15

DANNY YATOM
"Without a peace initiative…The fighting and violence will continue,…and our isolation process will deepen."
Ynet News, 11/2/15

SHABTAI SHAVIT
"[S]ome values are more sacred than land. Peace, which is the life and soul of true democracy, is more important than land."
Haaretz, 11/24/14

EFRAIM HALEVY
"'[N]o solution' means that there's going to be one state…it'll be a… non-democratic system for the majority, and this is unsustainable and untenable."
Wilson Center, 10/24/12

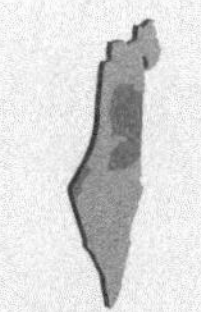

POPULATION BREAKDOWN[1]

2015 52% JEWISH
2020 49% JEWISH
2030 44% JEWISH

Israel can remain a Jewish, democratic state only if the Palestinians have a demilitarized Palestinian state.

It's Time: Two States for Two People

S. DANIEL ABRAHAM
CENTER FOR MIDDLE EAST PEACE
Hon. Robert Wexler, President
WWW.CENTERPEACE.ORG

1. S. DellaPergola, Professor Emeritus at The Hebrew University of Jerusalem. World Jewish Population 2015 in American Jewish Year Book 2015

New York Times ad, July 26, 2016

CHIEFS OF STAFF FROM THE ISRAEL DEFENSE FORCES:

SHAUL MOFAZ: "Time is not in favor of the state of Israel… The generation of the leaders today should decide. This year, next year — we have to decide." *(Washington Post, 7/19/12)*

DAN HALUTZ: "The question is whether there is a leadership who is willing to go the extra step to maintain a Jewish state, because the alternative is a bi-national state." *(Arutz Sheva, 4/8/11)*

AMNON LIPKIN-SHAHAK, Z"L: "I am afraid that it might come to a point in which it will be impossible to go back to a two-state solution, and then it's going to be a chaotic situation." *(J Street, 12/21/12)*

GABI ASHKENAZI: Israel will one day be "forced to separate from the Palestinians, in one way or another…time is not on our side." *(Jerusalem Post, 9/12/12)*

BENNY GANTZ: "This issue is important to us, it is important for ourselves, it is important for our connections with the international community." *(Times of Israel, 2/6/15)*

EHUD BARAK: "A two-state solution is the only viable long-term solution. It is a compelling imperative for us, in order to secure our identity and our future as a Jewish and democratic state; it's not a favor for the Palestinians." *(Haaretz, 3/4/13)*

SHIN BET (ISRAEL'S DOMESTIC SECURITY AGENCY) DIRECTORS:

AVI DICHTER: "Any intelligent person realizes that a one-state solution with the six million Jews and seven million non-Jews—mostly Muslims— is irresponsible." *(Arutz Sheva, 12/29/14)*

YUVAL DISKIN: "[T]he unsolved Israeli-Palestinian conflict represent[s] an existential threat…we need to reach an agreement now, before we reach the 'point of no return.'" *(Geneva Initiative 10 Year Conference, 12/4/13)*

AMI AYALON: "[T]he only way to sustain Zionism — by which I mean the perpetuation of a Jewish, democratic Israel in the spirit of the Declaration of Independence — is by making the two-state solution a reality." *(Jerusalem Post, 4/8/14)*

AVRAHAM SHALOM, Z"L: "If we do not turn away from adhering to the entire land of Israel [including the West Bank and Gaza] and begin to understand the other side, we will not get anywhere...If we don't change this there will be nothing there." *(The Guardian, 11/29/03)*

JACOB PERRY: "We're dealing with fateful issues in Israel, the peace process is deadlocked and we're heading rapidly towards a bi-national state. This is the end of Zionism, we need new leadership." *(Ynet News, 6/9/12)*

HEADS OF THE MOSSAD (ISRAEL'S INTELLIGENCE AGENCY):

MEIR DAGAN, Z"L: Netanyahu and Bennett "are leading us to a binational state which is a disaster and dangerous to Zionism." *(Arutz Sheva, 6/3/15)*

TAMIR PARDO: "The biggest threat [to Israel] is the Palestinian issue." *(Haaretz, 6/5/15)*

DANNY YATOM: "Without a peace initiative…The fighting and violence will continue,...and our isolation process will deepen." *(Ynet News, 11/2/15)*

SHABTAI SHAVIT: "[S]ome values are more sacred than land. Peace, which is the life and soul of true democracy, is more important than land." *(Haaretz, 11/24/14)*

EFRAIM HALEVY: "'[N]o solution' means that there's going to be one state…it'll be a... non-democratic system for the majority, and this is unsustainable and untenable." *(Wilson Center, 10/24/12)*

(a) How many different reasons are expressed in this ad in support of a two-state solution?

1		4	
2		5	
3		6	

(b) How many of these security experts base their support for a two-state solution on present safety and security considerations?

ISRAEL'S DEFENSIVE DEPTH WITHOUT THE WEST BANK

TEXT 12

RABBI OVADIAH YOSEF, CORRESPONDENCE, 23 SHEVAT 5763 [2003]

אֶל כְּבוֹד יַקִּירֵנוּ אַחֵינוּ בֵּית יִשְׂרָאֵל תּוֹשְׁבֵי יש"ע, הַשֵּׁם עֲלֵיהֶם יִחְיוּ שְׁלוֹמְכֶם יִשְׂגֶּא לָעַד.

בִּרְצוֹנִי לְהַבְהִיר אֶת עֶמְדָתִי בְּעִנְיַן יש"ע. לֹא פַּעַם הִסְבַּרְתִּי מִכְּבַר כִּי פְּסַק הַהֲלָכָה אֲשֶׁר נָתַתִּי בִּזְמַנּוֹ "שְׁטָחִים תְּמוּרַת שָׁלוֹם" אֵינוֹ תָּקֵף כְּלַל לְרֶגֶל הַמַּצָּב הַנּוֹכְחִי.

אֲנִי הִתְכַּוַּונְתִּי אַךְ וְרַק לְשָׁלוֹם אֱמֶת, בּוֹ יְרוּשָׁלַיִם וּסְבִיבוֹתֶיהָ יִשְׁכְּנוּ לָבֶטַח, בְּשָׁלוֹם בְּשַׁלְוָה. אוּלָם עַתָּה, עֵינֵינוּ רוֹאוֹת וְכָלוֹת כִּי אַדְרַבָּה, מְסִירַת שְׁטָחִים מֵאַרְצֵנוּ הַקְּדוֹשָׁה גּוֹרֶמֶת לְסַכָּנַת נְפָשׁוֹת. לֹא לְשָׁלוֹם כָּזֶה יִיחַלְנוּ וְלֹא לַנַּעַר הַזֶּה הִתְפַּלָּלְנוּ. לְפִיכָךְ הֶסְכֵּם אוֹסְלוֹ בָּטֵל וּמְבוּטָל, כִּי אֲנִי שָׁלוֹם וְכִי אֲדַבֵּר הֵמָּה לַמִּלְחָמָה. וְאֵין לָנוּ עַל מִי לְהִשָּׁעֵן אֶלָּא עַל אָבִינוּ שֶׁבַּשָּׁמַיִם.

To our honorable brothers residing in Judea, Samaria, and Gaza,

May God be with you, and may you be blessed with eternal peace!

I wish to clarify my position on the matter of Judea, Samaria, and Gaza. As I have explained in the past on more than one occasion, the halachic ruling that I issued in the past regarding [the permissibility of] returning land, "land for peace," is no longer relevant, given the present circumstance.

I had intended, only and purely, [that ceding territory is permitted if it leads to] authentic peace, one in which Jerusalem and its neighboring areas would dwell in peace and harmony. But we now see with our eyes that, to the contrary, giving away territory from our Holy Land puts lives in danger. It was not for this "peace" that we hoped and prayed. Therefore, the Oslo agreement is null and void. "I am at peace with them, but though I speak [of peace], they come to wage war" (PSALMS 120:7). We have no one on whom to rely other than our Father in heaven.

Jubilant families and greeters at Ben-Gurion Airport, where Entebbe hijacking victims were returned, 1976. (Photo credit: Magnum Photos; Micha Bar Am, photographer)

You deserve a factual look at . . .

The Two-State Illusion

Would it solve the Middle East problem?

There seems to be almost universal consensus that in order to bring peace to the Middle East the creation of a Palestinian state is unavoidable. What is more, such a "solution" is the policy of the United States.

What are the facts?

The lesson of Gaza. In previous *hasbarah* (educating and clarifying) messages we made clear that a Palestinian state would be impossible for Israel to accept. It would lead inevitably to Israel's destruction. The reason is primarily the lesson learned from the Gaza experiment. Under pressure from most of the world, Israel evacuated Gaza, displacing hundreds of families who had lived there for generations and who had built substantial communities and extensive agricultural installations. Instead of making even the least gesture of acknowledgment and gratitude, the Palestinians, almost from the very first day of their "liberation" from the hated Jews, began to lob rockets into Israel. Ultimately, Israel was forced to defend itself against those attacks and invaded Gaza in force. There was much damage and many casualties. As could be expected, "world opinion" condemned Israel's defensive action and called it "disproportionate."

"...the ultimate goal is not... a Palestinian state... but the destruction of Israel."

If Israel were foolish enough to yield to the unrelenting pressure and were to turn Judea/Samaria (the "West Bank") over to the Palestinians, it would find itself surrounded by enemies, whose ultimate goal is not the creation of a Palestinian state but the destruction of Israel – to use the common rhetoric, to wipe Israel off the map and push the Jews into the sea.

Statehood opportunities rejected. The reality is that the Palestinians are not really interested in their own independent state. Such a state never existed and the concept of a "Palestinian" people is a fairly new one. If the Palestinians were really interested in their own state, if that were their aspiration, they could have had such a state side-by-side with Israel, for a very long time. The first partition of Palestine – all of which, by the Balfour Declaration and by the mandate of the League of Nations was to be the Jewish home – occurred in 1921. Winston Churchill, who was then the Colonial Secretary, split the mandated territory, allocating the great bulk to the Arabs for the creation of what is now the Kingdom of Jordan. But, of course, that did not satisfy the Arabs. After much bloody fighting over the decades, other efforts were made to create an additional state for the Arabs (who by then called themselves "Palestinians"). There was the Peel Partition Plan of 1937, and, most importantly perhaps, the United Nations Partition Plan of 1947. Under the UN plan, the territory west of the Jordan River was to be split, with the major portion to be allocated to the Arabs and the smaller, disconnected, portion going to the Jews. Jerusalem, a bone of contention, was to be "internationalized" – it would not belong to either. The Jews, anxious to form their state, accepted this plan under which they were granted only a small fraction of the "Palestine" that they had been promised to be their homeland by the Balfour Declaration and by the mandate of the League of Nations. But the Arabs rejected the partition out of hand. Almost the same day that Israel declared its statehood and its independence, six Arab armies invaded Israel from north, east and south. In what could be called a Biblical miracle, the ragtag Jewish forces defeated the combined Arab might.

Following the Six-Day War of 1967, in which Israeli forces defeated the combined invasion forces of Egypt and Syria, Israel offered generous terms for the formation of a Palestinian state. But it was not accepted. Instead, the Arabs convened in Khartoum (Sudan) and pronounced their famous Three No's: No peace with Israel, No negotiations with Israel, No recognition of Israel. Other offers of statehood were made over the course of the years. Ehud Barak, then prime minister of Israel, and U.S. President Bill Clinton offered the Palestinians almost total withdrawal to the 1967 armistice lines. The Palestinians rejected the offer, presumably because it did not include Israel's willingness to accept hundreds of thousands of Palestinian "refugees," who would with one stroke accomplish what the Arabs had not accomplished in their wars: the destruction of Israel. The creation of a Palestinian state could have been accomplished many times. But it is the unalterable goal of the Palestinians, indeed of most Arabs and most Muslims, to destroy the Jewish state and never to recognize and legitimize Israel in whatever shape and size as a Jewish state.

It is important to understand that the creation of a Palestinian state is not the true ultimate goal of the Arabs. It is, at best, meant to be a stepping stone toward the ultimate goal: the destruction, the disappearance of Israel and of the hated Jews from any portion of what they consider "holy Muslim soil." The Arabs are not interested in putting an end to the suffering of the Palestinian people. That could have been accomplished long ago. On the contrary, to be martyrs is a source of pride and assurance of victory to the Arabs. They compare their willingness to sacrifice hundreds of thousands of their own with the Zionist enemy, who is concerned about combat losses or even the fate of one single abducted soldier.

This message has been published and paid for by

FLAME

Facts and Logic About the Middle East
P.O. Box 590359 ■ San Francisco, CA 94159
Gerardo Joffe, President

FLAME is a tax-exempt, non-profit educational 501 (c)(3) organization. Its purpose is the research and publication of the facts regarding developments in the Middle East and exposing false propaganda that might harm the interests of the United States and its allies in that area of the world. Your tax-deductible contributions are welcome. They enable us to pursue these goals and to publish these messages in national newspapers and magazines. We have virtually no overhead. Almost all of our revenue pays for our educational work, for these clarifying messages, and for related direct mail.

116

Ad published in Jewish media outlets, produced by Facts and Logic About the Middle East (FLAME)

TEXT 13a

LEVITICUS 18:5

וּשְׁמַרְתֶּם אֶת חֻקֹּתַי וְאֶת מִשְׁפָּטַי, אֲשֶׁר יַעֲשֶׂה אֹתָם הָאָדָם וָחַי בָּהֶם.

Observe My decrees and laws, for the person who obeys them will live by them.

TEXT 13b

TALMUD, YOMA 85B

"וָחַי בָּהֶם", וְלֹא שֶׁיָּמוּת בָּהֶם.

"Live by them"; do not die because of them.

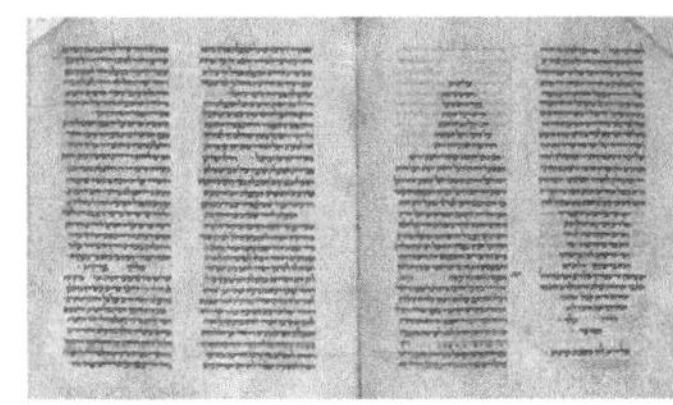

BABYLONIAN TALMUD

A literary work of monumental proportions that draws upon the legal, spiritual, intellectual, ethical, and historical traditions of Judaism. The 37 tractates of the Babylonian Talmud contain the teachings of the Jewish sages from the period after the destruction of the 2nd Temple through the 5th century CE. It has served as the primary vehicle for the transmission of the Oral Law and the education of Jews over the centuries; it is the entry point for all subsequent legal, ethical, and theological Jewish scholarship.

TEXT 13c

RABBI YOSEF YITSCHAK SCHNEERSOHN, CITED IN *HAYOM YOM*, 10 SHEVAT

אִמִּי זְקֶנְתִּי (הָרַבָּנִית מָרַת רִבְקָה נ"ע) בִּהְיוֹתָהּ כְּבַת שְׁמוֹנֶה עֶשְׂרֵה שָׁנָה - בִּשְׁנַת תרי"א - חָלְתָה, וְצִיוָּה הָרוֹפֵא אֲשֶׁר תֹּאכַל תֵּיכֶף בְּקוּמָהּ מִשְּׁנָתָהּ, אָמְנָם הִיא לֹא חָפְצָה לִטְעוֹם קוֹדֶם הַתְּפִלָּה, וְהָיְתָה מִתְפַּלֶּלֶת בְּהַשְׁכָּמָה וְאַחַר הַתְּפִלָּה הָיְתָה אוֹכֶלֶת פַּת שַׁחֲרִית.

כְּשֶׁנּוֹדַע הַדָּבָר לְחוֹתְנָהּ אדמו"ר הַצֶּמַח צֶדֶק, אָמַר לָהּ: "אַ אִיד דאַרְף זַיין געֶזוּנְד אוּן אַ בַּעַל כֹּחַ. אוֹיף מִצְוֹת שְׁטֵייט 'וָחַי בָּהֶם', אִיז דעֶר טַייטְשׁ וָחַי בָּהֶם, מעֶן דאַרְף אַרַיינְבְּרֵיינְגעֶן אַ חַיוּת אִין מִצְוֹת. בִּכְדֵי אַז מעֶן זאָל קעֶנעֶן אַרַיינְבְּרֵיינְגעֶן אַ חַיוּת אִין מִצְוֹת, מוּז מעֶן זַיין אַ בַּעַל כֹּחַ אוּן זַיין בְּשִׂמְחָה". וְסִיֵּים: "דוּ דאַרְפְסְט נִיט זַיין קֵיין נִיכְטעֶרעֶ. בְּעֶסעֶר עֶסעֶן צוּלִיב דאַוועֶנעֶן וִוי דאַוועֶנעֶן צוּלִיב עֶסעֶן". וּבֵירְכָהּ בַּאֲרִיכוּת יָמִים (נוֹלְדָה בִּשְׁנַת תקצ"ג וְנִפְטְרָה י' שְׁבָט תרע"ד).

When my grandmother, Rebbetzin Rivkah, of blessed memory, was eighteen years old (in 1851), she fell ill, and the physician ordered her to eat immediately upon awakening. As she did not wish to eat before morning prayers, she began praying earlier in the morning and then following this she would eat.

When her father-in-law, the *Tsemach Tsedek* [the third Chabad rebbe], learned of this, he said to her: "A Jew must be healthy and strong. The Torah says regarding *mitzvot*: 'Live by them.' [This verse] can also be interpreted to mean that we must infuse our *mitzvot* with life and vitality. To do so, one must be strong and joyful." He concluded: "You should not go without food. Better to

RABBI YOSEF YITSCHAK SCHNEERSOHN (RAYATS, FRIERDIKER REBBE, PREVIOUS REBBE) 1880–1950

Chasidic rebbe, prolific writer, and Jewish activist. Rabbi Yosef Yitschak, the 6th leader of the Chabad movement, actively promoted Jewish religious practice in Soviet Russia and was arrested for these activities. After his release from prison and exile, he settled in Warsaw, Poland, from where he fled Nazi occupation, and arrived in New York in 1940. Settling in Brooklyn, Rabbi Schneersohn worked to revitalize American Jewish life. His son-in law, Rabbi Menachem Mendel Schneerson, succeeded him as the leader of the Chabad movement.

eat in order to pray than to pray in order to eat." He then gave her a blessing for longevity. (She was born in 1833 and passed away in 1914).

Palestinians who had fled the war zone into Jordan crossing back into Israel over the Allenby Bridge, August 1967. (Photo credit: Magnum Photos; Micha Bar Am, photographer)

KEY POINTS

1 The "two-state solution" is a widely endorsed diplomatic solution for the Palestinian-Israeli conflict, with broad international support.

2 Various Torah laws and values have bearing on the permissibility of territorial concessions. From the halachic perspective, however, the overriding factor is the potential for *piku'ach nefesh* (danger to human life): If territorial concessions put lives at risk, it is forbidden; if territorial concessions save lives, then it is compulsory.

3 Non-*piku'ach-nefesh* arguments—such as ideological and demographic considerations, political or economic fallout, international standing, etc.—cannot override *piku'ach nefesh* considerations.

4 Present and immediate *piku'ach nefesh* overrides potential *piku'ach nefesh* in the future.

5 We turn to Israel's security experts with all questions relating to national security.

6 Israel must do its utmost to protect all lives, as well as seek to ease the plight of the Arabs under its control and provide for their needs.

7 "Land for peace" is a polarizing issue, one that causes rifts in the Jewish community. We must strive to genuinely listen to one another and appreciate the valid points that each side brings to the table, and thereby increase Jewish unity and mutual respect.

Appendix

TEXT 14

UNITED NATIONS SECURITY COUNCIL RESOLUTION 242, NOVEMBER 22, 1967

The Security Council,

Expressing its continuing concern with the grave situation in the Middle East,

Emphasizing the inadmissibility of the acquisition of territory by war and the need to work for a just and lasting peace in which every State in the area can live in security,

Emphasizing further that all Member States in their acceptance of the Charter of the United Nations have undertaken a commitment to act in accordance with Article 2 of the Charter,

1. *Affirms* that the fulfilment of Charter principles requires the establishment of a just and lasting peace in the Middle East which should include the application of both the following principles:

    (i) Withdrawal of Israel armed forces from territories occupied in the recent conflict;

    (ii) Termination of all claims or states of belligerency and respect for and acknowledgment of the sovereignty, territorial integrity and political independence of every State in the area and their right to live in peace within secure and recognized boundaries free from threats or acts of force;

2. *Affirms further* the necessity

   (a) For guaranteeing freedom of navigation through international waterways in the area;

   (b) For achieving a just settlement of the refugee problem;

   (c) For guaranteeing the territorial inviolability and political independence of every State in the area, through measures including the establishment of demilitarized zones;

3. *Requests* the Secretary-General to designate a Special Representative to proceed to the Middle East to establish and maintain contacts with the States concerned in order to promote agreement and assist efforts to achieve a peaceful and accepted settlement in accordance with the provisions and principles in this resolution;

4. *Requests* the Secretary-General to report to the Security Council on the progress of the efforts of the Special Representative as soon as possible.

Adopted unanimously at the 1382nd meeting.

Exercise 3

Consider the four arguments presented in Lesson One—Historical, International Law, Jewish Survival, and Biblical—to demonstrate the rightful claim of the Jewish nation to the Land of Israel. Which of them apply to the territories that Israel conquered during the Six-Day War?

	APPLICABLE	NON-APPLICABLE
Historical		
Jewish Survival		
International Law		
Biblical		

TEXT 15

MOSHE YAALON, "RESTORING A SECURITY-FIRST PEACE POLICY," *ISRAEL'S CRITICAL REQUIREMENTS FOR DEFENSIBLE BORDERS* (JERUSALEM: JERUSALEM CENTER FOR PUBLIC AFFAIRS, 2014), P. 13

Israel's situation prior to 1967 made it a "sitting duck" for enemy attack. Today, with all the new weaponry and technological developments available to its enemies—and with Hamas located approximately 70 km. from Tel Aviv—for Israel to revert to having a 14-km. waistline (the distance from Tulkarem to Netanya) would make it not only more vulnerable and inviting of attack, but virtually indefensible. Israel must be able to prevent hostile military forces and terror groups emanating from within and via a prospective Palestinian state from attacking Israel's narrow waistline, especially during a crisis that draws a large proportion of the IDF away from Israeli territory, such as into Lebanon or Syria.

MOSHE YAALON
1950–

Israeli army general and politician. Born and raised in Israel, Yaalon rose through the Israeli army ranks and served as IDF Chief of Staff from 2002–2005. After his military service, Yaalon joined the Likud party and served as Israel's Defense Minister from 2013–2016.

It must be emphasized that there are many unknowns when it comes to the future security of the Middle East and the stability of the regimes bordering Israel. This will become an especially grave concern should Iran achieve a nuclear weapons capability. Such a dramatic shift in the regional balance of power could destabilize Sunni regimes or compel them to cut deals with their new masters in Tehran that would compel them to join Iran in support of terror organizations. The terror groups themselves will be emboldened by their new nuclear patron and will speak about having acquired a protective nuclear umbrella for their attacks. Meanwhile, Hizbullah and Hamas are acquiring weapons with increasing range and lethality.

These terror groups are already penetrating land and sea barriers that had previously prevented states like Iran and Syria from transferring sophisticated weaponry. Israel must have robust borders in order to meet these possible challenges, including the threat of nonconventional attack, which cannot be ruled out. Israel is not alone in confronting these dangers, either currently or historically. The United States risked nuclear war to prevent the Soviet Union from deploying nuclear missiles 90 miles from its southern shore.

Israel's retaining control over its borders will make it more difficult for terror groups to use the territory of Israel's neighbors as a staging area for attacks. This will not only enhance Israel's security, but also the stability of neighboring governments and even distant Sunni regimes in the region. It is in the interest of all these actors for Israel to maintain defensible borders.

TEXT 16

UZI DAYAN, "DEFENSIBLE BORDERS TO ENSURE ISRAEL'S FUTURE," *ISRAEL'S CRITICAL REQUIREMENTS FOR DEFENSIBLE BORDERS* (JERUSALEM: JERUSALEM CENTER FOR PUBLIC AFFAIRS, 2014), PP. 35–37

Today it is often forgotten how vulnerable Israel was in the past. Before 1967 Israel's "narrow waist"—that is, the distance between the coastal cities of its central region and the West Bank under Jordanian occupation—was only about 8 miles (12 km.), not enough for minimal defensive depth in case of an invasion. Israel is a country about the size of New Jersey with a territory of only 16,100 square miles (25,900 sq. km.). Israel's small size alone is not the basis for its claim to defensible borders, but rather the fact that it has been a repeated victim of aggression caused the international community to recognize that right in the aftermath of the Six-Day War.

UZI DAYAN
1948–

Israeli army general. Born and raised in Israel, Dayan began his IDF service in 1966. He served as commander of the elite *Sayeret Matkal* commando unit and rose to the position of Deputy Chief of Staff. After his military service, Dayan served as chairman of Israel's National Security Council.

Israel's vulnerability is made all the more acute by the fact that 70 percent of the country's population, 80 percent of its industrial capacity, and crucial infrastructure targets (Ben-Gurion Airport, the Trans-Israel Highway [Route 6], the National Water Carrier, and high-voltage electrical power lines) are squeezed into that narrow coastal strip between the Mediterranean Sea and the West Bank. Moreover, the adjacent hills of the West Bank topographically dominate the low-lying and exposed coastal plain, affording an attacker clear advantages in terms of observation, fire, and defensive capability against an Israeli counterattack.

Thus the 1949 armistice lines were indefensible, leading the architects of Israel's national security doctrine, from Yigal Allon to Moshe Dayan to Yitzhak Rabin, to adamantly oppose a return to those lines, which they believed would invite aggression and endanger Israel's future instead of paving a path to peace.

TEXT 17

AHARON ZE'EVI FARKASH, "KEY PRINCIPLES OF A DEMILITARIZED PALESTINIAN STATE," *ISRAEL'S CRITICAL REQUIREMENTS FOR DEFENSIBLE BORDERS* (JERUSALEM: JERUSALEM CENTER FOR PUBLIC AFFAIRS, 2014), PP. 68–69

Israel is likely to face two main scenarios in the wake of the establishment of a Palestinian state, and in light of prevailing trends in the Middle East:

In the first scenario, the Palestinian state-in-formation would be a failed one, that serves as a convenient base for the development of terrorist infrastructures, as transpired in Gaza following Israel's 2005 unilateral withdrawal.

Such a situation would pose an ongoing challenge for Israel, which would likely face repeated assaults by terror squads attempting to penetrate its border, or by high-trajectory rockets launched into its heartland, as occurred following Israel's withdrawal from the territory. Hamas

AHARON ZE'EVI FARKASH
1948–

Israeli army general. Born in Romania, Farkash made *aliyah* to Israel in 1962 and began his IDF service in 1966. He served in military intelligence and was director of the Military Intelligence Directorate from 2001–2006.

rocket attacks on Israeli towns and cities increased by more than 500 percent between 2005 and 2006. In all likelihood, then, a withdrawal from the West Bank would lead to repeated armed confrontations, making it extremely difficult for Israelis to go about their daily lives, and severely hindering the implementation of peace agreements.

In the second scenario, involving the entire region, the threat to Israel would develop to the east of the Palestinian state, and Palestinian territory would be used as a base from which to attack Israel. Islamic radicalism would provide the context for this type of threat. The Iranian regime is on the verge of acquiring nuclear capabilities and already possesses ballistic missile capabilities that currently threaten Israel, its Arab neighbors, Russia and parts of Europe. The Islamic Revolutionary Guard Corps that controls Iran's most sensitive weapons systems, including its nuclear program, provides a strategic umbrella for the radical groups it mobilizes as proxies across the Middle East, from radical Shiite militias in Iraq and Hizbullah in Lebanon to Hamas and Palestinian Islamic Jihad in Gaza and the West Bank.

TEXT 18

UDI DEKEL, "CONTROL OF TERRITORIAL AIRSPACE AND THE ELECTROMAGNETIC SPECTRUM," *ISRAEL'S CRITICAL REQUIREMENTS FOR DEFENSIBLE BORDERS* (JERUSALEM: JERUSALEM CENTER FOR PUBLIC AFFAIRS, 2014), PP. 85–87

During the Camp David Summit in the summer of 2000, American military experts raised the question of whether the Israeli demand for control of a unified airspace over all the territory between the Mediterranean Sea and the Jordan River was essential. Among the justifications provided by Israeli representatives were the dangers of aerial terrorism. The Israelis explained the need to be prepared in the event of a suicide attack—carried out by a civilian aircraft laden with explosives—over a major Israeli urban center. One of the Americans present responded to this with disdain, asserting that the Israelis had a vivid imagination when it came to implausible threats, which they employed to justify exaggerated security demands.

UDI DEKEL
1957–

Israeli army general. Born and raised in Israel, Dekel began his IDF service in 1975. He served in various positions in military intelligence, rising to the rank of Brigadier General. Following his military service, Dekel was appointed by Prime Minister Ehud Olmert to head Israel's team for peace negotiations with the Palestinians. He is currently a researcher at the Jerusalem Center for Public Affairs.

A year later, on September 11, 2001, al-Qaeda sent airliners plunging into the World Trade Center in New York and the Pentagon in Washington, D.C., causing the death of thousands of people and illustrating the importance of creative thinking in assessing terrorist and national-security threat scenarios.

Such thinking is especially crucial for Israel, whose geography puts it at high military risk, in general, and at a great disadvantage in terms of its ability to prevent or respond to attacks from the air, in particular. . . .

This aerial threat creates a great defense challenge for Israel. It takes at least three minutes for a scramble takeoff of an interceptor aircraft that can identify such a potential enemy penetration—and this is without factoring in the flight time from the airbase until the interceptor engages the penetrating aircraft to identify it, or shoot it down if it is on a hostile mission.

In the event of an aerial attack aimed at Jerusalem, the hostile plane must be shot down at least 10 nautical miles east of the city—not directly over it. Otherwise, both the plane and its munitions would crash into population centers, with dire consequences.

In recent years, in addition to hostile planes, Israel must contend with unmanned aerial vehicles (UAVs), which pose more complex threats to Israel's security. According to reports, Iran has been developing a fleet of UAVs. Iranian technology is continuously improving, so the threat of an unmanned aircraft being launched from Iran towards Israel must be taken into account. Moreover, Iran has supplied UAVs to its proxy ally—Hizbullah, which in a future scenario could launch unmanned aircraft toward Israel not only from Lebanon, but also via Jordan and a future Palestinian state. This new route would enable them to fly undetected until they penetrate

Israel's major cities and strategic infrastructure. Most troublesome yet, the rapid and continuous advances in technology in this field have already put small drones within the reach of any terrorist organization. A civilian drone, purchased for a few thousands of dollars online, can easily be converted into a lethal weapon by fitting it to carry explosives and shrapnel and crashing it into a crowded street. Such an aircraft, if launched from the Jordanian border, could reach Israel within minutes.

TEXT 19a

TALMUD, ERUVIN 45A

נָכְרִים שֶׁצָּרוּ עַל עֲיָירוֹת יִשְׂרָאֵל, אֵין יוֹצְאִין עֲלֵיהֶם בִּכְלֵי זַיְינָן וְאֵין מְחַלְּלִין עֲלֵיהֶן אֶת הַשַּׁבָּת . . . בַּמֶּה דְּבָרִים אֲמוּרִים? כְּשֶׁבָּאוּ עַל עִסְקֵי מָמוֹן. אֲבָל בָּאוּ עַל עִסְקֵי נְפָשׁוֹת, יוֹצְאִין עֲלֵיהֶן בִּכְלֵי זַיְינָן וּמְחַלְּלִין עֲלֵיהֶן אֶת הַשַּׁבָּת.

וּבְעִיר הַסְּמוּכָה לַסְּפָר, אֲפִילוּ לֹא בָּאוּ עַל עִסְקֵי נְפָשׁוֹת אֶלָּא עַל עִסְקֵי תֶּבֶן וְקַשׁ, יוֹצְאִין עֲלֵיהֶן בִּכְלֵי זַיְינָן וּמְחַלְּלִין עֲלֵיהֶן אֶת הַשַּׁבָּת.

If Gentiles besiege Jewish cities, we do not initiate a military offensive against them, nor do we desecrate the Shabbat [to prepare a defense]. . . . This rule applies if the enemy's goal is solely monetary; if, however, they threaten lives, we initiate a military offensive against them, and we desecrate the Shabbat if necessary.

If the city abuts the border, even if the enemy does not seek to take any lives, rather, they only want to plunder straw and hay, we initiate a military offensive even if this entails desecrating the Shabbat.

TEXT 19b

RABBI YITSCHAK BEN MOSHE, *OR ZARU'A*, VOL. 2, LAWS OF SHABBAT, CH. 84

וְטַעֲמָא דְמִילְתָא, שֶׁמָא יִלְכְּדוּהָ וּמִשָּׁם תְּהֵא נוֹחָה לִיכְבֹּשׁ כָּל הָאָרֶץ לִפְנֵיהֶם.

Halachah views a city alongside the border differently for fear that if the enemy conquers it, it will be a launching pad that will allow them to conquer the entire land with greater ease.

RABBI YITSCHAK BEN MOSHE OF VIENNA CA. 1180–1250

Student of the German tosafists. His fame stems primarily from his influential halachic work and commentary to the Talmud, *Or Zaru'a*, which was subsequently quoted by many halachic authorities. His son Rabbi Chaim wrote a compendium of his father's work, which for many generations was the only widely used version of the *Or Zaru'a*. In the 19th century, the original work was found and published. Among his students was the Maharam of Rothenburg.

Additional Readings

LAND FOR PEACE

LETTERS BY THE LUBAVITCHER REBBE TO U.K. CHIEF RABBI, LORD IMMANUEL JAKOBOVITS

I am completely and unequivocally opposed to the surrender of any of the liberated areas currently under negotiation, such as Yehudah and Shomron, the Golan, etc., for the simple reason, and only reason, that surrendering any part of them would contravene a clear Psak-Din in Shulchan Aruch (Orach Chayim, sec. 329, par. 6, 7). I have repeatedly emphasized that this Psak-Din has nothing to do with the sanctity of Eretz Yisroel, or with "days of Moshiach," the Geula, and similar considerations, but solely with the rule of Pikuach-Nefesh. This is further emphasized by the fact that this Psak-Din has its source in the Talmud (Eiruvin 45a), where the Gemora cites as an illustration of a "border-town" under the terms of this Psak-Din—the city of Neharde'a in Babylon (present-day Iraq)—clearly not in Eretz Yisroel. I have emphasized time and time again that it is a question of, and should be judged purely on the basis of, Pikuach-Nefesh, not geography.

The said Psak-Din deals with a situation where gentiles (the term is *goyim* [nations], not enemies) besiege a Jewish border-town, ostensibly to obtain "straw and hay," and then leave. But because of the possible danger, not only to the Jews of the town, but also to other cities, the Shulchan Aruch rules that upon receiving news of the gentiles (even only preparations), the Jews must mobilize immediately and take up arms even on Shabbos—in accordance with the rule that "Pikuach-Nefesh supersedes Shabbos." Should there be a question whether the risk does in fact create a situation of Pikuach-Nefesh, then—as in the case of illness, where a medical authority is consulted—the authority to make a judgment is vested in the military experts. If military experts decide that there is a danger of Pikuach-Nefesh, there could be no other overriding considerations, since Pikuach-Nefesh overrides everything else. Should the military experts declare that while there is such a risk, yet it should be taken for some other reason, such as political considerations (good will of the gentiles)—this would clearly be contrary to the Psak-Din, for the Psak-Din requires that Pikuach-Nefesh, not political expediency, should be the decisive factor.

Now in regard to the liberated areas, all military experts, Jewish and non-Jewish, agree that in the present situation giving up any part of them would create serious security dangers. No-one says that giving up any part of them would enhance the defensibility of the borders. But some military experts are prepared to take a chance in order not to antagonize Washington and/or to improve the "International image," etc. To follow this line would not only go against the clear Psak-Din, but would also ignore costly lessons of the past. One glaring case in point is "the Yom Kippur War." Days and hours before the attack, there were urgent sessions of the government discussing the situation with the military. Military intelligence pointed to unmistakable evidence that an Egyptian attack was imminent, and the military experts advised a preemptive strike that would save many lives and prevent an invasion. However, the politicians, with the acquiescence of some military experts, rejected this action on

THE LUBAVITCHER REBBE, 1902–1994

The towering Jewish leader of the 20th century, known as "the Lubavitcher Rebbe," or simply as "the Rebbe." Born in southern Ukraine, the Rebbe escaped Nazi-occupied Europe, arriving in the U.S. in June 1941. The Rebbe inspired and guided the revival of traditional Judaism after the European devastation, impacting virtually every Jewish community the world over. The Rebbe often emphasized that the performance of just one additional good deed could usher in the era of Mashiach. The Rebbe's scholarly talks and writings have been printed in more than 200 volumes.

the ground that such a step, or even a general mobilization, before the Egyptians actually crossed the border, would mean being branded as the aggressor, and would jeopardize relations with the USA. This decision was contrary to the said Psak-Din of the Shulchan Aruch, as pointed out above. The tragic results of that decision bore out the validity of the Shulchan Aruch's position (as if it were necessary), for many lives were needlessly sacrificed, and the situation came close to total disaster, but for G-d's mercies. Suffice it to mention that the then Prime Minister later admitted that all her life she would be haunted by that tragic decision.

I know, of course, that there are Rabbis who are of the opinion that in the present situation, as they see it, it would be permissible from the viewpoint of the Shulchan Aruch to return areas from Eretz Yisroel. But it is also known on what information they based this view. One argument is that the present situation is not identical with the hypothetical case of a state of "being besieged by gentiles." A second argument is that the present surrendering of some areas would not endanger lives.

That these arguments are based on misinformation is patently clear. The Arab neighbors are prepared militarily; what is more, they do demand these areas as theirs to keep, and openly declare that if not surrendered voluntarily, they will take them by force, and eventually everything else. A Rabbi who says that the said Psak-Din of the Shulchan Aruch does not apply in the present situation is completely misinformed on what the situation actually is.

A further example of how facts can be publicly distorted is in connection with the surrender of the oil wells in Sinai. Some warned at that time that it would be a terrible mistake to give them up, since oil, in this day and age, is an indispensable vital weapon, for without it planes and tanks are put out of action as surely as if they had been knocked out. Nevertheless, there were Rabbis that defended the surrender of the oil wells—again having received and accepted the "information" that the country has ample oil reserves that would last for months. When it was suggested to them to verify this information with anyone who has some idea about the physical limitations of storing oil to build up reserves—especially in a small country with limited storage space—the suggestion was ignored. Sure enough, before long the Government found it necessary to demand from the USA urgent oil deliveries, because the reserves would last only a few days. Moreover, prominent members of the Government publicly admitted that it was a serious mistake to have surrendered the oil wells.

Be it also noted that since the surrender of the oil wells in Sinai—according to the Government's figures—some 2.5 billion dollars was paid by it to Egypt for oil from the very same wells that had been surrendered. Not to mention the fact of having to buy oil also in the spot market, all at exorbitant prices.

I was taken to task for placing so much emphasis on the security of Eretz Yisroel, the argument being that what has protected the Jewish people during the long Golus has been the study of Torah and the practice of Mitzvos; hence Torah-observant Jews should not make the inviolability of Eretz Yisroel as the overriding cause. I countered that they missed the point, for my position has nothing to do with Eretz Yisroel as such, but with the Pikuach-Nefesh of the Jews living there—which would apply to any part of the world.

It is said that my pronouncements on the issues are more political than Rabbinic. Inasmuch as the matter has to do with Pikuach-Nefesh, it is surely the duty of every Jew, be he Rabbi or layman, to do all permitted by the Shulchan Aruch to help forestall—or, at any rate, minimize—the danger. In a case of Pikuach-Nefesh, every possible effort must be made, even if there is a *safek* (doubt) and many doubts whether the effort will succeed.

*Chief Rabbi Jakobovits raised objections which are indicated with an * and were answered by the Rebbe as foll[ows].*

The only subject matter under discussion—at any rate, from my treatment of it—is the purely Halachic subject of Pikuach-Nefesh as it affects the question of returning any part of the liberated areas. Be it also remembered that we are not dealing with an academic question, but one of actuality and urgency, since definite action has been taken in regard to some areas (in Sinai), and as regards others (Yehudah, Shomron, Golan, etc.) commitments have been made, and some of them would have probably been surrendered long ago, but for the fact that the other side refused to take them, demanding more.

Since the subject matter, as noted, is purely Halachic, namely the question of Pikuach-Nefesh, the sanctity of the territories is irrelevant; so is irrelevant one's political affiliation or philosophy, or one's personal attitude to the Government, and the like. A Rabbi has to rule on the matter purely from the objective viewpoint of the Halachah, without allowing any other considerations or opinions, however strongly he may feel about them, to change, G-d forbid or to cloud his Halachic judgment.

> *There are Rabbis who have reached the same conclusion regarding the Territories precisely because of the sanctity of Eretz Yisroel.

I have stated repeatedly that my unequivocal stand against returning any part of Yehudah and Shomron, etc. is the same as on returning the Sinai oil wells, and any part of Sinai. Even those Rabbis who "reached the same conclusion on the territories precisely because of the sanctity of Eretz Yisroel" will admit that there is no question of sanctity involved in regard to Sinai and Sinai oil, but it is only a question of Pikuach-Nefesh, plain and simple.

> *Everyone agrees that "Pikuach-Nefesh supersedes Shabbos" as well as any other consideration. For this teaching we do not require the "Straw and Hay" rule. The argument among the Rabbis, as among others, is not about this teaching or this rule, but on what constitutes "Pikuach-Nefesh" in the present situation.

The contention that "the argument among Rabbis ... is not about (the rule of Pikuach-Nefesh), but on what constitutes Pikuach-Nefesh in the present situation" is true, of course. I already addressed that point in my previous letter, though I did not wish to overemphasize it, for obvious reasons. I pointed out that the other Rabbis based their evaluation of the present situation on misinformation presented to them together with the Shailah. I cited one glaring example of misinformation in that the Rabbis were told that the Government had ample oil reserves to last for months. Another item of misinformation was that the situation in Eretz Yisroel was described to them as not being comparable with the situation that the Gemora in Eiruvin speaks of, where the enemy is actually besieging the Jews, and there is the danger of further penetration. This is obviously a misrepresentation, for everybody knows that the Golan, Shomron and Yehudah are the very borders with Syria and Jordan, which are under strong influence of the PLO, etc. These avowed enemies are not only besieging Eretz Yisroel, but have actually carried out bloody attacks, and openly declared their determined intention to take everything back by force. A further "distinction" between the existing situation and that of the Gemora on which the opinion of those Rabbis was partially formulated was that in the case of the Gemora situation the enemy came to take "hay and straw" that belonged to Jews, whereas in the present situation, the enemy is demanding the return of territories that had been taken from them. This argument, too, has been published, and not anonymously.

Of course, I am not debating with those that believe that the Arabs have a legitimate Torah claim for the return of territories that "belong to them," because there is no common ground on which to debate. But, they should surely keep in mind that if the Arabs have a legitimate claim to the pre-'67 territories, they have an equally legitimate claim to the Old City. To be sure, "a Dayan must rule on the basis of testimony before his eyes"; but the public is entitled to know precisely on what arguments and reasons he arrived at his decision, and this is something one is entitled to know even If the Psak-Din concerns one Pruta, not to mention the Pikuach-Nefesh of three million Jews, and if there has been an error of facts, a Dayan should readily retract.

The Rabbis who declared that territories may be surrendered "for peace" based their opinion, among other things, on the information supplied to them (not by military experts) that territorial concessions would advance the cause of peace with the Arabs. Hence, they argued that the principle of Pikuach-Nefesh that is at the root of the "Straw and Hay" rule is not relevant to the situation at hand, but to the contrary.

Actually, it is clear from the said Halachah that the deciding factor is not what the enemy demands or promises, but whether it is a case of תפתח הארץ לעמהם—opening the land before the enemy; in other words, giving them an opportunity to breach the defenses. Whether or not the return of territories would indeed be such a case is, of course, for the military experts to decide, and not for politicians.

The fate of Israel and the lives of its Jews depend just as much on factors beyond the competence of military experts. For instance, Jewish lives could be endangered by sanctions or economic collapse leading to starvation; or by Arabs becoming a majority, by retaining over a million Arabs within Israel multiplying at twice the Jewish rate; or by a dramatic decline in the Jewish population through mass-emigration, itself caused by political and economic factors as well as the despair on the prospect of peace. Hence the opinion of political and other experts can have no lesser bearing on defining "Pikuach-Nefesh" than purely military calculations.

To argue that the fate of the country and the lives of the people depend also on factors beyond the competence of military experts, and that if political and economic factors will be ignored, it would lead to Pikuach-Nefesh later on, does not affect the immediate decision in relation to the return of territories. All the more so since it is certain that returning further territories will immediately weaken security, and would be an irreversible act, whereas the political and economic climate is unpredictable. So are, by and large, the other arguments that "territorial concessions under certain conditions might reduce the threat of war, or enhance Israel's ability to defend itself," etc. These are highly speculative conjectures, and I am certain that no military commander would bet on such chances. I repeat, the Halachah is clear—and it is, after all, the viewpoint of Halachah that is at the heart of the debate.

*Surely, any G-d fearing Jew, let alone Rabbi, must affirm that the ultimate security of Jews in the Land of Israel lies neither in armies nor in borders but in our spiritual worthiness through "the study of Torah and the practice of Mitzvos," and that this must be our over-riding and most urgent aim as well as the principal teaching of all Rabbis, as confirmed by the whole of our sources and our history.

Of course, every G-d fearing Jew must affirm that the security of Jews anywhere in the world, particularly in the Holy Land, lies with the study of the Torah and the practice of Mitzvos. But, when it comes to a question of Pikuach-Nefesh, as indeed in any situation, be it a matter of health or Parnossah, G-d Himself ordained that in addition to the strict observance of Torah and Mitzvos and absolute Bitochon in Him, a Jew is required to do what is necessary in the natural order of things. This, too, is part of the teachings of Rabbis.

Summary

1. The subject matter of the controversy centers on a Shailoh in Halachah, namely Pikuach Nefesh. Therefore, the position of both the Rabbis whose opinion differs from mine, as well as my position, must rest exclusively on the Halachah and treated purely as a Halachah-Shailoh.

2. The Shailoh is not a theoretical one, but a practical one that is high on the actual agenda, namely, whether—from the Halachah view—it is permitted, mandatory, or forbidden to return liberated areas in the so-called West Bank and Gaza, as well as in Sinai, including oil wells, military installations, etc. The Psak-Din on this Shailoh must, of course, be based on the actual and factual circumstances of the situation as they affect the security of Eretz Yisroel and of our brethren living there.

3. Both sides in the controversy, namely the Rabbis who ruled that it is Halachically permissible to make territorial concessions and those (myself included) who oppose this view, based their decisions on the principle of Pikuach Nefesh; the difference being that the former concluded that territorial concessions would avert or minimize Pikuach Nefesh, while the latter hold that any territorial concessions would create or aggravate Pikuach Nefesh.

4. There can be no difference of opinion among Rabbis that in a case of Pikuach Nefesh it is the duty of a Rabbi not to remain silent and wait until approached

to express his opinion. A Rabbi who waits to be approached in such a situation is termed meguneh (reproachable, blameworthy). Similarly there can be no difference of opinion about the duty of every Jew, without exception, to do everything possible (consistent with the Shulchan Aruch) to avert the danger of Pikuach Nefesh. The Rabbi himself may not consider his duty done simply by pronouncing his Psak-Din, but must take every possible action in this direction. Indeed, there are many precedents of Gedolei Yisroel actually doing things on Shabbos and Yom Kippur which but for the fact of Pikuach Nefesh would be most serious transgressions.

5. Since, as noted, the sole deciding factor is Pikuach Nefesh, it is quite irrelevant what political orientation or party the Rabbi issuing the Psak-Din subscribes to, for his Psak-Din must not be influenced in the slightest by anything except the Halachah alone.

6. The evidence on which a Rabbi or Beth Din bases the Psak-Din must strictly conform to the principle of דן דין אמת לאמתו [judging a case with ultimate truth]—that is to say, the judgment must be based on true facts and on objective truth. If there is any doubt about the veracity of the presented evidence, it is the duty of the Rabbi or Beth Din to investigate and verify the facts and ascertain the real and complete truth; and upon discovery that the Psak-Din was based on a misrepresentation of the Shailoh or of the facts submitted to them, they must, of course, promptly retract the erroneous Psak-Din and rectify it.

SAGE AND STRATEGIST

ARIEL SHARON

My first connection with the Rebbe was shortly after the death of my son, when I received from him a warm and moving condolence letter, delivered to our home by the Chabad people.

I first met the Rebbe face-to-face in the beginning of '68. Those were the days of the War of Attrition fought against the Egyptians at the Suez Canal. There were heated debates in the General Command over the way the war was being conducted and the troop deployment. I insisted on a mobile defense, which would prevent the needless bloodletting of our soldiers deployed along the canal. Among the generals in the General Command only General Yisrael Tal and I opposed the stationary defense approach. The result: I was sent on a lengthy tour of duty outside the country, until my future in the army could be decided . . .

My travels around the world brought me to the United States and to my first meeting with the Rebbe, which was followed by many subsequent meetings through the years. I remember our first meeting. His penetrating steel-gray eyes and the incredible knowledge he exhibited in global affairs left an especially strong impression on me.

I was particularly impressed by his tremendous knowledge and deep understanding in strategic and military matters. I remember his conversations and his letters to me on the subject of Israel's defense strategy in the Sinai—a subject that deeply troubled me at the time, even before the Yom Kippur War.

ARIEL SHARON, 1928–2014

Israeli military commander and politician. As a soldier and then a commander, Sharon participated prominently in Israel's War of Independence, the 1956 Suez Crisis, the Six-Day War, and the Yom Kippur War. Sharon was considered one of the greatest military commanders and strategists in Israel's history. As Minister of Defense, Sharon directed the 1982 Lebanon War. Ariel Sharon eventually entered politics and served as Israel's prime minister from 2001–2006. Though generally known for his right-wing political stances, he ordered the Israeli withdrawal from Gaza in 2005.

The Rebbe compared the line of fortifications along the Suez Canal—the Bar-Lev Line—to the Maginot Line the French built before World War Two as a defense against a German invasion. The Rebbe predicted—not by prophecy, but by rational analysis of the cold facts—that the Bar-Lev Line would be ineffectual and would, in the end, spell great disaster for Israel.

By the same token, he reacted severely, and with grave concern, to the fact that Israel did not react to Egypt's most serious violation of the cease-fire—on the very first night after it went into effect—that ended the War of Attrition. In August of 1970, the Egyptians advanced their Ground-to-Air missile batteries up to the banks of the Suez Canal, in blatant violation of the cease-fire agreement. Indeed, these missile batteries prevented the Israeli Air Force from disrupting and stopping the canal crossing by the Egyptian armies in the first stages of the Yom Kippur War.

I remember well the Rebbe's emphatic and uncompromising stance—primarily from a security perspective—against giving up territories from the Land of Israel, and even expressing willingness to give over these territories. He pointed out the security risks in giving up the territories. He was especially opposed, following the Camp David summits, to giving up the Sinai Peninsula to Egypt. His arguments were anchored in a realistic strategic analysis, which doubted the readiness of the Arabs in general, and the Egyptians in particular, to truly accept the existence of an independent Jewish state. The "cold peace" we have now with the Egyptians, the threat posed by an Egyptian military greatly strengthened by advanced Western weaponry, the hostility and incitement in the Egyptian press and school curriculum—these trends the Rebbe accurately foresaw more than 20 years ago, at the height of the peace euphoria in Israel, when public figures and commentators in Israel unanimously spoke about the "historical revolution" in Israeli-Arab relations.

The common thread running through the Rebbe's strategic thinking was always his concern for the continuity of the Jewish people. I remember a conversation I had with him, at the time, regarding the opening of the gates of the Soviet Union to Jewish immigration to Israel. I said to the Rebbe that, in my opinion, we should perhaps increase the pressure on the Soviets, that Jews across the world, and in Israel, should be more active in applying pressure to advance the opening of the borders. I remember what he said to me in this regard. The Rebbe said that he believes that the day is not far when the gates will open; but in the same breath he added that if we won't act to further Jewish education and to foster the connection with Judaism amongst the Jews inside the Soviet Union, then even when the gates do open, it won't accomplish anything! The Rebbe was adamant: Jewish education, strengthening the connection to our Jewish roots, awareness of Jewish traditions—these should be the singular, universal goal that takes precedence over every other national endeavor. In all our illuminating discussions and meetings, the primary subject was always his concern for the future, destiny, honor and integrity of the Jewish people.

The Rebbe was very careful about taking a stance on issues that were controversial within the Jewish community, such as the settlement of Chabad Chassidim in the Old City of Jerusalem, in Hebron, and in Judea and Samaria, though many of his followers did settle in those areas. He wrote to me that it seems to him that the Israeli government is not interested in seeing Jewish settlement in these areas. But just as he was careful in regard to controversial issues, so was he determined and tireless in his work to deepen and broaden the Jewish education amongst the young across the world: sending teachers to virtually every place on earth where Jews live, opening Jewish schools in Russia, North Africa, South and Central America, and across the United States. His uniqueness was that he "practiced what he preached."

I was distinctly privileged to meet with, and get to know up close, an acclaimed personality such as the Rebbe: a one-of-a-kind sage in the wisdom of Israel, but also a far-seeing strategist, whose focus was on guaranteeing the continued existence and security of the Jewish people, wherever they may find themselves. In the Rebbe, the age-old wisdom of Israel and a penetrating understanding of the security issues confronting the Jewish people merged in a single unique personality. "I have grown wise from my many teachers," our Sages say, but I learned most of all from the Rebbe, who in addition to teaching me many lessons in the wisdom of Israel also taught me an illuminating lesson in the subject of the security of the Jewish people and how we should act to ensure that "the eternity of Israel shall not falter."

In these days of confusion and faint-heartedness amongst the general public, and particularly many of our people, the Rebbe's statesmanship and strategic vision, together with all his other teachings, are a wellspring of living waters: original and eye-opening in the intellectual desert that characterizes the present era.

"Sage and Strategist," The Rebbe.org

THE DANGERS OF UNILATERAL ISRAELI WITHDRAWAL FROM THE WEST BANK AND EASTERN JERUSALEM

HIRSH GOODMAN

Executive Summary

- The main political parties in Israel now agree that a negotiated peace agreement with the Palestinians based on two-states-for-two-peoples, by trading territory for peace, is not attainable at this time.
- This comes in the wake of the recognition that the Palestinians have opted for a "Plan B" based on doing everything and anything to avoid recognizing Israel as the legitimate state of the Jewish People while, at the same time, focusing on delegitimizing Israel and seeking to isolate Israel internationally.
- Labor's policy of "constructive unilateralism" entails a withdrawal from some 80–85 percent of the West Bank, including dozens of neighborhoods in eastern Jerusalem; enticing, through incentives and legislation, 80–100,000 Israeli residents to give up their homes in the areas to be vacated and move to Israel proper or the settlement blocs; the completion of the security barrier; and maintaining a military presence on the Jordan River.
- Israel has withdrawn unilaterally twice before: from Lebanon in 2000 and Gaza in 2005. The unintended consequences of both these cases far outweighed the assumptions and predictions made at the time and did not foresee the collateral damage caused in their wake. These included four full-scale wars, thousands of cross-border incidents, and the transformation of tactical problems into strategic ones, all of which have left deep and indelible scars on Israel.
- The unilateralists say that by withdrawing, Israel is taking its future into its own hands and ending the "Palestinian veto" over our lives. The opposite is true. By standing firm and not running in the face of adversity, Israel controls its own destiny, maximizes security and fully maintains the only cards it has with which to negotiate its future.
- The way to make peace is not by giving away assets, but maintaining them until the partner comes to the table to negotiate, in accordance with the obligations to which it is committed and pursuant to its existing agreements with Israel.
- In *"Israel's Strategy of Unilateral Withdrawal,"* published by the Institute for National Security Studies in June 2009, Dr. Shmuel Even writes: "In the end, the strategy of unilateral withdrawal caused Israel significant damage.... The strategy of unilateral withdrawal did not meet expectations because of some erroneous basic assumptions, estimates, and concepts that lay at the heart of the approach"—precisely the same mistakes about to be repeated by those now propagating a unilateral withdrawal from the West Bank.
- "When standing on the edge of a cliff, it is wiser to keep still than step forward," Maj.-Gen. (ret.) Yaakov Amidror, a former head of the Israel National Security Council, wrote in June 2016. "It is wiser to defer action than to take unilateral steps that threaten to make a bad situation worse."

Introduction

The political debate in Israel took a remarkable turn in early 2016: Both sides of the spectrum, the Likud and Labor, came into alliance for one of the few times in Israel's history, openly admitting that the goal of achieving a negotiated solution with the Palestinians, based on two states for two peoples, was unattainable—a mirage, at this point in time.

One of the reasons for this was that they saw the Palestinians adopt what is known as "Plan B"—a policy based on the assumption that the best way to promote Palestinian goals and interests is through unilateral and prolific international activity, and that this policy will best be served by perpetuating current realities: violent attrition, sporadic terror, delegitimization, and boycott, which would weaken Israel internationally and keep the territorial debate in Israel alive to divide and weaken the country internally.

This also helps the Palestinians paper over their own deficiencies, including a seismically divided leadership, endemic corruption, and suppression of internal democracy, while pointing the finger at Israel's occupation as the perpetrator and themselves as the victims.

The Palestinian goal, Israel's two main political parties now agree, is not a two-states-for-two-peoples solution, based on trading territory for peace. Two attempts at doing so, by Ehud Barak in 2000 and Ehud Olmert in 2008—whose offer included giving up Israeli sovereignty over Jerusalem's Holy Basin—failed miserably because, it is now believed, the Palestinians want it all and will do everything and anything to avoid recognizing Israel as the legitimate state of the Jewish People. They want an eventual one-state reality in which the Palestinians will be the majority and Israel will cease to be a Jewish democratic state.

Therefore, those who promote unilateralism say, Israel should take control of its future by creating a new reality on the ground and changing the status quo to what they consider to be Israel's advantage. "Constructive unilateralism," as it is termed, entails a unilateral withdrawal from some 80–85 percent of the West Bank, including dozens of villages in eastern Jerusalem; enticing, through incentives and legislation, 80–100,000 Israeli residents to give up their homes in the areas to be vacated and move to Israel proper or the settlement blocs; the completion of the security barrier; and maintaining a military presence on the Jordan River.

The unilateralists believe that the status quo cannot be maintained; that Jewish population growth in the territories will, if unchecked, create a situation that will make any future solution based on land-for-peace un-implementable and that, in consequence, the result would be, de facto, one state with a Palestinian majority and the demise of Israel as a Jewish democratic state.

Unilateralism, like Brexit, is a term that has far deeper implications than the seeming logic and simplicity of the concept implies. Israel has withdrawn unilaterally twice before: from Lebanon in 2000 and Gaza in 2005, in both cases from uncontested land over which Israel had no claims, and, in the case of Gaza, not seen as territorially relevant in the context of any future agreement between the sides.

In the end, the unintended consequences of both these cases far outweighed the assumptions and predictions made at the time and did not foresee the collateral damage caused in their wake. These included four full-scale wars, thousands of cross-border incidents, and the transformation of tactical problems into strategic ones, all of which have left deep and indelible scars on Israel.

Here, the proposal is for a unilateral and unconditional Israeli withdrawal from 80–85 percent of the West Bank, to which Israel *does* have claims, to a line recognized by no party other than Israel itself.

The proposal gives these vacated territories de facto recognition as legitimately Palestinian, whereas, in reality, they are still in dispute and held by Israel in accordance with international norms and conventions pending a settlement.

It unilaterally relinquishes, without any quid-pro-quo and contrary to broad national consensus, the unity of Jerusalem as Israel's undivided capital.

Without an Israeli security presence, the illicit Palestinian arms industry in the West Bank will flourish, and terrorism will become legitimized and encouraged. Key strategic Israeli targets, like neighborhoods in Jerusalem, or Kfar Saba and the entire center of Israel, including Ben-Gurion Airport, could be menaced and closed down at will by a primitive rocket fired from a hill a few kilometers away or by a shoulder-fired, anti-aircraft missile. Recapturing these territories would be problematic, and the re-establishment of a reliable Palestinian Authority would be impossible.

This will blow wind into the sails of those who advocate Palestinian struggle, not compromise. And to argue that a unilateral withdrawal from the West Bank and eastern Jerusalem will abate terror flies in the face of the realities following Israel's unilateral withdrawal from Lebanon and Gaza.

Without Israel there to anchor Fatah's control of the PA, Hamas will soon take over, central government will break down, and chaos and factional violence will emerge, impacting on Jordan (as the Gaza withdrawal did in the case of Egypt) and regional stability in general.

Here again, as with Lebanon and Gaza, the proposal projects Israeli weakness in the face of adversity and, in a twist of logic, advocates for the erection of a barrier between peoples in the hope that it brings them closer toward peace.

There is also the internal Israeli dimension. It does not take much to imagine the political and social consequences that a unilateral relocation—probably forced—of 100,000 Israeli citizens from their homes would cause in the country. If the Gaza evacuation was a tremor, this would be an earthquake. Prime Minister Ariel Sharon's government tried for nearly a year to induce Gaza's Jewish residents to leave with appalling results. Here the scales are multiplied many times over. Having to give up one's home in the context of a negotiated settlement by a representative government is one thing; doing so for nothing in return seems patently incomprehensible.

Those who oppose this thinking transcend the usual political borders in Israel. They range from those who cannot understand why Israel should give up negotiating cards for nothing in return, to those who think Israel has a right to all the land.

In the not-too-distant future, the Israeli electorate may be asked to vote on the issue. There is now a public campaign afoot for a referendum on the issue.

Few, however, no matter from which side of the political spectrum, will fully understand the concept placed before them, or the importance of its implications. This essay is intended to fill that gap.

The Labor Party and Unilateral Withdrawal from the West Bank

In February 2016, the Labor Party Congress unanimously voted to make a unilateral disengagement from the Palestinians a central pillar of its platform, the first change to the party's platform since 2002.

Behind the decision were two motives: a loss of hope that a two-state solution based on territorial compromise is currently attainable, and that the status quo on the West Bank is unsustainable.

Unless Israel takes its future into its own hands, they argue, to change the current dynamic, the status quo will ultimately lead to a one-state reality in which the Palestinians will be the majority, and Israel will be doomed as a Jewish democratic state.

They fear that the current government's policy of allowing settlement expansion based upon natural population growth will lead to an irreversible situation on the West Bank, leaving nothing to negotiate if the Palestinians ever decide to come to the table.

In the words of Isaac Herzog, the Labor Party leader, in explaining the rationale for the change in Labor's platform:

> Separation and the prevention of the reality of a bi-national state is a top priority for Israel.... The goal of separation from our neighbors, the Palestinians, is of such vital strategic importance that if talks fail we will have to consider a proactive initiative of our own....

We can all say two states, while, in practice, the situation is moving toward one state and nothing is being done about it.

Labor's policy of unilateral separation from the Palestinians was born out of failure, not ideology; frustration, not vision.

As explained by Amos Yadlin, a former head of IDF intelligence and Labor's defense minister-designate in the 2015 national elections, in a 2016 post for the Brookings Institution:

- Reaching an agreement (with the Palestinians) is harder today than it was in either 2000 or 2008. Even the moderates among the Palestinians are unwilling to concede a right of return, to acknowledge an "end of conflict and end of claims," to recognize Israel as a Jewish state, or to allow basic security arrangements that will ease Israel's justified concerns.
- It appears that in 2016, the Palestinians do not view a two-state solution, along the Clinton Parameters, as a preferred outcome. Instead, their discourse is rooted in a "return of rights" in historic Palestine as a whole (including Israel), in

accordance with both the Hamas and Palestine Liberation Organization (PLO) ...

- For the Palestinian leadership, all paths lead to the same destination: either Israel accepts their conditions (which, through flooding Israel with refugees, will lead to the demise of Israel as a Jewish state) or the status quo persists, and Israel is supposedly lost.[1]

Unilateralism is not new to Israel in its interaction with its neighbors. In May 2000, after being in office for less than a year, the Labor prime minister, Ehud Barak, withdrew all Israeli forces from Lebanon after a two-decade presence there.

In August 2005, Ariel Sharon, then the prime minister, unilaterally withdrew all Israeli forces and settlers from Gaza in a process that fractured Israel internally and led to the mass eviction of 8,000 settlers and the razing of 21 settlements.

The most comprehensive, and recent, outline of Labor's proposal, is as follows:

- Israel should present an initiative for a final agreement with the Palestinians, based on the Clinton Parameters: generous borders for a future Palestinian state, demilitarized Palestinian state and no compromises on Israeli security, a commitment to an end of conflict and end of claims, and a Palestinian relinquishment of implementing a "right of return."
- Should the (preferable) bilateral track fail, Israel should move to a regional track, including the moderate Arab states—led by Egypt, Saudi Arabia, and Jordan—in an effort to reach a final-status agreement.
- If the moderate Arab states are unwilling or unable to contribute, Israel can aim to secure interim agreements with the Palestinians.
- Interim agreements would necessitate abandoning the principle of "nothing is agreed until everything is agreed" and shifting the paradigm to a principle of gradual implementation of any area of agreement, deferring talks on more contentious subjects to a later time.
- Only if all these paths fail, Israel should embark on a long-term independent strategy for shaping its borders.
- This strategy should be innovative and creative, removing the effective veto Palestinians have over Israel's future.
- It would require as much coordination as possible with the United States and the international community.
- It would leave open the option for a return to the negotiating table and to a negotiated settlement and reinforces the agreed two-state solution paradigm.
- Likewise, this route undermines and prevents the most problematic outcomes, namely, the continuation of the status quo or a final agreement without an end of conflict and security arrangements, and the flooding of Israel with refugees.[2]

An independent Israeli strategy would therefore involve:

- Israel's willingness to hand over 80 to 85 percent of the West Bank—a willingness demonstrated by undertaking concrete steps on the ground.
- Israel would need to initiate further redeployments from the West Bank, not including the Jordan Valley, the "settlement blocs," and eastern Jerusalem.
- The transfer of Area B and much of Area C to full Palestinian responsibility.
- The full completion of the security barrier in areas that are currently lacking in order to provide Israel with a contiguous and defensible border.
- A full cessation of Israeli settlement construction beyond the declared lines.
- A plan, preferably under an agreement, to resettle Israelis living east of these lines into Israel-proper, preferably to the Galilee, the Negev, and the main settlements blocs.
- Responsibility for the security of Israel remaining in the hands of the Israel Defense Forces (IDF) and the proper Israeli authorities.

- Israel must preserve its capacity to conduct preventive action, hot pursuit, border control, and air security.
- However, the IDF must try to minimize such operations in the evacuated territories.

Amos Yadlin, the primary architect of the plan, wrote in 2016:

> This independent strategy would allow Israel to pursue a solution from a point of strength, rather than being dictated by outside forces or waves of terror. It represents a long-term, paradigm-changing option which would preserve the two-state solution while removing several of the most serious obstacles to such a solution.[3]

Past experience, however, seems to prove that assessment optimistic. In the pullbacks from both Lebanon and Gaza there was an inherent logic, but in neither case did expectations meet reality.

Instead, in both cases, as outlined in detail below, unintended consequences prevailed over intentions, as will be the case here, but only with greater and more permanent damage to Israel and its future.

The Flaws and Consequences of a Unilateral Withdrawal from the West Bank

At the foundation of the thinking of those who propose a unilateral withdrawal from large tracts of the West Bank is that the status quo is untenable, certainly undesirable; that creeping Israeli settlement there will create an irreversible situation, making a two-state solution impossible, if and when the Palestinians want to come to the table.

This, they argue, will inexorably lead to the end of Israel as a Jewish and democratic state.

They claim there is a need to end "the Palestinian veto" over Israel's future, and that it is time for Israel to take the initiative to protect the country's nature and values and to protect it physically.

They concede that past unilateral moves had unintended consequences, but argue that these were the fault of poor execution, rather than flaws in the concept itself, which they now want to repeat in a much more complex environment with far higher stakes involved.

The Flaws in the Assumption

- The status quo *is sustainable*, governed by accepted norms of international law, the Israeli judiciary and the still valid principles evolved from the Oslo Accords.
- If those favoring unilateral separation were to be elected, there would be no need to retreat, as they could stop settlement activity and thereby keep the two-state option alive.
- Israel has formally committed itself in the Oslo Accords not to alter the status of the areas in question. Hence the assumption that their status will be changed and incorporated by osmosis into Israel is incorrect.
- Thus, regardless of which government comes to power, the status quo remains open-ended and sustainable, without any long- or short-term threat to Israel demographically or democratically.
- The incumbent Palestinian Authority in the West Bank has control and authority over the areas it governs, in accordance with the Oslo Accords, administratively and legislatively, including internal security.
- The PLO, at its own volition, was declared a "non-member observer state" by the UN General Assembly on November 14, 2012.
- It is highly unlikely that Israel would annex these areas, and thus they pose no threat to Israel's Jewish or democratic identity.
- What remains in question, therefore, is not whether there is a Palestinian representative entity, but its final borders and internal political nature, neither of which Israel can resolve unilaterally.
- While the unilateralists assume they will be able to get international and Palestinian cooperation and recognition for their move, in reality, it will be seen as a unilateral Israeli land-grab of 20 percent of the West Bank, in contravention of Israel's commitments in the Oslo Accords and vis-à-vis the international community, and as a provocation by the Palestinians.
- And while the unilateralists claim their withdrawal will cement the reality of a

two-states-for-two-peoples solution in the future, tampering with the status quo will derail these efforts, convincing the Palestinians that Israel wants a barrier, not peace, between the sides.

The Consequences

Few would argue that the current situation on the West Bank is desirable. Lack of clarity between neighbors is always problematic. The solution, however, is not to be found in defeatism or panic.

"When standing on the edge of a cliff, it is wiser to keep still than step forward," Maj.-Gen. (ret.) Yaakov Amidror, a former head of the Israel National Security Council, wrote in June 2016. "It is wiser to defer action than to take unilateral steps that threaten to make a bad situation worse."[4]

These are some of the potential consequences of unilateral withdrawal:

- The move will not enhance Israel's security as the unilateralists claim. It will harm it.
- The security cooperation Israel now has with the PA will dissipate.
- The security advantages provided by Israel's physical military deployment in the territories will be lost.
- The ability to contain, preempt, or respond to threats effectively and surgically will be limited.
- Re-entering these territories to cope with threats will open Israel up to charges against it and increase casualties on the Israeli side to do so.
- The intelligence benefits afforded by cooperation and current deployment will be adversely affected and, with it, Israel's ability to preempt terror.
- Again, Israel will be perceived as leaving the battlefield in the face of adversity.
- This will encourage the extremists and undermine Israeli deterrence. It will embolden the rejectionists.
- Palestinian terrorism will not be contained by the security barrier but will find a way under it, over it, and around it.
- Terror can be expected to intensify, given the economic and political realities Israel's unilateral withdrawal will create.
- Withdrawal from 80 percent of the West Bank will not clear Israel of the claim that it is still an occupying power.
- Nor will it lead to an abatement of Palestinian and pro-Palestinian efforts to delegitimize Israel and undermine its historic claims.
- It will not end efforts to boycott Israel, but will intensify them with claims that by creating a West Bank "prison," cut off by Israeli forces in all directions, Israel will be accused of human rights abuses, including ethnic cleansing.
- These charges will amplify with tens of thousands of Palestinians being cut off from their jobs in Israel and Palestinian residents of eastern Jerusalem unilaterally deprived of their existing rights and financial benefits as Israeli residents.
- Given the nature of the territory vacated, any Israeli retaliation to provocation will almost automatically be branded as a "disproportionate use of force."
- As opposed to the impression of unilateralism being a temporary move, it will be seen as a move by Israel to create a permanent new reality, a Palestinian ghetto in the West Bank, all talk of a future agreement being seen as lip service and not intent.
- The move will not move the Palestinians to the negotiating table as hoped but will be seen as further proof that Israel wants to expand its hold on territories those Palestinians who do support a two-state solution see as theirs.

By the Labor Party's own admission, unilateralism does not connote the quest for peace, but rather recognition that peace in a negotiated two-states-for-two-peoples framework with the Palestinians is not possible at this time. It connotes recognition of the true goal of the Palestinian leadership that wants it all and believes that with patience and fortitude, like Hizbullah and Hamas before them, they will eventually achieve their goal.

Those who oppose unilateralism, place as their baseline for future negotiation, not the security fence, but unequivocal and irreversible Palestinian recognition of Israel as the legitimate homeland of the Jewish

People and the legitimacy of Israel's historical bond to Jerusalem.

Until such time as this happens, they are prepared to maintain the status quo, taking into account the expansion of existing settlements on non-private land as dictated by natural growth and in accordance with Israeli law.

Logically, one would suppose this seepage should provide a massive incentive for the Palestinians to come to the table if they want a solution based on two states for two peoples. Until then, however, better Israeli boots on the ground than faith in a wall to protect Israel from violence.

The Conclusions to Be Drawn

The unilateralists seemed to have learned little from the lessons of the past.

- Once Israel is out of the territory, no one has direct control over how the vacuum will be filled.
- Pushing the Palestinians into a virtual ghetto, cutting them off from their sources of income and benefits, and limiting freedom of travel will not encourage moderation in the West Bank, but desperation, radicalization, and determination.
- Instead of a potential partner, no matter how slight the possibility, Israel will find yet another radicalized enemy on its border, atop existing PA and Hamas arsenals, capable of inflicting potentially serious damage to Israel's heartland that, in the end, will necessitate Israel re-taking the territories it unconditionally gave up.
- In order for the Palestinians to come to the table, they have to see a resilient Israel. The settlement reality should be their incentive, as should the fate of the territories in which radical Islam has begun to take hold.

The Palestinians have to understand and accept that modern Israel is not another foreign invader in the land, but a people with roots here and a long and painful history to prove it.

The unilateralists say that by withdrawing, Israel is taking its future into its own hands and ending the "Palestinian veto" over our lives. The opposite is true. By standing firm and not running in the face of adversity, Israel controls its own destiny, maximizes its security and fully maintains the only cards it has with which to negotiate its future.

Despite months of preparation and effort, the wrenching of 8,000 Israeli settlers from their homes and fields in Gaza left deep scars on Israeli society. It pitched soldiers against their families and brother against brother. It generated some of the largest and most violent protests in Israel's history.

Israel had no emotional or historical attachment to Gaza. In the West Bank, the territory in question is etched deep in the identity of every Jew, not just the Jewish residents of the West Bank. Scenes from the forced evacuation of three settlements in northern Samaria, as part of the Gaza withdrawal, were unique in the passion and determination demonstrated by those who opposed the move and an indication of things to come.

Thus:

- The belief that some 100,000 people will vacate their homes in return for incentives, including the ideologues among them, is a pipedream in the context of an unconditional withdrawal from the West Bank or Jerusalem.
- The move will tear Israel apart and pose a threat to democratic rule.
- It will cause dissent in the army and crack national unity, playing directly into the hands of those Palestinians who want a weak Israel.
- Borders drawn unilaterally will not receive international legitimacy.
- Neither will the Palestinians cooperate with having yet another 20 percent of their land unilaterally taken by Israel, albeit supposedly temporarily.
- It makes no sense for Israel to risk deep division, if not a civil war, for no Palestinian quid pro quo in return, or to risk creating a radicalized and bitter enemy on its border with the means and the will to cause it harm.

The way to make peace is not by giving away assets, but maintaining them until the partner comes to the table to negotiate, in accordance with the obligations to which it is committed and pursuant to its existing agreements with Israel.

The essence of peace is interaction between people, not a wall between them.

Maintaining the present is the path to the future, not repeating the mistakes of the past.

Assessing Past Strategies to Understand Future Implications The Case of Lebanon

Labor Party leader Ehud Barak had placed ending Israel's two-decade presence in Lebanon high on his agenda when running for prime minister in the 1999 elections. By May 24, 2000, the last Israeli left Lebanese territory, ending what the media called the "Lebanese quagmire."

The rationale for this was, among other reasons:

- Hizbullah had moved into Southern Lebanon.
- Israel's ally there, the South Lebanese Army, had collapsed.
- The main reason for Israel's presence, Palestinian terror, was no longer an issue.
- Hizbullah's campaign against Israel's presence on Lebanese territory was costing Israel mounting casualties in the face of diminished returns.
- It was assumed that by withdrawing, Israel would satisfy Hizbullah's stated cause-du-guerre, thus bringing peace and stability to Israel's northern frontier.
- It was also assumed that Israel's withdrawal to the internationally-recognized border would improve Israel's international relations.
- It would afford Israel legitimacy if it needed to attack against future aggression.
- The vast superiority of the Israel Defense Forces over those of Hizbullah would provide deterrence.
- It was hoped that the move would lead to international pressure on the Syrians to follow suit and remove their forces from Lebanon.

Few of these suppositions, however, came out as expected.

- Hizbullah moved into the vacuum left by Israel in Southern Lebanon and became highly militarized.
- Their self-declared victory propelled them into becoming the dominant force in Lebanon politically and militarily.
- Hizbullah and the Lebanese government insisted that Israel had not returned to the international border, but continued to occupy the Shab'a Farms, a sliver of land at the junction of Lebanon's border with Syria, claimed by the Syrians to be theirs.
- The conflict, in other words, remained open.
- The manner of Israel's withdrawal, done in secret and under cover of darkness to minimize potential casualties, was depicted as retreating like thieves in the night, playing into Hizbullah's narrative of achieving the first Arab victory over Israel in history.
- "Israel may have nuclear weapons and heavy weaponry, but, as God lives, it is weaker than a cobweb," Hizbullah leader Hassan Nasrallah boasted in his victory speech, pointedly made in the town of Bint Jebeil, once a South Lebanese Army stronghold.
- It turned Hizbullah into a role model for others fighting Israel.
- As Nasrallah told the Palestinians: "In order to liberate your lands, you do not need tanks or airplanes. Learn from the holy martyrs; you (too) can impose your demands on the Zionist aggressor"—a message that obviously resonated with the Palestinians. Arafat launched the Second Intifada some four months later.
- Hizbullah's perceived victory propelled it from a marginal Shia organization into the main force in Lebanon and, with it, Iran.
- Hizbullah's aggression against Israel did not end, but continued incessantly, culminating in the 2006 Lebanese War—a 34-day conflict Israel had wrongly assumed would be deterred by its disproportionate strength.
- The international support Israel thought would be forthcoming, if it needed to defend itself after leaving Lebanon, turned into international condemnation for "Israel's disproportionate response" in its use of force when it had to do so.

Also:

- The Syrians did not withdraw from Lebanon but remained entrenched for another five years.
- Hizbullah, and not the Lebanese government or army, filled the vacuum left by Israel's departure, opening the way for Iran to gain a major foothold in the country.
- Hizbullah, despite the heavy damage to its military infrastructure in the 2006 war, and despite Nasrallah being forced to live in hiding to this day, has become a major military force with tens of thousands of rockets and missiles in its arsenals, including those capable of striking deep into Israel's heartland.
- Using Lebanon as a base, Hizbullah has also grown into an Iranian expeditionary force involved in other conflicts in the region, specifically in Syria fighting on behalf of the regime and gaining valuable military experience in the process.
- Iran, by having a well-armed proxy under its direct command in close proximity to Israel and with the means to threaten Israel's heartland, has added a layer of deterrence against any Israeli designs on its nuclear facilities. Israel must now take a retaliatory attack from Lebanese territory into account.

There was logic in pulling Israeli forces out of Lebanon, but the pullback was done in haste. Not enough thought was given to the aftershock, to the resulting political chaos that would fill the vacuum caused by Israel's retreat, or capitulation, as some would say.

There were other, more measured, ways to solve the problem: negotiation; third-party intervention; tactical adjustments; better defensive measures; increasingly painful retaliation in the face of provocation; a targeted campaign against Hizbullah's leadership; exposing Iran's subterfuge and meddling in the region; forging new alliances with those of common cause—the list of options was endless.

Retreating under cover of darkness, in a move interpreted by Israel's enemies as weakness, and by Hizbullah as a victory, should not have been the prime option, however.

The Case of Gaza

Israel's withdrawal from Gaza in 2005 was a very different experience from that in Lebanon in all ways but one—the unexpected consequences of the move: the emergence, two years later, of an Iranian-supported Islamic fundamentalist proxy, Hamas, on Israel's southern border, and the three full-scale wars and countless attacks and counter-attacks that have ensued since.

Unlike Israel's withdrawal from Lebanon, however, Israel's disengagement from Gaza involved the uprooting of 21 settlements and eviction, mostly forcibly, of 8,000 Israeli residents from their homes.

The architect of the move was Ariel Sharon, elected prime minister in 2001, and an unlikely candidate to be the first Israeli leader to willingly and unconditionally uproot settlements and hand over territory to the Palestinians for nothing in return.

In the period leading up to Sharon's change in thinking, the Palestinian second intifada continued to flare, though Israel and the Palestinians had accepted the American-sponsored Roadmap to Peace in the spring of 2003. Sharon accused the Palestinians of having "sabotaged the process with a series of the most brutal terror attacks we have ever known."

In December 2003, with Israeli civilian casualties mounting, Sharon unveiled his "Disengagement Plan," named as such to avoid the negative connotations associated with "withdrawal."

In words reminiscent of those being used today by the proponents of unilateralism, he explained the logic behind his decision. Here follow key quotes from Sharon's 2003 address to the Fourth Herzliya Conference:[5]

- The purpose of the Disengagement Plan is to reduce terror as much as possible and grant Israeli citizens the maximum level of security.
- The process of disengagement will lead to an improvement in the quality of life and will help strengthen the Israeli economy.
- The unilateral steps which Israel will take in the framework of the Disengagement Plan will be fully coordinated with the United States.
- We must not harm our strategic coordination with the United States.

- We are interested in conducting direct negotiations, but do not intend to hold Israeli society hostage in the hands of the Palestinians.
- We will not wait for them indefinitely.
- The Disengagement Plan will include the redeployment of IDF forces along new security lines and a change in the deployment of settlements which will reduce as much as possible the number of Israelis located in the heart of the Palestinian population.
- Security will be provided by IDF deployment, the security fence, and other physical obstacles. The Disengagement Plan will reduce friction between the Palestinians and us.
- This reduction of friction will require the extremely difficult step of changing the deployment of some of the settlements.
- I would like to repeat what I have said in the past: In the framework of a future agreement, Israel will not remain in all the places where it is today.
- The relocation of settlements will be made, first and foremost, in order to draw the most efficient security line possible, thereby creating this disengagement between Israel and the Palestinians.
- This security line will not constitute the permanent border of the State of Israel; however, as long as implementation of the Roadmap is not resumed, the IDF will be deployed along that line.
- Settlements which will be relocated are those which will not be included in the territory of the State of Israel in the framework of any possible future permanent agreement.
- At the same time, in the framework of the Disengagement Plan, Israel will strengthen its control over those same areas in the Land of Israel which will constitute an inseparable part of the State of Israel in any future agreement.
- The Disengagement Plan is a security measure, not a political one and [does] not come in the way ... of reaching an agreed settlement.
- It is a step Israel will take in the absence of any other option, in order to improve its security.

Guiding his logic were the following elements:

- Gaza was never intended to be part of Israel under any arrangement with the Palestinians.
- It was, therefore, not disputed territory.
- Israel does not consider Gaza part of the Land of Israel and has no biblical, historical or emotional affinity there.
- Peace with Egypt had made the concept of a Gaza buffer zone anachronistic.
- He viewed Gaza as an impediment, an unnecessary and costly side-show to the main goal of securing Israel's hold over Judea and Samaria.
- He judged the Gaza settlements to be counterproductive, necessitating a disproportionally large military presence to defend them.
- He saw Israeli responsibility for over a million Palestinians in Gaza as a millstone around Israel's neck and a potential demographic danger to Israel's future as a Jewish and democratic state.
- It tightened Israel's relationship with the Bush Administration and was supported by President Bush in a letter that supported a non-return to the 1967 lines.

But, as in the case of Lebanon, in the end, it was the unintended consequences that shaped the future, not the logic behind the move. In the case of Gaza:

- In 2007, Hamas wrested control of Gaza from Fatah and the PA.
- Gaza came under the control of a rejectionist, Iranian-supported, Islamic fundamentalist enemy on its southern front—as had happened in the north.
- In consequence, Gaza went from being a tactical military problem to a strategic one, from a localized issue to a regional one.
- Instead of a negotiating partner in Gaza, Israel now had an implacable enemy.
- Instead of security cooperation with the PA in Gaza, Israel now had a well-armed, well-trained and dedicated enemy on its southern border.
- Expected international support for Israel's withdrawal from Gaza turned into condemnation of Israel for alleged use of "disproportionate force" when forced to defend itself.

- The withdrawal of forces was seen as weakness in the face of adversity by the Arab world, harming Israel's deterrence.
- This perception of weakness encouraged those who resisted compromise.
- Israel's willingness to uproot settlements in Gaza for no reward in return gave hope to the Palestinians that it would eventually do the same in the West Bank.
- Despite Sharon's assumption that the uprooting of the Gaza settlements could be done while maintaining national unity, the move, in fact, tore Israel apart internally and heightened the political rift in the country.
- The move did not improve Israel's security situation as expected, but worsened it in a fundamental way, as illustrated by the three full-scale wars and thousands of cross-border incidents that followed the withdrawal.

A General Assessment of Unilateralism in Lebanon and Gaza

A study titled "Israel's Strategy of Unilateral Withdrawal" by Dr. Shmuel Even, published by the Institute for National Security Studies in its journal *Strategic Assessment* in June 2009, was devastating in its conclusions. "In the end," he writes, "the strategy of unilateral withdrawal (in both cases) caused Israel significant damage."[6]

His main points:

- In both sectors from which Israel withdrew, the security threats grew stronger.
- The withdrawals hurt Israel's image as an entity that cannot be vanquished by military force and strengthened the radical axis in the Arab world.
- Secondary confrontation arenas turned into major fronts.
- Unilateral withdrawal and its implementation strengthened the image of the Shiite and Palestinian struggle and its values of patience, self-sacrifice, endurance, resistance, and devotion to the land.
- It demonstrated to the radical Islamic camp that it could achieve extraordinary success even without negotiations, which was quite perturbing to the pragmatic camp in the Arab world.

In Even's judgment, "the strategy of unilateral withdrawal did not meet expectations because of some erroneous basic assumptions, estimates, and concepts that lay at the heart of the approach,"—or precisely the same mistakes about to be repeated by those now propagating a unilateral withdrawal from the West Bank.

Hirsh Goodman, "The Dangers of a Unilateral Israeli Withdrawal from the West Bank and Eastern Jerusalem." *Jerusalem Center for Public Affairs: Israeli Security, Regional Diplomacy, and International Law*, 2017.

Endnotes

1 Amos Yadlin, "Two States, Four Paths for Achieving Them," *Brookings*, January 15, 2016, https://www.brookings.edu/blog/markaz/2016/01/15/two-states-four-paths-for-achieving-them/

2 Labor Party Platform: Yonatan Liss, "Labor Party Adopts Herzog's Plan for Separation from Palestinians," *Ha'aretz*, February 8, 2016. See also, Joshua Mitnick, "Labor Pains Over Two-State Solution," *The Jewish Week*, February 16, 2016, http://www.thejewishweek.com/news/israel-news/labor-pains-over-two-state-solution

3 Yadlin.

4 Yaakov Amidror, "Why Israel Should Not Adopt Unilateral Initiatives," BESA Center Perspectives Paper No. 343, Begin-Sadat Center for Strategic Studies, Bar-Ilan University, June 1, 2016,http://besacenter.org/perspectives-papers/israel-not-adopt-unilateral-initiatives/

5 Ariel Sharon, *Address at Fourth Herzliya Conference*, December 18, 2003, Israel Ministry of Foreign Affairs, http://mfa.gov.il/MFA/PressRoom/2003/Pages/Address%20by%20PM%20Ariel%20Sharon%20at%20the%20Fourth%20Herzliya.aspx

6 Shmuel Even, "Israel's Strategy of Unilateral Withdrawal," *Strategic Assessment*, Institute for National Security Studies, June 2009, http://www.inss.org.il/uploadImages/systemFiles/SA_12.1_English_Even.pdf

Lesson 5

ISRAEL IN PERSPECTIVE

VIEWPOINTS ON THE LAND'S IDENTITY

A woman greets Israeli soldiers returning from the conquest of East Jerusalem, Geulah Quarter of Jerusalem, 1967. (Photo credit: Magnum Photos; Micha Bar Am, photographer)

The Six-Day War had a profound impact on Diaspora Jewry. In its immediate aftermath, waves of new immigrants arrived in the Jewish state, while countless others experienced a spiritual reawakening. When the euphoria wore off, however, extreme diversity in perspective and reaction emerged—toward the war, and toward the State of Israel. What are the factors underwriting this fragmentation, and how do they influence Israel's political process today?

TEXT 1

LEON FESTINGER, *A THEORY OF COGNITIVE DISSONANCE* (STANFORD, CA: STANFORD UNIVERSITY PRESS, 1962), PP. 4–5

New events may happen, or new information may become known to a person, creating at least a momentary dissonance with existing knowledge, opinion, or cognition concerning behavior. Since a person does not have complete and perfect control over the information that reaches him and over events that can happen in his environment, such dissonance may easily arise. Thus, for example, a person may plan to go to a picnic with complete confidence that the weather will be warm and sunny. Nevertheless, just before he is due to start, it may begin to rain. The knowledge that it is now raining is dissonant with his confidence in a sunny day and with his planning to go to a picnic. Or, as another example, a person who is quite certain in his knowledge that automatic transmissions on automobiles are inefficient may accidentally come across an article praising automatic transmissions. Again, at least a momentary dissonance is created.

LEON FESTINGER
1919–1989

Social psychologist. Born to a Jewish family in Brooklyn, New York, Festinger received psychology degrees from the City College of New York and the University of Iowa and went on to serve as a professor at a number of American universities. Festinger was best known for his development of the theories of cognitive dissonance and social comparison, and is considered one of the most influential scholars in the field of social psychology.

TEXT 2

MICHAEL B. OREN, *SIX DAYS OF WAR: JUNE 1967 AND THE MAKING OF THE MODERN MIDDLE EAST* (OXFORD: OXFORD UNIVERSITY PRESS, 2002), PP. 135–136

Throughout the country, thousands were hurrying to dig trenches, build shelters, and fill sandbags. In Jerusalem, in particular, schools were refitted as bomb shelters, and air raid drills were practiced daily. Most buses and virtually all taxis were mobilized, and an emergency blood drive launched. An urgent request for surgeons—"in view of the tough conditions they must be physically fit and experienced"—was submitted to the Red Cross, and extra units of plasma ordered from abroad. Special committees were placed in charge of gathering essential foodstuffs, for replacing workers called to the front, and for evacuating children to Europe. Upward of 14,000 hospital beds were readied and antidotes stockpiled for poison gas victims, expected to arrive in waves of 200. Some 10,000 graves were dug.

The sole bright spot in these otherwise morbid preparations was the unprecedented outpouring of sympathy from around the Jewish world. . . . Yet these gestures did little to relieve the sense of approaching catastrophe, of the Jews' abandonment to yet another Holocaust. "What are you waiting for?" Hanna Zemer, deputy editor of the daily *Davar*, accosted [Prime Minister Levi] Eshkol. He retorted with a description of Israel's international isolation, of the massive casualties it would suffer. "Blut vet

MICHAEL B. OREN
1955–

Historian and diplomat. Born and raised in New York, Oren received degrees in international affairs from Columbia University. He made *aliyah* in 1979. Oren taught at several universities in Israel and the U.S. and wrote best-selling books about Israeli-American relations and the Six-Day War. In 2009 Oren was appointed Israel's ambassador to the U.S., a position he held until 2013. He currently serves as a member of Israel's parliament, representing the "Kulanu" party.

sich giessen vie vasser," he concluded in Yiddish: "Blood will run like water." . . . There was talk of the widespread bombing of Israeli cities, of an entire generation of soldiers being wiped out.

TEXT 3

TOM SEGEV, *1967: ISRAEL, THE WAR, AND THE YEAR THAT TRANSFORMED THE MIDDLE EAST* (NEW YORK: METROPOLITAN BOOKS, 2007), P. 15

The sense of total doom had all but disappeared; history was about to begin again. Two popular jokes drive home this reversal of mood. According to the first, told before the war, a sign hangs near the boarding gate at Lod Airport asking the last one out of the country to turn off the lights. In the second, after the war, two officers are talking about how to spend their day. "Let's conquer Cairo," one proposes. The other replies, "But what will we do after lunch?"

TOM SEGEV
1945–

Historian and author. Born and raised in Jerusalem, Segev received degrees in history and political science from Hebrew University and Boston University. He has written for various Israeli newspapers and lectured at a number of American universities. Segev has written a number of books about Israel and its society, and is associated with Israel's "New Historians," a group challenging many of the country's traditional narratives.

QUESTION FOR DISCUSSION

What are some of the ways in which Israel and Jews around the world rationalized the remarkable Six-Day War victory?

TEXT 4

DAPHNA BERMAN, "THE 40TH ANNIVERSARY OF THE SIX-DAY WAR RATE OF RETURN," *HAARETZ*, JUNE 1, 2007

According to numbers from the Jewish Agency, North American aliyah jumped from 739 in 1967 to nearly 6,500 two years later, peaking at over 8,000 immigrants by 1971. In the U.K., aliyah numbers were at 299 in 1967, with over 1,700 immigrants in 1969. Numbers from South Africa show a similar trend: Immigration was at 233 in 1967 and more than tripled to 803 olim [émigrés] by 1970.

"Until the Six-Day War, Western aliyah was not a major force," said Sidney Shapiro, director of Telfed, the Israel offices of the South African Zionist Federation. "The wave of post-1967 olim changed the face of aliyah. For the first time, there were sizable numbers of immigrants from the West, as compared to just a trickle."

DAPHNA BERMAN

Communications consultant. Berman is a consultant for the Strategic Impact Evaluation Fund at the World Bank. Previously, she was a correspondent for the *International Herald Tribune/ Haaretz* in Jerusalem, as well as a senior writer for *Moment Magazine*.

miracle

NOUN

1 An extraordinary and welcome event that is not explicable by natural or scientific laws and is therefore attributed to a divine agency.

2 A remarkable event or development that brings very welcome consequences.

Source: Online Oxford Dictionary

Some of the fiercest fighting in Sinai occurred at the Mitla Pass, directly east of Suez. Involving hundreds of tanks, the battle lasted an entire night and resulted in the almost complete destruction of the Egyptian equipment along the 16-mile-long pass. Most of the hardware was demolished by Israeli jet fighter bombers. A total of 536 Egyptian tanks were destroyed, June 8, 1967. (Photo credit: Magnum Photos; Rene Burri, photographer)

TEXT 5

RABBI SHMUEL BORNSTEIN, *SHEM MISHMUEL,* DEVARIM 5673

יֵשׁ שְׁנֵי מִינֵי הַנְהָגָה שֶׁהַשֵּׁם יִתְבָּרֵךְ מַנְהִיג אֶת עַמּוֹ יִשְׂרָאֵל. יֵשׁ הַנְהָגָה נִסִּית נִגְלֵית, כְּמוֹ מַן וּבְאֵר וְעַנְנֵי כָּבוֹד, וְיֵשׁ הַנְהָגָה הַמְלוּבֶּשֶׁת בְּטֶבַע, אֲבָל עַל יְדֵי נִסִּים נִסְתָּרִים . . .

וְהִנֵּה מוּבָן, שֶׁלְצוֹרֶךְ יִשְׂרָאֵל, לְרוֹמְמָם עַל כָּל גּוֹיֵי הָאָרֶץ, בְּוַדַּאי יוֹתֵר טוֹב וְיוֹתֵר כָּבוֹד וְשֵׂם תִּפְאֶרֶת לָהֶם בַּהַנְהָגָה הַנִּסִּית . . . אַךְ לְצוֹרֶךְ גָּבוֹהַּ, יֵשׁ לוֹמַר שֶׁיּוֹתֵר תּוֹעֶלֶת בַּהַנְהָגָה עַל יְדֵי נִסִּים נִסְתָּרִים הַמְלוּבָּשִׁים בְּטֶבַע . . . שֶׁהַהַנְהָגָה הַנִּסִּית הַמְלוּבֶּשֶׁת בְּטֶבַע מַגְבַּהַת גַּם אֶת עוֹלָם הַטֶּבַע וּמְזַכְּכָתוֹ.

There are two kinds of governance by which God leads His people Israel. There is an openly miraculous governance, as with the manna, the well [that sprang forth from a rock and provided the Jews with water throughout their desert sojourn], and the Clouds of Glory [that encompassed and protected the Jews in the desert]. There is also governance that is clothed in nature, in which miracles are hidden.

It is understood, that as far as Israel is concerned, revealed miracles are preferable, more glorious and more splendid, inasmuch as they elevate Israel's prestige and status among the nations. . . . For God's sake, however, one could say that the miracles that are cloaked in natural phenomena are of greater benefit. . . . For the miracles that are conveyed via natural means elevate and purify the natural world.

RABBI SHMUEL BORENSTEIN
1855–1926

Chasidic Rebbe. Rabbi Borenstein was born in Poland into a distinguished rabbinic family. His father and primary teacher, Rabbi Avraham—known by the title of his halachic responsa *Avnei Nezer*—was the first Rebbe of Sochatchov, and his maternal grandfather was Rabbi Menachem Mendel Morgenstern, the Rebbe of Kotzk. In 1910, Rabbi Shmuel succeeded his father as Rebbe of Sochatchov and established a yeshiva there. He is best known for the collection of his Chasidic sermons, *Shem MiShmuel,* which has gained wide popularity.

TEXT 6

GEORGE W. GAWRYCH, *KEY TO THE SINAI: THE BATTLES FOR ABU AGEILA IN THE 1956 AND 1967 ARAB-ISRAELI WARS* (FORT LEAVENWORTH, KS: U.S. ARMY COMMAND AND GENERAL STAFF COLLEGE, 1990), PP. 76–77

During the 1967 war, the Egyptian Army's command and control system down to division and brigade level broke down. The seeds of this problem were planted in the three weeks before the outbreak of hostilities. Earlier, in 1966, the Egyptians developed a new plan for the defense of the Sinai called *Qahir* (the victor). Plan *Qahir* placed control of combat forces in the Sinai under a field army commander directly responsible to GHQ (General Headquarters) in Cairo. But on 15 May, for reasons that still remain unclear, the Egyptian high command surprised its senior officers with the sudden creation of a front command and the appointment of General Abd al-Mohsen Kamal Murtagui to head it. . . .

GEORGE W. GAWRYCH
1950–

Historian and author. Gawrych received his doctorate in history from the University of Michigan. He is currently a professor of Middle Eastern History at Baylor University and has written a number of books about Middle Eastern history.

Murtagui, as the new front commander, would be plagued by a number of problems. Although a competent soldier, he had been commanding the Egyptian expeditionary force in Yemen and lacked intimate knowledge of the operational plan for Sinai. Furthermore, as a front commander in Sinai, he would receive a high degree of responsibility without the commensurate authority to carry out his mission. . . . Finally, Murtagui arrived at his command post in the Sinai (near Bir al-Thamada) on 29 May—only a week before the war and with a small staff of twenty officers. The Egyptian command and control system was further undermined when the high command replaced all twelve division commanders and chiefs of staff in the week or two after the creation of the front command. Then, the confusion seeped down to brigades and lower.

Israeli Army Chief of Staff Yitzhak Rabin surveys damage inflicted against Egyptian military installations along the Suez Canal during the Six-Day War, 1967. (Photo credit: Magnum Photos; Micha Bar Am, photographer)

TEXT 7a

LEVITICUS 26:7–8

> וּרְדַפְתֶּם אֶת אֹיְבֵיכֶם, וְנָפְלוּ לִפְנֵיכֶם לֶחָרֶב. וְרָדְפוּ מִכֶּם חֲמִשָּׁה מֵאָה, וּמֵאָה מִכֶּם רְבָבָה יִרְדֹּפוּ.

You will pursue your enemies, and they will fall before you by sword. Five of you will pursue a hundred [of your foe], and a hundred of you will pursue ten thousand.

TEXT 7b

DEUTERONOMY 28:7

> יִתֵּן ה' אֶת אֹיְבֶיךָ הַקָּמִים עָלֶיךָ נִגָּפִים לְפָנֶיךָ. בְּדֶרֶךְ אֶחָד יֵצְאוּ אֵלֶיךָ וּבְשִׁבְעָה דְרָכִים יָנוּסוּ לְפָנֶיךָ.

God will cause your enemies who rise up against you to be defeated before you. They will come out against you from one direction, but they will flee from you in seven directions.

TEXT 8

MICHAEL B. OREN, *SIX DAYS OF WAR: JUNE 1967 AND THE MAKING OF THE MODERN MIDDLE EAST*, OP. CIT., PP. 171–172

Supplied by Britain, Jordan's radar facility at 'Ajlun, near Jerash, was one of the most sophisticated in the Middle East. At 8:15 a.m., the station's screens were suddenly studded with blips. Though the Jordanians had grown accustomed to large numbers of Israeli aircraft heading out to sea, the density of the concentration was unprecedented. The officer on duty radioed in Grape—'*Inab,* in Arabic, the prearranged code word for war—to [Jordanian] Gen. Riyad's headquarters in Amman. Riyad, in turn, relayed the information to [Egyptian] Defense Minister Shams Badran in Cairo, and there it remained, undecipherable. The Egyptians had changed their encoding frequencies the previous day, but without updating the Jordanians. . . .

[Egyptian] air force intelligence also reported extensively on the Israeli attack, but the officers at Supreme Headquarters, devoted to [Field Marshal Abdel Hakim] 'Amer and distrustful of Nasser's loyalists in the air force, ignored them.

TEXT 9

STEVE LINDE, "ARAB ARMIES PLANNED TO DESTROY ISRAEL," *THE JERUSALEM POST*, JUNE 5, 2007

"The biggest myth going is that somehow there was not a real and immediate Arab threat, that somehow Israel could have negotiated itself outside the crisis of 1967, and that it wasn't facing an existential threat, or facing any threat at all," said [Michael] Oren, who is a senior fellow at the Adelson Institute for Strategic Studies at Jerusalem's Shalem Center and author of *Six Days of War: June 1967*. He noted that this was the premise of Tom Segev's book, *1967: Israel, the War, and the Year That Transformed the Middle East*. "What's remarkable is that all the people alleging this—not one of them is working from Arabic sources. It's quite extraordinary when you think about it. It's almost as if Israel were living in a universe by itself. It's a deeply solipsistic approach to Middle East history."

What's behind the myth, Oren argued, is "a more pervasive, ongoing effort to show that Israel bears the bulk, if not the sole responsibility, for decades of conflict in the Arab world, and that the Arabs are the aggrieved party.

"It's an attempt to show that Israel basically planned the Six Day War in advance, knowing that it was going to expand territorially. My position is that it was just the opposite. Israel was taken aback by the crisis, unprepared for it and panicked, believing it faced a true existential threat, and did not plan to expand territory.

"It did everything it could to keep Jordan and Syria out of the war. My reading of the Arabic documents show that the Arabs had real plans to attack and destroy the State of Israel."

General Moshe Dayan, Israeli Minister of Defense, at the Kalandiya Refugee Camp in the West Bank, 1967. (Photo credit: Magnum Photos; Micha Bar Am, photographer)

TEXT 10

TALMUD, KETUBOT 111A

> "הִשְׁבַּעְתִּי אֶתְכֶם בְּנוֹת יְרוּשָׁלַם . . . [אִם תָּעִירוּ וְאִם תְּעוֹרְרוּ אֶת הָאַהֲבָה עַד שֶׁתֶּחְפָּץ]" (שִׁיר הַשִּׁירִים ב, ז) . . .
>
> שֶׁלֹּא יַעֲלוּ יִשְׂרָאֵל בְּחוֹמָה.

"I adjure you, O daughters of Jerusalem [. . . that you neither awaken nor arouse the love until it is desirous]" (SONG OF SONGS 2:7). . . .

[In this verse, God imposes an oath upon the Jews,] that they not retake the Land of Israel by force.

BABYLONIAN TALMUD

A literary work of monumental proportions that draws upon the legal, spiritual, intellectual, ethical, and historical traditions of Judaism. The 37 tractates of the Babylonian Talmud contain the teachings of the Jewish sages from the period after the destruction of the 2nd Temple through the 5th century CE. It has served as the primary vehicle for the transmission of the Oral Law and the education of Jews over the centuries; it is the entry point for all subsequent legal, ethical, and theological Jewish scholarship.

A soldier's early morning prayers during the Six-Day War, Negev Desert, 1967. (Photo credit: Magnum Photos; Micha Bar Am, photographer)

TEXT 11a

MAX MANDELSTAMM, "OPEN LETTER," *HATSEFIRAH,* NISAN 13, 5659 [MARCH 24, 1899]

I have concluded that those Jews who are not Zionists—at least in their minds and hearts—are not Jews. To be a Zionist is to be a Jew. . . . There are many citizens of the world who are considered Jewish; who observe the commandments, such as circumcision, *tsitsit,* and *tefilin*; who are scrupulous regarding ritual slaughter; pray at the proper times; and fast on Jewish fast days. But in a national sense, these people have the right to the title Jew as much as I can rightfully identify myself as Chinese, were I to choose to abide by Chinese law.

MAX MANDELSTAMM
1839–1912

Zionist activist. Born in Lithuania, Mandelstamm studied ophthalmology and established and directed an ophthalmic hospital in Kiev, Ukraine. Mandelstamm was a prominent Zionist activist and served as the deputy chairman of the second Zionist Congress. He belonged to the Jewish Territorial Organization, which promoted the establishment of a Jewish state outside of the historical Land of Israel.

TEXT 11b

NACHMAN SYRKIN, *"MIN HACHUTSAH HA'OHELAH,"* CITED IN *KITVEI NACHMAN SYRKIN* (BERLIN: HASHACHAR, 1903), PP. 169–170

This [new, Zionist] Judaism stands in complete contrast to the Judaism of the medieval ages, religious Judaism, exilic Judaism. In fact, Zionism uproots religious Judaism in a stronger and more fundamental manner than does the Reform movement and assimilation. These uprooted Judaism in an artificial way, causing complete assimilation or allowing for the re-emergence of Talmudic and religious Judaism in a later period. Zionism, on the other hand, fundamentally uproots Judaism by creating new standards of Judaism and creating new Jewish spiritual values. This will successfully eradicate religious Judaism to the point that it will never again re-emerge.

NACHMAN SYRKIN
1868–1924

Political theorist and writer. Born and raised in Czarist Russia, Syrkin was both a Zionist and a socialist since his youth. He received his doctorate in philosophy from Berlin University and was a prominent participant of the Zionist Congresses. Syrkin dedicated himself to merging the ideologies of socialism and Zionism.

Jewish immigrants arrive in Palestine, facilitated by the Palmach, 1947. (Photo Credit: The Palmach Archive)

TEXT 12

RABBI YOEL TEITELBAUM, *DIVREI YOEL* VOL. 7, P. 415

אֵין לְסַפֵּר מֵנִסִים שֶׁנַּעֲשׂוּ עַל יְדֵי הַסִטְרָא אַחֲרָא, וְרָאוּי לְהִמָּנַע מִכַּךְ בְּכָל מַה דְּאֶפְשָׁר, כִּי הַדִּיבּוּר בָּזֶה עָלוּל לִגְרוֹם לְטָעוּת וּמִכְשׁוֹל לְקַלֵּי הַדַּעַת לוֹמַר שֶׁיֵּשׁ בָּהֶם מַמָּשׁ.

וַאֲפִילוּ אִם בֶּאֱמֶת נַעֲשׂוּ נִסִים צָרִיךְ לְהַעֲלִימָם וּלְהַלְבִּישׁ הַדָּבָר בְּטֶבַע כָּל מַה דְּאֶפְשָׁר. וּבַעֲוונוֹתֵינוּ הָרַבִּים בִּזְמַנֵּינוּ עוֹשִׂים הַהִיפּוּךְ מִזֶּה, שֶׁמְסַפְּרִים וּמְפַרְסְמִים נִסֵי הַס"מ דְבָרִים שֶׁאֵין בָּהֶם מַמָּשׁ, וְאֵינָם אֶלָּא נִסִים בְּדוּיִים שֶׁהִמְצִיאוּ כְּדֵי לְהַטְעוֹת אֶת הַבְּרִיּוֹת.

One should avoid, to the degree possible, recounting "miracles" performed by Satan. Such discussion causes people to err and misguides those who lack comprehension, leading them to ascribe significance to the events.

Even if in fact the victory was a supernatural phenomenon, it is necessary to conceal this fact and portray the events as natural. Sadly, today the opposite is occurring: people are discussing and publicizing nonexistent imaginary miracles, with the sole objective of deceiving the public.

RABBI YOEL TEITELBAUM
1887–1979

Chasidic Rebbe. Rabbi Teitelbaum was born in Sighet, Romania. Known for his scholarship from a young age, Rabbi Teitelbaum served as rabbi in a number of cities before being appointed rabbi of the city of Satmar, Romania. Rescued from the Holocaust on the Kastner train, Rabbi Teitelbaum settled in Williamsburg, Brooklyn (New York), where he reestablished the Chasidic community of Satmar. Under his leadership, Satmar grew from a small group to one of the largest Chasidic communities in the world. Rabbi Teitelbaum was known for his strictly isolationist line and vehement opposition to Zionism.

TEXT 13

RABBI TSVI YEHUDAH KOOK, CITED IN DAVID SINGER, "RAV KOOK'S CONTESTED LEGACY," *TRADITION*, 30:3, SPRING 1996

This is not a coincidental shaping of history. Rather, we must see God's guiding hand, and His divine ordering of events, for what they are—the fulfilment of, "When the Lord brings back the captivity of Zion [Psalms 126:1]." How fortunate are we to be a part of this national rebirth. . . .

All of the wars we have experienced have been a part of the process of redemption, whether they occurred before or after the establishment of the State; whether they were before or after the conquest of Jerusalem. . . . We are in the middle of the journey. . . . God causes salvation to appear, and brings redemption to completion, step by step.

RABBI TSVI YEHUDAH KOOK
1891–1982

Religious Zionist rabbi. Rabbi Tsvi Yehudah—son of Rabbi Avraham Yitschak Kook, the first Chief Rabbi of Mandatory Palestine—was born in Lithuania and made *aliyah* as a child with his family. Like his father, Rabbi Kook was a staunch religious Zionist, seeing the establishment and development of the State of Israel as part of the messianic process of redemption. He was the spiritual leader of the Gush Emunim settlement movement which established most of the Jewish communities in the West Bank and Gaza. Rabbi Kook is considered the most influential leader of the Religious Zionist movement in the period after the establishment of the State of Israel.

TEXT 14

THE REBBE, RABBI MENACHEM M. SCHNEERSON, *LIKUTEI SICHOS* 7:333–334

בְּקֶשֶׁר עִם הַמַּצָּב הַנּוֹכְחִי שֶׁל אֲחֵיכֶם וְאַחְיוֹתֵיכֶם - אַחֵינוּ וְאַחְיוֹתֵינוּ - הַנִּמְצָאִים בְּאֶרֶץ הַקּוֹדֶשׁ, בְּאֶרֶץ יִשְׂרָאֵל. הֵם עוֹמְדִים עַתָּה בְּמַצָּב כָּזֶה שֶׁהַקָּדוֹשׁ בָּרוּךְ הוּא מֵגִין עֲלֵיהֶם וְשׁוֹלֵחַ לָהֶם אֶת בִּרְכוֹתָיו וְאֶת יְשׁוּעָתוֹ בְּמִדָּה יְתֵרָה, כְּדֵי שֶׁיֵּצְאוּ - וְהֵם אָכֵן יֵצְאוּ - מֵהַמַּצָּב הַנּוֹכְחִי בְּהַצְלָחָה...

וְהוּא יוֹצִיאֵם, בְּיָדוֹ הַמְלֵאָה הַפְּתוּחָה הַקְּדוֹשָׁה וְהָרְחָבָה, מִכָּל הַקְּשָׁיִים, וְיָבִיא לָהֶם שָׁלוֹם וּבֶטַח בְּכָל הַמִּצְטָרֵךְ לָהֶם.

Regarding the current situation [in Israel]:

Our brothers and sisters that reside in the Holy Land, in the Land of Israel, are currently under God's protection. God is sending them His blessings and His salvation in great abundance, and they will successfully emerge from the present state of affairs. . . .

God—with His full, open, holy, and generous hand—will extricate the residents of Israel from all difficulty, and He will give them peace and security as per all their needs.

RABBI MENACHEM MENDEL SCHNEERSON 1902–1994

The towering Jewish leader of the 20th century, known as "the Lubavitcher Rebbe," or simply as "the Rebbe." Born in southern Ukraine, the Rebbe escaped Nazi-occupied Europe, arriving in the U.S. in June 1941. The Rebbe inspired and guided the revival of traditional Judaism after the European devastation, impacting virtually every Jewish community the world over. The Rebbe often emphasized that the performance of just one additional good deed could usher in the era of Mashiach. The Rebbe's scholarly talks and writings have been printed in more than 200 volumes.

TEXT 15

THE REBBE, RABBI MENACHEM M. SCHNEERSON, *IGROT KODESH* 24:332–333

אייבס, לאנגזם, רודל, שווארץ,
ישיבת תורת אמת
ת.ד. 5024 ירושלים

בְּמַעֲנֶה לְמִבְרָקָם - יִלְמְדוּ בְּהַתְמָדָה וּבִשְׁקִידָה וְכָל הַתַּלְמִידִים, וּבְוַדַּאי וּבְוַדַּאי לֹא יָנוּם וְלֹא יִישָׁן שׁוֹמֵר יִשְׂרָאֵל, וִיבַשְּׂרוּ טוֹב.

* * *

הַנִּישׂוּאִים יִהְיוּ בְּשָׁעָה טוֹבָה וּמוּצְלַחַת בִּזְמַנָּם בְּאֶרֶץ הַקֹּדֶשׁ כִּי שָׁם צִיוָּה ה' אֶת הַבְּרָכָה חַיִּים עַד הָעוֹלָם.

* * *

אֵין דַּעְתִּי נוֹחָה כְּלַל וּכְלַל מֵהַבֶּהָלוֹת וְהַגְזָמוֹת, וַה' יִשְׁמוֹר כָּל הַנַּ"ל בְּתוֹכְכֵי כָּל אַחֵינוּ בְּנֵי יִשְׂרָאֵל שְׁלִיטָ"א בְּכָל מָקוֹם שֶׁהֵם, וּבִפְרָט בַּמָּקוֹם אֲשֶׁר עֵינֵי ה' אֱלוֹקֶיךָ בָּהּ תָּמִיד.

Ives, Langsam, Rodal, Schwartz
Yeshiva Toras Emes
P.O.B. 5024, Jerusalem

In response to your telegram:

Continue your Torah study with complete dedication, along with all the other students. Without any shadow of a doubt, "the guardian of Israel neither slumbers nor sleeps" (PSALMS 121:4). May you share good news.

* * *

The wedding will be in an auspicious hour, in its designated time, in the Holy Land—"For there God has assured blessing and life for all eternity" (PSALMS 133:3).

* * *

I am very displeased by the panic and the exaggerations. God will protect all those whom you referenced among all our brethren, the children of Israel wherever they may be, and specifically those residing in the land where "God's eyes are constantly upon it" (DEUTERONOMY 11:12).

Israel from space, December 2014. (Photo credit: Barry Wilmore, NASA Astronaut to the International Space Station)

KEY POINTS

1 In the lead-up to the Six-Day War, extreme tension and trepidation mounted in Israel and around the globe. Preparations were made for worst-case scenarios. Then came the lightning quick, stunning victory. There was a large measure of collective cognitive dissonance that required reduction.

2 At the time, most ascribed the victory to divine intervention. The perception that a remarkable miracle had occurred led to a widespread religious reawakening, an uptick in *aliyah*, and an increase in Jewish pride around the world.

3 Some refused to accept the notion that a miracle had transpired. These people reevaluated how real the threat had been and concluded that Israel was not in as precarious a position as was thought. This perspective has become increasingly pervasive in recent years.

4 Some religious Jews staunchly oppose the State due to Zionism's deeply antireligious philosophic underpinnings. This group concluded that if there was supernatural intercession in Israel's victory, it was the Satan's work.

5 For the most part, religious communities today support the activities of the State that benefit the Jews residing in the Land—despite Zionism's philosophic roots—and view Israel's ability to self-govern as a gift from God.

6 Religious Zionists view the establishment of the State—and all the wars and conquests that followed—as evidence of the onset of the Messianic Redemption. The Six-Day War is seen as a most significant stage of the Redemption. Many, however, have difficulty defining the secular State in Messianic terms.

7 Many of the decisions that Israeli leaders contend with today are still shaped by the impact of the war. Their attempts to reconcile the cognitive dissonance produced by its outcomes mold their responses to this very day.

Additional Readings

THE RELIGIOUS MEANING OF THE SIX-DAY WAR: *A SYMPOSIUM*

RABBI SHEAR YASHUV COHEN, RABBI NORMAN LAMM, RABBI PINCHAS PELI,
RABBI WALTER S. WURZBURGER, DR. MICHAEL WYSCHOGROD

The Six-Day War has not only radically changed the political complexion of the Near East, but has wrought an upheaval in the consciousness of world Jewry. We witness considerable soul-searching among Jews all over the world who find themselves confronted with the challenge of re-examining their own personal relationship to the State of Israel. At the same time, there has developed, even in so-called secular circles, a new sensitivity and openness to questions pertaining to the religious significance of the establishment of an independent Jewish state.

To provide a forum for the discussion of some of these issues, involving the very roots of contemporary Jewish existence, the Editors of TRADITION brought together prominent Jewish thinkers from both Israel and America who were asked to respond to a series of questions previously submitted to them.

Rabbi Shear Yashuv Cohen is Deputy Mayor of Jerusalem and Director of the Harry Fischel Institute. Professor Pinchas Peli, editor of the well-known Israeli weekly, Panim El Panim, is a distinguished author and presently serves as Visiting Associate Professor of Hebrew Literature at Yeshiva University The American participants in this symposium consisted of the following members of our Editorial Board: Rabbi Norman Lamm, rabbi of the Jewish Center in New York and Erna Michael Professor of Jewish Philosophy at Yeshiva University; Dr. Michael Wyschogrod, Professor of Philosophy at the City University of New York; and Rabbi Walter S. Wurzburger, Editor of TRADITION, rabbi of Congregation Shaaray Tefila in Far Rockaway and Visiting Associate Professor of Philosophy at Yeshiva University.

Walter S. Wurzburger:

Orthodox Jewry is frequently accused of not facing up to the religious implications of the establishment of the State of Israel. As yet we have not formulated a proper response to the holocaust nor have we reacted in religious terms to the realities of Israel's independence. With only a few exceptions, both our religious consciousness and behavior have for all practical purposes ignored the historic dimensions that have been introduced by *Medinat Israel*. Although the panorama of Jewish existence has been completely overhauled, the area of religious life does not appreciably reflect the upheavals of our times.

Impatience with the religious community's reluctance to grapple with these issues has grown immeasurably as a result of the Six-Day War. Many maintain that the spectacular victories culminating with the recapture of Jerusalem represent an extraordinary manifestation of divine purpose in history. They are convinced that the events leading from the holocaust to present-day Israel reveal in a unique and special way that God acts in history. Others disagree. We cannot, they argue, presume any of God's purposes nor are we equipped to apprehend a special divine intervention. As rational human beings we must interpret historical events in purely naturalistic categories. Historic phenomena must, therefore, be explained exclusively in the light of political and military realities. However, even if we were to assume that the events in Israel were due to the direct intervention of the Almighty, we are still left with the formidable problem of establishing criteria by reference to which we can determine whether and to what extent a historic event or group of events should be directly attributed to the manifestation of Divine Providence. So far, apart from offering slogans, very little has been done to answer this question. But in the wake of developments since the Six-Day War and the "miraculous" conquest of Jerusalem, it is imperative that we come to grips with the historic realities of our time and account for them in theological terms.

To crystalize our thinking on this issue and to provide a framework for discussion of these events, TRADITION has invited you as sensitive Jewish thinkers representing both the perspective of Israelis and Americans to direct your attention to the following questions:

1. It has been said that the Six-Day War represents a unique demonstration of God's acting in history. Do you believe that the Six-Day War revealed God's operation in history to a far greater extent than other events since the establishment of the State? (For instance, the War of Liberation or the Sinai Campaign.)
2. Do the events in Israel reveal God's acting in history in a different way from other major events of our time which may also be said to reveal God's judgment in history—for example, the Cold War, Vietnam, race riots, etc.?
3. Do you look upon the events in Israel as a miracle that cannot be accounted for in terms of social, political, military or economic factors?
4. How would you compare the "miracles" of the Six-Day War with the miracles of Chanukah and Purim?
5. If you attribute theological significance to the events in Israel, what are the practical repercussions for our religious life today?
6. Do you believe that the rebirth of Israel culminating now with the recapture of Jerusalem indicates that we are on the verge of a Messianic Era?

Norman Lamm:
I am convinced that any attempt to explain the events in June 1967 as no more than a remarkable coincidence of natural factors reveals, on the part of the non-believer, an extraordinary act of naïve faith in the dogmas of agnosticism, and, on the part of the believer, a defense-mechanism by which to protect himself against possible future disappointment.

The Six-Day War was certainly a case of "revelation." But even more than a revelation of divine power and direction of history, it was a revelation in the sense that the author of the *Tanya* (R. Shneur Zalman Miladi) uses the term: a revealing to man's consciousness of the unsuspected reservoir of religious faith within him ("The hidden and natural love"). The sense of elation was universal amongst Jews, and it was authentically religious rather than nationalistic. It was the return to Mt. Moriah, not the capture of Mt. Scopus, that aroused this unparalleled exaltation. And, the existence of this inner Jewish religiousness, for whatever the reason, was not "revealed" to this extent before—neither in 1948 nor in 1956.

In attempting to understand these events in theological terms, I would rather *not* speak the language of messianism and redemption. Overloaded with centuries of sentiment, and so abused by repetition these past twenty years, terms such as *at'chalta di'geulah* (beginning of the Redemption) and *ikvata de'mashichah* (Messianic Era) inspire but do not clarify.

I prefer to analyze our situation in terms of the Biblical concept of *hester panim* ("the hiding of the face," i.e., God's withdrawal from a direct relationship with Israel). This is a concept which has been insufficiently explored but has immediate relevance to contemporary Jewish history. The need for brevity forces me to condense my remarks, perhaps beyond the limits of comprehensibility, and to eliminate mention of my sources. Nevertheless, I consider it a more fruitful approach than the language of Messianism.

The Torah considers *hester panim* the ultimate punishment, in that it severs the dialogue between God and Israel which is the totality of Judaism. It implies that man is henceforth deprived of divine Providence and subject to chance and the accidents of nature and history. The opposite pole is *nesiat panim*, the resumption of the dialogue. Although individuals may be entirely cut off from this relationship, this is not true of the people of Israel as a whole. Between these two poles there are, according to the Sages of the Talmud, two intermediate states. In the lower state, there is no relationship. Nonetheless, God does preserve Israel; His "hand is stretched forth" to protect us from oblivion. Other than mere survival, there is no real redemptive meaning to the vicissitudes of our history. But the second state, penultimate to *nesiat panim*, is that of "in a dream do I address him." There is a sudden, dreamlike, almost unreal and uncertain confrontation in which the two partners have caught a glimpse of each other's faces, and acknowledge each other's existence. There is no conversation—but the possibility exists. Israel must overcome its bashfulness, its cherished theories of divine absence, its rigid habits of despair, and face God directly. The "dream" must be interpreted and transformed into a reality. Then Israel must utter its first words to God and await His *nesiat panim*.

Purim represented such a dream state of transitional *hester panim*. (The Rabbis related the name Esther to *hester* [to hide].) The Purim events could also be viewed naturalistically. Yet, they were interpreted as miracles, such as a break in the silence between Israel and God and an opportunity for new dialogue. Tradition records a great religious revival as a result of the Purim story.

The Six-Day War was the emergence from the dreadful *hester panim* of mere survival to that of the dream confrontation, the state of new spiritual possibilities and historic meaningfulness. In three hours God turned to His people and for six days we looked at Him—and "when the Lord returned the captivity of Zion we were as dreamers."

What must we now do? We must undertake new and passionate campaigns to continue the dialogue. The "Yeshivah world" must break out of its stultifying withdrawal from Jewish society and embrace all Israel with love. The "Modern Orthodox" must abandon their self-consciousness, their apologetic stance, and their spiritual sterility and start advocating their ideals of a full Torah life within the context of Western culture without apprehension and superficiality together with a truly inspired commitment to Torah and *mitzvot*. Diaspora Jews, moreover, must take a fresh look at the question of *aliyah*. If we are, indeed, to understand contemporary events in terms of religious significance, we can no longer continue our ambivalent attitude, whereby we conceptually agree that we are to go on *aliyah*, but existentially live as though the *golah* were a permanent feature of Jewish history for all eternity. *Aliyah* for us must mean more than the fulfillment of an individual commandment, important as it is, and more than a sense of nationalistic identification. It must become an immediate personal imperative in consequence of a new relationship to which we have been privy, a new meaningfulness that has suddenly graced our history—perhaps for the first time since the destruction of the Temple. And above all, we must acknowledge—humbly and happily—that "they," the nonobservant Israelis, were right when they argued that Jews must forge their own destiny actively and not wait passively for heavenly miracles. Power, we must admit, is not necessarily antithetical to holiness. The "impulse from below," as the *Zohar* calls it, is necessary in order to evoke the "impulse from above."

A new awareness will come from our fellow-Jews that there did indeed occur this response to our efforts from Above, that we could never have done it alone, that "impulse" joined "impulse" and, as if in a dream, we saw the Lord God of Israel.

Before the dream vanishes and is "explained" in the trivial vocabulary of diplomacy and military strategy, we must all, together, build on it and reestablish the great *nesiat panim*, the prerequisite to true *shalom* (peace) in the Middle East and all the world.

Michael Wyschogrod:

No believing Jew who lived through that harrowing Monday in June of 1967 when the fate of the two million Jews of Israel hung in balance will ever forget the overwhelming gratitude that filled Jewish hearts when the magnitude of the Israeli victory became apparent. When for the first time in almost two thousand years many of the holiest places in the Land of Israel were once again under Jewish jurisdiction, it became difficult not to see the redeeming presence of God in the momentous events of the day. At such moments it is not easy to contain the pent-up messianism that in spite of the tragic disappointments of the past, is never far below the consciousness of the believing Jew. Nevertheless it is necessary to proceed with caution, listening obediently to the Divine Word, rather than human emotion, and to the judgment of God on the affairs of men.

All events, as events, are equivocal. To the eyes of non-belief there is always the natural explanation that refuses to transpose the historic order into a theological event. Concerning the events of the Six-Day War, I hear the voice of unbelief pose the following dilemma:

The government of Israel either had good military reasons to expect victory or it did not. If it did not and still embarked on the course it did it acted irresponsibly. And if it did have good reasons then the outcome was only as foreseen and no miraculous claims are justified. The voice of unbelief is difficult to still.

Jewish faith is therefore not based on events as such, be they events that appear redemptive or those, such as the holocaust, that seem to point to God's powerful anger with the people He loves above all other. Jewish faith is based on events as they are transformed by the Word of God from the realm of ambiguity to that of clarity. The events of the Red Sea become a fulcrum of Jewish faith because they are memorialized in the Biblical text by "And God on that day saved Israel from the hand of the Egyptians" (Ex. 14:30).

Without these clear and simple words which speak to the man of the 20th century as they have to all those who preceded him, the events of the past would have their inherent ambiguity compounded by the further shadow-existence that envelops events of the past, particularly the remote past. It is the Divine Word, not one of which "returns unfulfilled" (Isaiah 55: 11), which thus becomes not a report of the saving event but its theological center, the very meaning that God bestows on that which transpires.

Because we in our day do not have such a Word concerning the Six-Day War we remain in the realm of ambiguity. What we have witnessed may have been the opening of the redemption or it may have been merely one further chapter in a story that has many chapters.

That God's solicitude never leaves his people is certain; as such we must be grateful for his acts again and again. But to make solid messianic claims and to tie the fate of Judaism to the fortunes of the State of Israel, for whose preservation and prosperity we all fervently pray, is simply unauthorized and therefore irresponsible. Along this path could lurk, God forbid, a catastrophe similar to those that were the fate of other messianic claims.

Pinchas Peli:
The Six-Day War is just another chapter revealing God's hand in directing the Jewish people throughout its history. It is no different in *quality* from other events in the history of the people which exists, according to Scriptures, as a living testimony of God's sovereignty over human destiny ("Ye are My witnesses, saith the Lord." [Isaiah 43:10]). The Six-Day War is perhaps extraordinary, albeit not unique, in its *volume*. It has all the ingredients of a Biblical miracle (the many in the hands of the few, etc.) and it therefore commands our attention to this truth which is clearly one of the basic tenets of the Jewish faith—God's role in shaping Jewish history. We also hold that God's hand is manifested as well in the Cold War, on the battlefields of Vietnam and in the race riots. There is, however, as far as we are concerned, a substantial difference between our understanding of what happens to the people of Israel and the events which transpire in the rest of the world. While the ancient prophets of Israel proclaimed their prophecies even unto the Gentiles, they did so only inasmuch as those prophecies had an impact on Israel. The belief that God is inseparably involved in shaping human destinies and that He is concerned with their triumphs and failures, does not, however, necessarily imply that we can, at all times, decipher and spell out correctly every single move in history. Here it should be added, that God's acting in history and the foretelling of events in prophecy does not interfere with the exercise of "free will" endowed to Man. We are confronted here with one of the many dilemmas and conflicts of the human situation which hangs between man's full freedom and his simultaneous total dependence on God.

The history of the entire world is in God's hand. Where does He move the world? This is one of the great mysteries. We find ourselves in a relatively clearer position, however, when dealing with Jewish history. Here we encounter a peculiar process which operates on unique principles set forth by the early Hebrew prophets and fortified by the teachings of the Rabbis. Moving along against this setting, our task is not to probe whether we can see God's hand in the events which take place and then search for a theological interpretation of these events. Our method in this case is rather the reverse: we have to see how and to what extent the events fit into God's design of Jewish history as outlined and prescribed in such remarkable detail in the Torah and in the utterances of the prophets and sages. It is not God's intervention that we should take pains to seek, but rather examine our part in the events which we witness. The events themselves must be analyzed and verified vis-à-vis the prescription spelled out to us in Scriptures and tradition. When we have done this we may be shocked to discover that the word of God is being fulfilled in our own days not just in some general way, but to the most minute detail.

It is hard to find a more detailed description of the great holocaust visited on our people than the one which is rendered in the chapters of the Admonition (*Tokhechah*) in Deuteronomy and Leviticus. These chapters are a precise and concise summing up of the state of *Galut* as experienced by our people in the last two thousand years, reaching its bitter climax during the last, (alas, it was not the first) holocaust. Similarly, I can find no better description of the return of the Jews to the Land of Israel, the rehabilitation of the soil, the reestablishment of the state, the ingathering of the exiles and the regaining of Jerusalem—than in the prophecies recorded thousands of years ago by almost every prophet and psalmist of Israel.

Quotations from the Bible or sayings of the Rabbis to prove this are, I believe, not necessary. Open any book of the Bible or the *Midrash* and they are there, before you. All of these prophecies, if applied to recent events, or shall we better say, all the events which we have seen with our own eyes in recent years, if tested against these ancient-but-not-antiquated prophecies, point to one thing, namely the *kaytz*, the end of *galut*, and the beginning of *geulah* with all its implications.

The recent events in Israel can indeed, well be "accounted for in terms of social, political, military or economic factors." The miracle of the return of the Jewish people to its homeland (which, please mind, does not, as matter of fact, have any *equivalent* in world history) does not depend on the supernaturalness of these events, but in their very happening within nature. This, I believe, is the right concept of a miracle in Jewish thinking which emphasizes *nes* (miracle) within *teva* (nature). We do not require events which run contrary to nature as proof of God's role in this process of *geulah*. The greatest "miracle" of all is not that the victories of the Six-Day War came despite the prevailing "social, political, military or economic factors," but, that the Jews, with the help of the Almighty, have again created, in the last few decades, the conditions which made it possible for Israel to win the war for its survival in such an astonishing fashion. For us, the question should not be whether God is now on our side, but, whether we are on God's side, to fulfill His will and blueprint. As Jews, this second question is more meaningful to us on our unique march from Sinai to Sinai. It is of more vital significance than the question if the events are miraculous.

For the last hundred years we have had hints telling us Jews that the time of our exile is over. That Israel is established, that the land is being cultivated are signs of the *kaytz*. Now the Six-Day War has expressed this feeling more forcefully. Actually the first Jew who settled Rishon L'Zion or Zichron Yaakov evoked the same miracle, the same revelation of the hand of God as the Israeli Air Force which destroyed the Egyptian planes. It is all part of one story, one saga—the beginning of the re-establishment of Eretz Yisrael and the return of the exiles either out of their free will or of being forced to do so. It is the belief of many *gedolim* that the return of Jews to Eretz Yisrael will hasten the arrival of the Messiah. Everything in Jewish history so far points to this and we are witnessing its fulfillment. We already are on a very advanced stage of the arrival of the Messianic Era—not just on the verge of it. Our casting doubt on this is tantamount to questioning the validity of Torah and prophecy. It is a serious flaw in our faith.

Shear Yashuv Cohen:
The entire course of events of the Six-Day War is definitely more of a unique demonstration of *hashgachah* (what you have termed God's acting in history) than the events that preceded it. Somehow we awaited the establishment of the State of Israel; it was the result of long-time planning. Not so with the Six-Day War; it came as a surprise. Nobody in Israel had made plans for the quick course of events that took place. Rather I would say that every effort was made by Israel's leaders to delay any action leading to a war for survival. It all happened so suddenly. Nobody has logically explained what occurred: the blockade, the unusual pact between Hussein and Nasser which led to the

eventual liberation of Jerusalem. Your eyes have to be blind, your ears have to be deaf, your mind has to be closed to claim that the events were anything but unusual. It was as if the hand of God was pushing us towards the second stage of *at'chalta d'geulah* (beginning of redemption) and bringing us to *geulah* (redemption). Living through the danger of extermination and seeing the threat lifted miraculously through a stunning victory gives one the feeling that you are part of the historic divine planning, that you are only a tool in the hand of God. And the more you know about Israel's foreign policy and the struggles between different factions trying to delay war the more this feeling is reinforced. The miracles that happened during the war and the miracles that are occurring today—until this very moment—convince you that the Six-Day War was another sphere of *hitgalut hashechinah* (revelation of the Divine Presence).

There is no doubt in my mind that we are living now in *yemot ha-mashiach*. I have no explanation for the *shoah* (holocaust). I have no explanation for the miracles of the War of Independence. I have no other explanation for the miracles of the Six-Day War but the belief that we are part of the final geulah. Both Rav Kook *zt"l* and Rav Herzog *zt"l* had the same idea. It is tragic that the present leadership of the rabbinate in Israel and outside of Israel is afraid to rise to the moment by creating new means and methods. Our minds should be geared to making Israel the central abode of the Jewish people, to making it a *mamlekhet kohanim v' goi kadosh* (a kingdom of priests and holy nation). It's not a theological question anymore; it's admitting that what we see and hear is the hand of God acting in history.

I am sure that the Six-Day War has started a new era of understanding between religions. The Jew will not be an am *golah* (a people in exile), that lives among others and has to clarify the dividing principles between Jew and Gentile. It is now becoming an *or l'goyim* (a light for the nations). This, I think, is the deep meaning of the happening of the Six-Day War from a religious point of view.

Walter S. Wurzburger:
We have reached a stage where very sharp dichotomies come to the fore: On the one side you have the viewpoint that all of Jewish history should be conceived as the gradual unfolding of the Messianic Era; on the other side, you have the theory that without the Word we cannot possibly interpret any event as revealing God's acting in history. In between we have the view which placed the recent events somewhere between the absolute *hester panim* and, what Rabbi Lamm calls, *nesiat panim*.

My first question is to Professor Wyschogrod: Might one not be inclined to say that the Word of the Bible, as interpreted by Prof. Peli, is the Word which enables us to decipher the meaning of the event? Secondly, if you say that without the Word we cannot interpret the event, then how would it ever be possible for human beings to hear the Word unless they themselves are endowed with the gift of prophecy?

Norman Lamm:
May I amplify that question for Dr. Wyschogrod. If you're going to say that the event, by virtue of its being an event, is ambiguous, and, therefore, you await a word, then you remain with the question that a word, too, is ambiguous. People can hear a word and have doubts as to whether it is hallucinatory or real. The dichotomy that you make between word and event is not valid. I think you are taking the word "word" a bit too literally. Does the concept of *devar* Hashem (word of God) mean only a verbal or intellectual or prophetic communication, or can it be clothed in terms of an event so that an event becomes its own interpretation, as it were, or the event *is* the communication?

Pinchas Peli:
Is this word that you expect different from the words that you accepted for other *mitzvot*? In the case of all other *mitzvot* you accept the written word as handed down in tradition and do not wait for a new Word. Is not there a Word, and a very clear and explicit one, in regard to exile and redemption—why then wait for another one?

Shear Yashuv Cohen:
The historical approach provides Yehuda Halevi with this proof of the existence of God. The miracles experienced by the Jewish people constitute his evidence. Why should we not view the events of the last thirty years—the holocaust, the birth of Israel, and the Six-Day War—as events continuing to prove the existence of God and thus constituting *devar Hashem b'metsiut* (a manifestation of Divine Word in reality), if not *devar Hashem* literally?

Michael Wyschogrod:
Basically there are two questions addressed to me. First, is not the Biblical word which we have sufficient for the events of today? Must I have a new Word? And, secondly, does not God also speak through events rather than through Words? My understanding of the Messianic event is that it involves, in a necessary way, the reappearance of prophecy. That, of course, does not mean that the Biblical word, as we have it now, is not a guide for Jewish history. The crucial difference, however, between Jewish history under the Divine word in the Bible and the Messianic period is the end of *hester panim* in its most profound sense, namely, through the speaking of God.

Now there is something comical, of course, for someone to observe events and to refuse to recognize them unless he has read them in a text. But here I think I am adopting a comical position that is Jewish—waiting for the text. At present no text has evolved even though such events as *Medinat Yisrael*, the holocaust, and the Six-Day War have occurred. To me this is more than an unfortunate event, a shortcoming. But I must emphasize that I do not say *chas veshalom*, that I know that these events are not messianic. It is difficult for me to say this because everything that is Jewish and human in me pushes me to agree with you. But, at the same time, I cannot say what you say because I must hear the Word. One more observation and that will conclude my response. I observed that no one has referred to any of the catastrophes of false messianism in Jewish history. This is significant. In Shabtai Zvi there was the rousing of not one Jew or a hundred Jews but multitudes of Jews who heard the steps of the Messiah. And this event ended in one of the greatest tragedies in Jewish history. Can we, as we observe the events of Israel, simply forget about false messianism? They are unpleasant questions and. you don't want to think about it. But are you considering it?

Shear Yashuv Cohen:
All the false messianic movements arose as dreams and not as a result of an historic, long, physical process. They did not start from a national, economic, political involvement.

Norman Lamm:
You just spoke about the suddenness of the whole victory!

Shear Yashuv Cohen:
I don't speak specifically about the last event. I speak of the beginning of the revival of *Eretz Yisrael* fifty, sixty years ago. It was not a person coming to the Diaspora declaring himself the Messiah but a secular development generating a feeling of living in the days of the Messiah. This is the difference.

Walter S. Wurzburger:
But where are the universalistic implications that are associated with the Messianic Era? After all, Isaiah did not speak about a Messianic Era merely in terms of the restoration of the Jewish people, but he also predicted an era of universal peace and justice.

Shear Yashuv Cohen:
That's why I've mentioned interfaith relationships. I believe that the *techiat haguf* (the political and economic revival of the State of Israel) is only the beginning—a starting point. Miracles on the sphere of religious experience in the State of Israel will follow. Then we'll see the real Messiah.

Walter S. Wurzburger:
With the Vietnam War, the Cold War, race riots are you prepared to claim that we are in the midst of the Messianic age?

Shear Yashuv Cohen:
I feel these are additional reasons why I believe we are reaching that point.

Norman Lamm:
We are, I think, going very far astray if our two participants from Israel declare so positively and, to me, with shocking dogmatism, that we are presently in the midst of *yemot hamashiach*.

I must say I feel astounded. For if you accept this as the Messianic Era you have to draw certain consequences. First, what Dr. Wyschogrod said concerning pseudo-messianism. Second, you have to be aware that, unconsciously, you are adopting the Reform interpretation of the Messianic Era. *Mashiach* is no longer an individual personality.

Speaking of an era instead of a personality as the Messiah smacks more of 19th-century progressivism than it does of the original Jewish concept. I'd like to remind you that the Messiah according to the interpretation of our Sages, will come only *behesech hadaat* (by distraction). The more we talk about him, the less likely he's going to come. Perhaps, they meant that when you start talking about Messiah you become so involved trying to interpret him that when he'll come by and say, "Hello, I'm the Messiah," you'll be so busy at a *pilpul* about Messianic ages you won't even recognize him.

We should try to understand what has happened in terms of *hester panim* and *nesiat panim* because they have religious consequences. It means that our people have seen something and therefore the burden falls upon us as Orthodox, committed Jews to do something; whereas if the events are part of the Messianic Era the attitude may well be: "I'm satisfied with having built an army, let's forget the Messiah."

The point is that we are now in a stage where an entire people has once again seen the *penei HaShechinah, be'galuy*, here in America. Thus we have certain opportunities and we must draw certain consequences. Whereas, if you speak only in messianic terms, I'm afraid it is going to be as fruitless as it always has been.

Walter S. Wurzburger:
I see a certain danger in saying as our Israeli friends reiterate that every event in Jewish history is holy. If you endow everything with holiness then every natural event is holy. This leads to a rejection of our distinction between that which is holy and that which is not holy or "not yet holy." You are bound to end up with a complete repudiation of any kind of normative Judaism when you bestow holiness on every manifestation of Jewishness in Israel. It is this kind of mentality that prompts Prof. Peli to assert that every event in Jewish history is holy.

Pinchas Peli:
I would never say that the holocaust is holy although it is, perhaps messianic. It is an indication of a certain direction. You are going too far by saying that every historic movement is the realization of the Messiah. We do not know, our sages did not know. There are ups and downs. We don't make the events, God makes them. At most we know the *way* to the Messiah. We can shape them either in accordance with His will, or against His will. That is what we have to examine, not whether they are messianic or not. We do not decide when and how to cause the advent of the Messiah. This is God's business.

Shear Yashuv Cohen:
I must reject the idea that any discussion on the Messianic Era is futile. In the Talmud *Sanhedrin* there are many opinions expressed. Such a discussion is legitimate within the framework of *Emunah* (belief of Israel). Therefore I would not speak with such disdain about the *pilpul* of what the Messiah is. It is clear that as *Emunah* we speak about the personal Messiah that has to come. This, however, does not nullify my definition of the Messianic Era as a longer period in which the course of events leads us more and more towards the final stage of the Messiah.

I tend to agree with Prof. Peli that we are now closer to *acharit hayamim* (end of days). It is the first time in nineteen centuries that we have Jerusalem under Jewish dominion and a Jewish government controlling the Holy Land. Now it is possible for every Jew to visit or live in Eretz Yisrael. It did not happen before in history. It is this change in Jewish history that cannot be ignored. That is why I cannot accept or understand the resentment our American rabbis, our friends, have expressed today. I think it is a binding duty to admit that we live in a different era in Jewish history—an era that we have awaited for nineteen centuries. To ignore this would be to ignore *metsiut*

Hashem (existence of God) and *hitgalut Hashem* (revelation of God) on the course of history.

Norman Lamm:
I would like to say that I deny neither *metsiut Hashem* nor *hitgalut Hashem*, nor am I particularly resentful of *chachmei hamishnah* (the Talmudic Sages) and their discussion about the Messianic Era. Of course, I realize that we live in a unique time. That is why I specifically spoke about these events as a new stage in the relationship of *K'lal Yisrael* with God. Also as Maimonides in *Hilkhot Malackhim* states there were so many different conceptions of the Messianic Era that it was best not to go into all the details. Historically, wherever people started to interpret their own events as messianic events they ended up in trouble, from the great Rabbi Akiva down to the times of the false Messiahs. I prefer to think that the Messiah will come in his own good time. We have to work for redemption; we have to work for his coming. Our tasks are military, economic, religious and political. We have to get involved in these, and, above all, to integrate all these in a spiritual framework. Then the Messiah will come.

Michael Wyschogrod:
At this point I have a curious sense that there has been a little transformation here. Our Israeli friends have moderated their claim somewhat. This is regretful—I wanted to be convinced the other way.

Hester panim is something that has receded and returned throughout Jewish history. Wouldn't you say, for example, that at the height of the Spanish period there was a closeness of God to Israel that was ended in their expulsion? Or at the height of Eastern European life there was a closer and more cordial relation between God and Israel than there was starting September 1939? So if we examine it from that point of view I fully agree that the Six-Day War has brought us to a very unusual degree of closeness.

I just want to add one anecdote. A friend of mine, just days before the war, said to me that if Israel goes it will be the end of Judaism. At that time I did not know, of course, the outcome but I very strongly objected. We have lived through the destruction of six million Jews and yet we have not given up hope. We remain committed to the certainty of the Messianic coming. For us to change and say that the six million did not constitute the end of Judaism, but that God forbid if something happened to the *Yishuv* it would be very dangerous. While I love the people of Israel and the State of Israel as much as anyone, I love the goal of Jewish history even more, even more than the six million or the State of Israel. I am simply not prepared at this point to tie the end of one with the destruction of Jewish eschatology altogether.

Shear Yashuv Cohen:
I do not see the dichotomy between the goals of Jewish history and *emunah temimah* (simple faith) that nothing could happen to the State of Israel. Although it may sound illogical it did not occur to me for one single moment during the crises that Israel's destruction was imminently possible. This is not logical; but neither is *emunah*. I believe that Judaism is going to prevail and that the *Yishuv* in Israel is going to remain. I cannot even entertain any other thought or even discuss what would happen if. That is beyond the sphere of my basic beliefs. For me it is a matter of *emunah temimah*.

Walter S. Wurzburger:
How can you maintain such an *emunah temimah* about an empirical contingency? Naturally, we hope it won't ever happen but *emunah* does not warrant the belief that nothing can ever happen to Israel at any particular time, even though we have faith in *netzach Yisroel*—the indestructibility of the Jewish people as a whole.

Pinchas Peli:
This *emunah* was not shared by the head of the Israel Government. We were ready and prepared for the full destruction of Israel. Now the question is what theological implication it would have had.

Michael Wyschogrod:
May I make a confession here. There came a certain point in the events of May and June, before the outbreak of the war, when I was very pessimistic. Then it was asked, at what point it would be proper for Israel in order to save two million Jewish lives to make a very serious and compromising political settlement

involving Israeli sovereignty. Because we live in this unredeemed world, I think the Government of Israel must keep in mind that any other way of thinking would preclude taking such a step placing two million Jewish lives in jeopardy.

Shear Yashuv Cohen:
I must make a clarification. It is not the political independence of a state but the existence of a Jewish center in Israel that I had in mind. And while I agree it is not possible to maintain and lead a state based only upon religious assumption of *emunah,* deep in my heart I feel that it is contrary to *emunah* to believe that there will be a third destruction of the Yishuv in Israel. I don't see the contradiction. It's a different sphere. I speak from a theological viewpoint and not from a political viewpoint.

Norman Lamm:
I would like at this point, Prof. Wyschogrod, to take the side of our Israeli friends. The existence of the State is a fact that cannot be denied. And for a state to decide to surrender her sovereignty because it will cost a great number of human sacrifices in order to prevail is an act of suicide—the kind of national suicide that I think is impermissible, absolutely impermissible.

Michael Wyschogrod:
I am not, of course, advocating any such step. All I am saying is that any responsible secular government lives in a realistic world. It is conceivable that such a combination of circumstances could arise. Nations do surrender. Japan surrendered without knowing the future of its sovereignty. A state that thinks messianically and identifies its fate with the fate of the Jewish people cannot think that way. I want to preserve for the Israel Government the right under certain circumstances, which we pray will never happen, to act as any other secular political entity does. Without that we are on a track from which there is no getting off.

Pinchas Peli:
Well, as Jews, we are on that track anyway, whether we want it or not. Besides being Israelis, we are also Jews after Auschwitz. There is no such possibility that could ever occur for Israel to give up its statehood in order to save its Jews. Not only will it not save the Jews in Israel but it will also endanger Jewish lives throughout the world. We can't forget that we live after 1944 and that there was a "final solution" which the world silently ignored. This has religious implications for us. As Jews we cannot rely on any one. We must rely on our strength in Israel; this is God's pointing finger. This too was foretold thousands of years ago.

Norman Lamm:
I too have a confession but it is the reverse of Dr. Wyschogrod's. During June I felt that Israel had no way out; it must fight. This was not ideologically motivated—my feeling was simple *realpolitik*. As Prof. Peli said, after Auschwitz there no longer was any other way. I, too, felt that if, God forbid, Israel falls, it is the end of Judaism. Not that I had given up on the eschatology of Judaism, but rather it was a visceral feeling. Should this ever happen, God forbid, I throw the burden on God's shoulders. We are no longer responsible.

Michael Wyschogrod:
What Rabbi Lamm says merely confirms in my mind the magnitude of the dangers that face us. Now I am more distressed when I see an attitude placing the whole existence of the Jewish people in danger. This I am not prepared to accept.

Shear Yashuv Cohen:
Those who justify sacrificing Jewish lives in order to save *emunah* and *Torah*, but would not sacrifice Jewish lives to save a piece of land in Israel are acting contrary to the basic beliefs of *Torah*.

Michael Wyschogrod:
Gentlemen, the defenders of Masada were not normative Jews; those who surrendered were normative Jews.

Our Sages at a certain point, felt that it was proper to surrender, and they did surrender. Judaism is alive today because they surrendered instead of taking the other route.

Shear Yashuv Cohen:
That is a practical question; not a question of values.

Norman Lamm:
I don't think we have to agree with Rabbi Cohen's idea that the Land of Israel has suddenly been elevated to

a position of value it never had before. I think the historical evidence is against placing the country on the same level with *the people, the Torah, and the God of Israel*. But given the historical realities and political context in which we live, not because of ideological reasons, the destiny of the land is inextricably intertwined with the destiny of *the people* and vice versa.

Shear Yashuv Cohen:
So you argue on a pragmatic point?

Norman Lamm:
Purely pragmatic. The ideological point of view is *mufrach*, it is denied by the history of our people.

Walter S. Wurzburger:
I'd like to make an observation which I think is significant in terms of background. The people living in this part of the world tend to be less influenced by ideology and more prone to base their judgment upon considerations of expediency and the imperatives of the moment. We are reluctant to make our judgments in the light of what appears to be manifest destinies of peoples, or the inexorable unfolding of the Messianic Era or of a Divine purpose. Not to be overwhelmed by messianic categories represents to us an important *caveat* that must be observed in Jewish normative thinking—even when it addresses itself to the religious meaning of our time.

"The Religious Meaning of the Six-Day War: A Symposium," *Tradition: A Journal of Orthodox Thought*, Vol. 10, No. 1 (Summer 1968), pp. 5–20

REVISITING ZIONISM—CAN ISRAEL SURVIVE WITHOUT A SOUL?

RABBI YOSEF YITZCHOK JACOBSON

Defiance

The spies Moses sent to survey the land had done their job well. They convinced the entire nation that the advance to the Land of Israel was doomed and that Moses had misled them by taking them out of Egypt. A national hysteria consumed the nation. They demanded a new leader who would return them to Egypt.

In the continuation of this episode related in this week's portion (Shelach), Moses chastises the nation severely. He communicates to them G-d's pledge that their wish would be fulfilled: they would not enter the land but rather perish in the wilderness. Moses' words hit the people very hard and brought them to their senses. They decided to repent and advance toward the land. They exclaimed, "We are ready! We shall ascend to the place G-d has spoken; indeed we have sinned."

This time, though, Moses refused to go along.

> *"Why do you transgress the word of G-d; it will not succeed!" he tells them. "Do not ascend, for G-d is not in your midst! And you will be smitten before your enemies."*

But they refuse to obey. They are determined to mend their mistake and advance toward the Promised Land. "They defiantly ascended to the mountaintop, while the Ark of G-d's covenant and Moses did not move from the camp."

This path turned out to be ill advised. They were indeed struck down.

RABBI YOSEF YITSCAK JACOBSON, 1972-

Writer and lecturer. Born and raised in Brooklyn, Rabbi Jacobson was a member of the editorial team publishing the talks of the Lubavitcher Rebbe. He served as editor in chief of the Yiddish-English weekly, *The Algemeiner Journal,* and as spiritual leader of Congregation Beis Shmuel in Brooklyn. Rabbi Jacobson is a popular lecturer and teacher of Jewish thought and has written extensively on these subjects.

No Second Chance?

This story must be studied well.

The Bible often speaks of G-d as welcoming and embracing repentance. The Jews have repented in this case: they acknowledged their sin; they expressed remorse; they were determined to reverse their actions and follow the destination G-d envisioned for them at the outset of their journey. They were sincere in their repentance and conviction. But Moses warned them against it. Why? Doesn't Judaism believe in a second chance?

When we read the verses carefully, the answer becomes clear. Moses was not disputing the fact that their repentance was sincere. What he was telling them was that to conquer the Land of Israel they needed to have G-d in their midst. They could not do it alone. But G-d would not accompany them this time. He had decreed that this generation would remain in the desert. "The Ark of G-d's covenant and Moses did not move from the camp." And when the people attempted to take the land without the divine Ark at their side, failure was imminent.

The message Moses was communicating here was nothing less than revolutionary. He was telling them that for the Jewish people, nationalism divorced from spirituality and religion will not succeed.

Was he right?

Let us go forward a few thousand years and study the modern-day creation of the State of Israel.

Two Goals of Zionism

Zionism was a movement created more than a century ago with the goal of creating a national homeland for the Jewish people. Its founders believed that if a Jewish state were created, there would finally be one place on earth where Jews could be safe. Here, it was said, Jews would be able to defend themselves.

The early political Zionists also believed that having a country would normalize the condition of the Jew in the world. The Jews were singled out, they speculated, because there was something unnatural about a people not having a home. The French had France, the Italians had Italy. If the Jews had a country, the condition of the Jew would change. The world would cease its relentless attention on this tiny fraction of the world's population.

[One hundred and fourteen] years have passed since the first Zionist congress in Switzerland (in 1897), led by figures like Theodor Herzl, Max Nordau and Dr. Nathan Berenbaum (the latter coined the term Zionism). Israel today is a beautiful country that we love and cherish. Notwithstanding all of its challenges from within and without, it will soon boast the world's largest Jewish population and one of the greatest armies in the world. Its cultural, academic, social and religious achievements are extraordinary. It has become a home for millions of Jews and for their creativity in many diverse fields. We must support Israel in every possible way.

Yet, the sad truth is that the two primary and noble goals of Zionism—to create a safe haven for Jews and normalize their condition—have, sadly, not materialized in the State of Israel.

Only in the Jewish state were Jews subjected to daily missile attacks—for over six years!—on their children. Only in the Jewish State did a million Jews cower in bomb shelters to protect themselves from Hezbollah missiles. (In the end, the only thing that stopped the shelling of Israel's northern cities was the United Nations. We needed the gentiles again for our safety . . .)

Nor has Israel normalized the Jewish condition. Not only has it not assuaged the obsession with the Jewish people and extinguished the flames of anti-Semitism, on the contrary, the very existence of the State has become the target of enormous anti-Semitism the world over. Yugoslavia, Rwanda, Darfur—all conflicts that have taken countless more lives than the Israeli-Palestinian conflict—receive nowhere near the amount of attention that Israel does.

What did the ideologues of Zionism fail to understand? Where did they go wrong?

Too much is at stake for us to ignore this question. So many of our brothers and sisters have sacrificed—and continue to sacrifice—so much for our homeland, that we must not fail them by not attending to this question with the utmost sincerity and intellectual integrity.

What Makes Us a Nation?

Writing in the tenth century, the great Rabbi and philosopher Saadya Gaon pondered the question of what constituted the Jews as a nation. What was it that made us "one people" despite the fact that we did not share any of the conventional bases of nationhood? Lacking a homeland or political sovereignty, scattered around the world, speaking many languages and possessing a diversity of cultures, what defined the Jews as a single nation?

Rabbi Saadya's answer was straightforward: "Our nation is only a nation in virtue of its Torah." What he meant was this: The exclusive factor that defined Jewish nationhood—the thread that connected a Jew from Spain to a Jew from Tunisia—was their shared commitment to the same Torah and its Mitzvos.

The very genesis of Jewish nationhood attests to this, for our beginnings as a people differ from every other nationality on earth. Where the history of other nations begins with a piece of territory inhabited by many individuals who then form a nation and a constitution, Jewish history begins outside of their homeland, in the wilderness. What defines them as a nation is not the territory, but rather a single idea, a vision, a perspective, what we call today the Torah. For other nations, the homeland breeds the laws; for the Jews—whose very identity as a nation was defined by law, by Torah—the homeland is an outgrowth of Torah. The Torah defined the Land of Canaan as the suitable homeland for the Jews, the most conducive place on earth for them to carry out their mission and destiny.

It is fair to say that history has proven Rabbi Saadya right. Any Jewish movement over the last 3300 years that redefined Jewishness not in terms of Torah and Mitzvos—from the worshippers of the Baal during the First Temple era to the Sadducees in the Second Temple era, to the founders of the Enlightenment, the Yiddishisten and Bundesten in our own modern era—did not pass the test of time. Their great-grandchildren either returned to Torah or were lost to the Jewish people. The Jewish people could not sustain themselves as Jews without Torah.

What is even more: If we were to search for an objective, scientific answer to how the Jewish people have survived through millennia of unparalleled suffering and abuse, we would be compelled to search for the common thread that pervaded all of Jewish history from its very beginnings to this very day. And the only constant factor that has accompanied the Jewish people—through all its vicissitudes—was not land, language, culture, military prowess, etc., but its tenacious adherence to our spiritual heritage; its commitment to Torah and Mitzvos.

The New Jew

For close to eight centuries Rabbi Saadya's declaration went uncontested. Even those Jews, like Boruch Spinoza, who abandoned Jewish law, understood that this meant abandoning conscious membership of the Jewish people. Emancipation and Enlightenment in the 18th century gave birth, for the first time since Rabbi Saadya, to the idea of redefining the Jewish people outside of the context of Torah and Mitzvos.

Zionism followed suit. The leaders of secular Zionism sincerely believed that the new national identity of the Jewish people would create a new type of Jew, a "national creature" rather than a "religious creature." The founders of the State of Israel, too, tried hard to create the identity of an "Israeli." They believed that the Jewish religion served its purpose while in exile countries, giving Jews a distinct identity. But once they have created a national homeland for themselves, they could let go of their religious baggage and finally become a nation like all nations, a nation defined by its nationality, homeland and culture, not by its faith and spirituality.

The Israeli national anthem speaks of "the 2,000 year old Jewish hope to be a free people in its land, the land of Zion and Jerusalem." It makes no mention of the religious connection between the Jewish people and the Land. The signers of the Israeli Declaration of Independence, drawn up in May 1948, made no mention of G-d or Torah. After much debate, it was agreed upon to insert the ambiguous phrase "The Rock of Israel (Tzur Yisrael)," to be interpreted as one desired.

This seemed like a rational approach. Why mix religion and statehood? For a democracy to flourish, liberal pluralism must be maintained. Church and state need to be separated. Introducing biblical notions into the Zionist endeavor would only undermine Israel's success as a liberal democracy.

Buber's Warning

Writing from a very different paradigm, Martin Buber (in an essay titled "Zionism and the Other National Concepts") argued against the creation of a purely secular state of Israel.

"The secularizing trend in Zionism was directed against the mystery of Zion too. A people like other peoples, a land like other lands, a national movement like other national movements—this was and still is reclaimed as the postulate of common sense against every kind of 'mysticism.' And from this standpoint, the age-long belief that the successful reunion of this people with this land is inseparably bound up with a command and a condition was attacked. No more is necessary—so the watchword runs—than that the Jewish people should be granted the free development of all its powers in its own country like any other people. . . .

"The certainty of the generations of Israel testifies that this view is inadequate. The idea of Zion is rooted in deeper regions of the earth and rises into loftier regions of the air, and neither its deep roots nor its lofty heights, neither its memory of the past nor its ideal for the future, both of the selfsame texture, may be repudiated. If Israel renounces the mystery, it renounces the heart of reality itself. National forms without the eternal purpose from which they have arisen signify the end of Israel's specific fruitfulness. The free development of the latent power of the nation without a supreme value to give it purpose and direction does not mean regeneration, but the mere sport of a common self-deception behind which spiritual death lurks in ambush. If Israel desires less than it is intended to fulfill, than it will even fail to achieve the lesser goal."

Buber, himself quite distant from many aspects of Jewish faith and practice, talks of the "eternal purpose from which they have arisen." These are, like Buber himself, beautiful but nebulous words; but they can be taken in many directions. In fact, some of Buber's students at Hebrew University have become

Post-Zionist thinkers calling for the abolishment of Israel as a "Jewish State."

The Soul of a People

More than 3300 years ago Moses spoke clearly of the Jewish struggle for self-identity. He understood that nationality divorced from spirituality would not suffice for the Jewish soul. Our very identity is bound up with Torah; the definition of our nationhood is that we are carriers of Torah. If the Ark does not enter into the land with the Jewish people, their existence is in peril.

A national homeland on its own cannot do the trick for us. It can't "normalize" us, nor can give us the safety we crave. We need G-d in our midst; we need the Torah at our side.

This is not to suggest that citizens of Israel should legally be coerced to follow Jewish law. This would create an even deeper animosity to Judaism and its laws. In the world we live in, religion and spirituality must be a personal choice coming from within. What it is saying is that every nation needs a soul. Even Israel. And the soul of the Jewish people for 4,000 years has been the Torah.

Ancient Egypt and Rome built great monuments to outlive the winds and sands of time. What they built still stands, and in some respects has never been surpassed. But the civilizations that gave them life are long gone. The Jews became builders, too, but what they constructed were not monuments of stone. Instead they were summoned at Sinai to build a righteous world, worthy of becoming a home for the Divine presence. Its stones would be its holy deeds, mitzvot, and its mortar—Torah study and compassion. By teaching the Jews that the Architect of this world is G-d, and that the builders are all who wish to become His "partners in the work of creation," Moses turned a group of slaves into an eternal people.

"Revisiting Zionism—Can Israel Survive Without a Soul?" *The Algemeiner.* June 19, 2011.

Lesson 6

A NATION THAT DWELLS ALONE

ISRAEL'S RELATIONS WITH THE FAMILY OF NATIONS

Israeli paratrooper praying at the Western Wall, 1967. (Photo credit: Magnum Photos; Micha Bar Am, photographer)

One of Israel's principal dilemmas—one that grew more acute in the aftermath of the 1967 war—is its stance toward an often hostile international community. In disproportion to the size of both its land and population, Israel receives constant coverage in international media, and the majority of this coverage is uncomplimentary. Is the criticism and censure justifiable? Can Israel normalize its existence and affairs to the point that it will be viewed as equal to other players in the international community?

TEXT 1

DEUTERONOMY 11:10–11

כִּי הָאָרֶץ אֲשֶׁר אַתָּה בָא שָׁמָּה לְרִשְׁתָּהּ, לֹא כְאֶרֶץ מִצְרַיִם הִוא אֲשֶׁר יְצָאתֶם מִשָּׁם, אֲשֶׁר תִּזְרַע אֶת זַרְעֲךָ וְהִשְׁקִיתָ בְרַגְלְךָ כְּגַן הַיָּרָק.

וְהָאָרֶץ אֲשֶׁר אַתֶּם עֹבְרִים שָׁמָּה לְרִשְׁתָּהּ, אֶרֶץ הָרִים וּבְקָעֹת, לִמְטַר הַשָּׁמַיִם תִּשְׁתֶּה מָּיִם.

The land into which you are entering to possess is not like the land of Egypt from which you have left. There you planted your seed and watered [your fields by bringing water from the Nile] by foot, like a vegetable garden.

But the land that you are crossing [the Jordan River] to possess is a land of mountains and valleys that drinks rain from heaven.

Old Jerusalem, *Reuven Rubin, 1925. Oil on canvas. (Photo credit: University of California, S. Diego)*

Figure 6.1

Unbiased Critique

Fair	Equal and proportionate critique of all who are in violation of a consistently applied standard
Objective	Follows the facts wherever they lead; does not attempt to reconcile facts with a pre-scripted narrative or selectively focus on facts that are compatible with that narrative

TEXT 2a

MATTI FRIEDMAN, "AN INSIDER'S GUIDE TO THE MOST IMPORTANT STORY ON EARTH,"
TABLET MAGAZINE, AUGUST 26, 2014

Is there anything left to say about Israel and Gaza? Newspapers this summer have been full of little else. Television viewers see heaps of rubble and plumes of smoke in their sleep. A representative article from a recent issue of *The New Yorker* described the summer's events by dedicating one sentence each to the horrors in Nigeria and Ukraine, four sentences to the crazed *génocidaires* of ISIS, and the rest of the article—30 sentences—to Israel and Gaza. . . .

Israeli actions are analyzed and criticized, and every flaw in Israeli society is aggressively reported. In one seven-week period, from Nov. 8 to Dec. 16, 2011, I decided to count the stories coming out of our bureau on the various moral failings of Israeli society. . . . I counted 27 separate articles, an average of a story every two days. In a very conservative estimate, this seven-week tally was higher than the total number of significantly critical stories about Palestinian government and society, including the totalitarian Islamists of Hamas, that our bureau had published in the preceding three years.

The Hamas charter, for example, calls not just for Israel's destruction but for the murder of Jews and blames Jews for engineering the French and Russian revolutions and both world wars; the charter was never mentioned in

MATTI FRIEDMAN

Israeli journalist and author. A native Canadian, Friedman immigrated to Israel in 1995. His reporting has taken him to Lebanon, Morocco, Moscow, and the Caucasus, and his writing has appeared in the Wall Street Journal, the New York Times, the Washington Post, and elsewhere. He is the author of *The Aleppo Codex: A True Story of Obsession, Faith and the Pursuit of an Ancient Bible* (2012).

print when I was at the AP, though Hamas won a Palestinian national election and had become one of the region's most important players.

To draw the link with this summer's events: An observer might think Hamas' decision in recent years to construct a military infrastructure beneath Gaza's civilian infrastructure would be deemed newsworthy, if only because of what it meant about the way the next conflict would be fought and the cost to innocent people. But that is not the case. The Hamas emplacements were not important in themselves, and were therefore ignored. What was important was the Israeli decision to attack them.

There has been much discussion recently of Hamas attempts to intimidate reporters. Any veteran of the press corps here knows the intimidation is real, and I saw it in action myself as an editor on the AP news desk. During the 2008-2009 Gaza fighting I personally erased a key detail—that Hamas fighters were dressed as civilians and being counted as civilians in the death toll—because of a threat to our reporter in Gaza. (The policy was then, and remains, not to inform readers that the story is censored unless the censorship is Israeli. Earlier this month, the AP's Jerusalem news editor reported and submitted a story on Hamas intimidation; the story was shunted into deep freeze by his superiors and has not been published.)

TEXT 2b

IBID.

The Israel story is framed in the same terms that have been in use since the early 1990s—the quest for a "two-state solution." It is accepted that the conflict is "Israeli-Palestinian," meaning that it is a conflict taking place on land that Israel controls—0.2 percent of the Arab world—in which Jews are a majority and Arabs a minority. The conflict is more accurately described as "Israel-Arab," or "Jewish-Arab"—that is, a conflict between the 6 million Jews of Israel and 300 million Arabs in surrounding countries. (Perhaps "Israel-Muslim" would be more accurate, to take into account the enmity of non-Arab states like Iran and Turkey, and, more broadly, 1 billion Muslims worldwide.) This is the conflict that has been playing out in different forms for a century, before Israel existed, before Israel captured the Palestinian territories of Gaza and the West Bank, and before the term "Palestinian" was in use.

The "Israeli-Palestinian" framing allows the Jews, a tiny minority in the Middle East, to be depicted as the stronger party. It also includes the implicit assumption that if the Palestinian problem is somehow solved the conflict will be over, though no informed person today believes this to be true.

Video US World Politics Entertainment Health MoneyWa

AP | *February 3, 2016, 8:54 AM*

3 Palestinians killed as daily violence grinds on

Israeli policemen stand next to dead bodies at the scene where three Palestinians, who were shot dead by Israeli police after carrying out what Israeli police spokesman said was a shooting and stabbing attack outside Damascus Gate to Jerusalem's Old City, Feb. 3, 2016. **REUTERS**

CBSNEWS Video US World Politics Entertainment Health MoneyWat

AP | *September 19, 2016, 7:54 AM*

Another alleged Palestinian stabber shot by Israeli cops

Agence France-Presse
@AFP

Following

#BREAKING Police shoot man who stabbed passengers on Tel Aviv bus: police

GPXIII

RETWEETS 49 FAVORITES 11

8:02 AM - 21 Jan 2015

Israeli police shoot man in east Jerusalem

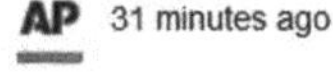

AP 31 minutes ago

JERUSALEM (AP) — Israeli police say they have shot a man whose car slammed into a crowded train stop in east Jerusalem, in what they suspect was an intentional attack.

Police spokeswoman Luba Samri says Wednesday's incident occurred near the national police headquarters. She says that nine people were wounded, some seriously.

QUESTION FOR DISCUSSION

Are these headlines fair and objective?

Photojournalists take pictures as the IDF operates inside the Gaza Strip during Operation Cast Lead, December 2008–January 2009. (Photo credit: Flash90; Kobi Gideon, photographer)

NOTABLE INCIDENTS OF ANTI-JEWISH PREJUDICE

c. 1429 BCE
Pharaoh enslaves the Jews.

c. 357 BCE
Haman plots to murder the Jews of the Persian Empire.

c. 350 BCE
Hecataeus of Abdera portrays Jews as misanthropic.

c. 170 BCE
Antiochus IV outlaws Jewish practice.

c. 150 BCE
Mnaseas of Patras: "Jews worship the head of an ass."

c. 35 CE
Apion, earliest known blood libel.

38
First real pogrom, Alexandria.

c. 125
Hadrian's decrees forbid Jewish practice.

135
Rome expels Jews from Jerusalem, renames Judea "Palestinae."

135
Rome expels Jews from Jerusalem, renames Judea "Palestinae."

150
Tacitus on the Jews: "Of all enslaved people the most contemptible."

306
Synod of Elvira: Jews and Christians not permitted to eat together.

415
Rome forbids construction of new synagogues.

535
Synod of Clermont: Jews forbidden to hold public office.

612
Spanish Visigoth realm expels Jews.

627
Muhammad beheads 600 Jews; women taken as slaves.

640
Caliph Omar makes Jews wear distinctive yellow belts.

640
Jews expelled from much of the Arabian Peninsula.

692
Trulanic Synod: Christians forbidden to use Jewish physicians.

1096
First Crusade: Thousands of Jews massacred.

1148
Almohads in Spain compel Jews to convert or die.

1179
Third Lateran Council: Jews may not be plaintiff or witness against Christians.

1190
All Jews of York, England, massacred.

1247
Jews of Beelitz, Prussia, accused of desecration of the Host and massacred.

1255
Lincoln blood libel: 18 Jews executed.

1267
Synod of Breslau: Jews compelled to live in ghettos.

1290
Edward I expels all Jews from England.

1306
Jews expelled from France.

1344
Black Death riots: Dozens of Jewish communities destroyed.

1389
3,000 Jews murdered in Prague riot.

1391
Thousands of Jews killed in riots in Spain.

1394
Charles VI expels French Jews.

1421
Massacre in Vienna: All Jews not killed are driven out.

1492
Expulsion of Spain's Jews.

1497
Forced conversion of all Jews in Portugal.

1543
Martin Luther writes *On the Jews and Their Lies.*

1648
Chmielnitzki Revolt; thousands of Jews massacred.

1744
Maria Theresa bans Jews from Hungary.

1776
Maryland requires Christian faith to hold public office.

1791
Russian Jews confined to Pale of Settlement.

1827
Tsar Nicholas I drafts young Jewish boys for 25 years of service.

1840
Damascus blood libel.

1850
Lionel de Rothschild denied seat in British Parliament.

1903

First printing of slanderous *Protocols of the Elders of Zion.*

1915

Leo Frank lynched in Georgia (U.S.).

1915

Russia removes 600,000 Jews to interior.

1919

Pogroms of Russian Civil War.

1921

Arab riots kill 43 Jews in Israel.

1938

Protocols of the Elders of Zion serialized by popular U.S. radio host; Evian Conference offers no help to European Jewish refugees; *Kristallnacht*: hundreds killed, 30,000 imprisoned, more than 1,000 synagogues ruined.

1939

Britain severely limits Jewish immigration to Palestine; Madison Square Garden packed by pro-Nazi rally; refugees on *MS S. Louis* turned away by Cuba, U.S.; Roper poll in US: 53% say Jews should be restricted; 10% say deported; ghettoization and mass shootings of Polish Jews by German police.

1940

Jews sent to slave labor camps in Poland; Britain turns back Jews escaping to Israel.

1946

Forty-two Holocaust survivors killed in Kielce, Poland.

1947

Riots in Aleppo, Syria; scores killed, more than 200 homes destroyed.

1948

Riots in Morocco; 250,000 Jews eventually flee.

1948

Pogroms in Libya; Jews flee.

1994

Jewish center in Buenos Aires bombed, killing 85.

2008

Jews targeted for slaughter in Mumbai.

AND VIOLENCE THROUGHOUT HISTORY

1861

Jewish U.S. Civil War chaplain in Union Army, Michael Allen, forced to resign for not being Christian.

1862

U.S. General Grant expels Jews from area he holds.

1881

Pogroms against Jews break out in Russia.

1894

The Dreyfus Affair.

1929

Arabs kill 133 Jews; Jews expelled from Hebron and Gaza.

1933

Riots against German Jews; German Jews banned from law, civil service, journalism, art, literature, music, broadcasting, and theater.

1941

Baghdad Pogrom: 179 Jews dead, more than 2,000 injured, 900 homes destroyed; SS kills more than 1 million Jews in Russia.

1942

Wannsee Conference organizes extermination of European Jewry; gassings start in Auschwitz and other camps.

1943

Warsaw Ghetto liquidated; Riegner Plan to save 70,000 Jews rejected by FDR; Greek Jews sent for extermination.

1944

Hungarian Jews sent for extermination; requests to bomb Auschwitz are rejected.

1945

Death marches through the winter; pogroms in Libya, more than 140 Jews killed.

1950

Synagogue bombings in Iraq spur exodus of 120,000.

1956

25,000 Jews forced to leave Egypt.

1975

UN General Assembly: "Zionism is a form of racism."

1991

Riots targeting Jews in Crown Heights, Brooklyn.

TEXT 3

PASSOVER *HAGGADAH*

שֶׁלֹּא אֶחָד בִּלְבָד עָמַד עָלֵינוּ לְכַלּוֹתֵנוּ. אֶלָּא שֶׁבְּכָל דּוֹר וָדוֹר עוֹמְדִים עָלֵינוּ לְכַלּוֹתֵנוּ.

It is not one individual alone who has risen against us to destroy us, but in every generation they rise against us to destroy us.

PASSOVER HAGGADAH

The Passover *Haggadah* was compiled during the Talmudic era. It incorporates verses from the Torah and Talmudic exegesis to tell the story of the Exodus. The *Haggadah*, which also establishes the structure of the seder, has been printed in thousands of editions and spawned thousands of commentaries, making it one of the most popular books in the history of literature.

Page from the Barcelona Haggadah *with the rubric "We were slaves to Pharaoh in Egypt," c. 1340, Spain. (The British Library, London)*

Exercise

Why are the Jews a consistent target for persecution and hatred throughout history?

Write down three issues that you would consider to be the primary causes of antisemitism.

1	
2	
3	

QUESTION FOR DISCUSSION

Can you identify any holes in the reasoning behind these causes?

TEXT 4

NATAN SHARANSKY, "ON HATING THE JEWS," *COMMENTARY MAGAZINE*, NOVEMBER 1, 2003

What makes the Soviet case instructive is, in no small measure, the fact that the professed purpose of Communism was to abolish all nations, peoples, and religions—those great engines of exclusion—on the road to the creation of a new world and a new man. . . .

In the eyes of Stalin and his henchmen, the Jews, starting with the loyal Communists among them, were always suspect—"ideological immigrants," in the telling phrase. But the animosity went beyond Jewish Communists. The Soviet regime declared war on the over 100 nationalities and religions under its boot; whole peoples were deported, entire classes destroyed, millions starved to death, and tens of millions killed. Everybody suffered, not only Jews. But, decades later, long after Stalin's repression had given way to Khrushchev's "thaw," only one national language, Hebrew, was still banned

NATAN SHARANSKY
1948–

Former Soviet dissident and Israeli politician. Sharansky is the chairman of the Jewish Agency. He spent years in Soviet prison as a political prisoner for his human rights activism. He was released after his wife led an international campaign for his freedom. He has served in various ministerial positions, and as deputy prime minister in the Israeli government.

in the Soviet Union; only one group, the Jews, was not permitted to establish schools for its children; only in the case of one group, the Jews, did the term "fifth line," referring to the space reserved for nationality on a Soviet citizen's identification papers, become a code for licensed discrimination.

TEXT 5

ESTHER 3:8–9

> וַיֹּאמֶר הָמָן לַמֶּלֶךְ אֲחַשְׁוֵרוֹשׁ, "יֶשְׁנוֹ עַם אֶחָד מְפֻזָּר וּמְפֹרָד בֵּין הָעַמִּים בְּכֹל מְדִינוֹת מַלְכוּתֶךָ. וְדָתֵיהֶם שֹׁנוֹת מִכָּל עָם וְאֶת דָּתֵי הַמֶּלֶךְ אֵינָם עֹשִׂים וְלַמֶּלֶךְ אֵין שֹׁוֶה לְהַנִּיחָם. אִם עַל הַמֶּלֶךְ טוֹב יִכָּתֵב לְאַבְּדָם".

Haman said to King Ahasuerus, "There is a certain people scattered among and separate from the peoples throughout all the provinces of your kingdom. Their laws differ from those of every people, and they do not keep the king's laws; it is therefore of no use for the king to let them be. If it pleases the king, let it be decreed to destroy them."

TEXT 6

RABBI MENACHEM ZEMBA, *CHIDUSHEI HAGA'ON RABBI MENACHEM ZEMBA*, CH. 48

יֶשְׁנָם אֲנָשִׁים הַחוֹשְׁבִים וּמְנַסִּים לִמְצוֹא אֶת הַנִּימוּקִים וְהַסִּיבּוֹת לְשִׂנְאָתָהּ שֶׁל הַגּוֹיִם כְּלַפֵּי הַיְהוּדִים. אוּלָם הַמְּצִיאוּת הוֹכִיחָה כִּי אֵין אַף סִיבָּה אַחַת נְכוֹנָה. שִׂנְאָה זוֹ הִיא חַסְרַת כָּל סִיבָּה וְכָל נִימּוּק . . .

כָּאן שׂוֹנְאִים אֶת הַיְהוּדִים עַל שׁוּם שֶׁהֵם קַפִּיטַלִיסְטִים. וְשָׁם עַל שׁוּם שֶׁהֵם סוֹצְיָאלִיסְטִים.

כָּאן עַל שׁוּם שֶׁהֵם זְרִיזִים וּפִקְחִים יֶתֶר עַל הַמִּידָה. וְשָׁם עַל שׁוּם שֶׁהֵם מְהַוִּים מַעֲמָסָה מִבְּלִי לְהָבִיא כָּל תּוֹעֶלֶת.

כָּאן עַל שׁוּם שֶׁהֵם חֲרֵדִים וְקַנָּאִים יֶתֶר עַל הַמִּידָה. וְשָׁם עַל שֶׁהֵם מִתְקַדְּמִים וּמְפִיצִים דֵּעוֹת חִילוֹנִיּוֹת.

כָּךְ תָּמִיד סוֹתְרִים הַנִּמּוּקִים זֶה אֶת זֶה. לְלֹא קוֹרְטוֹב שֶׁל הִגָּיוֹן וְשִׁיקּוּל דַּעַת.

Many seek to uncover the root cause and justifications for antisemitism. History has demonstrated, however, that not a single cause is correct. The hatred defies cause or reason.

Here they hate the Jews because they are capitalists; there they hate them because they are socialists.

Here they hate the Jews because they are industrious and shrewd; there they hate them because they are a burden on society who provide no benefit to the citizenry.

Here they hate the Jews because they are excessively religious and zealous; there they hate them because they are liberal, enlightened, and promulgate secular views.

The reasons are always contradictory.

RABBI MENACHEM ZEMBA
1883–1943

Pre-WWII Polish rabbi and halachist. Rabbi Zemba was a *chasid* of the Gur dynasty and a noted Torah scholar. He was active in communal Jewish life in Poland and served as honorary secretary in the Agudath Israel organization. Rabbi Zemba was gunned down by the Nazis in the Warsaw ghetto, and his entire family was killed in Treblinka. In 1958, his body was exhumed and reburied in Jerusalem. Thousands of pages of his scholarly works were destroyed in the burning of the ghetto.

TEXT 7

RABBI JONATHAN SACKS, "FUTURE TENSE—THE NEW ANTISEMITISM. WHAT IS IT AND HOW DO WE DEAL WITH IT?" *THE JEWISH CHRONICLE*, NOVEMBER 1, 2007

Antisemitism is not an ideology, a coherent set of beliefs. It is, in fact, an endless stream of contradictions. The best way of understanding it is to see it as a virus. Viruses attack the human body, but the body itself has an immensely sophisticated defence, the human immune system. How then do viruses survive and flourish? By mutating. Antisemitism mutates, and in so doing, defeats the immune systems set up by cultures to protect themselves against hatred.

In the first centuries of the Common Era, and again in the Middle Ages, this was religion. That is why Judeo-phobia took the form of religious doctrine. In the 19th century, religion had lost prestige, and the supreme authority was now science. Racial antisemitism was duly based on two pseudo-sciences, social Darwinism (the idea that in society, as in nature, the strong survive by eliminating the weak) and the so-called scientific study of race.

By the late 20th century, science had lost its prestige, having given us the power to destroy life on Earth. Today the supreme source of legitimacy is human rights. That is why Jews (or the Jewish state) are accused of the five primal sins against human rights: racism, apartheid, ethnic cleansing, attempted genocide and crimes against humanity.

RABBI JONATHAN SACKS, PHD
1948–

Former chief rabbi of the United Kingdom. Rabbi Sacks attended Cambridge University and received his doctorate from King's College, London. A prolific and influential author, his books include *Will We Have Jewish Grandchildren? and The Dignity of Difference.* He received the Jerusalem Prize in 1995 for his contributions to enhancing Jewish life in the Diaspora, was knighted and made a life peer in 2005, and became Baron Sacks of Aldridge in 2009.

TEXT 8

BENJAMIN WEINTHAL, "GERMAN COURT CALLS SYNAGOGUE TORCHING AN ACT TO 'CRITICIZE ISRAEL,'" *JERUSALEM POST*, JANUARY 13, 2017

Johannes Pinnel, a spokesman for the regional court [in the city of Wuppertal, Germany], explained the court's decision regarding the three German Palestinians who sought to firebomb the Wuppertal synagogue in July 2014. The court said in its 2015 decision that the three men wanted to draw "attention to the Gaza conflict" with Israel and deemed the attack not to be motivated by antisemitism. . . .

After the court's ruling, Volker Beck, a leading Green Party MP, said the "attack on the synagogue was motivated by antisemitism" and blasted the court for issuing a decision stating that the goal of the attack was to highlight the war in Gaza.

"This is a mistaken decision as far as the motives of the perpetrators are concerned," he said, adding that the burning of a synagogue in Germany because of the Middle East conflict can be attributed only to antisemitism.

"What do Jews in Germany have to do with the Middle East conflict? Every bit as much as Christians, non-religious people or Muslims in Germany, namely, absolutely nothing."

TEXT 9

BLAISE PASCAL, *THOUGHTS*, TRANS. W. F. TROTTER (NEW YORK: P. F. COLLIER & SON, 1910), PP. 209–210

The Jewish people at once attract my attention by the number of wonderful and singular facts which appear about them. . . . This family, or people, is the most ancient within human knowledge, a fact which seems to me to inspire a peculiar veneration for it. This people is not eminent solely by their antiquity, but is also singular by their duration, which has always continued from their origin till now. For whereas the nations of Greece and of Italy, of Lacedaemon, of Athens and of Rome, and others who came long after, have long since perished, these ever remain. And in spite of the endeavors of many powerful kings who have a hundred times tried to destroy them, as their historians testify, and as it is easy to conjecture from the natural order of things during so long a space of years, they have nevertheless been preserved (and this preservation has been foretold).

BLAISE PASCAL
1623–1662

French inventor, mathematician, physicist, and theological writer. In the 1640s, Pascal invented the Pascaline, an early calculator. In the 1650s, he laid the foundation of probability theory with Pierre de Fermat and published Les Provinciales, a groundbreaking work of religious theology. Pascal is also widely known for his body of notes, posthumously released as the Pensées.

Le traître, *Henri Meyer. Depiction of Alfred Dreyfus's degradation, from Le Petit Journal, January 18, 1895. (Bibliothèque Nationale de France)*

QUESTIONS FOR DISCUSSION

What is the secret of Jewish immortality?

Can we expect our immortality to continue? Is it possible for a little nation planted in a region of unrest to keep going alone?

TEXT 10

MIDRASH, *TANCHUMA, TOLDOT* 5

> אַדְרְיָאנוּס אָמַר לְרַבִּי יְהוֹשֻׁעַ, "גְדוֹלָה הַכִּבְשָׂה הָעוֹמֶדֶת בֵּין שִׁבְעִים זְאֵבִים!"
>
> אָמַר לֵיה, "גָדוֹל הוּא הָרוֹעֶה שֶׁמַּצִּילָהּ וְשׁוֹמְרָהּ וְשׁוֹבְרָן לִפְנֵיהָ".

The Roman Emperor Hadrian said to Rabbi Yehoshua: "Great is the sheep that survives in the midst of seventy wolves!"

Rabbi Yehoshua responded, "Great is the shepherd who saves the sheep, protects it, and vanquishes the wolves that wish to attack it."

MIDRASH TANCHUMA

A midrashic work bearing the name of Rabbi Tanchuma, a 4th century Talmudic sage quoted often in this work. Midrash is the designation of a particular genre of rabbinic literature usually forming a running commentary on specific books of the Bible. *Midrash Tanchuma* provides textual exegeses, expounds upon the biblical narrative, and develops and illustrates moral principles. *Tanchuma* is unique in that many of its sections commence with a halachic discussion, which subsequently leads into non-halachic teachings.

TEXT 11

NUMBERS 23:9

הֶן עָם לְבָדָד יִשְׁכֹּן, וּבַגּוֹיִם לֹא יִתְחַשָּׁב.

Behold! It is a people that dwells alone, and is not reckoned among the nations.

TEXT 12

RABBEINU BECHAYE BEN ASHER, DEUTERONOMY 11:17

לְכָךְ לֹא נָתַן לְךָ אֶרֶץ מַשְׁקֶה כְּאֶרֶץ מִצְרַיִם, כְּדֵי שֶׁלֹּא תִּהְיֶה הַהַשְׁקָאָה בְּיָדְךָ, וְיִהְיוּ תָּמִיד עֵינֶיךָ נְשׂוּאוֹת אֵלָיו לְמַפְתֵּחַ גְּשָׁמִים שֶׁבְּיָדוֹ.

God did not give you a self-irrigating land like Egypt so that you should not be able to water the land yourself. Instead, your attention will always turn to Him and the "key to the rain" that He holds.

RABBEINU BECHAYE BEN ASHER
1255–1340

Biblical commentator. Rabbeinu Bechaye lived in Spain and was a disciple of Rabbi Shlomo ben Aderet, known as Rashba. He is best known for his multifaceted commentary on the Torah, which interprets the text on literal, *midrashic*, philosophical, and kabbalistic levels. Rabbeinu Bechaye also wrote *Kad Hakemach*, a work on philosophy and ethics.

TEXT 13

DEUTERONOMY 11:11–12

וְהָאָרֶץ אֲשֶׁר אַתֶּם עֹבְרִים שָׁמָּה לְרִשְׁתָּהּ, אֶרֶץ הָרִים וּבְקָעֹת, לִמְטַר הַשָּׁמַיִם תִּשְׁתֶּה מָּיִם.

אֶרֶץ אֲשֶׁר ה' אֱלֹקֶיךָ דֹּרֵשׁ אֹתָהּ, תָּמִיד עֵינֵי ה' אֱלֹקֶיךָ בָּהּ, מֵרֵשִׁית הַשָּׁנָה וְעַד אַחֲרִית שָׁנָה.

But the land that you are crossing [the Jordan River] to possess is a land of mountains and valleys that drinks rain from heaven.

It is a land that your God cares for; the eyes of your God are continually upon it, from the beginning of the year to its end.

Religious man assists Israeli soldiers with donning tefillin at the Western Wall during the Six-Day War, 1967. (Photo credit: Magnum Photos; Leonard Freed, photographer)

TEXT 14

TALMUD, BERACHOT 6A

"וְרָאוּ כָּל עַמֵּי הָאָרֶץ כִּי שֵׁם ה' נִקְרָא עָלֶיךָ וְיָרְאוּ מִמֶּךָּ" (דְבָרִים כח, י).
וְתַנְיָא, ר' אֱלִיעֶזֶר הַגָּדוֹל אוֹמֵר: "אֵלּוּ תְּפִילִּין שֶׁבְּרֹאשׁ".

"All the nations of the earth will see that God's name is invoked upon you, and they will fear you" (DEUTERONOMY 28:10). It was taught that Rabbi Eliezer the Great said: "This is a reference to the tefillin of the head [upon which the name of God is written]."

BABYLONIAN TALMUD

A literary work of monumental proportions that draws upon the legal, spiritual, intellectual, ethical, and historical traditions of Judaism. The 37 tractates of the Babylonian Talmud contain the teachings of the Jewish sages from the period after the destruction of the 2nd Temple through the 5th century CE. It has served as the primary vehicle for the transmission of the Oral Law and the education of Jews over the centuries; it is the entry point for all subsequent legal, ethical, and theological Jewish scholarship.

TEXT 15

LEO SHAPIRO, "LUBAVITCHERS PUSH TEFILLIN CAMPAIGN," *THE BOSTON GLOBE*, NOV. 25, 1967

Since the Six-Day War in June which resulted in the creation of a united Jerusalem as part of Israel, more than 400,000 members of the Jewish faith are estimated to have observed the commandment to wear Phylacteries—Tefillin in Hebrew—at the city's Western, formerly known as the "Wailing," Wall.

Just before the outbreak of the war, an active campaign to push observance by Jewish males over 13 years of

Lubavitchers Push Tefillin Campaign

By LEO SHAPIRO
Staff Reporter

Since the Six-Day War in June which resulted in the creation of a united Jerusalem as part of Israel, more than 400,000 members of the Jewish faith are estimated to have observed the commandment to wear Phylacteries—called Tefillin in Hebrew—at the city's Western, formerly known as the "Wailing," Wall.

Just before the outbreak of the war, an active campaign to push observance by Jewish males over 13 years of age of the "mitzvah", blessing, of Tefillin, was launched by Rabbi Menachem M. Schneerson. the

and remodeling of three of the six floors of its building at 177 Tremont st., at a cocktail reception Tuesday at 4:30 p.m.

The organization is campaigning to raise funds for project so that it may better serve the entire community, in cooperation with the Massachusetts Board of Rabbis, the Vaad Harabonim (Orthodox) and its constituent congregations.

A number of people from this region will attend an institute this week-end at the Manor House of the Institute for Living Judaism in Great Barrington, sponsored by the Union of American Hebrew Congregations (Reform).

age of the "mitzvah," blessing, of Tefillin, was launched by Rabbi Menachem M. Schneerson, the "Lubavitcher Rebbe" in New York—leader of a Hasidic sect with branches throughout the world.

TEXT 16

SIFREI, DEUTERONOMY 15:18

"וּבֵרַכְךָ ה' אֱלוֹקֶיךָ בְּכָל אֲשֶׁר תַּעֲשֶׂה" (דְבָרִים טו, יח).
יָכוֹל אֲפִילוּ יוֹשֵׁב וּבָטֵל? תַּלְמוּד לוֹמַר, "בְּכָל אֲשֶׁר תַּעֲשֶׂה".

"Your God will bless you in all that you shall do" (DEUTERONOMY 15:18).

One might think [that one can be the beneficiary of God's blessing] even if sitting idly and not working. Therefore the verse says, "[God will bless you] *in all that you shall do.*"

SIFREI

An early rabbinic Midrash on the biblical books of Numbers and Deuteronomy. *Sifrei* focuses mostly on matters of law, as opposed to narratives and moral principles. According to Maimonides, this halachic Midrash was authored by Rav, a 3rd century Babylonian Talmudic sage.

TEXT 17

RABBI CHAIM OF VOLOZHIN (AS CITED IN *AVNEI CHEIN*, 1:791)

פֵּירוּשׁ רַשִׁ"י הַקָּדוֹשׁ עַל "וַיְמָאֵן לְהִתְנַחֵם" (בראשית לז, לה): "אֵין מְקַבְּלִין תַּנְחוּמִין עַל הַחַי". עַל מֵת אֲמִתִּי מְקַבְּלִין תַּנְחוּמִין, כִּי גְזֵרָה הִיא שֶׁיִּשְׁתַּכַּח מִן הַלֵּב; אֲבָל מִי שֶׁחוֹשְׁבִין עָלָיו שֶׁהוּא מֵת וּבֶאֱמֶת הוּא חַי, אֵין מְקַבְּלִין עָלָיו תַּנְחוּמִין.

וְכֵן הוּא גַּם בִּירוּשָׁלַיִם: אִילוּ הָיְתָה מֵתָה חַלִילָה וּבְלִי שׁוּם תִּקְוָה לָשׁוּב לִתְחִיָּה, הָיִינוּ שׁוֹכְחִים אוֹתָהּ כְּבַר, כְּמוֹ שֶׁשּׁוֹכְחִים כָּל מֵת; אוּלָם בִּרְאוֹתֵנוּ שֶׁכְּבָר עָבְרוּ כְּאַלְפַּיִם שָׁנָה, וִירוּשָׁלַיִם וְאֶרֶץ יִשְׂרָאֵל לֹא נִשְׁכְּחוּ מִלִּבֵּנוּ, סִימָן הוּא שֶׁהֵן חָיוֹת בְּקִרְבֵּנוּ.

Citing the words "Jacob refused to be consoled" (GENESIS 37:35), Rashi explains: "Because a person is not consoled over the living." Over one who has truly passed, a person is eventually consoled, because it has been decreed that the memory of the deceased should fade. But when a person is only thought to be dead but is in fact alive [as was the case with Joseph], those who mourn that person are not consoled.

The same is true regarding Jerusalem: Were she truly and hopelessly dead, God forbid, we would have long forgotten her, as every deceased is forgotten. But seeing that some two thousand years have elapsed, yet Jerusalem and the Land of Israel have not been forgotten from our hearts, this is a sure sign that they live within us.

RABBI CHAIM OF VOLOZHIN
1749–1821

Talmudist and philosopher. Born in Volozhin, Belarus, Rabbi Chaim was the protégé of Rabbi Eliyahu of Vilna (Gra) the most prominent scholar in Lithuania at the time. After the passing of his teacher, Rabbi Chaim established a yeshiva in Volozhin, which is considered the mother of the modern yeshiva system. He authored *Nefesh Hachayim*, an important work on philosophy and Kabbalah, and *Ru'ach Chayim*, a commentary on Ethics of the Fathers.

TEXT 18

MAIMONIDES, *MISHNEH TORAH*, LAWS OF KINGS 11:4 AND 12:5

יַעֲמוֹד מֶלֶךְ מִבֵּית דָוִד הוֹגֶה בַּתּוֹרָה וְעוֹסֵק בַּמִּצְוֹות כְּדָוִד אָבִיו כְּפִי תּוֹרָה שֶׁבִּכְתָב וְשֶׁבְּעַל פֶּה, וְיָכוֹף כָּל יִשְׂרָאֵל לֵילֵךְ בָּהּ וּלְחַזֵּק בִּדְקָהּ וְיִלָּחֵם מִלְחָמוֹת ה' . . . אִם עָשָׂה וְהִצְלִיחַ וּבָנָה מִקְדָּשׁ בִּמְקוֹמוֹ וְקִבֵּץ נִדְחֵי יִשְׂרָאֵל הֲרֵי זֶה מָשִׁיחַ בְּוַדַּאי. וִיתַקֵּן אֶת הָעוֹלָם כּוּלוֹ לַעֲבוֹד אֶת ה' בְּיַחַד . . .

וּבְאוֹתוֹ הַזְּמַן לֹא יִהְיֶה שָׁם לֹא רָעָב וְלֹא מִלְחָמָה וְלֹא קִנְאָה וְתַחֲרוּת שֶׁהַטּוֹבָה תִּהְיֶה מוּשְׁפַּעַת הַרְבֵּה וְכָל הַמַּעֲדַנִּים מְצוּיִין כְּעָפָר וְלֹא יִהְיֶה עֵסֶק כָּל הָעוֹלָם אֶלָּא לָדַעַת אֶת ה' בִּלְבַד . . . שֶׁנֶּאֱמַר, "כִּי מָלְאָה הָאָרֶץ דֵּעָה אֶת ה' כַּמַּיִם לַיָּם מְכַסִּים" (ישעיהו יא, ט).

A king from the House of David will arise, who studies Torah and fulfills its commandments like David his father in accordance with both the Written and Oral Torah, and he will compel all of Israel to walk in its ways and repair its breaches, and he will fight the battles of God. . . . If he does the above and is successful, and he builds the Temple in its place and gathers the dispersed of Israel [to the Land of Israel], then he is definitely the Mashiach. He will then improve the entire world to serve God in unison. . . .

In that time there will not be hunger or war, nor envy or competition, for good will flow in abundance and all the delights will be freely available as dust. The occupation of the entire world will be solely to know God . . . as it is written: "For the world will be filled with the knowledge of God as waters cover the sea bed" (ISAIAH 11:9).

RABBI MOSHE BEN MAIMON (MAIMONIDES, RAMBAM) 1135–1204

Halachist, philosopher, author, and physician. Maimonides was born in Cordoba, Spain. After the conquest of Cordoba by the Almohads, he fled Spain and eventually settled in Cairo, Egypt. There, he became the leader of the Jewish community and served as court physician to the vizier of Egypt. He is most noted for authoring the *Mishneh Torah*, an encyclopedic arrangement of Jewish law, and for his philosophical work, *Guide for the Perplexed*. His rulings on Jewish law are integral to the formation of halachic consensus.

KEY POINTS

1 Israel faces constant pressure and criticism in the international arena. While reasonable criticism is welcomed, many believe that Israel's treatment at the United Nations and by international media coverage is neither fair nor objective.

2 Antisemitism has been a historic constant, and it flourishes today too. Many theories have been suggested to explain the causes of antisemitism—e.g., the Jewish conviction of being the "chosen nation," the belief that Jews control the economy, and Christian or Islamic theology—but none of the reasons hold up to scrutiny.

3 Historically, Jews have tried to deal with antisemitism either by assimilating or by trying to find some sort of autonomy. Neither of these approaches has found lasting success.

4 There are several indicators that anti-Israel sentiment is simply a new form of antisemitism. As such, no true underlying cause can be found, and no change of lifestyle, conduct, or faith will solve the issue.

5 The survival of the Jewish nation is not natural; it is due to repeated divine intervention. When we rely on God, His protection is there for us to a far greater degree. Donning tefillin—by everyone, but especially by IDF soldiers—provides Israel with an added measure of divine protection.

6 Israel is not self-sufficient in terms of water supply and is reliant on rainfall. This is God's way of reminding us that our true security comes from Him—in all areas of life, society, and governance.

7 The same God in Whom we place our complete trust told us to be mindful of our ties with other nations: to maintain polite and respectful relationships.

8 Israel can't disengage from the world because it is her duty to provide the world with an example of a meaningful life of holiness, positive productivity, etc. Israel's disproportionate positive contributions to the world open the doors for her moral and spiritual message to be heard around the globe.

Appendix

TEXT 19

TODD M. ENDELMAN, "ASSIMILATION," *THE YIVO ENCYCLOPEDIA OF JEWS IN EASTERN EUROPE*

Assimilationists were wildly optimistic, at best, and woefully deluded, at worst, about the future. The integration and acceptance they envisioned depended not only on the transformation of the Jewish masses but equally on the transformation of the societies in which they lived. Specifically, their solution to the Jewish Question required the triumph of liberal individualism and religious tolerance, the emergence of political and social systems that would support these values, and the demise of corporate, organic notions of collective identity—none of which, it is now clear, was likely in Eastern Europe (with the possible exception of interwar Czechoslovakia). Symptomatic of their optimism was their attitude to antisemitism, whose threat to Jewish security and prosperity they minimized or even ignored. In their view, Jewish tribalism, as much as gentile ignorance, created antisemitism; as it weakened, they claimed, antisemitism would fade.

TODD ENDELMAN
1946–

Historian and author. Endelman is a historian specializing in modern Jewish history in Western Europe. He has taught at Yeshiva University and Indiana University and currently serves as a professor emeritus at the University of Michigan. Endelman is the author of a number of books.

TEXT 20

THEODORE HERZL, *THE JEWISH STATE* (MINEOLA, NEW YORK: DOVER PUBLICATIONS, 1988 ENGLISH EDITION), PP. 85–93

No one can deny the gravity of the situation of the Jews. Wherever they live in perceptible numbers, they are more or less persecuted. Their equality before the law, granted by statute, has become practically a dead letter. They are debarred from filling even moderately high positions, either in the army, or in any public or private capacity. And attempts are made to thrust them out of business also: "Don't buy from Jews!"

Attacks in Parliaments, in assemblies, in the press, in the pulpit, in the street, on journeys—for example, their exclusion from certain hotels—even in places of recreation, become daily more numerous. The forms of persecution varying according to the countries and social circles in which they occur. In Russia, imposts are levied on Jewish villages; in Rumania, a few persons are put to death; in Germany, they get a good beating occasionally; in Austria, Anti-Semites exercise terrorism over all public life; in Algeria, there are traveling agitators; in Paris, the Jews are shut out of the so-called best social circles and excluded from clubs. Shades of anti-Jewish feeling are innumerable. But this is not to be an attempt to make out a doleful category of Jewish hardships. . . .

THEODORE HERZL
1860–1904

Founder of modern political Zionism. Herzl was born to an assimilated Jewish family in Budapest, Hungary. After a brief legal career, Herzl turned to journalism, becoming the Paris correspondent for a Viennese newspaper. While in Paris, Herzl was deeply affected by the antisemitic Dreyfus affair and began searching for a solution to the problem of antisemitism. He eventually settled on the establishment of a Jewish State as the solution to antisemitism and published *Der Judenstaat* (*The State of the Jews*) in 1896. Herzl established and was elected President of the World Zionist Congress in 1897 and conducted a series of diplomatic initiatives to build support for a Jewish state.

Let the sovereignty be granted us over a portion of the globe large enough to satisfy the rightful requirements of a nation; the rest we shall manage for ourselves.

The creation of a new State is neither ridiculous nor impossible. We have in our day witnessed the process in connection with nations which were not largely members of the middle class, but poorer, less educated, and consequently weaker than ourselves. The Governments of all countries scourged by Anti-Semitism will be keenly interested in assisting us to obtain the sovereignty we want.

Additional Readings

THE ISRAEL STORY

AN INSIDER'S GUIDE TO THE MOST IMPORTANT STORY ON EARTH: A FORMER AP CORRESPONDENT EXPLAINS HOW AND WHY REPORTERS GET ISRAEL SO WRONG, AND WHY IT MATTERS

MATTI FRIEDMAN

Is there anything left to say about Israel and Gaza? Newspapers this summer have been full of little else. Television viewers see heaps of rubble and plumes of smoke in their sleep. A representative article from a recent issue of *The New Yorker* described the summer's events by dedicating one sentence each to the horrors in Nigeria and Ukraine, four sentences to the crazed *génocidaires* of ISIS, and the rest of the article—30 sentences—to Israel and Gaza.

When the hysteria abates, I believe the events in Gaza will not be remembered by the world as particularly important. People were killed, most of them Palestinians, including many unarmed innocents. I wish I could say the tragedy of their deaths, or the deaths of Israel's soldiers, will change something, that they mark a turning point. But they don't. This round was not the first in the Arab wars with Israel and will not be the last. The Israeli campaign was little different in its execution from any other waged by a Western army against a similar enemy in recent years, except for the more immediate nature of the threat to a country's own population, and the greater exertions, however futile, to avoid civilian deaths.

The lasting importance of this summer's war, I believe, doesn't lie in the war itself. It lies instead in the way the war has been described and responded to abroad, and the way this has laid bare the resurgence of an old, twisted pattern of thought and its migration from the margins to the mainstream of Western discourse—namely, a hostile obsession with Jews. The key to understanding this resurgence is not to be found among jihadi webmasters, basement conspiracy theorists, or radical activists. It is instead to be found first among the educated and respectable people who populate the international news industry; decent people, many of them, and some of them my former colleagues.

While global mania about Israeli actions has come to be taken for granted, it is actually the result of decisions made by individual human beings in positions of responsibility—in this case, journalists and editors. The world is not responding to events in this country, but rather to the description of these events by news organizations. The key to understanding the strange nature of the response is thus to be found in the practice of journalism, and specifically in a severe malfunction that is occurring in that profession—my profession—here in Israel.

In this essay I will try to provide a few tools to make sense of the news from Israel. I acquired these tools as an insider: Between 2006 and the end of 2011 I was a reporter and editor in the Jerusalem bureau of the Associated Press, one of the world's two biggest news providers. I have lived in Israel since 1995 and have been reporting on it since 1997.

MATTI FRIEDMAN

Israeli journalist and author. A native Canadian, Friedman immigrated to Israel in 1995. His reporting has taken him to Lebanon, Morocco, Moscow, and the Caucasus, and his writing has appeared in the *Wall Street Journal*, the *New York Times*, the *Washington Post*, and elsewhere. He is the author of *The Aleppo Codex: A True Story of Obsession, Faith and the Pursuit of an Ancient Bible* (2012).

This essay is not an exhaustive survey of the sins of the international media, a conservative polemic, or a defense of Israeli policies. (I am a believer in the importance of the "mainstream" media, a liberal, and a critic of many of my country's policies.) It necessarily involves some generalizations. I will first outline the central tropes of the international media's Israel story—a story on which there is surprisingly little variation among mainstream outlets, and one which is, as the word "story" suggests, a narrative construct that is largely fiction. I will then note the broader historical context of the way Israel has come to be discussed and explain why I believe it to be a matter of concern not only for people preoccupied with Jewish affairs. I will try to keep it brief.

How Important Is the Israel Story?

Staffing is the best measure of the importance of a story to a particular news organization. When I was a correspondent at the AP, the agency had more than 40 staffers covering Israel and the Palestinian territories. That was significantly more news staff than the AP had in China, Russia, or India, or in all of the 50 countries of sub-Saharan Africa combined. It was higher than the total number of news-gathering employees in all the countries where the uprisings of the "Arab Spring" eventually erupted.

To offer a sense of scale: Before the outbreak of the civil war in Syria, the permanent AP presence in that country consisted of a single regime-approved stringer. The AP's editors believed, that is, that Syria's importance was less than one-40th that of Israel. I don't mean to pick on the AP—the agency is wholly average, which makes it useful as an example. The big players in the news business practice groupthink, and these staffing arrangements were reflected across the herd. Staffing levels in Israel have decreased somewhat since the Arab uprisings began, but remain high. And when Israel flares up, as it did this summer, reporters are often moved from deadlier conflicts. Israel still trumps nearly everything else.

The volume of press coverage that results, even when little is going on, gives this conflict a prominence compared to which its actual human toll is absurdly small. In all of 2013, for example, the Israeli-Palestinian conflict claimed 42 lives—that is, roughly the monthly homicide rate in the city of Chicago. Jerusalem, internationally renowned as a city of conflict, had slightly fewer violent deaths per capita last year than Portland, Ore., one of America's safer cities. In contrast, in three years the Syrian conflict has claimed an estimated 190,000 lives, or about 70,000 more than the number of people who have ever died in the Arab-Israeli conflict since it began a century ago.

News organizations have nonetheless decided that this conflict is more important than, for example, the more than 1,600 women murdered in Pakistan last year (271 after being raped and 193 of them burned alive), the ongoing erasure of Tibet by the Chinese Communist Party, the carnage in Congo (more than 5 million dead as of 2012) or the Central African Republic, and the drug wars in Mexico (death toll between 2006 and 2012: 60,000), let alone conflicts no one has ever heard of in obscure corners of India or Thailand. They believe Israel to be the most important story on earth, or very close.

What Is Important About the Israel Story, and What Is Not

A reporter working in the international press corps here understands quickly that what is important in the Israel-Palestinian story is Israel. If you follow mainstream coverage, you will find nearly no real analysis of Palestinian society or ideologies, profiles of armed Palestinian groups, or investigation of Palestinian government. Palestinians are not taken seriously as agents of their own fate. The West has decided that Palestinians should want a state alongside Israel, so that opinion is attributed to them as fact, though anyone who has spent time with actual Palestinians understands that things are (understandably, in my opinion) more complicated. Who they are and what they want is not important: The story mandates that they exist as passive victims of the party that matters.

Corruption, for example, is a pressing concern for many Palestinians under the rule of the Palestinian Authority, but when I and another reporter once suggested an article on the subject, we were informed by the bureau chief that Palestinian corruption was "not the story." (Israeli corruption was, and we covered it at length.)

Israeli actions are analyzed and criticized, and every flaw in Israeli society is aggressively reported. In one seven-week period, from Nov. 8 to Dec. 16, 2011, I decided to count the stories coming out of our bureau on the various moral failings of Israeli society—proposed legislation meant to suppress the media, the rising influence of Orthodox Jews, unauthorized settlement outposts, gender segregation, and so forth. I counted 27 separate articles, an average of a story every two days. In a very conservative estimate, this seven-week tally was higher than the total number of significantly critical stories about Palestinian government and society, including the totalitarian Islamists of Hamas, that our bureau had published in the preceding three years.

The Hamas charter, for example, calls not just for Israel's destruction but for the murder of Jews and blames Jews for engineering the French and Russian revolutions and both world wars; the charter was never mentioned in print when I was at the AP, though Hamas won a Palestinian national election and had become one of the region's most important players. To draw the link with this summer's events: An observer might think Hamas' decision in recent years to construct a military infrastructure beneath Gaza's civilian infrastructure would be deemed newsworthy, if only because of what it meant about the way the next conflict would be fought and the cost to innocent people. But that is not the case. The Hamas emplacements were not important in themselves, and were therefore ignored. What was important was the Israeli decision to attack them.

There has been much discussion recently of Hamas attempts to intimidate reporters. Any veteran of the press corps here knows the intimidation is real, and I saw it in action myself as an editor on the AP news desk. During the 2008-2009 Gaza fighting I personally erased a key detail—that Hamas fighters were dressed as civilians and being counted as civilians in the death toll—because of a threat to our reporter in Gaza. (The policy was then, and remains, not to inform readers that the story is censored unless the censorship is Israeli. Earlier this month, the AP's Jerusalem news editor reported and submitted a story on Hamas intimidation; the story was shunted into deep freeze by his superiors and has not been published.)

But if critics imagine that journalists are clamoring to cover Hamas and are stymied by thugs and threats, it is generally not so. There are many low-risk ways to report Hamas actions, if the will is there: under bylines from Israel, under no byline, by citing Israeli sources. Reporters are resourceful when they want to be.

The fact is that Hamas intimidation is largely beside the point because the actions of Palestinians are beside the point: Most reporters in Gaza believe their job is to document violence directed by Israel at Palestinian civilians. That is the essence of the Israel story. In addition, reporters are under deadline and often at risk, and many don't speak the language and have only the most tenuous grip on what is going on. They are dependent on Palestinian colleagues and fixers who either fear Hamas, support Hamas, or both. Reporters don't need Hamas enforcers to shoo them away from facts that muddy the simple story they have been sent to tell.

It is not coincidence that the few journalists who have documented Hamas fighters and rocket launches in civilian areas this summer were generally not, as you might expect, from the large news organizations with big and permanent Gaza operations. They were mostly scrappy, peripheral, and newly arrived players—a Finn, an Indian crew, a few others. These poor souls didn't get the memo.

What Else Isn't Important?

The fact that Israelis quite recently elected moderate governments that sought reconciliation with the Palestinians, and which were undermined by the Palestinians, is considered unimportant and rarely mentioned. These lacunae are often not oversights but a matter of policy. In early 2009, for example, two colleagues of mine obtained information that Israeli Prime Minister Ehud Olmert had made a significant peace offer to the Palestinian Authority several months earlier, and that the Palestinians had deemed it insufficient. This had not been reported yet and it was—or should have been—one of the biggest stories of the year. The reporters obtained confirmation from both sides and one even saw a map, but the top editors at the bureau decided that they would not publish the story.

Some staffers were furious, but it didn't help. Our narrative was that the Palestinians were moderate and the Israelis recalcitrant and increasingly extreme. Reporting the Olmert offer—like delving too deeply into the subject of Hamas—would make that narrative look like nonsense. And so we were instructed to ignore it, and did, for more than a year and a half.

This decision taught me a lesson that should be clear to consumers of the Israel story: Many of the people deciding what you will read and see from here view their role not as explanatory but as political. Coverage is a weapon to be placed at the disposal of the side they like.

How Is the Israel Story Framed?

The Israel story is framed in the same terms that have been in use since the early 1990s—the quest for a "two-state solution." It is accepted that the conflict is "Israeli-Palestinian," meaning that it is a conflict taking place on land that Israel controls—0.2 percent of the Arab world—in which Jews are a majority and Arabs a minority. The conflict is more accurately described as "Israel-Arab," or "Jewish-Arab"—that is, a conflict between the 6 million Jews of Israel and 300 million Arabs in surrounding countries. (Perhaps "Israel-Muslim" would be more accurate, to take into account the enmity of non-Arab states like Iran and Turkey, and, more broadly, 1 billion Muslims worldwide.) This is the conflict that has been playing out in different forms for a century, before Israel existed, before Israel captured the Palestinian territories of Gaza and the West Bank, and before the term "Palestinian" was in use.

The "Israeli-Palestinian" framing allows the Jews, a tiny minority in the Middle East, to be depicted as the stronger party. It also includes the implicit assumption that if the Palestinian problem is somehow solved the conflict will be over, though no informed person today believes this to be true. This definition also allows the Israeli settlement project, which I believe is a serious moral and strategic error on Israel's part, to be described not as what it is—one more destructive symptom of the conflict—but rather as its cause.

A knowledgeable observer of the Middle East cannot avoid the impression that the region is a volcano and that the lava is radical Islam, an ideology whose various incarnations are now shaping this part of the world. Israel is a tiny village on the slopes of the volcano. Hamas is the local representative of radical Islam and is openly dedicated to the eradication of the Jewish minority enclave in Israel, just as Hezbollah is the dominant representative of radical Islam in Lebanon, the Islamic State in Syria and Iraq, the Taliban in Afghanistan and Pakistan, and so forth.

Hamas is not, as it freely admits, party to the effort to create a Palestinian state alongside Israel. It has different goals about which it is quite open and that are similar to those of the groups listed above. Since the mid-1990s, more than any other player, Hamas has destroyed the Israeli left, swayed moderate Israelis against territorial withdrawals, and buried the chances of a two-state compromise. That's one accurate way to frame the story.

An observer might also legitimately frame the story through the lens of minorities in the Middle East, all of which are under intense pressure from Islam: When minorities are helpless, their fate is that of the Yazidis or Christians of northern Iraq, as we have just seen, and when they are armed and organized they can fight back and survive, as in the case of the Jews and (we must hope) the Kurds.

There are, in other words, many different ways to see what is happening here. Jerusalem is less than a day's drive from Aleppo or Baghdad, and it should be clear to everyone that peace is pretty elusive in the Middle East even in places where Jews are absent. But reporters generally cannot see the Israel story in relation to anything else. Instead of describing Israel as one of the villages abutting the volcano, they describe Israel as the volcano.

The Israel story is framed to seem as if it has nothing to do with events nearby because the "Israel" of international journalism does not exist in the same geo-political universe as Iraq, Syria, or Egypt. The

Israel story is not a story about current events. It is about something else.

The Old Blank Screen

For centuries, stateless Jews played the role of a lightning rod for ill will among the majority population. They were a symbol of things that were wrong. Did you want to make the point that greed was bad? Jews were greedy. Cowardice? Jews were cowardly. Were you a Communist? Jews were capitalists. Were you a capitalist? In that case, Jews were Communists. Moral failure was the essential trait of the Jew. It was their role in Christian tradition—the only reason European society knew or cared about them in the first place.

Like many Jews who grew up late in the 20th century in friendly Western cities, I dismissed such ideas as the feverish memories of my grandparents. One thing I have learned—and I'm not alone this summer—is that I was foolish to have done so. Today, people in the West tend to believe the ills of the age are racism, colonialism, and militarism. The world's only Jewish country has done less harm than most countries on earth, and more good—and yet when people went looking for a country that would symbolize the sins of our new post-colonial, post-militaristic, post-ethnic dream-world, the country they chose was this one.

When the people responsible for explaining the world to the world, journalists, cover the Jews' war as more worthy of attention than any other, when they portray the Jews of Israel as the party obviously in the wrong, when they omit all possible justifications for the Jews' actions and obscure the true face of their enemies, what they are saying to their readers—whether they intend to or not—is that Jews are the worst people on earth. The Jews are a symbol of the evils that civilized people are taught from an early age to abhor. International press coverage has become a morality play starring a familiar villain.

Some readers might remember that Britain participated in the 2003 invasion of Iraq, the fallout from which has now killed more than three times the number of people ever killed in the Israel-Arab conflict; yet in Britain, protesters furiously condemn Jewish militarism. White people in London and Paris whose parents not long ago had themselves fanned by dark people in the sitting rooms of Rangoon or Algiers condemn Jewish "colonialism." Americans who live in places called "Manhattan" or "Seattle" condemn Jews for displacing the native people of Palestine. Russian reporters condemn Israel's brutal military tactics. Belgian reporters condemn Israel's treatment of Africans. When Israel opened a transportation service for Palestinian workers in the occupied West Bank a few years ago, American news consumers could read about Israel "segregating buses." And there are a lot of people in Europe, and not just in Germany, who enjoy hearing the Jews accused of genocide.

You don't need to be a history professor, or a psychiatrist, to understand what's going on. Having rehabilitated themselves against considerable odds in a minute corner of the earth, the descendants of powerless people who were pushed out of Europe and the Islamic Middle East have become what their grandparents were—the pool into which the world spits. The Jews of Israel are the screen onto which it has become socially acceptable to project the things you hate about yourself and your own country. The tool through which this psychological projection is executed is the international press.

Who Cares If the World Gets the Israel Story Wrong?

Because a gap has opened here between the way things are and the way they are described, opinions are wrong and policies are wrong, and observers are regularly blindsided by events. Such things have happened before. In the years leading to the breakdown of Soviet Communism in 1991, as the Russia expert Leon Aron wrote in a 2011 essay for *Foreign Policy*, "virtually no Western expert, scholar, official, or politician foresaw the impending collapse of the Soviet Union." The empire had been rotting for years and the signs were there, but the people who were supposed to be seeing and reporting them failed and when the superpower imploded everyone was surprised.

And there was the Spanish civil war: "Early in life I had noticed that no event is ever correctly reported in a newspaper, but in Spain, for the first time, I saw newspaper reports which do not bear any relation to the facts, not even the relationship which is implied in an ordinary lie. ... I saw, in fact, history being written not in terms of what had happened but of what ought to have happened according to various 'party lines.' " That was George Orwell, writing in 1942.

Orwell did not step off an airplane in Catalonia, stand next to a Republican cannon, and have himself filmed while confidently repeating what everyone else was saying or describing what any fool could see: weaponry, rubble, bodies. He looked beyond the ideological fantasies of his peers and knew that what was important was not necessarily visible. Spain, he understood, was not really about Spain at all—it was about a clash of totalitarian systems, German and Russian. He knew he was witnessing a threat to European civilization, and he wrote that, and he was right.

Understanding what happened in Gaza this summer means understanding Hezbollah in Lebanon, the rise of the Sunni jihadis in Syria and Iraq, and the long tentacles of Iran. It requires figuring out why countries like Egypt and Saudi Arabia now see themselves as closer to Israel than to Hamas. Above all, it requires us to understand what is clear to nearly everyone in the Middle East: The ascendant force in our part of the world is not democracy or modernity. It is rather an empowered strain of Islam that assumes different and sometimes conflicting forms, and that is willing to employ extreme violence in a quest to unite the region under its control and confront the West. Those who grasp this fact will be able to look around and connect the dots.

Israel is not an idea, a symbol of good or evil, or a litmus test for liberal opinion at dinner parties. It is a small country in a scary part of the world that is getting scarier. It should be reported as critically as any other place, and understood in context and in proportion. Israel is not one of the most important stories in the world, or even in the Middle East; whatever the outcome in this region in the next decade, it will have as much to do with Israel as World War II had to do with Spain. Israel is a speck on the map—a sideshow that happens to carry an unusual emotional charge.

Many in the West clearly prefer the old comfort of parsing the moral failings of Jews, and the familiar feeling of superiority this brings them, to confronting an unhappy and confusing reality. They may convince themselves that all of this is the Jews' problem, and indeed the Jews' fault. But journalists engage in these fantasies at the cost of their credibility and that of their profession. And, as Orwell would tell us, the world entertains fantasies at its peril.

"An Insider's Guide to the Most Important Story on Earth: A former AP correspondent explains how and why reporters get Israel so wrong, and why it matters," *Tablet Magazine*, August 26, 2014.

THE MUTATING VIRUS: UNDERSTANDING ANTISEMITISM

RABBI LORD JONATHAN SACKS

The hate that begins with Jews never ends with Jews. That is what I want us to understand today. It wasn't Jews alone who suffered under Hitler. It wasn't Jews alone who suffered under Stalin. It isn't Jews alone who suffer under ISIS or Al Qaeda or Islamic Jihad. We make a great mistake if we think antisemitism is a threat only to Jews. It is a threat, first and foremost, to Europe and to the freedoms it took centuries to achieve.

Antisemitism is not about Jews. It is about antisemites. It is about people who cannot accept responsibility for their own failures and have instead to blame someone else. Historically, if you were a Christian at the time of the Crusades, or a German after the First World War, and saw that the world hadn't turned out the way you believed it would, you blamed the Jews. That is what is happening today. And I cannot begin to say how dangerous it is. Not just to Jews but to everyone who values freedom, compassion and humanity.

The appearance of antisemitism in a culture is the first symptom of a disease, the early warning sign of collective breakdown. If Europe allows antisemitism to flourish, that will be the beginning of the end of Europe. And what I want to do in these brief remarks is simply to analyze a phenomenon full of vagueness and ambiguity, because we need precision and understanding to know what antisemitism is, why it happens, why antisemites are convinced that they are not antisemitic.

RABBI LORD JONATHAN SACKS, PHD, 1948–

Former chief rabbi of the United Kingdom. Rabbi Sacks attended Cambridge University and received his doctorate from King's College, London. A prolific and influential author, his books include Will We Have Jewish Grandchildren? and The Dignity of Difference. He received the Jerusalem Prize in 1995 for his contributions to enhancing Jewish life in the Diaspora, was knighted and made a life peer in 2005, and became Baron Sacks of Aldridge in 2009.

First let me define antisemitism. Not liking Jews is not antisemitism. We all have people we don't like. That's OK; that's human; it isn't dangerous. Second, criticizing Israel is not antisemitism. I was recently talking to some schoolchildren and they asked me: "Is criticizing Israel antisemitism?" I said No and I explained the difference. I asked them: "Do you believe you have a right to criticize the British government?" They all put up their hands. Then I asked, "Which of you believes that Britain has no right to exist?" No one put up their hands. "Now you know the difference," I said, and they all did.

Antisemitism means denying the right of Jews to exist collectively as Jews with the same rights as everyone else. It takes different forms in different ages. In the Middle Ages, Jews were hated because of their religion. In the nineteenth and early twentieth century they were hated because of their race. Today they are hated because of their nation state, the state of Israel. It takes different forms but it remains the same thing: the view that Jews have no right to exist as free and equal human beings.

If there is one thing I and my contemporaries did not expect, it was that antisemitism would reappear in Europe within living memory of the Holocaust. The reason we did not expect it was that Europe had undertaken the greatest collective effort in all of history to ensure that the virus of antisemitism would never again infect the body politic. It was a magnificent effort of antiracist legislation, Holocaust education and interfaith dialogue. Yet antisemitism has returned despite everything.

On 27 January 2000, representatives of 46 governments from around the world gathered in Stockholm to issue a collective declaration of Holocaust remembrance and the continuing fight against antisemitism, racism and prejudice. Then came 9/11, and within days conspiracy theories were flooding the internet claiming it was the work of Israel and its secret service, the Mossad. In April 2002, on Passover, I was in Florence with a Jewish couple from Paris when they received a phone call from their son, saying, "Mum, Dad, it's time to leave France. It's not safe for us here anymore."

In May 2007, in a private meeting here in Brussels, I told the three leaders of Europe at the time, Angela Merkel, President of the European Council, Jose Manuel Barroso, President of the European Commission, and Hans-Gert Pöttering, President of the European Parliament, that the Jews of Europe were beginning to ask whether there was a future for Jews in Europe.

That was more than nine years ago. Since then, things have become worse. Already in 2013, before some of the worst incidents, the European Union Agency for Fundamental Rights found that almost a third of Europe's Jews were considering emigrating because of antisemitism. In France the figure was 46 percent; in Hungary, 48 percent.

Let me ask you this. Whether you are Jewish, Christian, or Muslim: Would you stay in a country where you need armed police to guard you while you prayed? Where your children need armed guards to protect them at school? Where, if you wear a sign of your faith in public, you risk being abused or attacked? Where, when your children go to university, they are insulted and intimidated because of what is happening in some other part of the world? Where, when they present their own view of the situation they are howled down and silenced?

This is happening to Jews throughout Europe. In every single country of Europe, without exception, Jews are fearful for their or their children's future. If this continues, Jews will continue to leave Europe, until, barring the frail and the elderly, Europe will finally have become *Judenrein*.

How did this happen? It happened the way viruses always defeat the human immune system, namely, by mutating. The new antisemitism is different from the old antisemitism, in three ways. I've already mentioned one. Once Jews were hated because of their religion. Then they were hated because of their race. Now they are hated because of their nation state. The second difference is that the epicenter of the old antisemitism was Europe. Today it's the Middle East and it is communicated globally by the new electronic media. The third is particularly disturbing. Let me explain. It is easy to hate, but difficult publicly to justify hate. Throughout history, when people have sought to justify anti-Semitism, they have done so by recourse to the highest source of authority available within the culture. In the Middle Ages, it was religion. So we had religious anti-Judaism. In post-Enlightenment Europe it was science. So we had the twin foundations of Nazi ideology, Social Darwinism and the so-called Scientific Study of Race. Today the highest source of authority worldwide is human rights. That is why Israel—the only fully functioning democracy in the Middle East with a free press and independent judiciary—is regularly accused of the five cardinal sins against human rights: racism, apartheid, crimes against humanity, ethnic cleansing and attempted genocide.

The new antisemitism has mutated so that any practitioner of it can deny that he or she is an antisemite. After all, they'll say, I'm not a racist. I have no problem with Jews or Judaism. I only have a problem with the State of Israel. But in a world of 56 Muslim nations and 103 Christian ones, there is only one Jewish state, Israel, which constitutes one-quarter of one per cent of the land mass of the Middle East. Israel is the only one of the 193 member nations of the United Nations that has its right to exist regularly challenged, with one state, Iran, and many, many other groups, committed to its destruction.

Antisemitism means denying the right of Jews to exist as Jews with the same rights as everyone else. The form this takes today is anti-Zionism. Of course, there is a difference between Zionism and Judaism, and between Jews and Israelis, but this difference does not exist for the new antisemites themselves. It was Jews, not Israelis, who were murdered in terrorist attacks in Toulouse, Paris, Brussels and Copenhagen. Anti-Zionism is the antisemitism of our time.

In the Middle Ages Jews were accused of poisoning wells, spreading the plague, and killing Christian children to use their blood. In Nazi Germany they were accused of controlling both capitalist America and communist Russia. Today they are accused of running ISIS as well as America. All the old myths have been recycled, from the Blood Libel to the *Protocols of the Elders of Zion*. The cartoons that flood the Middle East are clones of those published in *Der Sturmer*, one of the primary vehicles of Nazi propaganda between 1923 and 1945.

The ultimate weapon of the new antisemitism is dazzling in its simplicity. It goes like this. The Holocaust must never happen again. But Israelis are the new Nazis; the Palestinians are the new Jews; all Jews are Zionists. Therefore the real antisemites of our time are none other than the Jews themselves. And these are not marginal views. They are widespread throughout the Muslim world, including communities in Europe, and they are slowly infecting the far left, the far right, academic circles, unions, and even some churches. Having cured itself of the virus of antisemitism, Europe is being reinfected by parts of the world that never went through the self-reckoning that Europe undertook once the facts of the Holocaust became known.

How do such absurdities come to be believed? This is a vast and complex subject, and I have written a book about it, but the simplest explanation is this. When bad things happen to a group, its members can ask one of two questions: "What did we do wrong?" or "Who did this to us?" The entire fate of the group will depend on which it chooses.

If it asks, "What did we do wrong?" it has begun the self-criticism essential to a free society. If it asks, "Who did this to us?" it has defined itself as a victim. It will then seek a scapegoat to blame for all its problems. Classically this has been the Jews.

Antisemitism is a form of cognitive failure, and it happens when groups feel that their world is spinning out of control. It began in the Middle Ages, when Christians saw that Islam had defeated them in places they regarded as their own, especially Jerusalem. That was when, in 1096, on their way to the Holy Land, the Crusaders stopped first to massacre Jewish communities in Northern Europe. It was born in the Middle East in the 1920s with the collapse of the Ottoman Empire. Antisemitism re-emerged in Europe in the 1870s during a period of economic recession and resurgent nationalism. And it is reappearing in Europe now for the same reasons: recession, nationalism, and a backlash against immigrants and other minorities. Antisemitism happens when the politics of hope gives way to the politics of fear, which quickly becomes the politics of hate.

This then reduces complex problems to simplicities. It divides the world into black and white, seeing all the fault on one side and all the victimhood on the other. It singles out one group among a hundred offenders for the blame. The argument is always the same. We are innocent; they are guilty. It follows that if we are to be free, they, the Jews or the state of Israel, must be destroyed. That is how the great crimes begin.

Jews were hated because they were different. They were the most conspicuous non-Christian minority in a Christian Europe. Today they are the most conspicuous non-Muslim presence in an Islamic Middle East. Antisemitism has always been about the inability of a group to make space for difference. No group that adopts it will ever, can ever, create a free society.

So I end where I began. The hate that begins with Jews never ends with Jews. Antisemitism is only secondarily about Jews. Primarily it is about the failure of groups to accept responsibility for their own failures, and to build their own future by their own endeavors. No society that has fostered antisemitism has ever sustained liberty or human rights or religious freedom. Every society driven by hate begins by seeking to destroy its enemies, but ends by destroying itself.

Europe today is not fundamentally antisemitic. But it has allowed antisemitism to enter via the new electronic media. It has failed to recognize that the new antisemitism is different from the old. We are not today back in the 1930s. But we are coming close to 1879, when Wilhelm Marr founded the League of Anti-Semites in Germany; to 1886 when Édouard Drumont published *La France Juive*; and 1897 when Karl Lueger became Mayor of Vienna. These were key moments in the spread of antisemitism, and all we have to do today is to remember that what was said then about Jews is being said today about the Jewish state.

The history of Jews in Europe has not always been a happy one. Europe's treatment of the Jews added certain words to the human vocabulary: disputation, forced conversion, inquisition, expulsion, auto-da-fé, ghetto, pogrom and Holocaust, words written in

Jewish tears and Jewish blood. Yet for all that, Jews loved Europe and contributed to it some of its greatest scientists, writers, academics, musicians, shapers of the modern mind.

If Europe lets itself be dragged down that road again, this will be the story told in times to come. First they came for the Jews. Then for the Christians. Then for the gays. Then for the atheists. Until there was nothing left of Europe's soul but a distant, fading memory.

Today I have tried to give voice to those who have no voice. I have spoken on behalf of the murdered Roma, Sinti, gays, dissidents, the mentally and physically handicapped, and a million and a half Jewish children murdered because of their grandparents' religion. In their name, I say to you: You know where the road ends. Don't go down there again.

You are the leaders of Europe. Its future is in your hands. If you do nothing, Jews will leave, European liberty will die, and there will be a moral stain on Europe's name that all eternity will not erase.

Stop it now while there is still time.

"A Mutating Virus: Understanding Antisemitism," rabbisacks.org, September 27, 2016.

WHY ISRAEL IS THE WORLD'S BEST NATION

GIULIO MEOTTI

I don't know another nation on earth which since its founding, less than seventy years ago, had to sacrifice 23,000 soldiers.

I don't know another nation on earth without recognized borders.

I don't know another nation on earth whose population lives under a perpetual emotional strain.

I don't know another nation on earth threatened to be wiped off the map.

I don't know another nation on earth so threatened by boycotts all over the world.

I don't know another nation on earth where the winners tend to lose wars.

I don't know another nation on earth which provides its own enemy with water, electricity, food, weapons, and medical treatment.

I don't know another nation on earth where guests on official visits utter disrespectful and offensive words.

But I also don't know another nation on earth which has recorded so many miracles.

Imagine a helpless, naked Jew at the gas ovens facing a Nazi official, who thinks he will get rid of the "Jewish cancer", get rid of this unique phenomenon of 2,000 years.

Could that helpless, naked Jew imagine that in 50 years other Jews will be flying F-16's in the skies over Israel?

Could that helpless Jew imagine that Israel's population today would be nine times that of 1948, the year of the state's creation?

Could that helpless Jew imagine that Israel is much happier than all the European countries?

Could that helpless Jew imagine that Israel has the highest production of scientific publications per capita in the world?

Could that helpless Jew imagine that Israel has the highest worldwide publication of new books?

Could that helpless Jew imagine that Israel is the only nation which began the XXI century with a net gain in the number of trees?

Could that helpless Jew imagine that Israel has with largest number of chess grandmasters per capita of any city in the world?

Could that helpless Jew imagine that Israel is the nation whose academics produce more scientific papers per capita than anywhere else in the world?

Could that helpless Jew imagine that Israel is the nation with the highest ratio of university degrees to the population in the world?

Could that helpless Jew imagine that Israel is the country which, in proportion to its population, with the largest number of startup companies in the world?

Could that helpless Jew imagine that Israel is the country with the highest percentage in the world of home computers per capita?

Could that helpless Jew imagine that Israel is the nation with the largest immigrant-absorbing model on earth?

Unfortunately, you will not find Israel's goodness and superiority in the media (also Israeli), because it doesn't fit in with the stereotype of the colonialist Zionist occupier.

In the world's consciousness, the word "Israel" must be equated with fear.

Israel just came out of another war against terrorists whose value is less than that of animals. Do you know of any animal species sheltering behind its own children?

But the Jewish State, despite its media, its cynical politicians, establishment, once again showed the world it is the best humanity has to offer.

This hope is impressed in the faces of Israel's fallen soldiers, its wounded and injured soldiers. In those faces there is joie de vivre, not sadness or hatred.

Terrorists and their Western appeasers want to destroy Israel because it is a light unto the nations.
The only one in the world in which we live.

"Why Israel Is the World's Best Nation," The Israel Forever Foundation, 2017

Bibliography

Bar-On, Mordechai. *Moshe Dayan: Israel's Controversial Hero*. New Haven: Yale University Press, 2012.

Collins, Larry, and Dominique Lapierre. *O Jerusalem*. New York: Simon and Schuster, 1972.

Dershowitz, Alan M. *The Case for Israel*. Hoboken, NJ: John Wiley and Sons, Inc., 2004

Eban, Abba Solomon. *Abba Eban: An Autobiography*. New York: Random House, 1977.

Gilbert, Martin. *Israel: A History*. New York: Harper Perennial, 2008.

Halevi, Yossi Klein. *Like Dreamers: The Story of the Israeli Paratroopers Who Reunited Jerusalem and Divided a Nation*. New York, NY: HarperCollins, 2013.

Hammel, Eric M. *Six Days in June: How Israel Won the 1967 Arab-Israeli War*. New York: Scribner's, 1992.

Kaplan, Aryeh. *Jerusalem, the Eye of the Universe: A Pictorial Tour of the Holy City*. New York, NY: National Conference of Synagogue Youth/Union of Orthodox Jewish Congregations of America, 1996.

Muravchik, Joshua. *Making David into Goliath: How the World Turned against Israel*. New York: Encounter Books, 2014.

Narkiss, Uzi. *The Liberation of Jerusalem: The Battle of 1967*. London, England: Vallentine, Mitchell, 1983.

Oren, Michael B. *Six Days of War: June 1967 and the Making of the Modern Middle East*. Oxford: Oxford University Press, 2002.

Rovner, Adam. *In the Shadow of Zion: Promised Lands before Israel*. New York: NYU Press, 2014.

Sacks, Jonathan. *Future Tense: Jews, Judaism, and Israel in the Twenty-First Century*. New York: Schocken, 2012.

Segev, Tom. *1967: Israel, the War, and the Year That Transformed the Middle East*. New York: Metropolitan, 2007. Print.

Touger, Eliyahu. *Eyes Upon the Land: The Territorial Integrity of Israel: a Life-Threatening Concern (Based on the Public Statements and Writings of the Lubavitcher Rebbe, Rabbi Menachem M. Schneerson)*. Brooklyn, NY: Sichos in English, 1997.

Acknowledgments

Pray for the peace of Jerusalem.
[Say to her:] "May those who love you enjoy tranquility.
May there be peace within your walls, tranquility in your palaces."

—PSALMS 122:6–7

Fifty years ago, in June of 1967, Israel was forced into a war of survival against the combined military weight of its mortal enemies. Hostilities halted with an Israeli victory that astounded the world and dramatically rewrote the country's borders and role in the Middle East. Israel's decisive victory on all fronts awoke the pride of post-Holocaust Jewry worldwide, but it failed to conclude Israel's struggle to thrive unhindered. In the half century that followed, Israel has unceasingly bled from the widest array of physical, political, and economic attacks.

If there are three overlapping rings to the history and destiny of the Jewish people, the first is the Jewish collective—the Nation of Israel. Another is its homeland—the Land of Israel. And yet another is its spiritual wisdom—the Torah of Israel. Marking the fiftieth anniversary of the Six-Day War, *Survival of a Nation* plumbs the strata of the Torah's formidable insights to provide clarity to the undying, albeit complicated, bond between the Nation and its Land, shedding critical light on the key issues that Israel faced half a century ago, and continues to grapple with today.

We extend our appreciation to **Rabbis Mordechai Dinerman** and **Naftali Silberberg**, who direct the JLI Curriculum Department and the Flagship editorial team; to **Rabbi Dr. Shmuel Klatzkin**, JLI's senior editor; and to **Rabbi Zalman Abraham,** charged with JLI strategic branding and marketing, who skillfully provides the vision for branding JLI course offerings.

We are grateful to **Rabbis Tzvi Kilov, Yanky Raskin, Motty Schochet, Shmuel Super, Yanki Tauber, Meir Wagner, Shaul Wolf, Mrs. Malky Bitton,** and **Mrs. Beruria Tenenbaum,** who extensively researched the topics for this course, wrote and edited lesson drafts, and made substantial contributions to the course content. **Rabbis Yakov Gershon** and **Eli Raksin** of JLI's **Machon Shmuel: The Sami Rohr Research Institute** and **Mrs. Leah Fridman** provided research assistance. This course also benefited greatly from a number of scholarly papers on various Israel-related topics produced by the Machon Shmuel Institute, headed by **Rabbi Avrohom Bergstein.**

We are thankful to **Rabbis Hesh Epstein, Zalman Gordon, Yitzchok Naparstek, Avrohom Sternberg,** and **Mrs. Layah Kranz-Lipskier,** members of the JLI editorial board, for providing countless useful suggestions that enhanced the course and ensured its suitability for a wide range of students.

We thank **Mrs. Rivki Mockin,** our exceptional Curriculum Coordinator, for streamlining the course production process and ensuring the smoothness, timeliness, and professionalism of the product; and **Rabbi Levi Kaplan** and **Mrs. Malka Solomon** for managing many of the components of book production. We are grateful to **Mendel Schtroks** and **Yosef Levertov** for designing the textbooks with taste, expertise and patience, and

Rabbi Mendel Sirota for directing the book publication. **Mrs. Lynne Clamage, Mrs. Ya'akovah Weber** and **Mrs. Rachel Witty** enhanced the quality and professionalism of the course with their copyediting and proofreading.

We thank **Baila Pruss, Mushka Pruss,** and **Mrs. Rivka Rapoport** for the design of the course's aesthetically pleasing PowerPoint presentations, and **Moshe Raskin** and **Getzy Raskin** for heading the team charged with the production of the videos for this course. The video scripts were masterfully written by **Rabbi Yaakov Paley**.

We acknowledge the hard work and efforts of JLI's support staff and administration, whose contributions to this course were critical, but whose names are too many to enumerate here.

We are immensely grateful for the encouragement of JLI's visionary chairman, and vice-chairman of Merkos L'Inyonei Chinuch—Lubavitch World Headquarters, **Rabbi Moshe Kotlarsky**. Rabbi Kotlarsky has been highly instrumental in building the infrastructure for the expansion of Chabad's international network, and is the architect of scores of initiatives and services to help Chabad representatives across the globe succeed in their mission. We are blessed to have the unwavering support of JLI's principal benefactor, **Mr. George Rohr**, who is fully invested in our work, continues to be instrumental in JLI's monumental growth and expansion, and is largely responsible for the Jewish renaissance that is being spearheaded by JLI and its affiliates across the globe.

The commitment and sage direction of JLI's dedicated executive board—**Rabbis Chaim Block, Hesh Epstein, Ronnie Fine, Yosef Gansburg, Shmuel Kaplan, Yisrael Rice,** and **Avrohom Sternberg**—and the countless hours they devote to the development of JLI, are what drive the vision, growth, and tremendous success of the organization.

Finally, JLI represents an incredible partnership of more than 1,400 *shluchim* and *shluchot* in over one thousand locations across the globe, who contribute their time and talent to further Jewish adult education. We thank them for generously sharing feedback and making suggestions that steer JLI's development and growth. They are our most valuable critics and our most cherished contributors.

Inspired by the call of the **Lubavitcher Rebbe**, of righteous memory, it is the mandate of the Rohr JLI to encourage all Jews throughout the world to experience and participate in their precious heritage of Torah learning. May this course succeed in fulfilling this sacred charge!

On behalf of the Rohr Jewish Learning Institute,

RABBI EFRAIM MINTZ
Executive Director

RABBI YISRAEL RICE
Chairman, Editorial Board

11 Nisan, 5777

The Rohr Jewish Learning Institute

AN AFFILIATE OF MERKOS L'INYONEI CHINUCH
THE EDUCATIONAL ARM OF THE CHABAD LUBAVITCH MOVEMENT
822 EASTERN PARKWAY, BROOKLYN, NY 11213

CURRICULUM DEVELOPMENT

Rabbi Mordechai Dinerman
Rabbi Naftali Silberberg
EDITORS-IN-CHIEF

Rabbi Dr. Shmuel Klatzkin
Rabbi Yanki Tauber
SENIOR EDITORS

Rabbi Binyomin Bitton
Rabbi Shlomie Chein
Rabbi Uri Gamson
Rabbi Eliezer Gurkow
Rabbi Ahrele Loschak
Rabbi Zalman Margolin
Rabbi Eliezer Raksin
Mrs. Rivka Rapoport
Rabbi Shmuel Raskin
Rabbi Yanky Raskin
Rabbi Mendel Rubin
Rabbi Michoel Shapiro
Rabbi Shmuel Super
Rabbi Boruch Werdiger
CURRICULUM TEAM

Mrs. Rivki Mockin
CONTENT COORDINATOR

MARKETING AND BRANDING

Rabbi Zalman Abraham
DIRECTOR

Mrs. Chaya Mushka Kanner
Mrs. Shevi Rivkin
Raizel Shurpin
Rikkie Winner
GRAPHIC DESIGN

Tzippy Blecher
Mendel Schtroks
Yossi Levertov
PUBLICATION DESIGN

Yisroel Beenstock
MARKETING FOR RESULTS

Rabbi Yaakov Paley
WRITER

Rabbi Simcha Backman
Rabbi Ronnie Fine
Rabbi Ovadia Goldman
Rabbi Mendy Halberstam
Rabbi Reuven New
Rabbi Yehuda Shemtov
MARKETING COMMITTEE

MARKETING CONSULTANTS

JJ Gross
Israel

Warren Modlin
MEDNETPRO, INC.
Orange County, CA

Alan Rosenspan
ALAN ROSENSPAN & ASSOCIATES
Sharon, MA

Gary Wexler
PASSION MARKETING
Los Angeles, CA

Joseph Jaffe
EVOL8TION
New York, NY

JLI CENTRAL

Ms. Rochel Karp
Mrs. Itta Kessler
Mrs. Malka Solomon
Mrs. Mussie Sputz
ADMINISTRATION

Rabbi Menachem Klein
PROJECT MANAGER

Rabbi Mendel Rosenfeld
EVENT COORDINATOR

Rabbi Mendel Sirota
Mrs. Mindy Wallach
AFFILIATE SUPPORT

Mrs. Bunia Chazan
Mrs. Mushka Lisker
Mushka Pruss
Mrs. Rivka Rapoport
Getzy Raskin
Moshe Raskin
Chani Tauber
MULTIMEDIA DEVELOPMENT

Rabbi Sholom Cohen
Rabbi Mendy Elishevitz
Rabbi Elchonon Korenblit
Avi J. Levy
Mrs. Rochie Rivkin
ONLINE DIVISION

Mrs. Lynne Clamage
Mrs. Ya'akovah Weber
Mrs. Rachel Witty
PROOFREADERS

Rabbi Mendel Sirota
PRINTING AND DISTRIBUTION

Mrs. Musie Liberow
Mrs. Shaina B. Mintz
Mrs. Shulamis Nadler
ACCOUNTING

Mrs. Musie Liberow
Mrs. Mindy Wallach
CONTINUING EDUCATION

JLI FLAGSHIP

Rabbi Yisrael Rice
CHAIRMAN

Rabbi Yisroel Altein
Rabbi Hesh Epstein
Rabbi Benzion Milecki
Rabbi Shalom Raichik
Rabbi Nochum Schapiro
Rabbi Shraga Sherman
Mrs. Rivkah Slonim
Rabbi Avraham Steinmetz
Rabbi Avrohom Sternberg
Rabbi Aryeh Weinstein
EDITORIAL BOARD

PAST FLAGSHIP AUTHORS

Rabbi Zalman Abraham
Brooklyn, NY

Rabbi Berel Bell
Montreal, QC

Rabbi Nissan D. Dubov
London, UK

Rabbi Tzvi Freeman
Toronto, ON

Rabbi Eliezer Gurkow
London, ON

Rabbi Aaron Herman
Pittsburgh, PA

Rabbi Simon Jacobson
New York, NY

Rabbi Dr. Chaim D. Kagan
Monsey, NY

Rabbi Yitschak M. Kagan
of blessed memory

Rabbi Dr. Shmuel Klatzkin
Dayton, OH

Rabbi Nochum Mangel
Dayton, OH

Rabbi Moshe Miller
Chicago, IL

Rabbi Yosef Paltiel
Brooklyn, NY

Rabbi Yehuda Pink
Solihull, UK

Rabbi Yisrael Rice
S. Rafael, CA

Rabbi Eli Silberstein
Ithaca, NY

Mrs. Rivkah Slonim
Binghamton, NY

Rabbi Avrohom Sternberg
New London, CT

Rabbi Shais Taub
Pittsburgh, PA

Rabbi Shlomo Yaffe
Cambridge, MA

ROSH CHODESH SOCIETY

Rabbi Shmuel Kaplan
CHAIRMAN

Mrs. Shaindy Jacobson
DIRECTOR

Mrs. Fraydee Kessler
ADMINISTRATOR

Mrs. Malka Bitton
Mrs. Shula Bryski
Mrs. Rochel Holzkenner
Mrs. Devorah Kornfeld
Mrs. Chana Lipskar
Mrs. Ahuva New
Mrs. Binie Tenenbaum
STEERING COMMITTEE

SINAI SCHOLARS SOCIETY
IN PARTNERSHIP WITH
CHABAD ON CAMPUS

Rabbi Menachem Schmidt
CHAIRMAN

Rabbi Dubi Rabinowitz
DIRECTOR

Mrs. Chana Wolosow
COORDINATOR

Mrs. Devorah Zlatopolsky
ADMINISTRATOR

Rabbi Moshe Chaim Dubrowski
Rabbi Yossy Gordon
Rabbi Efraim Mintz
Rabbi Menachem Schmidt
Rabbi Avi Weinstein
EXECUTIVE COMMITTEE

Rabbi Zalman Bluming
Rabbi Shlomie Chein
Rabbi Eli Gurevitch
CURRICULUM COMMITTEE

Rabbi Chaim Shaul Brook
Rabbi Shlomie Chein
Rabbi Zev Johnson
Rabbi Moshe Leib Gray
Rabbi Zalman Teichtel
Rabbi Shmuli Weiss
Rabbi Yisroel Wilhelm
STEERING COMMITTEE

JLI TEENS
IN PARTNERSHIP WITH
CTEEN: CHABAD TEEN NETWORK

Rabbi Chaim Block
CHAIRMAN

Rabbi Elya Silfen
DIRECTOR

Aliza Landes
PROGRAM ADMINISTRATOR

Rabbi Daniel Bortz
Rabbi Yossi Marrus
Mrs. Leah Rosenfeld
ADVISORY BOARD

TORAH STUDIES

Rabbi Yosef Gansburg
CHAIRMAN

Rabbi Zalman Margolin
DIRECTOR

Rabbi Ahrele Loschak
EDITOR

Rabbi Levi Fogelman
Rabbi Yaacov Halperin
Rabbi Nechemia Schusterman
Rabbi Ari Sollish
STEERING COMMITTEE

JLI INTERNATIONAL

Rabbi Avrohom Sternberg
CHAIRMAN

Rabbi Dubi Rabinowitz
DIRECTOR

Rabbi Berry Piekarski
ADMINISTRATOR

Mendel Schtroks
CONTENT MANAGER

Rabbi Yosef Yitzchok Noyman
ADMINISTRATOR, JLI ISRAEL
IN PARTNERSHIP WITH MIVTZA TORAH—ISRAEL

Rabbi Israel Ashkenazi
DIRECTOR, JLI ISRAEL

Rabbi Eli Wolf
ADMINISTRATOR, JLI IN THE CIS
IN PARTNERSHIP WITH THE FEDERATION OF JEWISH COMMUNITIES OF THE CIS

Rabbi Shevach Zlatopolsky
EDITOR, JLI IN THE CIS

Dr. Arye Olman
TRANSLATOR, RUSSIAN

Rabbi Nochum Schapiro
REGIONAL REPRESENTATIVE, AUSTRALIA

Rabbi Avraham Golovacheov
REGIONAL REPRESENTATIVE, GERMANY

Rabbi Shmuel Katzman
REGIONAL REPRESENTATIVE, NETHERLANDS

NATIONAL JEWISH RETREAT

Rabbi Hesh Epstein
CHAIRMAN

Mrs. Shaina B. Mintz
ADMINISTRATOR

Bruce Backman
Rabbi Menachem Klein
COORDINATORS

Rabbi Shmuly Karp
SHLUCHIM LIAISON

Mrs. Chana Dechter
Mrs. Fraydee Kessler
Aliza Landes
SERVICE AND SUPPORT

JLI LAND & SPIRIT

ISRAEL EXPERIENCE

Rabbi Shmuly Karp
DIRECTOR

Mrs. Shaina B. Mintz
ADMINISTRATOR

Rabbi Yechiel Baitelman
Rabbi Dovid Flinkenstein
Rabbi Chanoch Kaplan
Rabbi Levi Klein
Rabbi Mendy Mangel
Rabbi Sholom Raichik
STEERING COMMITTEE

SHABBAT IN THE HEIGHTS

Shmuly Karp
DIRECTOR

Mrs. Shulamis Nadler
SERVICE AND SUPPORT

Rabbi Chaim Hanoka
Rabbi Zalman Marcus
STEERING COMMITTEE

MYSHIUR

ADVANCED LEARNING INITIATIVE

Rabbi Shmuel Kaplan
CHAIRMAN

Rabbi Levi Kaplan
DIRECTOR

TORAHCAFE.COM

ONLINE LEARNING

Rabbi Levi Kaplan
DIRECTOR

Rabbi Mendy Elishevitz
Rabbi Elchonon Korenblit
WEBSITE DEVELOPMENT

Moshe Levin
CONTENT MANAGER

Avrohom Shimon Ezagui
FILMING

MACHON SHMUEL

THE SAMI ROHR RESEARCH INSTITUTE

Rabbi Avrohom Bergstein
DEAN

Rabbi Moshe Miller
Rabbi Gedalya Oberlander
Rabbi Chaim Rapoport
Rabbi Chaim Schapiro
RABBINIC ADVISORY BOARD

Rabbi Yakov Gershon
RESEARCH FELLOW

FOUNDING DEPARTMENT HEADS

Rabbi Mendel Bell
Rabbi Zalman Charytan
Rabbi Mendel Druk
Rabbi Menachem Gansburg
Rabbi Meir Hecht
Rabbi Yoni Katz
Rabbi Chaim Zalman Levy
Rabbi Benny Rapoport
Dr. Chana Silberstein
Rabbi Elchonon Tenenbaum
Rabbi Mendy Weg

Faculty Directory

ALABAMA

BIRMINGHAM
Rabbi Yossi Friedman 205.970.0100

MOBILE
Rabbi Yosef Goldwasser 251-265-1213

ALASKA

ANCHORAGE
Rabbi Yosef Greenberg 907.279.1200

WASILLA
Rabbi Mendy Greenberg 907.357.8770

ARIZONA

FLAGSTAFF
Rabbi Dovie Shapiro 928.255.5756

FOUNTAIN HILLS
Rabbi Mendy Lipskier 480.776.4763

GILBERT
Rabbi Shimi Ash 480.269.6680

ORO VALLEY
Rabbi Ephraim Zimmerman 520.477.8672

PHOENIX
Rabbi Zalman Levertov
Rabbi Yossi Friedman 602.944.2753

PRESCOTT
Rabbi Elie Filler 928.362.8924

SCOTTSDALE
Rabbi Yossi Levertov 480.998.1410

TUCSON
Rabbi Yehuda Ceitlin 520.881.7956

CALIFORNIA

AGOURA HILLS
Rabbi Moshe Bryski
Rabbi Yisroel Levine 818.991.0991

BAKERSFIELD
Rabbi Shmuli Schlanger 661.331.1695

BEL AIR
Rabbi Chaim Mentz 310.475.5311

BEVERLY HILLS
Rabbi Chaim I. Sperlin 310.734.9079

BURBANK
Rabbi Shmuly Kornfeld 818.954.0070

CARLSBAD
Rabbi Yeruchem Eilfort
Mrs. Nechama Eilfort 760.943.8891

CHATSWORTH
Rabbi Yossi Spritzer 818.718.0777

CONTRA COSTA
Rabbi Dovber Berkowitz 925.937.4101

CORONADO
Rabbi Eli Fradkin 619.365.4728

ENCINO
Rabbi Aryeh Herzog 818.784.9986
Chapter founded by Rabbi Joshua Gordon, OBM

FOLSOM
Rabbi Yossi Grossbaum 916.608.9811

FREMONT
Rabbi Moshe Fuss 510.300.4090

GLENDALE
Rabbi Simcha Backman 818.240.2750

HUNTINGTON BEACH
Rabbi Aron Berkowitz 714.846.2285

LA JOLLA
Rabbi Baruch Shalom Ezagui 858.455.5433

LAGUNA BEACH
Rabbi Elimelech Gurevitch 949.499.0770

LOMITA
Rabbi Eli Hecht
Rabbi Sholom Pinson 310.326.8234

LONG BEACH
Rabbi Abba Perelmuter 562.621.9828

LOS ANGELES
Rabbi Leibel Korf 323.660.5177

MARINA DEL REY
Rabbi Danny Yiftach-Hashem
Rabbi Dovid Yiftach 310.859.0770

NORTH HOLLYWOOD
Rabbi Nachman Abend 818.989.9539

NORTHRIDGE
Rabbi Eli Rivkin 818.368.3937

OAKLAND
Rabbi Dovid Labkowski 510.545.6770

PACIFIC PALISADES
Rabbi Zushe Cunin 310.454.7783

PALO ALTO
Rabbi Yosef Levin
Rabbi Ber Rosenblatt 650.424.9800

PASADENA
Rabbi Chaim Hanoka 626.564.8820
Rabbi Sholom Stiefel 626-539-4578

RANCHO MIRAGE
Rabbi Shimon H. Posner 760.770.7785

RANCHO PALOS VERDES
Rabbi Yitzchok Magalnic 310.544.5544

RANCHO S. FE
Rabbi Levi Raskin 858.756.7571

REDONDO BEACH
Rabbi Yossi Mintz
Rabbi Zalman Gordon 310.214.4999

S. BARBARA
Rabbi Mendel Loschak 805.683.1544
Chapter founded by Rabbi Yosef Loschak, OBM

S. CLEMENTE
Rabbi Menachem M. Slavin 949.489.0723

S. DIEGO
Rabbi Rafi Andrusier 619.387.8770
Rabbi Motte Fradkin 858.547.0076

S. FRANCISCO
Rabbi Peretz Mochkin 415.571.8770
Rabbi Shlomo Zarchi 415.752.2866

S. LUIS OBISPO
Rabbi Chaim Leib Hilel 805.706.0256

S. MONICA
Rabbi Boruch Rabinowitz 310.394.5699

S. RAFAEL
Rabbi Yisrael Rice 415.492.1666

SOUTH LAKE TAHOE
Rabbi Mordechai Richler 530.314.7677

STUDIO CITY
Mrs. Chanie Baitelman
Rabbi Yossi Baitelman 818.508.6633

TEMECULA
Rabbi Yonasan Abrams 951.234.4196

THOUSAND OAKS
Rabbi Chaim Bryski 805.493.7776

TUSTIN
Rabbi Yehoshua Eliezrie 714.508.2150

VENTURA
Rabbi Yakov Latowicz
Mrs. Sarah Latowicz 805.658.7441

WEST HILLS
Rabbi Avi Rabin 818.337.4544

WEST HOLLYWOOD
Rabbi Mordechai Kirschenbaum 310.275.1215

WEST LOS ANGELES
Rabbi Mordechai Zaetz 424.652.8742

YORBA LINDA
Rabbi Dovid Eliezrie 714.693.0770

COLORADO

ASPEN
Rabbi Mendel Mintz 970.544.3770

DENVER
Rabbi Yossi Serebryanski 303.744.9699

FORT COLLINS
Rabbi Yerachmiel Gorelik 970.407.1613

HIGHLANDS RANCH
Rabbi Avraham Mintz 303.694.9119

VAIL
Rabbi Dovid Mintz 970.476.7887

WESTMINSTER
Rabbi Benjy Brackman 303.429.5177

CONNECTICUT

FAIRFIELD
Rabbi Shlame Landa 203.373.7551

GREENWICH
Rabbi Yossi Deren
Rabbi Menachem Feldman 203.629.9059

MILFORD
Rabbi Schneur Wilhelm 203.878.4569

NEW LONDON
Rabbi Avrohom Sternberg 860.437.8000

ORANGE
Rabbi Shea Hecht 203-795-7095

STAMFORD
Rabbi Yisrael Deren
Rabbi Levi Mendelow 203.3.CHABAD

WEST HARTFORD
Rabbi Shaya Gopin 860.232.1116

WESTPORT
Rabbi Yehuda L. Kantor
Mrs. Dina Kantor 203.226.8584

DELAWARE

WILMINGTON
Rabbi Chuni Vogel 302.529.9900

DISTRICT OF COLUMBIA

WASHINGTON
Rabbi Levi Shemtov
Rabbi Shua Hecht 202.332.5600

FLORIDA

BAL HARBOUR
Rabbi Dov Schochet 305.868.1411

BOCA RATON
Rabbi Zalman Bukiet
Rabbi Arele Gopin 561-994-6257
Rabbi Moishe Denburg 561.526.5760

BOYNTON BEACH
Rabbi Yosef Yitzchok Raichik 561.732.4633

BRADENTON
Rabbi Menachem Bukiet 941.388.9656

BROWARD CO.: SOUTHWEST
Rabbi Mordechai Andrusier 954.874.2280

CAPE CORAL
Rabbi Yossi Labkowski 239-963-4770

CORAL GABLES
Rabbi Avrohom Stolik 305.490.7572

CORAL SPRINGS
Rabbi Yankie Denburg 954.471.8646

DELRAY BEACH
Rabbi Sholom Ber Korf 561.496.6228

EAST BOCA RATON
Rabbi Ruvi New 561.417.7797

FLEMING ISLAND
Rabbi Shmuly Feldman 904.290.1017

FORT LAUDERDALE
Rabbi Yitzchok Naparstek 954.568.1190

FORT MYERS
Rabbi Yitzchok Minkowicz
Mrs. Nechama Minkowicz 239.433.7708

HALLANDALE BEACH
Rabbi Mordy Feiner 954.458.1877

HOLLYWOOD
Rabbi Leizer Barash 954.965.9933
Rabbi Leibel Kudan 954.801.3367

KENDALL
Rabbi Yossi Harlig 305.234.5654

LAKELAND
Rabbi Moshe Lazaros 863.510.5968

LONGWOOD
Rabbi Yanky Majesky 407.636.5994

MAITLAND
Rabbi Sholom Dubov
Rabbi Levik Dubov 470.644.2500

OCALA
Rabbi Yossi Hecht 352.291.2218

ORLANDO
Rabbi Yosef Konikov 407.354.3660

ORMOND BEACH
Rabbi Shmuel Konikov 386.672.9300

PALM BEACH GARDENS
Rabbi Dovid Vigler 561.624.2223

PALM CITY
Rabbi Shlomo Uminer 772.288.0606

PALMETTO BAY
Rabbi Zalman Gansburg 786.282.0413

PLANTATION
Rabbi Pinchas Taylor 954.644.9177

PONTE VEDRA BEACH
Rabbi Nochum Kurinsky 904.543.9301

SARASOTA
Rabbi Chaim Shaul Steinmetz 941.925.0770

SATELLITE BEACH
Rabbi Zvi Konikov 321.777.2770

SOUTH PALM BEACH
Rabbi Leibel Stolik 561.889.3499

SOUTH TAMPA
Rabbi Mendy Dubrowski 813.922.1723

SUNNY ISLES BEACH
Rabbi Alexander Kaller 305.803.5315

VENICE
Rabbi Sholom Ber Schmerling 941.493.2770

WESTON
Rabbi Yisroel Spalter 954.349.6565

WEST PALM BEACH
Rabbi Yoel Gancz 561.659.7770

GEORGIA

ALPHARETTA
Rabbi Hirshy Minkowicz 770.410.9000

ATLANTA
Rabbi Yossi New
Rabbi Isser New 404.843.2464
Rabbi Ari Sollish 404-898-0434

GWINNETT
Rabbi Yossi Lerman 678.595.0196

MARIETTA
Rabbi Ephraim Silverman 770.565.4412

HAWAII

PRINCEVILLE
Rabbi Michoel Goldman 808.647.4293

IDAHO

BOISE
Rabbi Mendel Lifshitz 208.853.9200

ILLINOIS

CHAMPAIGN
Rabbi Dovid Tiechtel 217.355.8672

CHICAGO
Rabbi Meir Hecht 312.714.4655
Rabbi Yosef Moscowitz 773.772.3770
Rabbi Levi Notik 773.274.5123

ELGIN
Rabbi Mendel Shemtov 847.440.4486

GLENVIEW
Rabbi Yishaya Benjaminson 847.998.9896

HIGHLAND PARK
Mrs. Michla Schanowitz 847.266.0770

NAPERVILLE
Rabbi Mendy Goldstein 630.778.9770

NORTHBROOK
Rabbi Meir Moscowitz 847.564.8770

OAK PARK
Rabbi Yitzchok Bergstein 708.524.1530

PEORIA
Rabbi Eli Langsam 309.692.2250

ROCKFORD
Rabbi Yecheskel Rothman 815.596.0032

SKOKIE
Rabbi Yochanan Posner 847.677.1770

VERNON HILLS
Rabbi Shimmy Susskind 847.984.2919

WILMETTE
Rabbi Dovid Flinkenstein 847.251.7707

INDIANA

INDIANAPOLIS
Rabbi Dr. Shmuel Klatzkin 317.251.5573

KANSAS

OVERLAND PARK
Rabbi Mendy Wineberg 913.649.4852

KENTUCKY

LOUISVILLE
Rabbi Avrohom Litvin 502.459.1770

LOUISIANA

METAIRIE
Rabbi Yossie Nemes
Rabbi Mendel Ceitlin 504.454.2910

MARYLAND

BALTIMORE
Rabbi Elchonon Lisbon 410.358.4787
Rabbi Velvel Belinsky 410.764.5000
Classes in Russian

BEL AIR
Rabbi Kushi Schusterman 443.353.9718

BETHESDA
Rabbi Sender Geisinsky 301.913.9777

COLUMBIA
Rabbi Hillel Baron
Rabbi Yosef Chaim Sufrin 410.740.2424

FREDERICK
Rabbi Boruch Labkowski 301.996.3659

GAITHERSBURG
Rabbi Sholom Raichik 301.926.3632

OLNEY
Rabbi Bentzy Stolik 301.660.6770

OWINGS MILLS
Rabbi Nochum H. Katsenelenbogen 410.356.5156

POTOMAC
Rabbi Mendel Bluming 301.983.4200
Rabbi Mendel Kaplan 301.983.1485

ROCKVILLE
Rabbi Moishe Kavka 301.836.1242

MASSACHUSETTS

BOSTON
Rabbi Yosef Zaklos 617.297.7282

CAPE COD
Rabbi Yekusiel Alperowitz 508.775.2324

LONGMEADOW
Rabbi Yakov Wolff 413.567.8665

NEWTON
Rabbi Shalom Ber Prus 617.244.1200

SUDBURY
Rabbi Yisroel Freeman 978-443-0110

SWAMPSCOTT
Mrs. Layah Lipsker 781.581.3833

MICHIGAN

ANN ARBOR
Rabbi Aharon Goldstein 734.995.3276

GRAND RAPIDS
Rabbi Mordechai Haller 616.957.0770

WEST BLOOMFIELD
Rabbi Elimelech Silberberg 248.855.6170

MINNESOTA

MINNETONKA
Rabbi Mordechai Grossbaum
Rabbi Shmuel Silberstein 952.929.9922

S. PAUL
Rabbi Shneur Zalman Bendet 651.998.9298

MISSOURI

S. LOUIS
Rabbi Yosef Landa 314.725.0400

NEVADA

SUMMERLIN
Rabbi Yisroel Schanowitz
Rabbi Tzvi Bronchtain 702.855.0770

NEW JERSEY

BASKING RIDGE
Rabbi Mendy Herson
Rabbi Mendel Shemtov 908.604.8844

CHERRY HILL
Rabbi Mendy Mangel 856.874.1500

CLINTON
Rabbi Eli Kornfeld 908.623.7000

FAIR LAWN
Rabbi Avrohom Bergstein 201.362.2712

FORT LEE
Rabbi Meir Konikov 201.886.1238

FRANKLIN LAKES
Rabbi Chanoch Kaplan 201.848.0449

HASKELL
Rabbi Mendy Gurkov 201.696.7609

HILLSBOROUGH
Rabbi Shmaya Krinsky 908.874.0444

HOLMDEL
Rabbi Shmaya Galperin 732.772.1998

MADISON
Rabbi Shalom Lubin 973.377.0707

MANALAPAN
Rabbi Boruch Chazanow
Rabbi Levi Wolosow 732.972.3687

MOUNTAIN LAKES
Rabbi Levi Dubinsky 973.551.1898

MULLICA HILL
Rabbi Avrohom Richler 856.733.0770

OLD TAPPAN
Rabbi Mendy Lewis 201.767.4008

PASSAIC
Rabbi Yitzchak Sebbag
Dr. Michael Akerman 973.246.5251

RANDOLPH
Rabbi Avraham Bekhor
Mrs. Chava Bekhor 973-895-3070

ROCKAWAY
Rabbi Asher Herson
Rabbi Mordechai Baumgarten 973.625.1525

TEANECK
Rabbi Ephraim Simon 201.907.0686

TENAFLY
Rabbi Mordechai Shain 201.871.1152

TOMS RIVER
Rabbi Moshe Gourarie 732.349.4199

WEST ORANGE
Rabbi Mendy Kasowitz 973.486.2362

WOODCLIFF LAKE
Rabbi Dov Drizin 201.476.0157

NEW YORK

BAY SHORE
Rabbi Shimon Stillerman 631.913.8770

BEDFORD
Rabbi Arik Wolf 914.666.6065

BINGHAMTON
Mrs. Rivkah Slonim 607.797.0015

BRIGHTON BEACH
Rabbi Moshe Winner 718.946.9833

BROOKVILLE
Rabbi Mendy Heber 516.626.0600

CEDARHURST
Rabbi Zalman Wolowik 516.295.2478

COMMACK
Rabbi Mendel Teldon 631.543.3343

DIX HILLS
Rabbi Eli Laufer
Rabbi Yaakov Saacks 631.351.8672

DOBBS FERRY
Rabbi Benjy Silverman 914.693.6100

EAST HAMPTON
Rabbi Leibel Baumgarten
Rabbi Mendy Goldberg 631.329.5800

ELLENVILLE
Rabbi Shlomie Deren 845.647.4450

FOREST HILLS
Rabbi Yossi Mendelson 917.861.9726

GREAT NECK
Rabbi Yoseph Geisinsky 516.487.4554

JAMAICA ESTATES
Rabbi Shmuel Kogan 718.480.0100

KINGSTON
Rabbi Yitzchok Hecht 845.334.9044

LARCHMONT
Rabbi Mendel Silberstein 914.834.4321

LONG BEACH
Rabbi Eli Goodman 516.897.2473

NYC KEHILATH JESHURUN
Rabbi Elie Weinstock 212.774.5636

NYC MIDTOWN
Mrs. Raizy Metzger 212.758.3770

NYACK
Rabbi Chaim Zvi Ehrenreich 845.356.6686

OCEANSIDE
Rabbi Levi Gurkow 516.764.7385

OSSINING
Rabbi Dovid Labkowski 914.923.2522

PARK SLOPE
Rabbi Menashe Wolf 347.957.1291

PORT WASHINGTON
Rabbi Shalom Paltiel 516.767.8672

PROSPECT HEIGHTS
Rabbi Mendy Hecht 347.622.3599

RIVERDALE
Rabbi Levi Shemtov 718.549.1100

ROCHESTER
Rabbi Nechemia Vogel 585.271.0330

ROSLYN
Rabbi Yaakov Reiter 516.484.8185

SCARSDALE
Rabbi Avrohom Butman 914.527.2077

SEA GATE
Rabbi Chaim Brikman 917-975-2792

SOUTHAMPTON
Rabbi Chaim Pape 917.627.4865

STATEN ISLAND
Rabbi Mendy Katzman 718.370.8953

STONY BROOK
Rabbi Shalom Ber Cohen 631.585.0521

SUFFERN
Rabbi Shmuel Gancz 845.368.1889

WESTBURY
Rabbi Mendy Brownstein 516.850.4486

NORTH CAROLINA

ASHEVILLE
Rabbi Shaya Susskind 828.505.0746

CARY
Rabbi Yisroel Cotlar 919.651.9710

CHAPEL HILL
Rabbi Zalman Bluming 919.630.5129

CHARLOTTE
Rabbi Yossi Groner
Rabbi Shlomo Cohen 704.366.3984

GREENSBORO
Rabbi Yosef Plotkin 336.617.8120

RALEIGH
Rabbi Pinchas Herman
Rabbi Lev Cotlar 919.637.6950

WILMINGTON
Rabbi Moshe Lieblich 910.763.4770

OHIO

BEACHWOOD
Rabbi Shmuli Friedman 216.370.2887

BLUE ASH
Rabbi Yisroel Mangel 513.793.5200

COLUMBUS
Rabbi Yitzi Kaltmann 614.294.3296

DAYTON
Rabbi Nochum Mangel
Rabbi Shmuel Klatzkin 937.643.0770

OKLAHOMA

OKLAHOMA CITY
Rabbi Ovadia Goldman 405.524.4800

TULSA
Rabbi Yehuda Weg 918.492.4499

OREGON

BEND
Rabbi Yitzchok Feldman 541.633.7991

PORTLAND
Rabbi Mordechai Wilhelm 503.977.9947

SALEM
Rabbi Avrohom Yitzchok Perlstein 503.383.9569

PENNSYLVANIA

AMBLER
Rabbi Shaya Deitsch 215.591.9310

BALA CYNWYD
Rabbi Shraga Sherman 610.660.9192

CLARKS SUMMIT
Rabbi Benny Rapoport 570.881.1833

LAFAYETTE HILL
Rabbi Yisroel Kotlarsky 484.533.7009

LANCASTER
Rabbi Elazar Green 717.368.6565

NEWTOWN
Rabbi Aryeh Weinstein 215.497.9925

PHILADELPHIA: CENTER CITY
Rabbi Yochonon Goldman 215.238.2100

PITTSBURGH
Rabbi Yisroel Altein ..... 412.422.7300 EXT. 269
Rabbi Ely Rosenfeld 412.781.1800

PITTSBURGH: SOUTH HILLS
Rabbi Mendy Rosenblum 412.278.3693

RYDAL
Rabbi Zushe Gurevitz 267.536.5757

WYNNEWOOD
Rabbi Moishe Brennan 610.529.9011

PUERTO RICO

CAROLINA
Rabbi Mendel Zarchi 787.253.0894

RHODE ISLAND

WARWICK
Rabbi Yossi Laufer 401.884.7888

SOUTH CAROLINA

COLUMBIA
Rabbi Hesh Epstein
Rabbi Levi Marrus 803.782.1831

GREENVILLE
Rabbi Leibel Kesselman 864.256.1770

TENNESSEE

CHATTANOOGA
Rabbi Shaul Perlstein 423.490.1106

MEMPHIS
Rabbi Levi Klein 901.754.0404

TEXAS

ARLINGTON
Rabbi Levi Gurevitch 817.451.1171

AUSTIN
Rabbi Mendy Levertov 512.905.2778

BELLAIRE
Rabbi Yossi Zaklikofsky 713.839.8887

DALLAS
Rabbi Mendel Dubrawsky
Rabbi Moshe Naparstek 972.818.0770
Rabbi Zvi Drizin 214.632.2633

FORT WORTH
Rabbi Dov Mandel 817.263.7701

HOUSTON
Rabbi Dovid Goldstein
Rabbi Zally Lazarus 281.589.7188
Rabbi Moishe Traxler 713.774.0300

HOUSTON: RICE UNIVERSITY AREA
Rabbi Eliezer Lazaroff 713.522.2004

LEAGUE CITY
Rabbi Yitzchok Schmukler 281.724.1554

MISSOURI CITY
Rabbi Mendel Feigenson 832.758.0685

PLANO
Rabbi Mendel Block
Rabbi Yehudah Horowitz 972.596.8270

S. ANTONIO
Rabbi Chaim Block
Rabbi Levi Teldon 210.492.1085

THE WOODLANDS
Rabbi Mendel Blecher 281.719.5213

UTAH

SALT LAKE CITY
Rabbi Benny Zippel 801.467.7777

VERMONT

BURLINGTON
Rabbi Yitzchok Raskin 802.658.5770

VIRGINIA

ALEXANDRIA/ARLINGTON
Rabbi Mordechai Newman 703.370.2774

FAIRFAX
Rabbi Leibel Fajnland 703.426.1980

HERNDON
Rabbi Leibel Fajnland 571.594.6490

NORFOLK
Rabbi Aaron Margolin
Rabbi Levi Brashevitzky 757.616.0770

TYSONS CORNER
Rabbi Chezzy Deitsch 703.829.5770
Chapter founded by Rabbi Levi Deitsch, OBM

WASHINGTON

BELLINGHAM
Rabbi Yosef Truxton 617.640.8841

MERCER ISLAND
Rabbi Elazar Bogomilsky 206.527.1411

SPOKANE COUNTY
Rabbi Yisroel Hahn 509.443.0770

WISCONSIN

KENOSHA
Rabbi Tzali Wilschanski 262.359.0770

MADISON
Rabbi Avremel Matusof 608.231.3450

MILWAUKEE
Rabbi Mendel Shmotkin 414.961.6100

WAUKESHA
Rabbi Levi Brook 925.708.4203

ARGENTINA

CAPITAL FEDERAL
Rabbi Mendy Gurevitch 54.11.4545.7771

PALERMO NUEVO
Rabbi Mendy Grunblatt 54.11.4772.1024

AUSTRALIA

NEW SOUTH WALES

DOUBLE BAY
Rabbi Yanky Berger
Rabbi Yisroel Dolnikov 612.9327.1644

DOVER HEIGHTS
Rabbi Motti Feldman 612.9387.3822

NORTH SHORE
Rabbi Nochum Schapiro
Mrs. Fruma Schapiro 612.9488.9548

SOUTH HEAD
Rabbi Benzion Milecki 612.9337.6775

QUEENSLAND

BRISBANE
Rabbi Levi Jaffe 617.3843.6770

VICTORIA

BENTLEIGH EAST
Rabbi Mendel Raskin 613.9570.6707

CAULFIELD NORTH
Rabbi Menachem Stern 614.4850.4301

ELSTERNWICK
Rabbi Chaim Cowen 614.3330.8584

MELBOURNE
Rabbi Sholem Gorelik 614.5244.8770

MOORABBIN
Rabbi Elisha Greenbaum 614.0349.0434

WESTERN AUSTRALIA

PERTH
Rabbi Shalom White 618.9275.2106

BRAZIL

RIO DE JANEIRO
Rabbi Yehoshua Binyomin Goldman
Rabbi Avrohom Tsvi Beuthner 55.21.2294.3138

S. PAULO
Rabbi Avraham Steinmetz 55.11.3081.3081
Rabbi Yerachmiel Belinow 55.11.3663.2838

CANADA

ALBERTA

CALGARY
Rabbi Mordechai Groner 403.281.3770

EDMONTON
Rabbi Ari Drelich
Rabbi Mendy Blachman 780.851.1515

BRITISH COLUMBIA

OKANAGAN
Rabbi Shmuly Hecht 250.575.5384

RICHMOND
Rabbi Yechiel Baitelman 604.277.6427

VANCOUVER
Rabbi Dovid Rosenfeld 604.266.1313

VICTORIA
Rabbi Meir Kaplan 250.595.7656

MANITOBA

WINNIPEG
Rabbi Shmuel Altein 204.339.8737

ONTARIO

LAWRENCE/EGLINTON
Rabbi Menachem Gansburg 416.546.8770

LONDON
Rabbi Mordechai Silberberg 519.434.3623

MISSISSAUGA
Rabbi Yitzchok Slavin 905.820.4432

NIAGARA FALLS
Rabbi Zalman Zaltzman 905.356.7200

OTTAWA
Rabbi Menachem M. Blum 613.843.7770

RICHMOND HILL
Rabbi Mendel Bernstein 905.770.7700

GREATER TORONTO REGIONAL OFFICE & THORNHILL
Rabbi Yossi Gansburg 905.731.7000

WATERLOO
Rabbi Moshe Goldman 226.338.7770

YORK MILLS
Rabbi Levi Gansburg 416-551-9391

QUEBEC

CÔTE-S.-LUC
Rabbi Levi Raskin 514.485.7221

MONTREAL
Rabbi Ronnie Fine
Pesach Nussbaum 514-738-3434

TOWN OF MOUNT ROYAL
Rabbi Moshe Krasnanski
Rabbi Shneur Zalman Rader 514.739.0770

WESTMOUNT
Rabbi Yossi Shanowitz
Mrs. Devorah Leah Shanowitz 514.937.4772

SASKATCHEWAN

REGINA
Rabbi Avrohom Simmonds 306.585.1359

SASKATOON
Rabbi Raphael Kats 306.384.4370

CAYMAN ISLANDS

GRAND CAYMAN
Rabbi Berel Pewzner 717.798.1040

DENMARK

COPENHAGEN
Rabbi Yitzchok Loewenthal 45.3316.1850

ESTONIA

TALLINN
Rabbi Shmuel Kot 372.662.30.50

GEORGIA

TBILISI
Rabbi Meir Kozlovsky 995.593.23.91.15

GERMANY

BERLIN
Rabbi Yehuda Tiechtel 49.30.2128.0830

HAMBURG
Rabbi Shlomo Bistritzky 49.40.4142.4190

HANNOVER
Rabbi Binyamin Wolff 49.511.811.2822

GREECE

ATHENS
Rabbi Mendel Hendel 30.210.520.2880

GUATEMALA

GUATEMALA CITY
Rabbi Shalom Pelman 502.2485.0770

ISRAEL

ASHKELON
Rabbi Shneor Lieberman 054.977.0512

BALFURYA
Rabbi Noam Bar-Tov 054.580.4770

CAESAREA
Rabbi Chaim Meir Lieberman 054.621.2586

EVEN YEHUDA
Rabbi Menachem Noyman 054.777.0707

GANEI TIKVA
Rabbi Gershon Shnur 054.524.2358

GIV'ATAYIM
Rabbi Pinchus Bitton 052.643.8770

HAIFA
Rabbi Yehuda Dunin 054.426.3763

KARMIEL
Rabbi Mendy Elishevitz 054.521.3073

KFAR SABA
Rabbi Yossi Baitch 054.445.5020

KIRYAT BIALIK
Rabbi Pinny Marton 050.661.1768

KIRYAT MOTZKIN
Rabbi Shimon Eizenbach 050.902.0770

KOCHAV YAIR
Rabbi Dovi Greenberg 054.332.6244

MACCABIM-RE'UT
Rabbi Yosef Yitzchak Noiman 054.977.0549

MODIIN
Rabbi Boruch Slonim 054.300.1770

NES ZIYONA
Rabbi Menachem Feldman 054.497.7092

NETANYA
Rabbi Schneur Brod 054.579.7572

RAMAT GAN-KRINITZI
Rabbi Yisroel Gurevitz 052.743.2814

RAMAT GAN-MAROM NAVE
Rabbi Binyamin Meir Kali 050.476.0770

RAMAT YISHAI
Rabbi Shneor Zalman Wolosow 052.324.5475

RISHON LEZION
Rabbi Uri Keshet 050.722.4593

ROSH PINA
Rabbi Sholom Ber Hertzel 052.458.7600

YEHUD
Rabbi Shmuel Wolf 053.536.1479

KAZAKHSTAN

ALMATY
Rabbi Shevach Zlatopolsky 7.7272.77.59.77

LATVIA

RIGA
Rabbi Shneur Zalman Kot 371.6733.1520

NETHERLANDS

ALMERE
Rabbi Moshe Stiefel 31-36-744-0509

AMSTERDAM
Rabbi Jaacov Zwi Spiero 31-652-328-065

THE HAGUE
Rabbi Shmuel Katzman 31-70-347-0222

HEEMSTEDE-HAARLEM
Rabbi Shmuel Spiero 31-23-532-0707

NIJMEGEN
Rabbi Menachem Mendel Levine 31-621-586-575

ROTTERDAM
Rabbi Yehuda Vorst 31-10-265-5530

PANAMA

PANAMA CITY
Rabbi Ari Laine
Rabbi Gabriel Benayon 507.223.3383

RUSSIA

ASTRAKHAN
Rabbi Yisroel Melamed 7.851.239.28.24

BRYANSK
Rabbi Menachem Mendel Zaklas 7.483.264.55.15

CHELYABINSK
Rabbi Meir Kirsh 7.351.263.24.68

MOSCOW: MARINA ROSHA
Rabbi Mordechai Weisberg 7.495.645.50.00

NIZHNY NOVGOROD
Rabbi Shimon Bergman 7.920.253.47.70

OMSK
Rabbi Osher Krichevsky 7.381.231.33.07

PERM
Rabbi Zalman Deutch 7.342.212.47.32

ROSTOV
Rabbi Chaim Danzinger 7.8632.99.02.68

S. PETERSBURG
Rabbi Zvi Pinsky 7.812.713.62.09

SAMARA
Rabbi Shlomo Deutch 7.846.333.40.64

SARATOV
Rabbi Yaakov Kubitshek 7.8452.21.58.00

TOGLIATTI
Rabbi Meier Fischer 7.848.273.02.84

UFA
Rabbi Dan Krichevsky 7.347.244.55.33

VORONEZH
Rabbi Levi Stiefel 7.473.252.96.99

SINGAPORE

SINGAPORE
Rabbi Mordechai Abergel 656.337.2189
Rabbi Netanel Rivni 656.336.2127
Classes in Hebrew

SOUTH AFRICA

CAPE TOWN
Rabbi Levi Popack 27.21.434.3740

JOHANNESBURG
Rabbi Dovid Masinter
Rabbi Ari Kievman 27.11.440.6600
Rabbi Dovid Hazdan
Rabbi Shmuel Simpson 27.11.728.8152

SWEDEN

STOCKHOLM
Rabbi Chaim Greisman 468.679.7067

SWITZERLAND

BASEL
Rabbi Zalmen Wishedsky 41.41.361.1770

LUZERN
Rabbi Chaim Drukman 41.41.361.1770

UKRAINE

DNEPROPETROVSK
Rabbi Dan Makagon 380.504.51.13.18

NIKOLAYEV
Rabbi Sholom Gotlieb 380.512.37.37.71

ODESSA
Rabbi Avraham Wolf
Rabbi Yaakov Neiman .... 38.048.728.0770 EXT. 280

ZHITOMIR
Rabbi Shlomo Wilhelm 380.504.63.01.32

UNITED KINGDOM

CARDIFF
Rabbi Michoel Rose 44.792.866.9536

CHEADLE
Rabbi Peretz Chein 44.161.428.1818

LEEDS
Rabbi Eli Pink 44.113.266.3311

LONDON
Rabbi Mendel Cohen 44.77.7261.2661
Rabbi Nissan D. Dubov 44.20.8944.1581
Rabbi Mendy Korer 44.794.632.5444
Rabbi Gershon Overlander
Rabbi Dovid Katz 44.207.624.2770
Rabbi Yossi Simon 44.20.8458.0416

MANCHESTER
Rabbi Levi Cohen 44.161.792.6335
Rabbi Shmuli Jaffe 44.161.766.1812

THE JEWISH LEARNING MULTIPLEX

Brought to you by the Rohr Jewish Learning Institute

In fulfillment of the mandate of the Lubavitcher Rebbe, of blessed memory, whose leadership guides every step of our work, the mission of the Rohr Jewish Learning Institute is to transform Jewish life and the greater community through the study of Torah, connecting each Jew to our shared heritage of Jewish learning.

While our flagship program remains the cornerstone of our organization, JLI is proud to feature additional divisions catering to specific populations, in order to meet a wide array of educational needs.

THE ROHR JEWISH LEARNING INSTITUTE,
a subsidiary of *Merkos L'Inyonei Chinuch*,
is the adult education arm of the Chabad-Lubavitch Movement.

Torah Studies provides a rich and nuanced encounter with the weekly Torah reading.

MyShiur courses are designed to assist students in developing the skills needed to study Talmud independently.

IN PARTNERSHIP WITH CHABAD ON CAMPUS

This rigorous fellowship program invites select college students to explore the fundamentals of Judaism.

IN PARTNERSHIP WITH CTEEN: CHABAD TEEN NETWORK

Jewish teens forge their identity as they engage in Torah study, social interaction, and serious fun.

The Rosh Chodesh Society gathers Jewish women together once a month for intensive textual study.

TorahCafe.com provides an exclusive selection of top-rated Jewish educational videos.

This yearly event rejuvenates mind, body, and spirit with a powerful synthesis of Jewish learning and community.

Participants delve into our nation's rich past while exploring the Holy Land's relevance and meaning today.

Select affiliates are invited to partner with peers and noted professionals, as leaders of innovation and excellence.

THE SAMI ROHR
RESEARCH INSTITUTE

Machon Shmuel is an institute providing Torah research in the service of educators worldwide.